ER

LAROUSSE
cocktails

LAROUSSE
cocktails

FERNANDO CASTELLON

hamlyn

I would like to thank all the people who have encouraged and helped me in my profession: Sylvain Solignac, Pierre Chapeau, Jean-Michel Cochet, Gérard Martron, Jean-Pierre Cointreau, Gérard Chausée, Colin Peter Field, Charles Schumann, Rafael Ballesteros, Ted Haigh, Philippe Vic, also my wife, Murielle Legrand-Castellon for her support throughout.

Fernando Castellon

First published in Great Britain in 2005 by
Hamlyn, a division of Octopus Publishing Group Ltd
2–4 Heron Quays, London E14 4JP

Copyright © English edition Octopus Publishing Group Ltd 2005

Copyright © original French edition Larousse 2004

Editor-in-Chief: Carola Strang

Editorial Director: Colette Hanicotte

Editor: Aude Mantoux-Nicolas
in collaboration with Françoise Maitre *and* Martine Willemin

Cocktail Snacks Recipes created by: Coco Jobard

Artistic Director: Emmanuel Chaspoul
assisted by Jacqueline Bloch *and* Martine Debrais

Graphic Designer: Jacqueline Bloch

Layout: Sophie Compagne

Cartography: Laurent Blondel

Iconography: Bridgett Noizeux

Photography of cocktails, cocktail snacks and bar interiors: Nicolas Bertherat
Stylist: Coco Jobard
See other photographic credits at the end of the book

Revision Correction: Annick Valade
assisted by Madeleine Biaujeaud

Index: Marie-Thérèse Ménager

Production: Annie Botrel

English translation provided by: Translate-A-Book, Oxford, England

ISBN 0 600 61261 9
EAN 9780600612612

e record for this book is available from the British Library

Printed and bound in Canale, Italy

Preface

It has given me great pleasure to write this preface to *Larousse Cocktails*; the author, Fernando Castellon, has been my friend for almost ten years. Fernando has put together an impressive collection of documentary information on the subject of cocktails. We spent hours together, retracing the true origin of some of them, comparing ingredients and historical data. It was a laborious process.

Of course, before one can make any progress one has to establish a basis of incontrovertible facts on which to build. The publication date of a book providing information can very often serve as a reference point, as with the first mention of distillation, made in 1309 in the writings of Arnaud de Villeneuve (1245–1313), of the Salerno school in Italy. The process may possibly have already existed before that date but there is no documentary evidence to confirm it.

Like the plays of William Shakespeare, the art of preparing cocktails lends itself to a thousand and one interpretations, so it is not surprising that there are, for instance, three different ways of making crustas or scaffas.

A definitive reference book on the subject, written by a specialist, was clearly lacking and this was what was in mind when the author began his work; without waiting for the Muse to inspire him, he undertook painstaking research of the subject, scouring the books in his own library as well as those in my own collection and those of established experts in the USA. *Larousse Cocktails* is the fruit of ten years' work and the meticulous study and comparison of all the various interpretations previously put forward. Where others have come up with their own versions, this author set out to find an objective answer, which is what makes this book so illuminating.

Larousse has produced a book that will fascinate professionals, but is also perfectly suited to those just starting out in this highly coloured world. The technical information on the preparation of cocktails has never been so clearly explained nor the historical facts so captivatingly set out.

I find this book a source of inspiration, and each page awakens a longing to pick up the telephone and talk to Fernando. It is a work that I value most sincerely and one that, from now on, will never be far from my cocktail shaker.

Colin Peter Field
Head Barman at The Ritz Hotel in Paris

Contents

Recipes for cocktails
and cocktail snacks   60

For a deeper insight   289

How to use
Larousse Cocktails

REFERENCE TO THE TYPE OF BASIC ALCOHOL USED, chapter by chapter, making recipes easy to find.

Vodka: *liqueur-based cocktails*

Vodka Stinger
Short drink to serve as a digestif

FOR 1 GLASS
3–4 ice cubes
1¼ measures vodka
½ measure white crème de menthe

• Place the ice and all the ingredients in a rocks glass.
• Stir with a mixing spoon for 8–10 seconds. Serve immediately.

The Vodka Stinger is also known as the White Spider. Its flavour is reminiscent of mint pastilles.

CLASSIFICATION OF RECIPES according to their consistency and flavour helps one to choose a suitable cocktail: dry, thirst-quenching, fruit-based, liqueur-based, smooth or hot.

Smooth cocktails

On the trail of Hemingway
The Bloody Mary (▷ right), the precise origins of which are unknown, has been given any number of names: Mary Rose in 1939, Red Snapper in 1944 and Bloody Mary in 1946. Ernest Hemingway (pictured here) worked hard on making it widely known, even as far away as China. In a letter to Bernard Peyton in 1947 he wrote, 'When I introduced this cocktail in Hong Kong in 1941 I believe I contributed more than any other single factor – with the possible exception of the Japanese army – to the fall of this Crown Colony'.

Bloody Mary
Long drink to serve at any time

FOR 1 GLASS
5–6 ice cubes
1 measure vodka
3 measures tomato juice
1 teaspoon fresh lemon juice
1 teaspoon Worcestershire sauce
3 drops red Tabasco sauce
1 pinch celery salt
1 pinch black pepper
1 small stick (stalk) celery

• Place the ice and all the ingredients except the celery stick in a mixing glass. Stir with a mixing spoon for 8–10 seconds.
• Strain into a highball glass using a cocktail strainer.
• Wash the piece of celery and place it in the glass. Serve immediately.

BOXES FOR EMBLEMATIC COCKTAILS revealing the picturesque history of the drinks and the famous people who enjoyed them.

86

Recipes for cocktails and cocktail snacks pages 60–288

550 recipes for both alcoholic and non-alcoholic cocktails

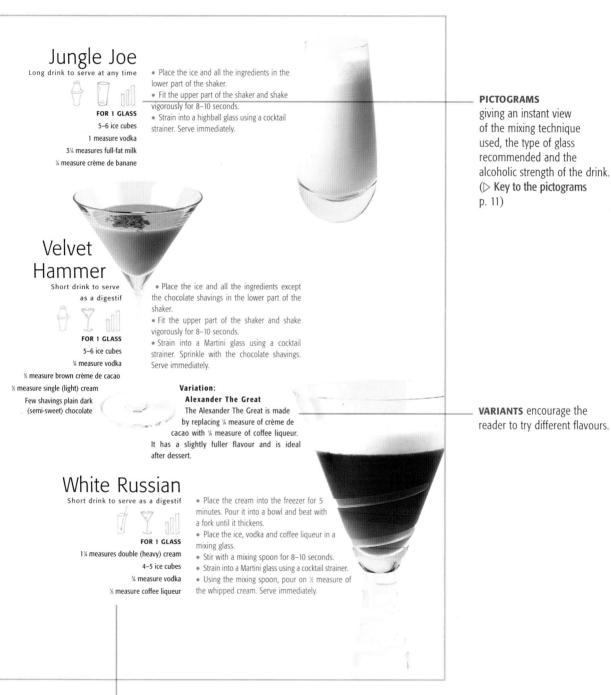

Jungle Joe
Long drink to serve at any time

FOR 1 GLASS
5–6 ice cubes
1 measure vodka
3¼ measures full-fat milk
¼ measure crème de banane

- Place the ice and all the ingredients in the lower part of the shaker.
- Fit the upper part of the shaker and shake vigorously for 8–10 seconds.
- Strain into a highball glass using a cocktail strainer. Serve immediately.

PICTOGRAMS
giving an instant view of the mixing technique used, the type of glass recommended and the alcoholic strength of the drink.
(▷ **Key to the pictograms** p. 11)

Velvet Hammer
Short drink to serve as a digestif

FOR 1 GLASS
5–6 ice cubes
¾ measure vodka
½ measure brown crème de cacao
½ measure single (light) cream
Few shavings plain dark (semi-sweet) chocolate

- Place the ice and all the ingredients except the chocolate shavings in the lower part of the shaker.
- Fit the upper part of the shaker and shake vigorously for 8–10 seconds.
- Strain into a Martini glass using a cocktail strainer. Sprinkle with the chocolate shavings. Serve immediately.

Variation:
Alexander The Great
The Alexander The Great is made by replacing ¼ measure of crème de cacao with ¼ measure of coffee liqueur. It has a slightly fuller flavour and is ideal after dessert.

VARIANTS encourage the reader to try different flavours.

White Russian
Short drink to serve as a digestif

FOR 1 GLASS
1¼ measures double (heavy) cream
4–5 ice cubes
¾ measure vodka
½ measure coffee liqueur

- Place the cream into the freezer for 5 minutes. Pour it into a bowl and beat with a fork until it thickens.
- Place the ice, vodka and coffee liqueur in a mixing glass.
- Stir with a mixing spoon for 8–10 seconds.
- Strain into a Martini glass using a cocktail strainer.
- Using the mixing spoon, pour on ½ measure of the whipped cream. Serve immediately.

INGREDIENTS ARE PRESENTED IN A VERY PRACTICAL WAY
the items are listed in the order in which they are used in the recipe.
Note that professionals and hotel schools often work differently.
(▷ **The basic rules of mixing** p. 48)

■ 45 recipes for cocktail snacks to accompany cocktails.

A few ideas for snacks to serve with cocktails based on other forms of alcohol:
■ bite-sized pieces of polenta with Parma ham (prosciutto)
■ bruschetta with mozzarella and artichokes
■ prawns (shrimp) flavoured with almonds and paprika
■ aubergine (eggplant) rolls with tomatoes and (bell) peppers
■ cream of chestnut delight
▶ recipes page 284

▶ In each chapter, **SUPERB DOUBLE-PAGE ILLUSTRATIONS** offer suggestions for cocktail snacks when having friends in for an aperitif, organizing a cocktail party or other festive occasion.

▶ Whether **SAVOURY OR SWEET**, the recipes (▷ pp. 268–288) offer original flavours and are always easy to prepare.

The art of the successful cocktail

■ Preparing cocktails
pages 52–59

▶ **THE TECHNIQUES TO MASTER** are explained and illustrated step-by-step: how to use a shaker or mixing glass; how to frost a glass; how to make crushed ice, etc.

▶ **THE BOXES** explain the academic method, which is often adopted by professionals, especially in competitions.

Cocktail preparation

Preparing in a shaker
This method is used when the ingredients will only be thoroughly mixed if shaken vigorously. It may be the case with a syrup, a more or less thick fruit juice or a rich substance such as coconut milk, or egg whites or yolks. One can equally well use either a shaker with an integral strainer (the most common nowadays) or a Boston or continental shaker.

SHAKER WITH STRAINER The shaker with an integral strainer is made up of three metallic parts: the lower part, the upper part, which includes the strainer, and the lid.

1. Slightly more than half-fill the lower part of the shaker with the amount of ice indicated in the recipe, then pour in the ingredients in the order and quantities indicated.

2. Fit the upper part and the lid.

3. Hold the shaker firmly, placing the thumb of the right hand (if you are right-handed) on the lid and the index and middle fingers of the other hand under the lower part. Shake vigorously for about 8–10 seconds. When the drink is well chilled the outside of the shaker will become frosted.

4. Remove the lid and, keeping hold of the upper part, pour the contents into the appropriate glass; any solid particles (including the ice cubes) will be held back by the integral strainer. Decorate the cocktail if necessary and serve immediately.

The academic method
1. Slightly more than half-fill the lower part of the shaker with the amount of ice indicated in the recipe. Fit the upper part and the lid in place. Hold the shaker firmly, placing the thumb of the right hand (if you are right-handed) on the lid and the index and middle fingers of the other hand under the lower part. Shake vigorously for 4–5 seconds. Take off the lid and pour away any accumulated water. Remove the upper part of the shaker and pour in the cocktail ingredients in the order and quantities stated in the recipe.
Follow stages **2, 3, 4** as above.

55

CONVERSION TABLES

The volumes given in tenths and ounces are rounded to the nearest point.

Millilitres	Measures	Tenths		Ounces	
		For a 70 ml short drink	For a 180 ml long drink	Imperial ounce = 2.843 ml	American ounce = 2.957 ml
10 ml	¼ measure	1/10	1/10	¼ oz	¼ oz
20 ml	½ measure	3/10	1/10	¾ oz	¾ oz
30 ml	¾ measure	4/10	2/10	1 oz	1 oz
40 ml	1 measure	6/10	2/10	1½ oz	1¼ oz
50 ml	1¼ measures	7/10	3/10	1¾ oz	1¾ oz
60 ml	1½ measures	9/10	3/10	2 oz	2 oz
70 ml	1¾ measures	10/10	4/10	2½ oz	2¼ oz
80 ml	2 measures		4/10	2¾ oz	2¾ oz
90 ml	2¼ measures		5/10	3¼ oz	3 oz
100 ml	2½ measures		6/10	3½ oz	3½ oz
110 ml	2¾ measures		6/10	3¾ oz	3¾ oz
120 ml	3 measures		7/10	4¼ oz	4 oz
130 ml	3¼ measures		7/10	4½ oz	4½ oz
140 ml	3½ measures		8/10	5 oz	4¾ oz
150 ml	3¾ measures		8/10	5¼ oz	5 oz
160 ml	4 measures		9/10	5¾ oz	5½ oz
170 ml	4¼ measures		9/10	6 oz	5¾ oz
180 ml	4½ measures		10/10	6¼ oz	6 oz

The measure that has been used in this book is based on a standard measure of 40 ml (1½ fl oz). If preferred, a different volume can be used providing the proportions are kept constant within a drink and suitable adjustments are made to spoon measures.

KEY TO THE PICTOGRAMS

MIXING METHOD	GLASS RECOMMENDED	ALCOHOLIC CONTENT
Directly in the serving glass	Martini	Weak in alcohol (≤16% Vol/≤ 32° proof)
In a mixing glass	Tulip	
	Wine	Moderately alcoholic (17–22% Vol/34–44° proof)
In a shaker	Flute	Strongly alcoholic (≥ 23% Vol/≥ 46° proof)
In a blender	Shot	
	Rocks	
	Highball	
	Toddy	

The art of the
successful
cocktail

The history of cocktails

The story of cocktails, which stretches back more than two centuries, is rich in characters and anecdotes, but first of all we need to look into the history of the word itself, which has undergone changes of meaning over the years.

The history of the term 'cocktail'

Uncertain origin

First of all, where did this word come from? There is no precise answer to that question. At one time in England it was used to describe a non-thoroughbred horse in which the muscles below the tail had been severed so that it remained in a permanently high, flowing curve like that of a cock's tail. Others believe the word 'cocktail' is a corruption of the *coquetier* (eggcup) in which a certain Frenchman served strange concoctions called *coquetel* – he may have been a pharmacist from New Orleans…

Still others place the origin of the term in Mexico, where the father of a princess called Coctel was known for mixing mysterious potions. A further theory is that, possibly, tavern-keepers used cock's tail feathers to mark the various kinds of drink. We will probably never know, but no matter; these legends should be allowed to carry on being a part of the folklore of the world's bars.

The first mention in print

On the other hand, we do know exactly when the word 'cocktail' first appeared in print. The details are as follows: in May 1806, in *The Balance and Colombian Repository*, a newspaper of the town of Hudson in New York State, a curious reader asked the editor, 'Sir, I have read your article which appeared on the sixth of this month regarding the accounts submitted by a Democrat candidate … under the title of Loss, 25 *do. cock tail*. Would you be good enough to inform me as to what is understood by this form of refreshment? … I have heard talk of *jorum*, of *phlegm cutter*, of *fog-driver*, … but never before in my life, and I have lived for a good number of years, have I heard tell of a *cocktail*. Is it a speciality of the area, or is it a new invention? Does the name describe the effect the drink has on a particular part of the body? …'

The editor replied on 13 May 1806: 'A *cock tail* is a stimulating drink made with all manner of spirits, sugar, water and bitters; it is commonly known as *bittered sling* and is thought to be an excellent potion during the electoral campaign because it emboldens the heart and befuddles the head … It is also said to be particularly useful to a Democrat candidate, because anyone who will swallow a glass of it will swallow anything.'

Subsequent meanings

Nowadays the word 'cocktail' is used to describe any mixed drink containing at least two ingredients, but the meaning of the word has evolved significantly. When it first appeared in the United States at the beginning of the nineteenth century, the term 'cocktail' meant a very specific mixture of brandy, sugar, water and bitters. By the 1890s the word 'cocktail' was used to describe a drink prepared in a mixing glass or a shaker and served 'straight-up' (without ice in the glass). The other mixed drinks were simply referred to as 'mixed drinks'.

From the 1920s onwards, the meaning of the word 'cocktail' continued to extend its influence until it finally included all forms of mixed drinks. Cocktail parties and cocktail dresses also became part of the language.

Cocktails in ancient times

Mankind has been making mixtures since time immemorial. The Ancients drank combinations of wine, honey, herbs and spices. Much later, when spirits and liqueurs came on the scene, the monks and apothecaries made up preparations, primarily for medicinal use, which eventually became used as aperitifs and digestifs. Punch, made with tea, rum, sugar and spices, was already known in the Caribbean at the end of the seventeenth century, and grog made its appearance in the ships of the Royal Navy around 1740 when Admiral Vernon, nicknamed 'Old Grog' by the sailors, made them dilute their daily ration of rum with water. For their part, the British Army in India came up with the idea of mixing gin with the quinine-based soft drink (soda) that they drank to ward off malaria, thus inventing 'Gin and Tonic'.

Around the same time, in English clubs and American taverns, it was customary to serve mixed drinks made in copious amounts in large bowls. The drinks, prepared in these bowls and ladled into glasses, were served either hot (as with certain types of punch), at room temperature or even chilled, since establishments in the major cities had access to ice, either via ice sellers or from nearby snow-capped mountains.

HARRY JOHNSON

Harry Johnson was the author of the first bartender's manual, written in New York in 1882 and entitled, *New and Improved Bartender's Manual*. Unlike Jerry Thomas's first cocktail book (▷ p. 16), Johnson's book includes chapters on organizing the bar, equipment, ingredients and the art of mixing, as well as service. It also reveals that from adolescence onwards Johnson had spent his life in the saloon and hotel environment, that he learned to mix drinks in San Francisco, and had worked for 40 years in the leading establishments in New York and other parts of the country, as well as in Europe, etc. At a competition held in New Orleans in 1869 he even won the title of United States Champion Bartender.

The rapid rise of the cocktail (1800–1850)

As we have seen, the word 'cocktail' first appeared at the beginning of the 1800s, but we had to wait until 50 years later to see the consumption of mixed drinks really take off in America. In that era, while alcoholic liquor, such as brandy, rum and rye whiskey was available all over the United States, only places like New York, New Orleans and San Francisco had access to ice and various kinds of liqueurs. It is significant that all the great pioneers of the American bar, like Jerry Thomas, Harry Johnson and William Boothby, who is mentioned later, worked in one or more of these cities.

▶ Engraving showing Harry Johnson, taken from the cocktail manual *How to Mix Drinks of the Present Style* (1888). The bartender is pouring a cocktail made in a Boston shaker into ten glasses simultaneously.

Transition from tavern to bar (1850–1890)

While Viennese-type cafés became popular in Europe, on the other side of the Atlantic the tavern eventually became the bar. The bar was the immediate descendant of the saloon – a term that was coined at the start of the nineteenth century to define the room reserved for drinking that was set apart from the dining room. At that time the word 'bar' referred to the item of furniture on which the drinks were prepared – in other words, the counter, which often had a bar running along its front – and it only superceded the term 'saloon' at the end of the nineteenth century, once it had come into common use as the place where the drinks were served.

The invention of the ice machine

In the middle of the nineteenth century another novelty emerged in Europe: machine-made ice, which played a defining role in the history of the cocktail. Already in 1834 a machine using ether as a refrigerant, invented in London by an American called Jacob Perkins (1766–1849), kept ice collected from the mountains from melting for quite long periods. A new machine, using ammonia, was perfected in 1859 by the Frenchman Ferdinand Carré (1824–1900) and for the first time permitted the production of ice on a large scale.

The first practical manuals

All the conditions were now in place for the successful launch of the mixed drink. Among the many barmen who practised this art, one in particular stands out as destined to become famous. His name was Jeremiah P Thomas, known as Jerry Thomas, and in 1862 in New York he published the first book of cocktails and mixed drinks under the French-inspired title of *The Bon Vivant's Companion or How to Mix Drinks*. It listed 236 recipes for those that were most popular at the time. A manual on the manufacture of liqueurs and syrups, written by Christian Schultz, was also included so that anyone who had difficulty in obtaining some of the ingredients could produce products with a

▲ The Hoffman House Bar, popular New York meeting place for businessmen and fashionable artists, reproduced from a lithograph from the end of the nineteenth century.

similar flavour. A second revised edition was published in 1876 under the title of *The Bar-Tender's Guide*, and added 50 or so new recipes to the original ones. In 1887, a third edition was published posthumously and contained a fresh selection of more than 280 cocktails.

The first of the great figures associated with the American bar

In the nineteenth century two 'mixologists', Harry Johnson and William Boothby, contributed – like Jerry Thomas before them – to the prestige of the barman's trade by publishing their own works, each in three successive editions. These books are interesting because they give an overview of the way bar keeping evolved over the years.

They offer little information about the authors themselves but fortunately vast numbers of articles about the great American barmen appeared in local newspapers. There was an interview with Jerry Thomas, published 28 March 1882 in the *New York Sun*, on the occasion of the sale by auction of his collection of caricatures and drawings by American artists. The article offers a few insights into the life of 'The Professor', as he was known to his admiring customers.

The following is an extract: '... "An American?" continued Mr Thomas, in a tone of surprise. "Dear me, yes, and a sailor. I was born in Watertown, Jefferson County, fifty-two years ago, and sailed all about the world before the mast. I landed in San Francisco in 1849, and ran off into the mountains after gold: ... came back to New York with $16,000, and walked about with kid gloves for some time, to the great delight of myself and a select company; started a bar with George Earle under Barnum's Museum where the Herald building is now; in '53 went as a bartender to the Mills House in Charleston; followed that up by similar professional efforts in Chicago, St Louis, and along the Mississippi; came back and mixed excellent drinks at the Metropolitan; crossed over to the Heenan-Sayers fight in 1859, having seen twenty-one prize fights before; have seen seven since; turned up barkeeper in the Occidental Hotel in San Francisco in 1863; took a turn at Virginia City, and was back here in 1866, when, with my brother George M, who is now retired from business and living in Twenty-first Street, I [rented?] the place at 937 Broadway [running?] through to Fifth Avenue, where Johnson's now is, just below Twenty-second Street. It was a great place. After two years our bar receipts ran $400 a day, and the way people used to drop in to look at Mr Thomas Nast's pictures was a pleasing thing to us, who stood ready to serve them what they wished to drink when they were done. ... We quit in 1871, and went up to where the Bijou[?] is now, where we stopped for some time, with all the pictures around us. But in 1876 I sold that out too. John Morrissey buying and running it for a pool room.'"

In another article in the *New York Times* of 15 December 1885, we learn that Jerry Thomas died the day before, at his New York home, of an apoplectic fit. He was 55 years old and the article cites two of his famous creations: the Tom & Jerry (▷ p. 169) and the Blue Blazer (▷ p. 139).

The American School (1860–1890)

The first barmen's associations

Professional bar-workers quickly began to organize themselves. In Chicago, in 1866, they got together and set up the Bartenders' and Waiters' Union and in the 1890s the National Bartenders' Association also came into being. During that time a number of books on bar keeping and cocktails were published – no less than 40 between 1860 and 1900. They contain precious information for us today, about both the ingredients used in the different eras and the development of great classics like the John Collins (▷ p. 101) in the 1860s, the Gin Fizz (▷ p. 100) in the 1870s, the Manhattan (▷ p. 122) in the 1880s and the Old-Fashioned (▷ p. 122) in the 1890s.

WILLIAM BOOTHBY

In San Francisco in 1891, a few years after Harry Johnson (▷ p. 15), William Boothby published his first book under the title *Cocktail Boothby's American Bartender*, which was presented as the only practical treaty on 'mixology', or the 'science of mixing'. The terms 'mixology' and 'mixologist' were coined in San Francisco at the end of the 1880s. Known as 'Cocktail Boothby' in the profession, the author claimed to be the first mixologist but no one knows whether he actually invented the word. From the various re-editions of his manual, we have been able to gather valuable information about the evolution of the cocktail and of bar practices.

▲ Poster by Henri Toulouse-Lautrec, illustrating a scene in an American bar at 33, Rue Royale, Paris (1895), commissioned by the magazine *The Chap Book*.

The fate of the great classics

Thanks to these numerous works, we can establish that certain recipes, like the Manhattan, have remained unaltered for more than a century. But we also find that other famous cocktails have changed completely over the decades showing the way barmen adapted to evolving customer taste. This is illustrated by development of the Dry Martini (▷ p. 92), which was called a Martinez when it first appeared in

FRANK NEWMAN

Frank Newman, an English national, took over the bar of the Grand Hotel, opposite the Opéra Garnier in Paris just before 1900. To gain recognition he published a book called 'American-Bar', a revised edition of which was published in 1904 and contained the first written reference to the Dry Martini. Newman subsequently opened his own establishment under the name of 'The Cosmopolitan' at Asnières, in the Hauts-de-Seine region near Paris. In 1927 he created the Diabola (▷ p. 92), a short drink made with gin, red Dubonnet and orgeat syrup.

1884; it became the Martini in 1888 (a name that confuses Europeans, since the Martini – or Dry Martini – has nothing whatsoever to do with the Italian aperitif created by Martini & Rossi in 1863). The recipe for the Martini included gin, red vermouth and concentrated bitters (similar to today's Angostura bitters), garnished with a lemon twist.

The first change to the Martini recipe occurred during the 1890s when orange bitters were substituted for the Angostura type and a maraschino cherry replaced the lemon twist. At the start of the 1900s the name of the cocktail and its ingredients changed again; it became the Dry Martini, using dry vermouth rather than red, and a new garnish – a green olive, which underlined the dry nature of the drink. Frank Newman, head barman at the Grand Hotel in Paris, published this recipe in 1904, in the second edition of his book, *American-Bar*.

The cocktail goes international around 1900

Drink-mixing had become an American speciality and American barmen were on hand to initiate the rest of the world into the charm of American drinks at the various Universal Exhibitions, which took place on both sides of the Atlantic in the nineteenth century. When the first cocktail bars opened in England, France and Germany they inevitably became known as 'American bars'. As a consequence, by the early 1900s the cocktail habit had already become widespread in Europe.

In London, among the pioneers of this expansion, was the American barman Leo Engel who, at the end of the 1870s, was responsible for introducing the clientele of the famous Criterion restaurant in Piccadilly Circus to American drinks. Shortly afterwards, a professional magazine called *Barman and Barmaid* began publication in the British capital.

In France, the fashion for the English language and the attraction of everything that came from the New World, fuelled the craze for cocktails. In Paris, Louis Fouquet offered a wide range of American drinks in Fouquet's, his restaurant on the Champs Élysées, which opened shortly after he published a book on cocktails in 1896. In the same era, the American tourists congregating in the area around the Paris Opera, were delighted to be able to sip their favourite cocktails at the Grand Hotel, Rue Daunou, the Chatam and the New York Bar (later to become Harry's Bar).

Prohibition (1919–1933) and the post-war period

The Prohibition period constituted an important stage in the history of the cocktail. The ban on the consumption of alcohol in the United States brought in its wake an immediate reaction that had not been foreseen by the legislators. Clandestine distilleries multiplied, smuggling became organized, gang warfare raged and 'speakeasies' selling illegal alcohol prospered.

CONSTANTINO RIBALAIGUA VERT

Originally from Catalonia, Constantino Ribalaigua Vert (?–1952) landed in Cuba around 1910. He found a job at La Florida in Havana, where he excelled in the preparation of cocktails and was christened 'Constant' by the customers because the quality of his drinks never varied. In 1918 he bought La Florida and under his ownership it became a very famous establishment indeed. It used to serve Daiquiris 'frappé' – with crushed ice – until the advent of the electric blender, at which time Ribalaigua offered his customers a new version, the Frozen Daiquiri (▷ p. 148). His bar, which was re-named 'Floridita' ('little Florida' in Spanish) around 1940, became the acknowledged temple of the Daiquiri.

The Americans in Cuba

During that time American tourists from the coastal areas began flocking to Cuba, where they could enjoy the latest novelties created by expatriate barmen from the local rum, untroubled by restrictive laws.

▼ Police control operation, checking a stock of alcohol in Philadelphia (Pennsylvania) in 1924, when Prohibition was in full swing.

HARRY McELHONE

Before opening his establishment in Paris in 1923 (Harry's New York Bar), Harry McElhone (1890–1958) worked at the Plaza in New York, then in the casinos at Enghien and Nice, also Ciro's in London and at Deauville. British by birth, he made his name in the profession in London in 1919 when he published a small book called the *ABC of Mixing Cocktails*. A few years later he started a club for cocktail enthusiasts called 'International Bar Flies', and set up a worldwide network of establishments willing to accommodate them. McElhone made a great contribution to the prestige of the profession of barman, and invented several cocktails that have since become classics, such as the French 75 (▷ p. 220) and the Monkey Gland (▷ p. 109).

In Havana, known at the beginning of the twentieth century as the 'Paris of the Caribbean', a roaring trade was enjoyed by establishments where one could drink excellent, refreshing cocktails like Mint Julep (▷ p. 131) made with rum rather than bourbon. The professional barmen of Cuba soon became organized and, in 1924, created the 'Club des Cantineros', which oversaw the training of the island's bar staff, thus ensuring the delivery of the kind of service their American clients expected. The first of the club's manuals, issued in 1930 and containing no less than 600 recipes, illustrates the scope of the Cuban barman's knowledge. This was the era when legendary bars like La Florida, Sloppy Joe's and the Bodeguita del Medio came into being. Many now-classic cocktails were invented in Cuba – the Daiquiri (▷ p. 147), the Presidente (▷ p. 142), the Mary Pickford (▷ p. 161), the Cuba Libre (▷ p. 146) and the Mojito (▷ p. 151).

The vitality of Europe's barmen

The main cities of Europe also saw a proliferation of American bars and cocktail bars attached to hotels, all serving the most sophisticated cocktails. And so, while Prohibition held sway in the United States, the internationalization of the cocktail carried on apace. Many American barmen became voluntary exiles, like Harry Craddock, who joined the staff of the Savoy Hotel in London. In Paris, the cosmopolitan clientele also attracted the great European barmen, some of whom stayed on permanently, like Frank Meier, an Austrian by birth, who took over the management of the bar at The Ritz Hotel, in Rue Cambon, when it opened in 1921. In 1923, Englishman Harry McElhone bought the New York Bar in Rue Daunou and renamed it Harry's New York Bar; today it is known simply as Harry's Bar.

A number of classics, such as the Americano (▷ p. 233), the Sidecar (▷ p. 201), the French 75 (▷ p. 220) and the Red Lion (▷ p. 111) were invented in this era.

The end of Prohibition

The ineffectiveness of the Prohibition law in the United States led to its repeal in 1933, but

▶ The American singer, Josephine Baker (1906–1975) drinking a cocktail.

▲ The terrace of the American bar Le Select, on the Champs Élysées – typical of the establishments that were opened in Europe by American barmen forced into self-exile by Prohibition during the 1920s.

enthusiasm for cocktails persisted and their development continued to grow. It became fashionable to keep a bar at home and cocktail parties, to which friends were invited for drinks before dinner, became a feature of popular culture.

Around 1930, the 'Maison du Cocktail' – a company specializing in the sale of equipment and bars for private apartments – opened in Paris. The craze was at its height, driven by Hollywood movies in which cocktail drinking was depicted as the acme of sophistication. Maison Nicolas, specialist in fine wines, rebelled against this mounting tide and asked designer Paul Iribe (1883–1935), companion of Coco Chanel, to provide the illustrations for a violently anti-cocktail publicity campaign.

FRANK MEIER AND JEAN AZIMONT

Frank Meier, an Austrian national, began working at The Ritz Hotel in Paris in 1921, when it opened its Café Parisien in Rue Cambon. To welcome his first customers he invented the Royal Highball (▷ p. 226), an elegant combination of Cognac, Champagne and fresh strawberries. Once the venture was a success it became his custom to greet and mingle with his clients on the public side of the bar, leaving the preparation of the cocktails to a team of barmen. In 1936, the Petit Bar was opened beside the Café Parisien and entrusted to one of the barmen, Jean Azimont, otherwise known as 'Bertin', who was taken on in 1926. After the death of Meier in 1947, Azimont took over and ran the business until 1975; during this period he became friendly with writer, Ernest Hemingway, who was one of the bar's regulars. Today the Café Parisien has become the Cambon Bar and the Petit Bar is now the Hemingway Bar.

21

VICTOR BERGERON, ALIAS TRADER VIC

American Victor Bergeron (1902–1984) opened an establishment called Hinky Dink's in 1932 at Oakland in San Francisco Bay. The décor, the cuisine and the drinks all drew heavily on Polynesian culture. At the end of Prohibition he began offering tropical cocktails, as did Don the Beachcomber (▷ p. 23) in Hollywood. His business did very well and he re-named it Trader Vic – the name his customers had dubbed him. He wrote several benchmark books on Polynesian drinks and cuisine, including the *Trader Vic Bartender's Guide*, published in 1947 and revised in 1972. It contains recipes for several of the cocktails he invented, such as the Scorpion (▷ p. 164) and the Mai Tai (▷ p. 150), which is also attributed to him.

The cocktail in limbo (from 1945-1980)

After World War II the circumstances that had made cocktails such a significant part of European popular drinking culture gave way to more difficult times. Though new recipes such as the Bellini (▷ p. 224), Irish Coffee (▷ p. 139) and the Black Russian (▷ p. 84) were invented, the attraction of cocktails declined until they virtually fell into disuse. When someone found a cocktail shaker in the attic, or in a curio store, they used it as an ornament rather than for its original purpose. But despite that, the art of cocktail preparation carried on, thanks to the international clientele frequenting the bars in the grander hotels. Cocktails fared rather better in their native land. Classics like the Bronx (▷ p. 107), the Clover Club (▷ p. 116) or the Sazerac (▷ p. 123) were replaced by novelties such as the Mai Tai (▷ p. 150), the Moscow Mule (▷ p. 73) and the Margarita (▷ p. 176). The success of vodka in the United States played a big part in the development of the long drink; what could be easier than making a long drink, such as a Screwdriver (▷ p. 82), simply by adding a measure of vodka to fruit juice?

▲ A 1952 cover of the German magazine *Er, Die Zeitschrift für den Herrn* ('Him, the Man's Magazine').

The Renaissance of the Cocktail (1980 to today)
The 'flair' phenomenon

In 1988, a new phenomenon appeared on the scene with the release of Roger Donaldson's movie *Cocktail*, starring Tom Cruise. In this movie, the actor is seen tossing the bottles up in the air and catching them as he prepares the cocktails, watched by his astonished customers. This technique, known as 'flair', is now the subject of competitions and it enjoys considerable success among professionals, who give displays at festive gatherings.

There are two categories of flair: 'working flair' – which has the bartender throwing the bottles in the air and catching them as he prepares the drinks directly in the glass or in a shaker – and 'exhibition flair'. Working flair can be performed with full bottles fitted with a pourer; exhibition flair, however, requires special techniques and great dexterity. The thrown bottles must rotate through 360°, which is impossible if the bottles contain more than about 60 ml (2 fl oz) of liquid. That said, both types of flair require extensive training on the part of the operator, since throwing bottles about in this way could have dangerous consequences, both for barman and customers. These displays of technical skill have engendered a revived interest in cocktails.

Adapting to the needs of a new clientele

Since the 1980s, many new recipes have appeared and rapidly gained a foothold on the international scene. Among these ubiquitous novelties is the Cosmopolitan (▷ p. 64) which, in less than ten years, has secured a place among the Top 10 of all categories. It is perfectly in tune with the expectations of customers who require fairly low-alcohol cocktails of which they can drink safely several in the course of an evening.

'Less quantity, more quality' seems to be the thinking behind this new tendency. Barmen have adapted to modern tastes and rediscovered the virtues of fresh fruit that made the Cuban cocktails so successful in their day. The new family of cocktails, fresh fruit Martinis, such as the Melon Martini (▷ p. 65), are some of the best. They are made with fresh fruit or vegetable juices with vodka, or other neutral alcohol, added to produce a mixture that is fruity without being too sweet. But for those who continue to prefer strong cocktails there is always the Vodka Martini Extra-Dry (▷ p. 67), the Dry Martini (▷ p. 92), the Old-Fashioned (▷ p. 122) and the Sazerac (▷ p. 123).

▲ Actor Tom Cruise in a 'flair' scene from Roger Donaldson's film *Cocktail* (1988).

DONN BEACH, ALIAS DON THE BEACHCOMBER

Donn Beach (1907–1989) arrived in Hollywood at the age of 24 after travelling around Jamaica, Australia and Tahiti. He became involved with people linked with the movie industry, who called him in to act as an advisor on production sets in the South Seas. In 1933 he opened a small restaurant in Hollywood and called it Don the Beachcomber. At the end of Prohibition he collaborated with Trader Vic (▷ p. 22) in the 'Tiki' movement (Tiki's being statues representing the Polynesian goddess of that name), invented numerous tropical cocktails, the best known being the Zombie (▷ p. 165), and did much to popularize Polynesian culture.

The cocktail 'families'

Since the beginning of the nineteenth century, in both America and Europe, mixed drinks have been prepared according to precise written recipes. Professionals of the drinks industry have gone to great lengths to classify the different kinds of cocktails according to the types of alcohol and other ingredients that go into their making. A single recipe has been known to give rise to a whole category.

A family of cocktails is defined according to three criteria – a given mixture of ingredients, a specific method of preparation (directly in the glass or in a shaker or blender) and the way the resulting mixture is served.

Note that each category is served in its own special type of glass (▷ p. 46).

The forgotten categories

Cobblers This family of short drinks appeared in the United States before 1810. Originally a cobbler was made with still, sparkling or even fortified wine. The most popular cobblers were Sherry Cobbler and Whiskey Cobbler. A cobbler is prepared directly in a rocks glass or tumbler with ice cubes. It is made with spirit and sugar, and is garnished with orange slices or berries in season.

THE TWO TYPES OF COCKTAIL

Short drink. This term defines a mixture of varying strength, depending on the proportion of alcoholic ingredients; its volume should not exceed 120 ml (4 fl oz).

Long drink. This describes a drink of more than 120 ml (4 fl oz) in which the alcohol content has been diluted.

Cocktail A generic term the meaning of which has changed significantly over the years (▷ p. 14). Nowadays it covers any drink, alcoholic or not, made with two or more ingredients.

Crustas This family of short drinks was invented in the 1840s by Joseph Santini at the City Exchange in New Orleans. The best-known examples were Brandy Crusta and Whiskey Crusta. A crusta, prepared directly in a small wine glass, with ice, consists of the basic spirit, lemon juice, sugar and bitters, and is garnished with a long strip of lemon peel (zest) strewn around the rim of the glass.

Daisies This type of long drink appeared in the United States in the 1870s. The most popular recipes were the Brandy Daisy and the Gin Daisy. A daisy is prepared directly in a highball glass and is made up of spirit, lemon juice, sugar, curaçao and soda water (club soda).

Eggnogs This family of long drinks was invented in the United States before 1800. The most popular versions were Brandy Eggnog or Rum Eggnog. Eggnog is made in a shaker, with ice, and is served in a highball glass. It consists of spirit, egg yolk, milk and sugar. It would appear to be the descendant of an English drink called 'posset', made with similar ingredients but using a fortified wine instead of spirits. It was particularly popular for New Year celebrations and could also be drunk hot.

Fixes This family of short drinks was already known in the United States before the 1860s, the most popular ones being Brandy Fix and Gin Fix. They are simply 'sours' ($\triangleright$ p. 26) garnished with berries in season.

Flips These short drinks originated in England prior to 1810. Like the cobbler, the flip was originally made with fortified wine. In the 1860s they were prepared in a shaker with ice cubes and served in a wine glass. The most popular ones were Port Flip ($\triangleright$ p. 203) and Brandy Flip. A flip is made with spirit, egg yolk and sugar, topped with a sprinkling of nutmeg.

Puffs This family of long drinks appeared in the United States in the 1890s. The most popular ones were Whiskey Puff and Brandy Puff. They are prepared directly in a highball glass, with ice, a spirit, milk, sugar and sometimes soda water (club soda).

Sangarees This category of drink came to light in the British Antilles before 1820. The most popular recipes were for Brandy Sangaree and Gin Sangaree. A sangaree is made in a shaker, with ice, and served in a wine glass. The ingredients are spirit, ruby port and sugar, with nutmeg grated over the top.

Slings This category of short drinks originated in the United States before 1800. The most popular ones were Brandy Sling and Whiskey Sling. Slings were also drunk hot. Prepared directly in a rocks glass with ice, they are made up of spirit, still or sparkling mineral water and sugar, topped with a sprinkling of nutmeg.

Smashes This family of short drinks first saw the light in the 1850s in the United States. The most popular versions were the Brandy Smash and the Gin Smash. A smash is a form of julep ($\triangleright$ p. 26) made with just two or three

fresh mint leaves so as to attenuate the mint flavour, and garnished with slices of orange and berries in season.

The families still in current use

Bucks This family of short drinks was invented in London, supposedly in the 1920s, possibly at Buck's Club. They are prepared directly in a rocks glass from ice, spirit, lemon juice and a little ginger ale, garnished with a strip of lemon peel (zest).

Coladas These long drinks were invented at the start of the 1950s in Puerto Rico. The best known are Piña Colada ($\triangleright$ p. 162) and Blue Hawaiian ($\triangleright$ p. 162). A colada is prepared in a shaker or a blender and is served in a highball glass. It is made with spirit, fruit juice and coconut milk.

Collins This family of long drinks appeared in the United States at the end of the 1860s, and was invented in the 1800s by John Collins, Maître d'Hôtel at Limmer's Coffee House in London. One of the most popular versions is the John Collins ($\triangleright$ p. 101). Prepared directly in a highball glass, with ice, a collins consists of spirit, lemon juice, soda water (club soda) and sugar.

Coolers This family of long drinks appeared in the United States at the end of the 1880s. The cooler seems to have been invented to promote a device of the same name, which was used to chill ginger ale. One of the most popular versions is the Remsen Cooler ($\triangleright$ p. 100). A cooler consists of spirit, sugar and ginger ale, mixed with ice directly in a highball glass. Nowadays the term 'cooler' is used to indicate drinks containing fruit juice.

Fizzes This long drink family appeared in the United States in the 1870s. A fizz is made in a shaker, with ice, and is served in a highball glass. One of the most popular ones is Gin Fizz

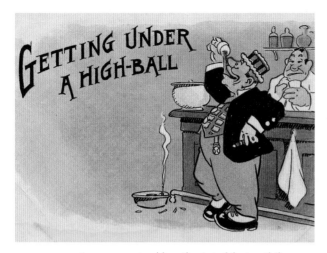

▲ Humorous postcard from the start of the twentieth century, showing a man drinking a long drink.

(▷ p. 100). A fizz is prepared in the same way as a collins (▷ p. 25), but with less lemon juice, which makes it less acidic. Originally, both these long drinks were made in a shaker, and the soda water (club soda) added at the end, but today they are prepared in different ways.

Highballs This type of long drink was invented in New York in the 1890s. The recipe was perfected by Bradley Martin, and was subsequently popularized by Patrick Gavin Duffy. One of the most popular is the Brandy Highball (▷ p. 196). A highball is made directly in a highball glass, with ice, and consists of spirit with a carbonated drink. It can be garnished with a strip of lemon peel (zest).

Juleps This family of short drinks already existed in the United States before 1800. The best-known versions are the Mint Julep (▷ p. 131) and the Mojito (▷ p. 151). A julep is made directly in a rocks glass, with crushed ice, and is made from spirit, fresh mint and sugar. It can also be made as a long drink.

Pousse-café ▷ Shooters

Punches This family of long drinks appeared in the British Antilles pre-1700, probably in Barbados. The most well-known recipes are Planter's Punch (▷ p. 152) and Fish House

Punch (▷ p. 168). Often fruit juice replaces part of the water. A long drink, punch is made in a highball glass, with crushed ice, and is made with spirit, citrus juice, soda water (club soda) and grenadine. It has changed little from the original recipe, which was sweetened with sugar, used still water and had spices added. It was sometimes drunk hot.

Rickeys This family of long drinks was invented at Shoemaker's in Washington, around 1900. A rickey is prepared directly in a highball glass, with ice, and consists of spirit, lime juice and soda water (club soda).

Shooters This family of short drinks, nowadays known as shooters, was already popular in New Orleans in the 1840s. It is probably of French origin. A shooter is made directly in a shot glass and consists of several different basic spirits and/or liqueurs superimposed on each other without being allowed to mix (▷ p. 58). At one time one drank the different layers one after the other. The best-known versions are Santina's Pousse-Café (▷ p. 211) and the B-52 (▷ p. 243).

Sours These short drinks originated in England, where they appeared around the middle of the 1700s. One of the best known is the Whiskey Sour (▷ p. 132). A sour is made in a shaker and is served in a rocks glass. It contains spirit, lemon juice and sugar.

Toddies This hot drink family originated in the British Antilles, where it has been known since the 1760s. A toddy is prepared directly in a heat-resistant toddy glass, from spirit, boiling water and sugar. In France, this drink, with added lemon juice, is called a Grog (▷ p. 168).

A chronological overview

The following are a few dates in the history of the most famous recipes and the origins of great cocktail families of our times.

1860–1870

How to Mix Drinks	the first book about cocktails, written by Jerry Thomas and published in New York in 1862.	▷ p. 16
Lime juice cordial	a sweetened lime juice product invented in 1865 by Lachlan Rose, Edinburgh.	p. 318
Collins family	first appeared in the United States.	▷ p. 25

1870–1880

Sazerac	perfected at the start of the 1870s by Thomas H. Handy at Sazerac House in New Orleans.	▷ p. 123
Daisy family	first appeared in the United States.	▷ p. 24
Fizz family	first appeared in the United States.	▷ p. 26

1880–1890

Martinez	invented at the start of the 1880s in the United States; attributed to Jerry Thomas.	▷ p. 95
Manhattan	appeared in 1884 in the United States; its origin is unknown.	▷ p. 122
East India	invented in 1888 in the United States; attributed to Harry Johnson.	▷ p. 202
Spritzer	introduced to the United States around 1888; originally made with Rhine wine and Seltzer.	▷ p. 235
Bijou	invented at the end of the 1880s in the United States; attributed to Harry Johnson.	▷ p. 113
Turf	invented between 1888 and 1895 in the United States; attributed to Harry Johnson.	▷ p. 96
Black Velvet	popularized in the United States; originally called Champagne Velvet in the United States.	▷ p. 228
Horse's Neck	appeared in the United States.	▷ p. 198
Ramos Gin Fizz	invented by Henry C Ramos at the Imperial Cabinet Saloon in New Orleans.	▷ p. 117

1890–1900

Stinger	appeared at the start of the 1890s in the United States; originally called Judge Cocktail.	▷ p. 211
Highball family	invented between 1890 and 1895 by Bradley Martin on the occasion of a grand reception in the United States.	▷ p. 26
Remsen Cooler	invented before 1895 by a naval officer, William Remsen, at the Union Club in New York.	▷ p. 100
Daiquiri	invented in 1898 by a group of engineers at the Venus Hotel in Santiago de Cuba.	▷ p. 147
Bull's Eye	popularized in the United States.	▷ p. 249
Champagne Julep	invented in New York; attributed to William Schmidt.	▷ p. 220
Puff family	first appeared in the United States.	▷ p. 25

1900–1910

Bronx	appeared between 1899 and 1908 in the United States; attributed to Johnnie Soloon of the hotel Old Waldorf-Astoria in New York.	▷ p. 107
Pisco Punch	appeared around 1900 in the United States.	▷ p. 200
Lone Tree	invented between 1900 and 1904 at the Myopia Hunt Club in Hamilton (Massachusetts).	▷ p. 95
Old-Fashioned	invented between 1900 and 1907 at the Pendennis Club in Louisville (Kentucky).	▷ p. 122
Clover Club	invented between 1900 and 1908 at the Bellevue-Stratford Hotel in Philadelphia for the members of the Clover Club.	▷ p. 116
Rickey family	invented around 1900 at Shoemaker's in Washington for Colonel Joe Rickey.	▷ p. 26
Grasshopper	appeared in the United States around 1900; attributed to Harry O'Brien of the Palace Hotel in San Francisco.	▷ p. 245

Dry Martini	recipe published for the first time in 1904 in Paris, in the book *American-Bar* by Frank Newman.	▷ p. 92
Zaza	invented between 1904 and 1907 by Frank Newman at the Grand Hotel in Paris.	▷ p. 96
Rose	invented in 1906 by Johnny Milta at the Chatam in Paris.	▷ p. 195
Absinthe Veilleuse	invented before 1908 in Paris by Paul Geoffroy.	▷ p. 232
Bamboo	invented before 1908 in Yokohama by Louis Eppinger.	▷ p. 233
Tomate à l'Absinthe	invented before 1908 in France.	▷ p. 235
Jack Rose	invented in New York; it was created by Jacob Rosenzweig, nicknamed Bald Jack Rose.	▷ p. 199

1910–1920

Singapore Sling	invented between 1910 and 1915 by Ngiam Tong Boon at the Raffles Hotel in Singapore.	▷ p. 105
Ward Eight	invented between 1918 and 1922 in the United States, perhaps in the 8th district of Washington, also known as Ward Eight.	▷ p. 134

1920–1930

Pussy Foot	invented in London in 1920 by Robert Vermeire.	▷ p. 267
Whizz-Bang	invented in 1920 by Tommy Burton at the Sports' Club in London.	▷ p. 124
Mary Pickford	invented in Cuba between 1920 and 1926, by Fred Kaufman.	▷ p. 161
Royal Highball	invented in 1921 by Frank Meier, for the opening of The Ritz Hotel's Cambon Bar.	▷ p. 226
Alexander	invented in 1922 by Harry McElhone at Ciro's in London; originally called Princess Mary.	▷ p. 116
Bloodhound	introduced in 1922 in London by the Duke of Manchester.	▷ p. 90
Florida	popularized in London in 1922.	▷ p. 250
Monkey Gland	invented before 1922 by Harry McElhone.	▷ p. 109
Paradise	popularized in 1922 in London.	▷ p. 110
Queen Cocktail	invented in 1922 in New York by Harry Craddock.	▷ p. 110
Sidecar	introduced in 1922 in London, by McGarry, head barman at Buck's Club.	▷ p. 201
White Lady	invented between 1922 and 1923 in France, probably at the Carlton hotel in Cannes.	▷ p. 106
Scoff-Law	invented in 1924 by Jock at Harry's Bar in Paris.	▷ p. 123
French 75	invented in 1925 by Harry McElhone at Harry's Bar in Paris.	▷ p. 220
Mimosa	invented in 1925 in Paris and attributed to The Ritz Hotel bar.	▷ p. 225
Blue Bird	invented in 1927 by Frank Meier.	▷ p. 98
Claridge	invented before 1927 by Léon, barman at the Claridge Hotel in Paris.	▷ p. 91
Diabola	invented before 1927 by Frank Newman in Paris.	▷ p. 92
Acacias	invented in 1928 by Mademoiselle Doudjam for an amateur cocktail competition at Biarritz.	▷ p. 112
Americano	invented in Italy before 1928 and popularized in France.	▷ p. 233
Frozen Daiquiri	invented between 1928 and 1930 by Constantino Ribalaigua Vert at the Florida in Cuba.	▷ p. 148
Negroni	invented before 1929 by Albert of the Chatam in Paris under the name of Camparinete.	▷ p. 235
Buck Family	probably invented in London, by McGarry of Buck's Club.	▷ p. 25
Alfonso	popularized in France during the visit of King Alphonse XIII of Spain to Deauville.	▷ p. 216
Commodore	appeared in the United States; attributed to Phil Gross who worked in Cincinnati.	▷ p. 125
Depth Bomb	invented in England.	▷ p. 197
Mojito	first appeared in Cuba; nowadays it is made without bitters.	▷ p. 151
Presidente	invented by Constantino Ribalaigua Vert at the Florida in Cuba.	▷ p. 142

1930–1940

Macka	invented in France at the start of the 1930s, probably at the Bar Basque at St-Jean-de-Luz.	▷ p. 101
Olympic	invented between 1930 and 1934 by Frank Meier at The Ritz Hotel bar in Paris.	▷ p. 203
Bee's Knees	invented between 1930 and 1936 by Frank Meier at The Ritz Hotel bar in Paris.	▷ p. 112
Red Lion	invented in London in 1933 by Arthur A Tarling.	▷ p. 111
Cuba Libre	recipe first published in 1935 in the United States by Albert S Crockett in his book: *The Old Waldorf-Astoria Bar Book*.	▷ p. 146
B & B	probably appeared in 1937 in New York; attributed to the Club 21.	▷ p. 203
Black Rose	invented before 1936 by Frank Meier at The Ritz Hotel bar in Paris.	▷ p. 144
Green Hat	invented before 1936 by Frank Meier at The Ritz Hotel bar in Paris.	▷ p. 100
Highbinder	invented before 1936 by Frank Meier at The Ritz Hotel bar in Paris.	▷ p. 209
Prince of Wales	appeared in 1936 in France; attributed to Jack Van Land of Harry's Bar in Le Touquet.	▷ p. 229
Bloody Mary	recipe first published in Cuba in 1939, under the name of Mary Rose.	▷ p. 86
Hemingway Special	invented for Ernest Hemingway in 1939 by Antonio Melan in Cuba.	▷ p. 149
Pink Daiquiri	invented in 1939 in Cuba; also known as a Daiquiri No 5.	▷ p. 152
Doctor Funk	invented by Don the Beachcomber in California.	▷ p. 148
Floridita Daiquiri	invented by Benjamin Orbon at the Florida in Cuba.	▷ p. 148
Hurricane	invented by Pat O'Brien in New Orleans.	▷ p. 160
Marama Rum Punch	invented by Don the Beachcomber in California.	▷ p. 150
Pearl Diver	invented by Don the Beachcomber in California.	▷ p. 162
Zombie	invented by Don the Beachcomber in California.	▷ p. 165

1940–1950

Moscow Mule	invented in 1941, probably at the Cock 'n' Bull restaurant in Hollywood.	▷ p. 73
Irish Coffee	invented in 1943 by Joe Sheridan at Foynes airport in Ireland.	▷ p. 139
Mai Tai	attributed to Trader Vic, who would have invented it in 1944.	▷ p. 150
Scorpion	recipe published in 1946 by Trader Vic, who invented it in Oakland, California.	▷ p. 164
Vodka Martini Extra-Dry	appeared at the Stork Club in New York in 1946.	▷ p. 67
Bellini	invented in 1948 at Harry's Bar in Venice by Arrigo Cipriani.	▷ p. 224
El Diablo	recipe first published at the end of the 1940s in the United States.	▷ p. 175
Red Snapper	first publication of the name given to a Bloody Mary at the Saint Regis Hotel in New York.	▷ p. 117

1950–1960

Black Russian	invented around 1950, probably by Gustave Tops at the Métropole Hotel in Brussels.	▷ p. 84
Piña Colada	appeared at the start of the 1950s in Puerto Rico; attributed to Ramon Marrero Perez, barman at the Caribe Hilton Hotel.	▷ p. 162
Tamanaco Dry	invented at the start of the 1950s by Jacques Hébrard at the Tamanaco Hotel in Caracas; initially known as the Jack'artini.	▷ p. 106
Kir	invented in 1904 at Dijon; renamed Blanc Cassis (1951).	▷ p. 234
Golden Dream	invented by LeRoy Sharon at Marineland in California.	▷ p. 244

1960–1970

Blue Lagoon	invented in 1960 by Andy McElhone at Harry's Bar in Paris.	▶ p. 68
Screwdriver	extremely popular all over the United States at the start of the 1960s.	▶ p. 82
Harvey Wallbanger	appeared between 1968 and 1970 in California;	
	attributed to Pancho's Bar on Manhattan Beach.	▶ p. 79
Tequila Sunrise	invented at the end of the 1960s in the United States.	▶ p. 186
Banana Daiquiri	invented by Trader Vic.	▶ p. 158
Bossa Nova	invented by Cecil E Roberts at the Nassau Beach Hotel in the Bahamas.	▶ p. 158
Joe Kanoo	invented by D R Lunan at the Sheraton Hotel in Kingston;	
	initially called the Jonkanoo Screwdriver.	▶ p. 161
Margarita	popularized in the United States; its origin is unknown.	▶ p. 176
Montego Bay	invented by Trader Vic.	▶ p. 151
Mulata	invented in Cuba and attributed to José Maria Vasquez.	▶ p. 167

1970–1980

Blue Hawaiian	invented at the start of the 1970s in the United States.	▶ p. 162
Cape Codder	invented at the start of the 1970s in the United States.	▶ p. 69

1980–1990

Apple Sunrise	invented in 1980 by Charles Schumann in Munich.	▶ p. 201
Midnight Moon	invented in 1982 by Colin Peter Field in Paris.	▶ p. 228
Aristo	invented in 1984 by Duschan Tistler at Passau in Germany.	▶ p. 156
Carol Channing	invented in 1984 by Dick Bradsell in London.	▶ p. 217
Creativity	invented in 1984 by Peter Roth in Zurich.	▶ p. 125
Lady Killer	invented in 1984 by Peter Roth at the Kronenhalle Bar in Zurich.	▶ p. 108
Basic	invented in 1986 by Duschan Tistler at Passau in Germany.	▶ p. 237
Long Island Iced Tea	invented between 1980 and 1987 at the Balboa Café in San Francisco.	▶ p. 73
Purple Hooter	invented between 1980 and 1987 at the Balboa Café in San Francisco.	▶ p. 74
Sex on the Beach #2	invented between 1980 and 1987 at the Balboa Café in San Francisco.	▶ p. 83
Bramble	invented in London by Dick Bradsell.	▶ p. 98
Fuzzy Navel	appeared in San Francisco; attributed to Pat O'Shea's Mad Hatter.	▶ p. 241

Since 1990

Black Widow	invented in 1992 in New York by Dale DeGroff, author of *The Craft of the Cocktail*.	▶ p. 166
Woo Woo	invented in 1993 at Julie's Supper Club in San Francisco.	▶ p. 83
Apple Pilar	invented in 1994 by Colin Peter Field in Paris.	▶ p. 248
Serendipiti	invented in 1994 by Colin Peter Field in Paris.	▶ p. 227
Añejo Highball	invented in New York in 1995 by Dale DeGroff, author of *The Craft of the Cocktail*.	▶ p. 143
Burgos	invented in 1995 by Colin Peter Field in Paris.	▶ p. 205
Ginger Champagne	invented in 1995 by Colin Peter Field in Paris (or Benderitter).	▶ p. 218
Beam Me Up Scotty	invented in 1996 by Willi Haase at the Hudson Bar in Berlin.	▶ p. 132
Cable Car	invented in 1996 in San Francisco by Tony Abou-Ganim.	▶ p. 145
Dusty Rose	invented in New York in 1996 by Dale DeGroff, author of *The Craft of the Cocktail*.	▶ p. 244
Tropicana	invented in 1996 by Willi Haase at the Hudson Bar in Berlin.	▶ p. 164
Fiesta	invented in 1997 by Colin Peter Field in Paris.	▶ p. 65
Expresso Martini	invented in London by Dick Bradsell in 1998.	▶ p. 71
Just Try	invented by Mauro Mahjoub at the Negroni Bar in Munich in 1998.	▶ p. 115

Agave Punch	invented in New York in 1999 by Dale DeGroff, author of *The Craft of the Cocktail*.	▶	p. 181
Baccarat	invented by Peter Roth in Zurich in 1999.	▶	p. 157
Breakfast Martini	invented in 1999 in London, by Salvatore Calabrese, author of *Classic Cocktails*.	▶	p. 98
Betty Blue	invented in 2000 by Mauro Mahjoub at the Negroni Bar in Munich.	▶	p. 84
G.G.	invented in 2000 in London, by Salvatore Calabrese, author of *Classic Cocktails*.	▶	p. 101
Apple Martini	appeared in the United States around 2000, no doubt in New York (recipe given is European version).	▶	p. 78
French Spring Punch	invented in London between 2000 and 2003 by Dick Bradsell.	▶	p. 226
Russian Spring Punch	invented in London between 2000 and 2003 by Dick Bradsell.	▶	p. 226
Treacle	invented in London between 2000 and 2003 by Dick Bradsell.	▶	p. 143
Clockwork Orange	invented in 2001 in Paris by Colin Peter Field.	▶	p. 70
Delmarva	invented in Los Angeles in 2001 by Ted Haigh, known by the nickname of 'Dr Cocktail'.	▶	p. 134
Jam Daiquiri	invented in Valencia (Spain) in 2001 by Rafael Ballesteros.	▶	p. 160
Meringue	invented in Los Angeles in 2001 by Ted Haigh	▶	p. 221
Evolution	invented in Valencia (Spain) in 2002 by Rafael Ballesteros.	▶	p. 114
Francis the Mule	invented in Los Angeles in 2002 by Ted Haigh.	▶	p. 126
Gotham	invented in 2002 in Seattle, Washington, by Robert Hess, also known by the name 'Drinkboy'.	▶	p. 194
Jaizkibel	invented in Valencia (Spain) in 2002 by Rafael Ballesteros.	▶	p. 100
Twistin	invented by Peter Roth in Zurich in 2002.	▶	p. 136
European Beauty	invented in Valencia (Spain) in 2003 by Rafael Ballesteros.	▶	p. 120
Hondarribia	invented in Valencia (Spain) in 2003 by Rafael Ballesteros.	▶	p. 121
Lemony Snicket	invented in Los Angeles in 2003 by Ted Haigh.	▶	p. 115
Cosmopolitan	invented at Julie's Supper Club in San Francisco.	▶	p. 64
Playa del Mar	invented by Navajoe Joe in London.	▶	p. 185

Cocktails created by Fernando Castellon

1997	Maxim's Coffee *(in Brussels)*	▶	p. 213
1999	Apple Sparkle *(in France)*	▶	p. 248
	Chocolate Bliss *(in London)*	▶	p. 204
	Mango Sparkle *(in France)*	▶	p. 251
2000	Asian Passion *(in France)*	▶	p. 249
	Dee-Light *(in Sydney)*	▶	p. 197
	El Ultimo *(in Bogota)*	▶	p. 202
	Passion Cooler *(in France)*	▶	p. 251
2001	Amber Twist *(in Seoul)*	▶	p. 194
2002	Cassisina *(in France)*	▶	p. 70
	Cranberry Colada *(in France)*	▶	p. 256
	Milky Mango *(in France)*	▶	p. 265
	My Sky *(in France)*	▶	p. 257
	Planter's Punchless *(in France)*	▶	p. 252
	Purple Pash *(in France)*	▶	p. 252
	Redwood *(in France)*	▶	p. 142
2003	Berry Blush *(in France)*	▶	p. 68
	Bounty Boat *(in France)*	▶	p. 204

Ingredients used in the bar

All the alcohols and other ingredients used in the recipes contained in this book are listed here according to type, not omitting the decorative elements, which are always appreciated, and the ice, which plays a paramount role. At the end of the chapter is a table that lists all the ingredients, set out according to the needs of the different users: beginners, amateurs or professionals.

The different kinds of alcohol

There is a wide variety of alcohols that serve as a basis for cocktails. They are listed in the same order as in the chapter on recipes – grain alcohols, plant alcohols and, finally, distilled wines.

For more details see the chapter on the manufacture of alcoholic drinks (▷ p. 290).

Vodka This white spirit is distilled from a mash made with potatoes, rye or even a mixture of cereals. The process of distilling it to the degree of 96% Vol/192° proof causes it to lose almost all the aromas found in the basic ingredients. Filtration further removes any residual aromas. Water is added to reduce the degree of alcohol to 40% Vol/80° proof. Vodka is correctly described as a 'neutral' alcohol. There are some vodkas that are flavoured with fruit or plants, such as lemon, blackcurrant and bison grass, but these are rarely used in cocktails.

Gin This spirit, generally obtained from cereals, is the basis of a great many cocktails. Ordinary gin is a neutral alcohol, flavoured with extract of juniper berries.

■ **London gin** London gin, which can be produced anywhere in the world, is distilled with juniper berries and other spices (cardamom seeds, angelica root, coriander seeds, etc.).

■ **Plymouth gin** This gin is also distilled with juniper berries and other spices, but it may only be made at Plymouth in England. In this respect it benefits from a controlled appellation of origin.

Scotch whiskies To qualify for the name Scotch, whisky must have been produced, and have aged for at least three years in the barrel, in Scotland.

■ **Scotch whisky (single malt)** Single malt is made solely from malted barley, a part of which has been dried over a peat fire. After double distillation it is aged in barrels for at least three years. The aromas of single malt whiskies are more complex than those of blended whiskies.

■ **Scotch whisky (blended)** Blended whisky is a mixture of malt whisky and grain whisky. The flavour is lighter than that of the single malts.

Irish whiskeys Among the Irish whiskeys there are the 'pure pot still', made with a mixture of malted barley and un-malted barley, and the 'single grain', based on other cereals. After triple distillation Irish whiskey is aged for three years.

American whiskeys A number of cocktails are based on bourbon, rye whiskey or Tennessee whiskey.

■ **Straight bourbon** Straight bourbon, made from a mixture of cereals of which maize (corn) comprises the major part, may only be produced in the United States. After triple distillation it must have been aged for at least two years in new barrels, the interiors of which have been charred.

■ **Straight rye** This American whiskey is made in the same way as bourbon, but using rye instead of maize (corn) as the major component.

■ **Straight Tennessee whiskey** This whiskey is made from a mixture of cereals of which one – generally maize (corn) – is predominant. It must be produced in the State of Tennessee. After double distillation the spirit obtained is filtered through maple-wood charcoal, which attenuates some of the aromas. It is then aged for at least two years in new barrels, the interiors of which have been charred.

■ **Canadian whisky** Canadian whisky is made from a mixture of cereals, generally predominantly rye. After single distillation it is aged for at least three years. Whisky produced in Canada is marketed under several names: Canadian Whisky, Canadian Rye Whisky or simply Rye Whisky. The expression 'straight rye' is reserved for rye whiskey produced in the United States.

Rums ■ **Puerto Rican rum** This Hispanic type of rum is made from molasses, the by-product of sugar cane refining. Puerto Rican rum, which is multiple-column distilled, is filtered in order to obtain a lighter, less pronounced flavour.

■ **Cuban rum** This is made by the same process as Puerto Rican rum but is produced in Cuba, where the making of rum originated.

■ **Jamaican rum** This rum, also made from sugar cane molasses and single-column distilled, is generally aged in casks that had previously contained 'straight bourbon', which is what gives it its woody flavour.

■ *Rhum agricole* Principally produced in the French Antilles, *rhum agricole*, 'agricultural rum', is unusual in that it is distilled from sugar cane juice rather than molasses. It is the most aromatic of all the rums. The one from Martinique has been granted an AOC (controlled appellation of origin). According to the length of time it is aged, *rhum agricole*, like the various rums produced by sugar refineries, can be white, amber, dark, etc.

■ **Cachaça** This Brazilian spirit can be distilled from molasses or sugar cane juice, which is why some varieties of cachaça are very similar to *rhum agricole* or 'agricultural rum'.

Tequila Tequila is a Mexican spirit, made from a tropical plant called agave. Used on its own, the word 'tequila' indicates a mixed tequila made with a minimum of 51% of agave. Tequila 100% Agave is made solely from a cultivated variety of agave called *Agave tequilana* 'Weber blue'. The names 'gold' or 'joven abocado' indicate tequila that has been coloured and sweetened.

■ **Tequila blanco** Tequila blanco (or silver) has not undergone any ageing process whatsoever.

■ **Tequila reposado** Tequila reposado has spent at least two months in cask or barrel.

■ **Tequila añejo** Tequila añejo has been aged for at least one year in barrel. It is rarely aged for more than eight to ten years as the bitter taste of the alcohol increases over time.

▶ This advertisement for Old St Croix rum appeared in a 1943 issue of the American magazine *Life*.

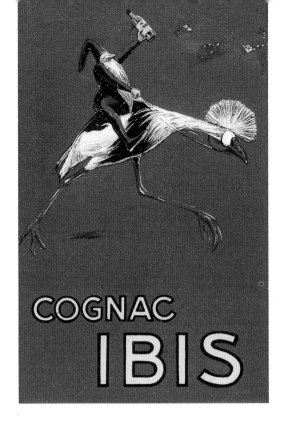

◀ An advertisement for a brand of Cognac that no longer exists.

Kirsch This cherry alcohol is produced principally in France, Switzerland and Germany. After distillation, kirsch is aged for several months in glass carboys.

Wines, aperitifs, bitters, aniseed-based products

Apart from distilled alcohols, other alcoholic drinks are used in the making of cocktails. Some, like Champagne, wine and port wine are known the world over, while others are regional products or commercial brands. They are listed in alphabetical order.

Angostura bitters These concentrated bitters, invented in 1824 by Dr Siegert at Ciudad Bolivar (formerly Angostura) in Venezuela, are produced nowadays in Trinidad in the British Antilles. They are made up of rum flavoured with gentian, spices and plant extracts (44.7% Vol/89.4° proof).

Beer This universal drink is produced by fermenting a barley-based mash, flavoured with hops. Its alcohol content is from 4–7% Vol/8–14° proof. Lager is the most widely drunk variety. In England and Ireland 'ale' refers to a brown beer; 'stout' is the darkest of all beers.

Campari This bitter drink, invented by Gaspare Campari in Milan in the 1860s, is flavoured with extracts of roots, fruit and herbs, and is coloured red (25% Vol/50° proof).

Champagne Made from black and/or white grapes, Champagne is a sparkling wine obtained by procuring a second fermentation in bottle. It is made only in the Champagne area in France (around 12% Vol/24° proof). In the preparation of cocktails it is preferable to use a Champagne Brut.

Brandies ▪ **Cognac** Better known in many countries as 'brandy', Cognac is produced in the Charentes region of France and is made from white wine. After double distillation in a simple alembic still, the spirit must be aged for at least two and a half years in barrel. Cognac is an AOC (controlled appellation of origin) and it must be harvested, distilled and aged exclusively within the designated zone.

▪ **Pisco** This alcohol is made in Chile from white wine and is known as Chilean Brandy. After distillation, pisco is marketed at several different alcoholic strengths (35%, 40% or 45% Vol/70°, 80° or 90° proof), either aged for at least two months, or not at all. A spirit also named pisco is produced in Peru, but by another process, which gives it a different flavour.

▪ **Calvados** This French spirit is made from cider (with 30% pear juice added in the case of Calvados Domfrontais). The area covered by the Calvados AOC is almost entirely confined to Lower Normandy. The Calvados from the Pays d'Auge AOC is essentially the product of the Calvados region and after double distillation it is aged for at least two years. Calvados produced in the Domfrontais AOC must be aged for more than three years.

▶ A Champagne advertisement created in 1949 by poster designer and illustrator René Gruau (1909–2004).

Dubonnet This aromatic, deep red wine with a bitter flavour was invented in Paris in 1846 by Joseph Dubonnet. It is 14.8% Vol/29.6° proof. Another red Dubonnet and a white Dubonnet, 19% Vol/38° proof, were created later for the American market.

Fernet-Branca This bitter was invented in Milan in 1845 by Bernardino Branca. Fernet-Branca, in which the bitterness is very marked, indeed, is made by macerating 40 medicinal plants and aromatic herbs (aloes, camomile, gentian, quinine, saffron, sage, etc.) in neutral alcohol. It is 40% Vol/80° proof.

Orange bitters These concentrated bitters are made from neutral alcohol and extract of bitter oranges, which gives them their orange flavour (30–40% Vol/60–80° proof). The most common commercial brand in France is Reimerschmidt.

Pernod This aniseed-flavoured liquor was created by Pernod Fils and Hémard in 1922, when the production of aniseed-based alcohol was legalized following the ban on absinthe in 1915 (45% Vol/90° proof). The flavour of Pernod is different from that of pastis.

Peychaud's bitters These concentrated bitters were invented by Antoine A Peychaud in New Orleans, in the 1830s, based on a secret family recipe jealously guarded since 1793 (30% Vol/60° proof).

Pimm's This bitter was invented in London in the 1840s and was first marketed in 1859. Pimm's No 1 is made by flavouring gin with herbs and spices (25% Vol/50° proof).

Port Port is a wine fortified with alcohol distilled from wine produced in the vineyards of the Douro valley in Portugal (around 20% Vol/40° proof). The entire production is carried out in wine and spirit stores situated in the town of Porto. Vintage ports, and late-bottled vintage ports (LBV), are made by blending several wines from the same vintage before ageing. 'Ruby' and 'tawny' ports are produced from blends of different vintages.

Sherry Sherry (called *jerez* in Spain and *xérès* in France) is a white wine fortified with alcohol distilled from wine, produced in Andalusia in the south of Spain. It is about 15% Vol/30° proof. The production of sherry sticks rigidly to traditional techniques. Besides the pale, dry Finos one also finds the deeper coloured, stronger Olorosos.

Spirits flavoured with absinthe This liquor is made by flavouring neutral alcohol with extracts of absinthe (45–70% Vol/90–140° proof). The noxious substances that resulted in the ban on the production of absinthe in 1915 are thus present only in infinitesimal amounts.

Vermouth The Italian origins of this aperitif date back to the seventeenth century.
■ **Dry vermouth** Pale coloured dry vermouth, containing 50–60 g (2–2¼ oz) of sugar per litre (1¾ pints), is made with white wine, fortified with neutral alcohol and flavoured with more or less bitter herbs, including absinthe. It is 14.5–22% Vol/29–44° proof.
■ **Red vermouth** This sweet vermouth, containing 100–150 g (4–5 oz) of sugar per litre (1¾ pints), is also made from white wine and coloured with caramel. Like the white, it is 14.5–22% Vol/29–44° proof.

Wine Several kinds of wine are used in cocktails, notably white wines of the Aligoté type, used in the preparation of the famous Kir (▷ p. 234), red Bordeaux for hot wine drinks and rough, strong red wine for Sangria (▷ p. 242).

Liqueurs

Liqueurs are generally made by distilling neutral alcohol in which fruits, plants, spices and/or rinds have macerated for several weeks. Crèmes are liqueurs with a strong sugar content 250 g (9 oz) per litre (1¾ pints).

Amaretto This liqueur, an Italian speciality, is made by macerating apricot kernels and alcohol with the addition of water and sugar (25–28% Vol/50–56° proof). The best-known brand is Amaretto Disaronno, created in 1817.

Apricot brandy This liqueur is made by macerating apricots in alcohol distilled from wine with the addition of at least 100 g (4 oz) of sugar per litre (1¾ pints) (24–30% Vol/48–60° proof).

Banane (crème de) Crème de banane is made by flavouring neutral alcohol with an extract taken from the skins of bananas, coloured yellow and containing at least 250 g (9 oz) of sugar per litre (1¾ pints) (24–30% Vol/48–60° proof).

Benedictine This plant- and spice-based liqueur, invented by Benedictine monks in the sixteenth century, was first marketed commercially in 1863 at Fécamp, by a man called Alexandre le Grand (40% Vol/80° proof).

Cacao (crème de) Crème de cacao is the result of flavouring neutral alcohol with a cocoa extract; it may be brown in colour but this is not always the case. It contains at least 250 g (9 oz) of sugar per litre (1¾ pints) (24–30% Vol/48–60° proof).

Cassis (crème de) Crème de cassis has been a speciality of Dijon since 1845, and is made by macerating blackcurrants in neutral alcohol and adding water and at least 400 g (14 oz) of sugar per litre (1¾ pints) (15–20% Vol/30–40° proof).

Chartreuse The liqueur made by the Chartreuse monks, inspired by a recipe dating back to the start of the seventeenth century, is flavoured with more than one hundred plants and spices. There are two types: green Chartreuse (55% Vol/110° proof), created in 1764, and yellow Chartreuse (40% Vol/80° proof), perfected in 1838.

Cherry brandy This is made by macerating cherries in wine-based alcohol with the addition of at least 100 g (4 oz) of sugar per litre (1¾ pints) (24–30% Vol/48–60° proof). The best-known brands are Cherry Heering, created in Denmark in 1818 (24.7% Vol/49.4° proof) and Cherry Rocher, perfected in the middle of the nineteenth century at La Côte-Saint-André in the Isère region (24% Vol/48° proof).

Coconut (liqueur) This liqueur is made by macerating extract of coconut in rum or a neutral alcohol and contains at least 100 g (4 oz) of sugar per litre (1¾ pints) (20–24% Vol/40–48° proof). The best-known brand name is Vedrenne.

Coffee (liqueur) Coffee liqueur is produced by flavouring neutral alcohol with coffee

◀ Poster created in 1935 for the famous aperitif, from a drawing by Cassandre (1901–1968).

extract; it is coloured brown and contains at least 100 g (4 oz) of sugar per litre (1¾ pints) (24–26.5% Vol/48–53° proof).

Curaçao Curaçao is an orange liqueur originally developed by the Dutch with the peel of bitter oranges imported from the island of Curaçao in the Dutch Antilles.
■ **Curaçao triple sec** This is made by flavouring neutral alcohol with an extract of both bitter and sweet oranges (35–40% Vol/70–80° proof).
■ **Blue curaçao** This is a curaçao triple sec with the alcohol content reduced to 25% Vol/50° proof and coloured blue.
■ **Orange curaçao** This is a curaçao triple sec with the alcohol content reduced to 30% Vol/60° proof and coloured orange with caramel.

Drambuie This liqueur, whose origins go back to the eighteenth century, is made from a blend of Scotch malt whisky and Scotch grain whisky, flavoured with spices and sweetened with heather honey (40% Vol/80° proof). It was marketed commercially from 1909 by Malcolm Mackinnon, but of course the recipe remains a secret.

Fraise (crème de) Crème de fraise is made by macerating strawberries in neutral alcohol with the addition of water and at least 250 g (9 oz) of sugar per litre (1¾ pints) (15–20% Vol/30–40° proof).

Framboise (crème de) Crème de framboise is made by macerating raspberries in neutral alcohol with the addition of water and at least 250 g (9 oz) of sugar per litre (1¾ pints) (15–20% Vol/ 30–40° proof).

Galliano This liqueur was invented in 1896 in Tuscany by Arturo Vaccari. It is made by flavouring alcohol with plant extracts (star anise, lavender, vanilla, etc.) and colouring it yellow (30% Vol/60° proof).

Grand Marnier Cordon Rouge Invented in 1880, this liqueur allies bitter oranges with rigorously selected Cognac (40% Vol/80° proof).

Irish cream This creamy liqueur of Irish origin is made with Irish whiskey, fresh cream and cocoa (17% Vol/34° proof). The best-known one is made by Bailey's, who invented this new category of liqueur in 1974 in Dublin.

Krupnik This traditional Polish liqueur is a combination of vodka, spices and honey (40% Vol/80° proof).

Limoncello An Italian liqueur produced in the Amalfi region by macerating lemon rinds in neutral alcohol with sugar and water added (30% Vol/60° proof). The original brand, Limoncello di Capri, was created in 1988.

Lychee/litchi (liqueur) This liqueur is made by flavouring neutral alcohol with an extract of lychees (litchis) and at least 100 g (4 oz) of sugar per litre (1¾ pints) (20–24% Vol/40–48° proof).

Manzana verde Of Spanish origin, this recently invented liqueur is made by flavouring neutral alcohol with an extract of green apples (Granny Smith) and contains at least 100 g (4 oz) of sugar per litre (1¾ pints) (18–20% Vol/36–40° proof). In English it is called apple schnapps. Izarra and Vedrenne are the main commercial brands of manzana verde in France.

Maraschino (liqueur) This liqueur was originally Italian and was first made at Zara (now Zadar in Croatia) in 1821 by Girolamo Luxardo. It is the product of distilling a mash of *marasca* – bitter wild cherries – and adding at least 100 g (4 oz) of sugar per litre (1¾ pints) (30–32% Vol/60–64° proof). Luxardo is still the principal producer.

Melocoton This liqueur, made by flavouring neutral alcohol with peach extract, contains at least 100 g (4 oz) of sugar per litre (1¾ pints) (18–20% Vol/36–40° proof). This kind of liqueur is generally called peach schnapps in English. The principal commercial brands of melocoton in France are Archer's and Vedrenne.

Melon (liqueur) Melon liqueur, made by flavouring a neutral alcohol with extract of winter melons (those having orange or greenish flesh), contains at least 100 g (4 oz) of sugar per litre (1¾ pints) (20–25% Vol/40–50° proof). The Japanese company Midori first created the green melon liqueur in 1978.

Menthe (crème de) Crème de menthe (white or green) is a liqueur that was originally made in England and which became popular in the eighteenth century. It is made by flavouring neutral alcohol with mint extract that is then sweetened and often coloured green (21–24% Vol/42–48° proof). Get 27 is a green crème de menthe, whereas Get 31 is colourless.

Mûre (crème de) Crème de mûre is made by macerating blackberries in neutral alcohol with the addition of water and 250 g (9 oz) of sugar per litre (1¾ pints) (15–20% Vol/30–40° proof).

Southern Comfort This liqueur was invented in New Orleans in 1874 by M W Heron and marketed commercially in 1889. It is made with American whiskey and other ingredients, which are kept secret, and contains at least 100 g (4 oz) of sugar per litre (1¾ pints) (40% Vol/80° proof).

▲ An advertisement for Monin orangeade.

Fruit juices and fruit nectars

Among the non-alcoholic ingredients used in the preparation of cocktails, fruit juices and nectars hold pride of place. They are marketed with labels that carry precise information about their composition and method of production. When there is a choice it is better to opt for fresh fruit juice.

Fresh fruit juice These fruit juices are the nearest thing to the freshly squeezed juices one makes at home. They are sold from refrigerated counters and carry a 14-day 'sell-by' date. They must be used within two days of being opened. They are simply fresh fruit juices bottled without any additives or treatment. This is the best category to use for those cocktail recipes that call for lemon, lime, orange or grapefruit juice.

Fruit juice and concentrate-based fruit juice Made up of 100% fruit juice, 'fruit juice' has undergone flash pasteurization, during which it is subjected briefly to a high temperature, which sterilizes it while retaining all its qualities. As to concentrate-based fruit juice, this has had water added before being offered for sale. The fruit is squeezed at the production source and is concentrated by evaporation to simplify stocking and transport. Pineapple, cranberry, mango, apple and passion fruit juices come in both these categories, as well as tomato and carrot juices, which are used in many cocktails.

Fruit nectars Fruit nectars are drinks that contain less fruit and are sweetened with sugar. In cocktail recipes the one most frequently used is banana nectar.

Mineral water and mixers

Mineral water Among the various kinds of bottled water are 'spring water' and many 'natural mineral waters' known for their therapeutic value (mineral salts, trace elements). They may be still, naturally effervescent or carbonated.

Soda water (club soda) is a carbonated mineral water, formerly sold in siphons but nowadays in bottles. It is often used to dilute spirits and fruit juices.

Mixers These are effervescent drinks often made by flavouring purified water with aromatic extracts and adding carbonic gas.

Cola This effervescent drink, flavoured with plant extracts and coloured with caramel, was perfected in the United States in the 1880s.

Ginger ale This drink is lightly flavoured with ginger. The best-known brand, Canada Dry, was created in Toronto in 1904 by John J McLaughlin.

Ginger beer This effervescent drink results from a liquid based on fresh ginger that is bottled at the start of fermentation. It is mainly produced in Jamaica and the main brands are D & G and Reed's.

Lemon-lime soda This effervescent drink flavoured with lemon and lime extracts was invented in 1928 by Charles Grigg under the name of 7 UP which, even today, is still the main brand.

Tonic water Schweppes Tonic Water, an effervescent drink flavoured with quinine, was invented in the 1870s in England and is the most famous of the tonic waters.

Syrups and sweeteners

Syrups Syrups are made by dissolving sugar or other sweet substances in water, with or without flavourings. They add flavour, sweetness and colour to alcoholic cocktails.

Grenadine Formerly made with pomegranate juice, grenadine is now based on any red fruit juice, vanilla and sometimes lemon.

Lime juice cordial This syrup, originally from Scotland, is lime juice sweetened with sugar. The most famous brand is Rose's Lime Juice Cordial.

Orgeat syrup A syrup flavoured with almonds.

Raspberry syrup Syrup flavoured with raspberries.

Sugar cane syrup This is simply cane sugar dissolved in water. It is essential to the preparation of a number of cocktails.

Sweeteners

Coconut milk This thick, non-alcoholic liquid has been produced in the Caribbean since the 1950s and is made from pulverized coconut and cane sugar.

Honey This is made by bees, from the nectar they collect from flowers. Liquid honey, made from acacia or other flowers, is used in the making of certain cocktails.

Sugar This is made from sugar cane or sugar beet. In preparing cocktails one can use lump sugar, brown or white, or caster (superfine) sugar, which has fine grains that dissolve easily in alcohol.

Eggs and dairy products

Towards the end of the nineteenth century, many cocktails were made with the yolk or white of an egg, or even milk. They were greatly valued for their reputed fortifying properties. Some of the recipes have become classics. Nowadays, the dairy products used in cocktails are both full-fat amd semi-skimmed milk, and single (light) and double (heavy) cream. Egg yolk forms part of the ingredients of some cocktails, while the white is used to give a frothy consistency to certain mixtures.

▶ In the table opposite, the stock for beginners ℐ is sufficient to prepare many of the recipes that require the most commonly used products. The stock for amateurs ℐ ℐ allows for the preparation of a wider range of drinks, whereas with the professional stock ℐ ℐ ℐ it is possible to make all the drinks mentioned in this book.

BAR STOCKS

Spirits

Spirits	Y	YY	YYY
Vodka	●	●	●
Gin and London gin	●	●	●
Plymouth gin			●
Scotch whisky (blended)	●	●	●
Scotch whisky (single malt)			●
Irish whiskey		●	●
Straight bourbon	●	●	●
Straight Tennessee whiskey		●	●
Straight rye whiskey			●
Canadian whisky		●	●
Rum (Puerto Rican)		●	●
Rum (Cuban)	●	●	●
Rum (Jamaican)		●	●
Rhum agricole, 'agricultural rum'			●
Cachaça			●
Tequila blanco (100% agave)	●	●	●
Tequila reposado (100% agave)		●	●
Tequila añejo (100% agave)			●
Cognac	●	●	●
Pisco			●
Calvados		●	●
Kirsch			●

Wines, aperitifs, bitters, etc.

Wines, aperitifs, bitters, etc.	Y	YY	YYY
Angostura bitters	●	●	●
Beer		●	●
Campari		●	●
Champagne	●	●	●
Dubonnet			●
Fernet-Branca			●
Orange bitters		●	●
Pernod			●
Peychaud's bitters			●
Pimm's			●
Port			●
Sherry (jerez or xérès)			●
Spirits made with absinthe			●
Vermouth, dry	●	●	●
Vermouth, red	●	●	●
Wine	●	●	●

Liqueurs

Liqueurs	Y	YY	YYY
Amaretto		●	●
Apricot brandy		●	●
Banane (crème de)		●	●
Benedictine			●
Cacao (crème de)	●	●	●
Cassis (crème de)	●	●	●
Chartreuse			●
Cherry brandy		●	●
Coconut liqueur			●
Coffee liqueur	●	●	●
Curaçao triple sec	●	●	●
Curaçao, blue		●	●
Curaçao, orange			●

Liqueurs

Liqueurs	Y	YY	YYY
Drambuie			●
Fraise (crème de)			●
Framboise (crème de)			●
Galliano		●	●
Grand Marnier Cordon Rouge			●
Irish cream		●	●
Krupnik			●
Limoncello			●
Lychee (litchi) liqueur			●
Manzana verde			●
Maraschino liqueur			●
Melocoton (peach schnapps)		●	●
Melon liqueur			●
Menthe (crème de)	●	●	●
Mûre (crème de)		●	●
Southern Comfort			●

Fruit juices and fruit nectars

Fruit juices and fruit nectars	Y	YY	YYY
Apple juice		●	●
Banana nectar		●	●
Carrot juice		●	●
Cranberry juice	●	●	●
Grapefruit juice		●	●
Lemon juice	●	●	●
Lime juice	●	●	●
Lychee (litchi) juice		●	●
Mango juice		●	●
Orange juice	●	●	●
Passion fruit juice		●	●
Pineapple juice	●	●	●
Tomato juice		●	●

Mineral waters and mixers

Mineral waters and mixers	Y	YY	YYY
Still mineral water		●	●
Sparkling mineral water	●	●	●
Cola		●	●
Ginger ale	●	●	●
Ginger beer			●
Lemon-lime soda	●	●	●
Tonic water			●

Syrups and sweeteners

Syrups and sweeteners	Y	YY	YYY
Grenadine	●	●	●
Lime juice cordial			●
Orgeat syrup			●
Raspberry syrup			●
Sugar cane syrup			●
Coconut milk		●	●
Liquid honey			●
Sugar	●	●	●

Eggs and dairy products

Eggs and dairy products	Y	YY	YYY
Eggs			●
Cream		●	●
Milk		●	●

Condiments and sauces

A number of condiments are used to accentuate the flavour of certain cocktails, mainly salt, celery salt and pepper, but also such spices as cinnamon and cloves. Some recipes call for the use of specific sauces.

Tabasco This highly spiced sauce was invented in Louisiana in 1868 by Edmund McIlhenny. It is made up of vinegar, chilli peppers and salt.

Worcestershire sauce This sauce was invented in 1837 in the English county of Worcester. The longest established make is Lea & Perrins. The ingredients include vinegar, anchovies, tamarind, garlic and onion.

▲ 1951 American advertisement for a 'tele-bar' – a unit combining television set, radio and refrigerated drinks bar.

Garnishes

Garnishes added to certain cocktails include such fresh fruits as lemon, lime, orange, pineapple, strawberries, raspberries, also fresh mint leaves and even vegetables such as celery sticks and cucumber. Maraschino cherries, green olives and tiny white onions preserved in vinegar are other additions. Some cocktails can be topped with shaved chocolate or grated nutmeg. Orange or blackcurrant conserves are occasionally used in cocktails but only rarely.

Cocktail decorations

While it is not essential, a number of cocktail recipes call for decoration, which should be just enough to enhance the contents of the glass without turning the cocktail into an object of fantasy. The garnishes already mentioned above play an important role in the decoration. These so-called functional garnishes add to the flavour to a greater or lesser degree. This also applies to citrus peel (zest) or fresh mint leaves, which contribute a pronounced aroma. Merely decorative garnishes are there to enhance the final appearance of the cocktail – a pineapple leaf placed on the rim of the glass being a perfect example. As to frosting the rim of the glass with salt or icing (confectioners') sugar (▷ p. 59), it may be classed as a functional decoration, since the flavour of the salt or sugar affects the taste of the drink.

Ice

A great deal of ice is used in the mixing of cocktails. It is important to ensure that you have an adequate stock before your guests arrive. The more ice used, the more refreshing the resulting drinks. If too little is used, the ice cubes melt too quickly and the resulting cocktail is over-diluted.

On the other hand, with abundant ice the drink chills rapidly and dilution is reduced to a minimum. In hard water areas it is better to make the ice with mineral water.

Crushed ice, indispensable for some drinks, is made by smashing up ice cubes in a cloth (▷ p. 59). It is used to make 'frappé' drinks.

Bar equipment

A number of manufacturers make all kinds of bar equipment but these items should be chosen carefully, as it is only with use that one can really judge their value. As to glasses, these should not be seen as simple receptacles; careful attention should be given to their selection because the different shapes and weights contribute greatly to the ultimate enjoyment of the drink.

The utensils

Boston shaker This was the first shaker used in America by the pioneer barmen of the nineteenth century. The Boston shaker consists of a large glass (which can also be used as a mixing glass, even though it lacks a spout) and a metal tumbler of a larger diameter than the glass. When the ingredients are shaken, the cooling effect of the ice causes the metal to contract and make a hermetic seal with the glass (but without ever blocking it tightly shut).

Continental shaker As its name indicates, the continental shaker originated in Europe at the start of the twentieth century. It is a development of the Boston shaker, but both elements are made of metal. Elegantly shaped, it is used in the same way as the Boston shaker.

Shaker with strainer This shaker appeared at the end of the nineteenth century. Its special feature is an incorporated strainer that does away with the need to use a cocktail strainer. This form of shaker is the one most used by the general public. It does have the effect, however, of diluting the drinks to a greater extent since, when pouring the drink into the glass the ice accumulates in a restricted space and consequently melts more rapidly.

Mixing spoon This special spoon is an essential tool for mixing cocktails directly in the glass or in the mixing glass, and also for making shooters (▷ p. 58). It is also useful for measuring ingredients (it holds the same amount as a teaspoon). The stem is often twisted, to provide a good grip even when wet from contact with the ice. The flat, disk-shaped end of the stem serves as a pestle for crushing mint leaves. More solid ingredients (pieces of lemon, orange, melon, cucumber, etc.) require a proper wooden pestle.

mixing spoon

shaker with strainer

Boston shaker

mixing glass

sommelier

pulp strainer

ice scoop

nutmeg grater

cocktail strainer

paring knife

spirit measure

Rinse it out immediately after use to make it easier to clean.

Spirit measure This allows one to measure the exact amount of alcohol specified in the recipes. Generally it consists of two linked measures holding different quantities, which differ from one country to another according to the units of capacity in use there. In France, for example, these measures hold 20 ml (¾ fl oz) and 40 ml (1¼ fl oz). In the UK the measure used (a jigger) is 25 ml (1 fl oz), or 50 ml (1¾ fl oz) for a double, while in the United States it is 45 ml (1½ fl oz).

Pourer cork A pourer cork is made of soft plastic, which adapts to fit most bottle necks. It is fitted with two metal tubes of different diameters, one through which the liquid pours and a second that extends down into the bottle and controls the intake of air, ensuring a regular, uninterrupted flow. A stock of several pourer corks is recommended.

Cocktail strainer This is a perforated metal plate with a metal spiral, like a spring, around its edge. It is used to hold back the ice when pouring cocktails that are served 'straight up' from a Boston shaker or mixing glass.

Crushed-ice strainer This is a round perforated metal disk that fits over the rim of the glass. It is used to filter out crushed ice from drinks served 'straight up'.

Pulp strainer This strainer serves as a sieve for liquids containing elements in suspension. It is used in addition to the crushed ice strainer and is held over the serving glass while the preparation is poured.

Lemon squeezer This can be manual or electric, and is used to extract the juice from citrus fruits. It is important to press the sides of the fruit and not the top so as not to damage the white pulp under the skin, which gives a bitter taste to the juice. A lemon squeezer should be rinsed immediately after use to make cleaning easier.

Mixing glass This is used for mixing cocktails that are to be served 'straight up', that is without ice in the glass. It consists of a large glass furnished with a spout. It must hold at least 500 ml (17¼ fl oz) if used to mix a single drink or 650 ml (22½ fl oz) for two. Its height must be such that the mixing spoon can be manipulated without the fingers coming into contact with the glass during preparation.

Blender This electric appliance is essential to the preparation of 'frozen' cocktails. The length of time needed to achieve a homogeneous result depends on the power of the blender. If its speed is less than 18,000 rpm then it is better to use crushed ice when preparing 'frozen' cocktails.

Pestle This implement is made of wood or hard plastic and is used to crush mint leaves or fruit for the purpose of bringing out the aromas or reducing them to a purée.

Crown top bottle-opener This object is used to remove the metal tops from mixer bottles but more and more often nowadays these bottles come with screw-tops.

Sommelier This form of corkscrew comes complete with a serrated blade for cutting around the capsule covering the cork, a long metal spiral (with 5 turns) that pierces the cork without damaging it, and a crown top bottle opener.

Ice tongs These are used to transfer ice cubes from the ice bucket to the glass, shaker or blender, and also for handling the fruit used as garnish.

Ice scoop This is used for shovelling crushed ice into the glass, mixing glass, shaker or blender.

Paring knife A knife with a smooth, 10 cm (4 in) blade used for cutting regular strips of peel (zest) from citrus fruits.

Slicing knife This knife has a serrated blade around 15 cm (6 in) long and is used in preference to a smooth blade for quartering or slicing fruit, as it separates the slices rather than allowing these to stick to each other.

Cutting board This board, made of wood, polyethylene (a hard plastic) or toughened glass, is used for cutting fruit. It must be rinsed after use with an anti-bacterial cleaning medium.

Nutmeg grater A small grater used to grate nutmeg or chocolate. Nutmeg must be grated at the last moment to preserve all its flavour.

Straws A straw allows one to drink a cocktail without making contact with the ice cubes or crushed ice, which is a boon to people with sensitive teeth. Straws are mainly used with long drinks and short drinks served 'frozen' or 'on the rocks', but never with drinks served 'straight up'.

Mixing sticks These little tools generally accompany cocktails served 'on the rocks'. They are used to stir the mixture when the melting ice forms a layer on the surface.

Drink mats Whether made of absorbent paper or tissue, a drink mat is there to absorb any condensation that drips down on the surface of the cold glass, or an accidental spillage.

▼ In the table below the utensils marked with a dot correspond to the needs of different categories of user. Some are indispensable, even to beginners ¥, others are only needed by amateurs ¥ ¥ or professionals ¥ ¥ ¥.

BAR EQUIPMENT

	¥	¥ ¥	¥ ¥ ¥
Shaker, Boston or continental		●	●
Shaker with strainer	●		
Mixing spoon	●	●	●
Mixing glass	●	●	●
Blender		●	●
Spirit measure	●	●	●
Pourer cork		●	●
Cocktail strainer		●	●
Crushed-ice strainer			●
Pulp strainer			●
Lemon squeezer	●	●	●
Pestle	●	●	●
Crown top bottle-opener	●	●	●
Sommelier		●	●
Ice tongs	●	●	●
Ice scoop			●
Paring knife		●	●
Slicing knife	●	●	●
Cutting board	●	●	●
Grater		●	●
Straws	●	●	●
Mixing sticks	●	●	●
Drinks mats		●	●

Glassware

Martini glass The name is taken from the famous Dry Martini that is usually served in it; it is also known as a cocktail glass. It holds about 200 ml (7 fl oz). The Martini glass is recommended for short drinks served 'straight up', 'frappé' and often also for 'frozen' drinks. It is particularly suitable for cocktails like the Cosmopolitan (▷ p. 64), the Manhattan (▷ p. 122) and the Sidecar (▷ p. 201).

Tulip glass This holds about 120 ml (4 fl oz) and is the ideal shape for assessing the quality of alcoholic drinks. It allows the most volatile aromas to rise and secondary aromas to be detected when the contents are swirled. Generally speaking, cocktails are not served in tulip glasses, with the exception of the Nikolaschka (▷ p. 210).

Wine glass This holds around 250 ml (8½ fl oz) and is used for wine and for cocktails such as Spritzer (▷ p. 235), and Absinthe Drip (▷ p. 232).

Champagne flute The shape of this glass, which holds about 180 ml (6¼ fl oz), helps to bring out the full finesse of Champagne. The flute is also used for Champagne-based cocktails, except those served with ice in a highball glass. It is an absolute must for, among others, Champagne Cocktail (▷ p. 217), Kir Royal (▷ p. 218) and the Bellini (▷ p. 224).

Shot glass This holds about 60 ml (2 fl oz) and its compact shape makes it ideal for drinks intended to be 'knocked back' in one go. Shooters are always served in this type of glass. Tequila and vodka are served neat in shot glasses. They are also suitable for such cocktails as the Kamikaze (▷ p. 71), Tequila Straight (▷ p. 173) and the B-52 (▷ p. 243).

Rocks glass Its name comes from the term 'on the rocks', used to describe spirits served with ice. It is also called an old-fashioned and a small tumbler. It holds around 300 ml (10¼ fl oz) and is used for cocktails like the Caïpirinha (▷ p. 145), the Black Russian (▷ p. 84) and the Gimlet (▷ p. 99).

Highball glass The name of this glass is the same as the Highball cocktail family. It is also known as a Collins glass or a large tumbler. It holds approximately 350 ml (12 fl oz) and is used for such cocktails as the Sea Breeze (▷ p. 82), El Diablo (▷ p. 175) and Gin Fizz (▷ p. 100).

Toddy glass The name of this glass is also that of a family of cocktails – the Toddies. Intended for the service of hot cocktails, it is made of heatproof glass that is proofed against being filled with boiling liquid. It holds about 250 ml (8½ fl oz) and is used for Irish Coffee (▷ p. 139), Fish House Punch (▷ p. 168) and Mexican Tea (▷ p. 191).

| Martini | tulip | wine | flute | shot | rocks | highball | toddy |

The basic rules of cocktail mixing

The art of cocktail making lies in mixing ingredients in a way that combines the different aromas to produce a new, more subtle result. In 1948, American David Embury, who was passionately interested in the art of cocktail mixing, established a system of classification that is still used in professional circles. He divided the ingredients into three groups: a base; a modifying, smoothing or aromatizing agent; and additional special flavouring and colouring ingredients. According to the author, this classification applied only to cocktails served 'straight up' (▷ p. 49) – in a Martini glass – but it is perfectly adapted to long drinks as well.

The three components of a cocktail

The base

The base is the ingredient that contributes the organoleptic qualities (aroma, taste, colour) and is responsible for the first impression. The cocktail is built around this unique base that is almost always some kind of spirit: vodka, gin, the various kinds of whisky, rum, tequila, Cognac and Calvados. Champagne is also used as the basis of some cocktails, though its sparkling character makes it equally suitable as the modifier ingredient.

The proportion of the other ingredients to the base varies according to whether one is making a short or a long drink.

The proportion of the alcohol base in a short drink, especially one served in a Martini glass, is generally 50–70% but it can be as high as 90% (for an Extra-Dry Martini, ▷ p. 92). The alcoholic strength of the base counterbalances the flavours contributed by the modifier and any flavouring or colouring agents used. The taste of the alcohol will always remain perceptible and recognizable, which is why short drinks are classified according to the spirit they are based on – gin, whisky or rum cocktails, etc.

In the case of long drinks the base represents only 20–30% of the total volume so the flavour of the basic alcohol will, of necessity, be much less pronounced on the palate, although the marked flavour of alcohols such as tequila made from 100% agave remains easily identifiable.

The modifier

The modifier is the ingredient, or group of ingredients, which has the most effect on the consistency of the cocktail and also contributes extra flavours that complement those of the base.

It may consist of wine, a sparkling wine such as Champagne, an aromatic wine such as vermouth or a fortified wine such as port. Mixed with the alcohol base, these vinous products make for a fluid texture, and in some cases add a touch of sweetness. They are used mainly in short drinks, however, it is not unusual to find Champagne used as a mixer in a long drink.

Mineral water, still or sparkling, or carbonated mixers like soda water (club soda), cola, tonic water, lemon-lime soda, ginger ale or ginger beer can all form the body of the drink. These give a light sensation on the palate, particularly in the case of long, refreshing drinks, but care has to be taken not to drown the other ingredients.

Fruit or vegetable juice, used as the modifying agent of the drink, will affect its consistency. Cranberry juice, for instance, will produce a fluid drink, whereas tomato juice will make it thicker and smoother. When making short drinks, lemon or lime juice should be used sparingly because their acidity can overshadow the flavours of the other ingredients.

Finally, the modifier may be a rich substance like milk or cream, or the white or yolk of egg. These ingredients make for a creamy, smooth mixture but they should be measured very accurately as a cocktail that is excessively thick or rich could be off-putting.

The flavouring and colouring agents

These are the complementary elements that add sweetness or bitterness to a cocktail and perhaps colour too.

Bitters like Campari, and concentrates such as Angostura bitters, add a bitter flavour in varying degrees and, in some cases, also add colour.

Sweeteners, which include syrups and liqueurs, add extra flavour and also attenuate the strength of the base. Their colour, too, can give a fanciful touch, as does the grenadine in a Tequila Sunrise (▷ p. 186).

In every case, whether using bitters, syrups or liqueurs, one must be careful to maintain the balance of the cocktail. In short drinks, where the modifier makes up only a small part of the whole, using a liqueur as a flavouring agent will greatly influence the nature of the cocktail. Taken to its limit, if the cocktail is made entirely from a base and a liqueur additive, with no added modifier whatsoever, it will be very strong in alcohol.

In the case of cocktails that are made up of just base and a flavouring agent with no spirit base (a Kir ▷ p. 234, for example, or a Vermouth-Cassis ▷ p. 236), one must, of course, increase the quantity of additive used in order to give the desired alcoholic strength.

▲ 1961 American advertisement for the 'Cocktailamatic' – a machine for the preparation of cocktails.

The order of the ingredients

In order to make this book practical to use, the ingredients that go to make up the cocktails are set out in the recipes in the order that they are used.

Professionals often use the ingredients in a different order – base, then flavouring or colouring agent, then modifier – depending on the way they work.

When in doubt, the beginner could also adopt the procedure recommended by the hotel schools: begin by pouring the cheapest ingredient and finish with the most expensive, thus minimizing the waste if a mistake is made halfway through!

The three conditions for a successful cocktail

In order for a cocktail to become popular with a wide range of people and find a place among the cocktail classics, there are three conditions that have to be met: the taste, the appearance and the name.

The taste

In the matter of the taste, naturally the choice of ingredients and the measures used must be absolutely right. All the aromas must complement each other. To be sure of this happening there is a set of rules that professionals may or may not strictly adhere to, depending on their knowledge and their character. One of these forbids the mixing of grain alcohol (whisky or gin, for example) with alcohol distilled from the grape (Cognac and other brandies). This ban can even be extended to cover the practice of mixing spirits made from the same basic materials (two different kinds of grain alcohol, for example). Other rules condemn unnatural unions such as, among others, rum/Calvados, Cognac/rum, rum/gin and whisky/rum.

Note that mixing vodka with alcohol that has been aged is not a good idea either; the vodka, a notable neutral alcohol, would have a negative effect on the aromas that have developed during the ageing process. All these principles have not prevented long drinks like Long Island Iced Tea (▷ p. 73), which contains vodka, gin, rum and even occasionally tequila, from becoming internationally successful and acknowledged classics.

The appearance

This is all-important as it is the first thing that awakens the interest of a potential drinker. But while cocktails should always be attractive, excessive decoration should be avoided. One must also bear in mind that very different results can be obtained using the same ingredients. A Daiquiri (▷ p. 147), for example, served 'straight up' in a Martini glass, or a Caïpirinha (▷ p. 145), served 'frappé' in a rocks glass, are both made from rum, lime juice and sugar but are totally different in appearance. Colour, too, plays a significant role in the success of a cocktail. It can, for example, add a feminine touch.

The name

The name of a cocktail is also integral because it stirs the imagination. Consciously or not, the customer will detect a hidden meaning or an innuendo. The name can indicate the degree of alcohol in a cocktail or whether it is non-alcoholic; whether it was invented for a particular occasion or in honour of an important person. It can, like the colour, give an impression of femininity, as in the Pink Daiquiri (▷ p. 152), or be clearly masculine, like the Kamikaze (▷ p. 71).

Ever since cocktails came into being, barmen have cultivated the knack of giving apt

THE DIFFERENT WAYS OF SERVING COCKTAILS

Float. This term is used when the alcohol is poured over the mixing spoon so that it floats on top of the other ingredients.

Frappé. This describes a drink served on a bed of crushed ice in a Martini glass. This way of producing a drink with the consistency of the modern 'frozen' cocktails was very popular in hot climates at the start of the 1930s, before the electric blender came into general use.

Frozen. This term indicates the sorbet- (sherbet-) or snow-like consistency of drinks made in an electric blender when the quantity of ice used is greater than that of the rest of the ingredients.

On the rocks. This expression indicates a drink that is poured into a glass part-filled with ice cubes. These keep the drink cold while it is being consumed. Many people prefer their spirits 'on the rocks' as the melting ice attenuates the strength of the alcohol.

Straight up. This refers to a drink pre-cooled in a mixing glass or shaker then strained, usually into a Martini glass, to remove the ice cubes.

PRECISE MEASURES

Simply mixing the ingredients is not in itself a complex operation but when making something that has to satisfy one's own or one's guests' palate, it tends to become more demanding, so it is essential to stick to the measures indicated in the recipes.

Any change in the proportions, however small, is to be avoided since it is easy to upset the balance of a cocktail, especially in the case of short drinks. One should be careful, for example, not to over-dilute the other components by adding too much soda water (club soda) to a long drink, or using too much lemon juice, which would make the cocktail excessively acidic, or of overdoing the quantity of egg or dairy produce, which could spoil the appetite.

For this reason, the use of a spirit measure is strongly recommended. Only those who, from extensive experience, are totally familiar with the flavour and nature of the ingredients, are able to judge quantities without measuring them.

and memorable names to even the simplest of drinks, so that they go on to become legendary. This was the case with the Screwdriver ($\triangleright$ p. 82), for example, which in reality is nothing more than vodka with orange juice. A whole international language of the cocktail bar has developed in which one finds, apart from the specific terms like 'on the rocks', 'shorts', etc., a long list of cocktails with evocative names, borrowed for the most part from Anglo-Saxon culture, regardless of their country of origin.

The range of flavours

The vast choice of ingredients listed in the previous chapter ($\triangleright$ pp. 33–42) brings into play a wide variety of flavours and aromas, ranging from strong to mild. One can classify all the products and substances used in cocktail making by their flavours.

Remember that while the sensory organs are capable of recognizing a multitude of taste sensations, there are only four primary flavours: sweet, salt, acid and bitter. According to the complexity of the cocktail, one, or a contrasting combination of several of these basic flavours, may predominate.

Sweetness is the most common flavour found in cocktails because so many of the essential ingredients – syrups, fruit juices (especially fruit nectars), liqueurs and even some mixers – are sweet.

Acid is also very much in evidence, since highly acidic ingredients, like lemon and lime juice, are used to counterbalance the sweetness of one or more of the other ingredients. And many fruits are both sweet and acid at the same time.

Bitterness is less frequently encountered, although it does serve a similar purpose to acid flavours in counteracting sweetness. In cocktails, it is present in such ingredients as bitters (concentrated or otherwise), grapefruit juice and tonic water.

Salt flavours are found in only a very few cocktails since saline ingredients – such as tomato juice with its 7 g (¼ oz) of salt per litre (1¼ pints), salt and celery salt – are used relatively little. They are, of course, present in those cocktails served in a glass with a salt-frosted rim ($\triangleright$ p. 59).

The best combinations

Combining some types of alcohol is definitely inadvisable, as we have seen ($\triangleright$ p. 49). On the other hand, experience shows that in many cases remarkable results can be obtained from a combination of a base, a modifier and a flavouring or colouring agent. The most accessible way of listing the combinations that offer the most interesting results is by setting them out in a table and marking them with a cross.

In the table on the opposite page, the vertical columns represent the principal kinds of alcohol used as a base in cocktails, and the horizontal columns the ingredients most widely used as the modifier and the flavouring or colouring agents. This table is not exhaustive, it is merely based on professional experience. Everyone is free to think up new mixtures, to try new combinations, but it is as well to bear in mind that alcohol should always be taken in moderation.

THE BEST COMBINATIONS

	MODIFIER	Vodka	Gin	Scotch whisky/ Irish whiskey	American whiskeys	White rum (Cuban, Jamaican)	Pale rum (Cuban, etc.)	Tequila	Cognac	Calvados	Champagne
Various wines	Sherry (*jerez* or *xérès*)			•					•		
	Vermouth, dry	•	•	•		•		•	•		
	Vermouth, red			•	•	•	•	•	•	•	
	Port								•		
Fruit juices	Apple	•				•	•		•	•	•
	Cranberry	•				•	•				
	Grapefruit	•				•	•				
	Lemon/lime	•	•	•		•	•	•	•		
	Orange	•	•	•		•	•	•	•		
	Pineapple					•	•	•			•
	Tomato	•									
Waters and mixers	Sparkling/still water		•	•	•	•	•	•	•	•	
	Cola					•	•	•			
	Ginger ale		•	•		•	•	•			
	Ginger beer	•				•	•	•			
	Lemon-lime soda	•				•	•	•			
	Tonic water							•			
Other	Single (light)	•	•					•	•		
	Milk		•			•	•		•	•	
	Egg		•	•					•		

FLAVOURING/COLOURING AGENTS

	MODIFIER	Vodka	Gin	Scotch whisky/ Irish whiskey	American whiskeys	White rum (Cuban, Jamaican)	Pale rum (Cuban, etc.)	Tequila	Cognac	Calvados	Champagne
Bitters and aniseed-based ingredients	Angostura bitters			•			•	•	•		•
	Campari		•								
	Dubonnet										•
	Orange bitters		•			•			•		
	Pernod		•								
	Peychaud's bitters				•				•		
	Pimm's										•
Liqueurs and crèmes	Amaretto	•		•					•	•	•
	Apricot brandy		•		•	•			•		•
	Banane (crème de)						•	•			•
	Benedictine				•				•		•
	Cacao (crème de)		•			•	•		•		•
	Cassis (crème de)	•				•	•		•	•	•
	Chartreuse		•	•							
	Cherry brandy	•	•	•	•				•		•
	Coconut liqueur								•	•	
	Coffee liqueur	•					•	•	•		•
	Curaçao	•	•	•	•	•	•	•	•	•	•
	Galliano	•				•	•				
	Manzana verde	•								•	
	Maraschino liqueur		•			•					
	Melocoton (peach schnapps)	•									
	Menthe (crème de)	•							•		
	Mûre (crème de)	•				•	•		•	•	•
Sweeteners	Coconut milk	•				•	•				
	Honey		•			•	•	•	•		
	Grenadine	•	•	•	•	•	•	•	•	•	
	Lime juice cordial	•	•	•		•					
	Sugar cane syrup	•	•	•	•	•	•	•	•	•	•

51

Cocktail preparation

In England, as in America, long before the cocktail made its appearance, taverns and clubs offered mixed drinks called punches or cups that were served from large-capacity receptacles called bowls. The preparation of mixed drinks evolved progressively in the course of the nineteenth century, especially once it became possible to make ice artificially.

In the first book about cocktails, published in New York in 1862, the 236 recipes offered were, for the most part, prepared individually. All the techniques used today, such as the use of mixing glasses and shakers (and even shooters), are mentioned in it, except of course the blender, which was not invented until the end of the 1920s.

Until that time a distinction was made between 'cocktails' – drinks made with specific utensils (mixing glass or shaker) and served 'straight up', without ice in the glass – and 'mixed drinks' that were generally prepared directly in the glass. Nowadays the word 'cocktail' covers all prepared drinks.

Making a cocktail means first selecting several drinks, alcoholic or non-alcoholic, then mixing them together, generally using ice to cool them, which has the added effect of diluting the alcohol contained in them.

While an unlimited number of combinations can be made from the ingredients, there are only four main ways of actually preparing cocktails (they are indicated in the little pictogram that accompanies each of the recipes in this book):

■ directly in the glass (▷ p. 53), used when the recipe's ingredients are easily mixed

■ in a mixing glass (▷ p. 54), notably used when all the ingredients are alcoholic
■ in a shaker (▷ pp. 55–6), which thoroughly mixes the ingredients
■ in a blender (▷ p. 57), which is essential for making 'frozen' cocktails.

There is a fifth way, but this is only used in the very specialized preparation of shooters (▷ p. 58).

The preparation of cocktails calls for a certain amount of practice in some indispensable techniques, such as preparing crushed ice (▷ p. 59) and frosting a glass (▷ p. 59).

For each cocktail recipe, the method of preparation recommended in this book is the one which is most widely used in Europe and the rest of the world.

Sometimes it is possible to change the texture of a cocktail by preparing it in a different way. For example, both Margaritas (▷ p. 176) and Daiquiris (▷ p. 147) can be served 'straight up' when made in a shaker, or 'frozen', with a sorbet-like (sherbet-like) texture, when made in a blender.

Using a shaker can give a cocktail a frothy appearance.

Finally, when using a mixing glass, a shaker or a blender, one can generally make a cocktail large enough to serve two people.

Preparing directly in the glass

This method is used when the ingredients in the recipe are easily mixed. For the most part we are dealing with a spirit and a sweetener – a syrup or a liqueur – or non-sweet liquids such as fruit juice or soda water (club soda). The ice cubes in the glass serve to cool the drink. Drinks are also prepared directly in the glass if the recipe includes a solid ingredient (a herb or citrus fruit) that has to be crushed with a pestle, but only if the item is destined to remain in the drink; if not, then a mixing glass must be used and the mixture strained (▷ p. 54). Finally, hot cocktails are also prepared directly in the glass.

If there are no solid ingredients in the recipe go directly to stage **2**, otherwise proceed as follows:

1. If required by the recipe, crush the quarter of lime with a pestle to extract the juice and the aromatic oils contained in the rind, or lightly press the fresh mint leaves to extract the aroma, being careful not to break them up.

2. Two-thirds fill the glass in which the cocktail is to be served with the number of ice cubes (crushed if necessary) indicated in the recipe.

3. Pour in the ingredients in the order and quantities given.

4. Stir with the mixing spoon using a rotating movement from base to top. After a few seconds condensation will give the outside of the glass a frosted appearance, which indicates that the drink is cold enough. Add any necessary decoration and serve immediately.

Preparing in a mixing glass

This method is used when all the ingredients in the cocktail recipe are alcoholic and therefore will mix easily. It is also used when a small quantity of syrup is to be added. It is often used when a cocktail cannot be prepared directly in the glass because it needs to be strained to remove any pulp from a citrus fruit or ice, for example.

1. Half-fill the mixing glass with the number of ice cubes called for in the recipe.

2. Pour the ingredients into the mixing glass in the order and quantities given in the recipe.

3. Stir with the mixing spoon using a rotating movement from base to top. After a few seconds condensation will gather on the outside of the glass, giving it a frosted appearance, which indicates that the drink is sufficiently cooled.

4. Strain the contents through a cocktail strainer into an appropriate serving glass, add any desired decoration and serve immediately.

The academic method
1. Slightly more than half-fill the mixing glass with the amount of ice called for in the recipe. Stir it for 4–5 seconds with the mixing spoon. Pour off the resulting water, holding back the ice with the cocktail strainer.
Stages **2, 3, 4** as above.

Preparing in a shaker

This method is used when the ingredients will only be thoroughly mixed if shaken vigorously. It may be the case with a syrup, a more or less thick fruit juice or a rich substance such as coconut milk, or egg whites or yolks. One can equally well use either a shaker with an integral strainer (the most common nowadays) or a Boston or continental shaker.

SHAKER WITH STRAINER The shaker with an integral strainer is made up of three metallic parts: the lower part, the upper part, which includes the strainer, and the lid.

1. Slightly more than half-fill the lower part of the shaker with the amount of ice indicated in the recipe, then pour in the ingredients in the order and quantities indicated.

2. Fit the upper part and the lid.

3. Hold the shaker firmly, placing the thumb of the right hand (if you are right-handed) on the lid and the index and middle fingers of the other hand under the lower part. Shake vigorously for about 8–10 seconds. When the drink is well chilled the outside of the shaker will become frosted.

4. Remove the lid and, keeping hold of the upper part, pour the contents into the appropriate glass; any solid particles (including the ice cubes) will be held back by the integral strainer. Decorate the cocktail if necessary and serve immediately.

The academic method
1. Slightly more than half-fill the lower part of the shaker with the amount of ice indicated in the recipe. Fix the upper part and the lid in place. Hold the shaker firmly, placing the thumb of the right hand (if you are right-handed) on the lid and the index and middle fingers of the other hand under the lower part. Shake vigorously for 4–5 seconds. Take off the lid and pour away any accumulated water. Remove the upper part of the shaker and pour in the cocktail ingredients in the order and quantities stated in the recipe.
Follow stages **2, 3, 4** as above.

BOSTON SHAKER OR CONTINENTAL SHAKER   The Boston shaker, developed in the United States, is made up of two parts that fit together. The lower part consists of a large glass, while the upper part is a type of metal tumbler with a slightly larger diameter than the glass. When the ingredients and ice are shaken in the Boston shaker the metal contracts under the action of the cold and forms a hermetic seal, which, however, is never tight enough to make it difficult to open.

In the continental shaker, an elegantly shaped European invention, both parts are made of metal. Both these shakers are used in the same way.

1. Half-fill the lower part of the shaker with the specified amount of ice then pour in the ingredients in the order and quantities stated in the recipe.

2. Press the upper part of the shaker firmly on to the lower part. Hold the shaker firmly, placing the index finger of the right hand (if you are right-handed) on the upper part and the thumb of the other hand under the base of the lower part.

3. Shake vigorously for 8–10 seconds. The frosted appearance of the metal tumbler shows when the drink is cool enough. Turn the shaker upside down. With the left hand hold the shaker by the part that is now underneath while supporting the upper part with the index finger of the same hand. Then with the palm of the right hand give a light tap near the junction of the two parts, which should release the upper part.

4. If necessary, strain the contents into an appropriate serving glass using a cocktail strainer and/or a pulp strainer. Otherwise pour straight into the serving glass and decorate as required. Serve immediately.

The academic method

1. Slightly more than half-fill the lower half of the shaker with the amount of ice indicated in the recipe. Shake the ice for a few seconds to cool the shaker thoroughly then open it up as indicated in stage 3.

2. Pour away the water accumulated in the lower part, retaining the ice with the cocktail strainer. Pour the ingredients, in the order and quantities indicated in the recipe, into the upper part of the shaker, and press the two halves firmly together. Hold and shake the shaker as indicated above. Stages **3** and **4** as above.

Preparing in a blender

The blender may be replaced by the shaker for a number of recipes but it is the only way of achieving the 'frozen' texture, which is similar to that of a sorbet (sherbet).

1. Fill the blender goblet with the quantity of crushed ice stated in the recipe.

2. Pour the ingredients into the goblet in the order and quantities stated in the recipe.

3. Put the cover on the goblet and blend at slow speed for 5–10 seconds. For a 'frozen' result, blend at maximum speed for 15–30 seconds until the liquids and the ice are perfectly mixed and take on the appearance of a sorbet (sherbet), by which time the liquid will have begun to congeal on the walls of the goblet.

4. Remove the cover and pour the contents of the goblet into the appropriate glass for the recipe, add decoration if required and serve immediately.

The academic method
This method is applied when using a domestic blender, which is less powerful than a professional one.
1. As above.
2. Put all the ingredients except the spirit into the goblet.
3. Place the cover on the goblet and blend at slow speed for 5–10 seconds, then on maximum speed for 15–30 seconds, until the liquids and the ice are perfectly blended and have the appearance of a sorbet (sherbet). Turn the speed back to slow, remove the central stopper from the cover and pour in the alcohol, then replace the stopper and turn the speed back up to maximum and run until the mixture has once more taken on the appearance of a sorbet.
4. As above.

Preparing a shooter

A shooter is a specific form of cocktail usually made up of several superimposed layers of spirits and/or liqueurs that are not mixed together. Shooters are served in shot glasses holding about 60 ml (2 fl oz) and are intended to be knocked back in one go!

1. Pour the first of the ingredients listed in the recipe into a shot glass, making sure you progress from the sweetest or most dense to the least sweet, or least dense.

2. Hold the mixing spoon in such a way that it just makes contact with the surface of the liquid. Pour the second ingredient very slowly on to the spoon to slow the rate of flow (if you are using a pourer cork, reduce the flow still further by blocking the air intake with the thumb of the hand holding the bottle). As you pour, gently raise the spoon so that the second liquid lies on top of the first without mixing with it.

3. Repeat the process with the third ingredient. Serve immediately.

Alice in
Wonderland

Santina's
Pousse-Café

Fiesta

B-52

Making crushed ice

Cocktails that are to be served 'frappé' require the use of crushed ice. It is recommended, too, for preparations made in a blender. Crushed ice can also fulfil the role of filter; in the Mojito (▷ p. 151), for example, it traps the essential crushed mint leaves that might otherwise spoil the drinker's enjoyment of the cocktail.

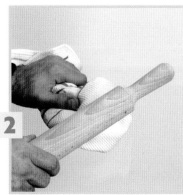

1. Place the number of ice cubes stated in the recipe into a clean cloth. Fold in the four corners and gather them firmly in the left hand (if you are right-handed).

2. Give the ice contained in the cloth a few sharp blows with a wooden rolling pin held in the other hand.

Frosting the rim of a glass

For certain cocktails, frosting the glass with sugar or salt not only adds an imaginative touch but also improves the taste. In the Margarita (▷ p. 176), for example, the salt adhering to the rim of the glass enhances the impact of the flavour.

1. Pour a layer of salt (or sugar) about 5 mm (¼ in) deep into a saucer. Rub a quarter of a cut lime right around the rim of the glass.

2. Turn the glass upside down and twist it around in the salt (or sugar), making sure that the edge of the glass becomes coated all the way round.

Recipes for
cocktails and
cocktail snacks

Vodka-based cocktails

Originally Polish or Russian, vodka is now internationally produced. It is distilled from potatoes, barley or a mixture of cereals, and is popular more for its purity than any specific flavour. There are also aromatic vodkas, flavoured with fruit (lemon or blackcurrant, for example) or plants (bison grass). These may form part of certain cocktails but, for the most part, a completely neutral vodka, which gives strength to the cocktail without influencing its taste, is the one used. Vodka is unobtrusive when added to fruit juices, such as cranberry juice in the Cape Codder (▷ p. 69) or Sea Breeze (▷ p. 82), orange juice in a Screwdriver (▷ p. 82) or grapefruit in the Salty Dog (▷ p. 81).

It mixes equally well with coffee liqueur in a Black Russian (▷ p. 84) and an Expresso Martini (▷ p. 71), and with crème de cacao in a Chocolate Martini (▷ p. 84) or a Velvet Hammer (▷ p. 87).

Finally, vodka is the ideal spirit for making fresh fruit Martinis, like the Cucumber Martini (▷ p. 64) because its neutrality gives full rein to the flavour of the chosen fruit.

Vodka is produced under many brands in about 30 countries, the principal ones being Poland, Russia and the United States. Great Britain, Finland, the Netherlands and Sweden are also major vodka producers.
▷ *See also p. 294*

THE 10 INDISPUTABLE CLASSICS

Apple Martini ▷ p. 78
Black Russian ▷ p. 84
Bloody Mary ▷ p. 86
Caipirovska ▷ p. 69
Cosmopolitan ▷ p. 64
Harvey Wallbanger ▷ p. 79
French Martini ▷ p. 79
Sea Breeze ▷ p. 82
Sex on the Beach ▷ p. 83
Vodka Martini ▷ p. 67

Dry cocktails

A glamorous short drink

The Cosmopolitan (▷ right), a recent cocktail, was invented at the start of the 1990s at Julie's Supper Club in San Francisco. It quickly established itself as an international classic and has become for women what the Dry Martini (▷ p. 92) is to men – a sophisticated and glamorous drink. It was Madonna (photographed here) who popularized the Cosmopolitan among the evening partygoers in New York and London.

Cosmopolitan

Short drink to serve at any time

FOR 1 GLASS

5–6 ice cubes

1 measure vodka

½ measure cranberry juice
(based on fruit concentrate)

1 teaspoon fresh lime juice

1 teaspoon curaçao triple sec

1 strip unwaxed lime peel (zest)

● Place the ice in the lower part of the shaker then add the vodka, cranberry juice, lime juice and curaçao. Fit the upper part of the shaker and shake vigorously for 8–10 seconds.
● Strain it into a Martini glass using a cocktail strainer.
● Cut the strip of lime peel with a paring knife. Over the glass, pinch it between the fingers to release the oils then drop it into the cocktail. Serve immediately.

Cucumber Martini

Short drink to serve at any time

FOR 1 GLASS

½ cucumber

5–6 ice cubes

1 measure vodka

1 teaspoon sugar cane syrup

● Peel the cucumber and cut it into small pieces.
● Place the pieces in the lower part of the shaker and crush them to a purée with a pestle.

● Add the ice, vodka and sugar cane syrup.
● Fit the upper part of the shaker and shake vigorously for 10 seconds.
● Strain the mixture through a pulp strainer into a Martini glass. Serve immediately.

 This cocktail belongs to a new family of fresh fruit Martinis based on the principle of one or more types of fresh fruit reduced to a purée to extract the juice.

Fiesta

Short drink to serve in the evening

FOR 1 GLASS

¼ measure curaçao triple sec

1 teaspoon grenadine

¼ measure vodka

1 teaspoon Campari

- Pour the ¼ measure curaçao triple sec into a shot glass.
- Slowly add the grenadine, which will sink to the bottom of the glass.
- In a separate glass, mix the vodka and Campari to obtain a red liquid.
- Carefully pour this vodka-Campari mix on top of the curaçao triple sec, using a mixing spoon to ensure that the liquids remain in layers (▷ p. 58). Serve immediately.

Melon Martini

Short drink to serve at any time

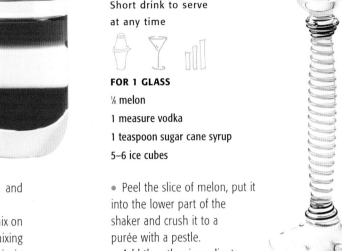

FOR 1 GLASS

⅛ melon

1 measure vodka

1 teaspoon sugar cane syrup

5–6 ice cubes

- Peel the slice of melon, put it into the lower part of the shaker and crush it to a purée with a pestle.
- Add the other ingredients and ice.
- Fit the upper part of the shaker and shake vigorously for 10 seconds.
- Strain the mixture into a Martini glass using a cocktail strainer and a pulp strainer. Serve immediately.

Metropolitan

Short drink to serve at any time

FOR 1 GLASS

5–6 ice cubes

1 measure blackcurrant-flavoured vodka

½ measure cranberry juice (based on fruit concentrate)

1 teaspoon fresh lime juice

1 teaspoon curaçao triple sec

1 strip unwaxed lime peel (zest)

- Place the ice in the lower part of the shaker and add the vodka, cranberry juice, lime juice and curaçao.
- Fit the upper part of the shaker and shake vigorously for 8–10 seconds.
- Strain the mixture into a Martini glass using a cocktail strainer.
- Cut the strip of lime peel with a paring knife. Over the glass, pinch it between the fingers to release the oils then drop it into the cocktail. Serve immediately.

Pineapple & Ginger Martini

Short drink to serve at any time

FOR 1 GLASS

1 piece fresh root ginger

½ slice fresh pineapple 1 cm (½ inch) thick

5–6 ice cubes

1 measure vodka

1 teaspoon sugar cane syrup

1 pineapple leaf

• Wash and peel the ginger and cut a slice about 1 cm (½ inch) diameter and 2 mm (¹⁄₁₆ inch) thick. Peel the half slice of pineapple and cut into small pieces.
• Crush the ginger with a pestle in the lower part of the shaker. Add the pineapple pieces and also crush to obtain a purée.
• Add the ice, vodka and sugar cane syrup.
• Fit the upper part of the shaker and shake vigorously for 10 seconds.
• Strain the mixture into a Martini glass using a cocktail strainer and a pulp strainer. Make 2 slits in the pineapple leaf and slot it onto the edge of the glass. Serve immediately.

James Bond, Vodka Martini's ambassador

The Vodka Martini (▷ p. 67), a variation of the Dry Martini made with vodka, is intimately linked with the character of James Bond. Since 1962, with the film Dr No, *the famous British secret agent, played by Sean Connery (photographed here), has boosted the fame of this cocktail, even though the questionable taste he shows by insisting on his Vodka Martini being 'shaken not stirred' risks upsetting the purists.*

Raspberry & Mint Martini

Short drink to serve at any time

FOR 1 GLASS

12–15 fresh raspberries

5–6 ice cubes

1¼ measures vodka

1 teaspoon sugar cane syrup

3–4 fresh mint leaves

• Crush the raspberries with a pestle in the lower part of the shaker.
• Add the ice, vodka, sugar cane syrup and whole mint leaves.
• Fit the upper part of the shaker and shake vigorously for 10 seconds.
• Strain the mixture into a Martini glass using a cocktail strainer and a pulp strainer. Serve immediately.

Vodka Martini Extra-Dry

Short drink to serve as an aperitif

FOR 1 GLASS

6–7 ice cubes

⅓ measure dry vermouth

1¾ measures vodka

1 green olive or an unwaxed lemon

• Place the ice and vermouth in a mixing glass.

• Stir it with an up and down circular motion for 6–8 seconds to flavour the ice cubes with the vermouth then discard the liquid, using a cocktail strainer to retain the ice.

• Pour the vodka onto the flavoured ice and stir with an up and down circular motion for 6–8 seconds.

• Pour into a Martini glass using a cocktail strainer.

• Add the olive to the drink. Alternatively, cut a strip of lemon peel (zest) with a paring knife. Over the glass, pinch it between the fingers to release the oils then drop it into the cocktail. Serve immediately.

 This cocktail is also called a Vodkatini.

Variation: Vodka Dry Martini
Vodka Dry Martini is made using 1¼ measures of vodka and ½ measure of vermouth. It is less dry and is an excellent short drink for an aperitif.

Thirst-quenching cocktails

Balalaïka

Short drink to serve at any time

FOR 1 GLASS

5–6 ice cubes

1 measure vodka

⅓ measure curaçao triple sec

⅓ measure lemon juice

• Place the ice, vodka, curaçao and lemon juice in the lower part of the shaker.

• Fit the upper part of the shaker and shake vigorously for 8–10 seconds.

• Strain the mixture into a Martini glass using a cocktail strainer. Serve immediately.

Ballet Russe

Short drink to serve at any time

FOR 1 GLASS

5–6 ice cubes

1 measure vodka

¼ measure crème de cassis

⅓ measure fresh lime juice

• Place the ice and all the ingredients in the lower part of the shaker.

• Fit the upper part of the shaker and shake vigorously for 8–10 seconds.

• Strain the mixture into a Martini glass using a cocktail strainer. Serve immediately.

Berry Blush

Long drink to serve
at any time

FOR 1 GLASS

5 fresh strawberries

8–10 ice cubes

1 measure vodka

1 measure cranberry juice
(based on fruit concentrate)

¼ measure fresh lemon juice

1 teaspoon sugar cane syrup

1½ measures soda water (club soda)

- Crush 4 strawberries with a pestle in the lower part of the shaker.
- Add 5–6 ice cubes, the vodka, cranberry juice, lemon juice and sugar cane syrup.
- Fit the upper part of the shaker and shake vigorously for 8–10 seconds.
- Place 3–4 ice cubes in a highball glass then strain the contents of the shaker into it using a cocktail strainer and pulp strainer.
- Top up (top off) with soda water and place the remaining strawberry, sliced in half, into the glass. Serve immediately.

Blue Lagoon

Short drink to serve at any time

FOR 1 GLASS

5–6 ice cubes

1 measure vodka

⅓ measure fresh
lemon juice

⅓ measure blue curaçao

- Place the ice and all the ingredients in the lower part of the shaker. Fit the upper part of the shaker and shake vigorously for 8–10 seconds.
- Strain the mixture into a Martini glass using a cocktail strainer. Serve immediately.

Variation:
Blue Lagoon Highball
The same recipe served in a highball glass and topped up (topped off) with lemon-lime soda is called a Blue Lagoon Highball, a sweeter long drink, which is ideal at any time.

Bull-Frog

Long drink to serve
at any time

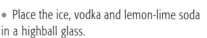

FOR 1 GLASS

4–5 ice cubes

1 measure vodka

3½ measures lemon-lime soda

⅛ unwaxed lime

- Place the ice, vodka and lemon-lime soda in a highball glass.
- Stir with an up and down circular motion for 8–10 seconds.
- Squeeze the lime segment then drop it in the glass. Serve immediately.

Burgundy Juicer

Long drink to serve
at any time

FOR 1 GLASS

5–6 ice cubes

1¼ measures vodka

2 measures pure
grapefruit juice

¼ measure crème de cassis

1¼ measures Caipirovska
(club soda)

• Place the ice, vodka, grapefruit juice and crème de cassis in the lower part of the shaker.
• Fit the upper part of the shaker and shake vigorously for 8–10 seconds.
• Strain into a highball glass using a cocktail strainer.
• Top up (top off) with the soda water. Serve immediately.

Caipirovska

Short drink to serve
at any time

FOR 1 GLASS

½ unwaxed lime

2 mixing spoons caster
(superfine) sugar

3–4 crushed ice cubes (▷ p. 59)

1¼ measures vodka

• Cut the lime half into 4 pieces.
Place the sugar in a rocks glass and add the lime pieces. Crush them with a pestle, then fill the glass with the crushed ice.
• Pour in the vodka and stir with a mixing spoon for 8–10 seconds. Serve immediately.

This cocktail was created for a Swedish brand of vodka in the 1990s in order to promote the product on the Brazilian market. Nowadays the Caipirovska is a very popular drink in Scandinavia.

Cape Codder

Long drink to serve
at any time

FOR 1 GLASS

4–5 ice cubes

1 measure vodka

3½ measures cranberry juice
(based on fruit concentrate)

½ slice unwaxed lime

• Place the ice, vodka and cranberry juice in a highball glass.
• Stir for 8–10 seconds with a mixing spoon.
• Add the lime slice and serve immediately.

Variation: Cape Cod Cooler
The Cape Cod Cooler is made by replacing 1½ measures of cranberry juice with 1½ measures of soda water (club soda), giving a more thirst-quenching long drink that is ideal in the late afternoon.

Cassisina

Short drink to serve
at any time

FOR 1 GLASS

⅛ unwaxed lime

3–4 crushed ice cubes (▷ p. 59)

1¼ measures vodka

½ measure crème de cassis

• Squeeze the lime segment into a rocks
glass.
• Fill the glass with the crushed ice and add
the other ingredients.
• Stir the mixture with a mixing spoon for
8–10 seconds. Serve immediately.

Clockwork Orange

Short drink to serve
at any time

FOR 1 GLASS

½ unwaxed orange

2 mixing spoons caster
(superfine) sugar

3–4 crushed ice cubes
(▷ p. 59)

1¼ measures vodka

• Cut the orange half
into 4 pieces.
• Place the sugar in a
rocks glass and add the oranges pieces.
• Crush them on the sugar with a pestle,
then fill the glass with the crushed ice.
• Add the vodka and stir with a mixing
spoon for 8–10 seconds. Serve immediately.

Double Vision

Short drink to serve
at any time

FOR 1 GLASS

5–6 ice cubes

⅓ measure blackcurrant-flavoured vodka

⅓ measure lemon-flavoured vodka

½ measure pure apple juice

¼ measure fresh lime juice

1 teaspoon sugar cane syrup

2–3 drops Angostura bitters

• Place the ice and all the ingredients in the
lower part of the shaker.
• Fit the upper part of the shaker and shake
vigorously for 8–10 seconds.
• Strain into a Martini glass using a cocktail
strainer. Serve immediately.

 The Double Vision can also be
made as a long drink, served in a highball
glass, by further adding ¼ measure of
each type of vodka, 2 measures of apple
juice, ¼ measure of lime juice, 1 teaspoon
of sugar cane syrup and 2 drops of
Angostura bitters.

Espresso Martini

Short drink to serve in the evening

FOR 1 GLASS

5–6 ice cubes

¾ measure vodka

¾ measure cold espresso coffee

1 teaspoon coffee liqueur

1 teaspoon sugar cane syrup

- Place the ice and all ingredients in the lower part of the shaker.
- Fit the upper part of the shaker and shake vigorously for 8–10 seconds.
- Strain into a Martini glass using a cocktail strainer. Serve immediately.

 Invented in 1998 by Dick Bradsell at the Pharmacy, in London, this cocktail was originally called the Pharmaceutical Stimulant.

Frisky Bison

Short drink to serve in the evening

FOR 1 GLASS

5–6 ice cubes

¾ measure bison grass-flavoured vodka

½ measure pure apple juice

¼ measure manzana verde liqueur

1 teaspoon fresh lime juice

1 teaspoon sugar cane syrup

3–4 fresh mint leaves

- Place the ice and all the ingredients in the lower part of the shaker.
- Fit the upper part of the shaker and shake vigorously for 8–10 seconds.
- Strain into a Martini glass using a cocktail strainer. Serve immediately.

Kamikaze

Short drink to serve in the evening

FOR 1 GLASS

3–4 ice cubes

⅓ measure vodka

¼ measure curaçao triple sec

1 teaspoon fresh lime juice

- Place the ice and all the ingredients in the lower part of the shaker.
- Fit the upper part of the shaker and shake vigorously for 8–10 seconds.
- Strain into a shot glass using a cocktail strainer. Serve immediately.

Killer Punch

Long drink to serve
at any time

FOR 1 GLASS

4–5 ice cubes

1 measure vodka

1 teaspoon green melon liqueur

1 teaspoon amaretto

3¼ measures cranberry juice
(based on fruit concentrate)

- Place the ice and all the ingredients in a highball glass.
- Stir with a mixing spoon for 8–10 seconds. Serve immediately.

Variation: Koolaid

Prepared in a Martini glass, using the same quantities of liqueurs but only ¾ measure of vodka and ⅓ measure of cranberry juice. With the addition of ⅓ measure of pure orange juice, this drink becomes a Koolaid, a sweeter short drink, ideal at any time.

Kremlin Cooler

Long drink to serve at any time

FOR 1 GLASS

4–5 ice cubes

1 measure vodka

⅛ measure fresh lime juice

1 teaspoon sugar cane syrup

3 measures soda water
(club soda)

1 slice unwaxed lime

- Place the ice with all the ingredients except the lime slice in a high-ball glass.
- Stir with a mixing spoon for 8–10 seconds.
- Add the lime slice. Serve immediately.

Lemon Drop

Short drink to serve
at any time

FOR 1 GLASS

5–6 ice cubes

1 measure lemon-flavoured vodka

¼ measure fresh lemon juice

2 teaspoons sugar cane syrup

1 strip unwaxed lemon peel (zest)

- Place the ice, vodka, lemon juice and sugar cane syrup in the lower part of the shaker.
- Fit the upper part of the shaker and shake vigorously for 8–10 seconds.
- Strain into a Martini glass using a cocktail strainer.
- Cut the strip of lemon peel with a paring knife. Over the glass, pinch it between the fingers to release the oils then drop it into the cocktail. Serve immediately.

Long Island Iced Tea

Long drink to serve in the evening

FOR 1 GLASS

8–10 ice cubes

⅛ measure vodka

1 measure fresh lemon juice

⅛ measure gin

⅛ measure Puerto Rican rum

⅛ measure curaçao triple sec

1 measure cola

½ slice unwaxed lemon

• Place 5–6 ice cubes and all the ingredients except the cola and lemon slice in the lower part of the shaker.
• Fit the upper part of the shaker and shake vigorously for 8–10 seconds.
• Place 3–4 ice cubes and the cola in a highball glass.
• Slowly add the contents of the shaker, pouring them through a cocktail strainer so they form graduated layers with the cola.
• Add the lemon slice. Serve immediately, leaving the stirring to your guest.

This drink was reputedly invented in the Balboa Café in San Francisco. It made its appearance in the middle of the 1980s and was especially successful with the men. The original recipe also included tequila.

Variation: Long Island Lemonade
This lemon-flavoured long drink, which is ideal for drinking in the evening, is made by using lemon-lime soda in place of the cola.

Moscow Mule

Long drink to serve at any time

FOR 1 GLASS

4–5 ice cubes

1 measure vodka

¼ measure fresh lime juice

2–3 drops Angostura bitters (optional)

3¼ measures ginger beer

1 slice unwaxed lime

• Place the ice, vodka, lime juice and Angostura bitters (if used) in a highball glass. Add the ginger beer.
• Stir with a mixing spoon for 8–10 seconds.
• Add the lime slice and serve immediately.

Created for publicity purposes

The Moscow Mule (▷ above) was the first promotional cocktail in the history of vodka. It was created in 1941 at the Cock 'n' Bull restaurant in Hollywood. In that period the Heublein Company had just bought the Smirnoff brand and was looking for an original drink to introduce its vodka that was, at the time, unknown in the United States. The proprietor of the Cock 'n' Bull had a large stock of ginger beer and collaborating with the Director of Heublein to create the Moscow Mule provided an excellent way of unloading it.

Napoli

Long drink to serve
at any time

FOR 1 GLASS

4–5 ice cubes

1 measure vodka

¼ measure Galliano

3¼ measures ginger ale

1 strip unwaxed orange peel
(zest)

• Place the ice, vodka, Galliano
and ginger ale in a highball glass.
• Stir with an up and down
circular motion for 8–10 seconds.
• Cut the strip of orange peel with
a paring knife. Over the glass, pinch
it between the fingers to release the oils then
drop it into the cocktail. Serve immediately.

Purple Haze

Short drink to serve in the evening

FOR 1 GLASS

3–4 ice cubes

⅛ measure vodka

¼ measure fresh lime juice

1 teaspoon sugar cane syrup

1 teaspoon crème de mûre

• Place the ice, vodka, lime juice
and sugar cane syrup in the lower
part of the shaker.
• Fit the upper part of the
shaker and shake vigorously for
4–6 seconds.
• Strain into a shot glass using a
cocktail strainer.
• Add the crème de mûre, which
should sink to the bottom of the
glass. Serve immediately.

Purple Hooter

Long drink to serve
at any time

FOR 1 GLASS

4–5 ice cubes

1 measure vodka

½ measure fresh lime juice

¼ measure crème de mûre

2¾ measures lemon-lime soda

• Place the ice, vodka, lime juice and crème
de mûre in the lower part of the shaker.
• Fit the upper part of the shaker and shake
vigorously for 4–6 seconds.
• Pour into a highball glass. Add the lemon-
lime soda.
• Stir for 2–3 seconds. Serve immediately.

Raspberry Mule

Long drink to serve at any time

FOR 1 GLASS

14–15 fresh raspberries

8–10 ice cubes

1 measure vodka

¼ measure fresh lime juice

2¾ measures ginger beer

1 slice unwaxed lime

- Crush the raspberries with a pestle in the lower part of the shaker.
- Add 5–6 ice cubes, the vodka and lime juice.
- Fit the upper part of the shaker and shake vigorously for 8–10 seconds.
- Place 3–4 ice cubes in a highball glass then strain the contents of the shaker into it using a cocktail strainer and pulp strainer.
- Add the ginger beer and stir for 3–4 seconds with a mixing spoon.
- Add the lime slice. Serve immediately.

Testa Rossa

Long drink to serve as an aperitif

FOR 1 GLASS

4–5 ice cubes

¾ measure vodka

½ measure Campari

3¼ measures soda water (club soda)

¼ slice unwaxed orange

- Place the ice, vodka, Campari and soda water into a highball glass.
- Stir with a mixing spoon for 8–10 seconds.
- Add the orange slice and serve immediately.

Uncle Vanya

Short drink to serve in the evening

FOR 1 GLASS

5–6 ice cubes

1 measure vodka

⅓ measure crème de mûre

⅓ measure fresh lime juice

- Place the ice, vodka, crème de mûre and lime juice in the lower part of the shaker.
- Fit the upper part of the shaker and shake vigorously for 8–10 seconds.
- Strain into a wine glass using a cocktail strainer. Serve immediately.

A few ideas for cocktail snacks to serve with
vodka-based cocktails:

- potato canapés with marinated salmon
- herring tartare and beetroot (beet) on canapés
- cucumber 'tagliatelle' with taramasalata
- cherry tomatoes with two garnishes
- chopped pineapple and strawberries with rosemary

▶ **recipes page 270**

Vodka Gimlet

Short drink to serve at any time

FOR 1 GLASS

3–4 ice cubes

1 measure vodka

½ measure lime cordial

• Place the ice and all the ingredients in a rocks glass.
• Stir with a mixing spoon for 8–10 seconds. Serve immediately.

Variation: Vodka Lime Sour
Replacing the lime cordial with ½ measure of fresh lime juice and 2 teaspoons of sugar cane syrup results in a Vodka Lime Sour, a more acidic short drink that is ideal at any time.

Fruit-based cocktails

Apple Martini

Short drink to serve at any time

FOR 1 GLASS

5–6 ice cubes

¾ measure vodka

½ measure manzana verde liqueur

½ measure pure apple juice

• Place the ice and all the ingredients in the lower part of the shaker.
• Fit the upper part of the shaker and shake vigorously for 8–10 seconds.
• Strain into a Martini glass using a cocktail strainer. Serve immediately.

Aquamarine

Long drink to serve at any time

FOR 1 GLASS

5–6 ice cubes

¾ measure vodka

3 measures pure apple juice

½ measure peach schnapps

1 teaspoon blue curaçao

• Place the ice and all the ingredients in the lower part of the shaker.
• Fit the upper part of the shaker and shake vigorously for 8–10 seconds.
• Pour the contents of the shaker into a highball glass. Serve immediately.

If you want a cocktail with a more pronounced blue colour, use apple juice based on concentrate, which is much paler.

Chi Chi

Long drink to serve
at any time

FOR 1 GLASS

1 slice pineapple about
1 cm (½ inch) thick

5–6 ice cubes

1 measure vodka

2 mixing spoons coconut
milk (canned)

3 measures pure pineapple juice

- Cut a triangular piece from the pineapple slice leaving the skin in place.
- Place the ice and all the ingredients except the pineapple piece in the lower part of the shaker.
- Fit the upper part of the shaker and shake vigorously for 8–10 seconds.
- Strain into a highball glass, using a cocktail strainer.
- Make a slit in the pineapple triangle and fix it to the edge of the glass. Serve immediately.

French Martini

Short drink to serve
at any time

FOR 1 GLASS

5–6 ice cubes

¾ measure vodka

¾ measure pure pineapple juice

1 teaspoon crème de mûre

- Place the ice and all the ingredients in the lower part of the shaker.
- Fit the upper part of the shaker and shake vigorously for 8–10 seconds.
- Strain into a Martini glass using a cocktail strainer. Serve immediately.

Harvey Wallbanger

Long drink to serve
at any time

FOR 1 GLASS

5–6 ice cubes

1 measure vodka

3¼ measures pure orange juice

¼ measure Galliano

- Place the ice, vodka and orange juice in the lower part of the shaker.
- Fit the upper part of the shaker and shake vigorously for 8–10 seconds.
- Strain into a highball glass using a cocktail strainer.
- Pour in the Galliano. Serve immediately.

Variation: Henrietta Wallbanger
The Henrietta Wallbanger, a long drink with a bitter flavour, ideal to drink at any time, is made with pure grapefruit juice instead of the orange juice.

The appropriately named Harvey Wallbanger
According to popular legend, the Harvey Wallbanger (▷ p. 79) owes its name to a Californian surfer called Harvey, who habitually drank Screwdrivers (▷ p. 82) laced with Galliano. One day, after a heavy session, his friends watched him weave his way out of the beach bar, banging his board against the walls as he went, and christened his favourite drink the Harvey Wallbanger.

Lychee Martini
Short drink to serve at any time

FOR 1 GLASS

5–6 ice cubes

¾ measure vodka

¾ measure lychee (litchi) juice (based on fruit concentrate)

¼ measure lychee (litchi) liqueur

- Place the ice and all the ingredients in the lower part of the shaker.
- Fit the upper part of the shaker and shake vigorously for 8–10 seconds.
- Strain into a Martini glass using a cocktail strainer. Serve immediately.

 Lychee juice is sold in stores selling exotic products.

Madras
Long drink to serve at any time

FOR 1 GLASS

4–5 ice cubes

1 measure vodka

1¾ measures pure orange juice

1¾ measures cranberry juice (based on fruit concentrate)

1 segment unwaxed orange

- Place the ice and all the ingredients except the orange segment in a highball glass and stir for 8–10 seconds.
- Make a slit in the orange segment and fix it to the rim of the glass. Serve immediately.

Polish Martini

Short drink to serve
at any time

FOR 1 GLASS

5–6 ice cubes

⅛ measure vodka

⅛ measure bison
grass-flavoured vodka

¾ measure pure apple juice

¼ measure Krupnik liqueur

1 apple

- Place the ice, both vodkas, apple juice
and Krupnik liqueur in the lower part of
the shaker.
- Fit the upper part of the shaker and shake
vigorously for 8–10 seconds.
- Strain into a Martini glass using a cocktail
strainer.
- Wash the apple, cut it in half and remove
the core. Cut a few thin slices and place
them in the glass. Serve immediately.

Salty Dog

Short drink to serve at any time

FOR 1 GLASS

Fine salt

5–6 ice cubes

¾ measure vodka

¾ measure fresh pink
grapefruit juice

- Frost the rim of a Martini glass with salt
(▷ p. 59).
- Place the ice and all the ingredients in the
lower part of the shaker.
- Fit the upper part of the shaker and shake
vigorously for 8–10 seconds.
- Strain into a Martini glass using a cocktail
strainer. Serve immediately.

San Francisco

Long drink to serve at any time

FOR 1 GLASS

1 slice fresh pineapple,
about 1 cm (½ inch) thick

5–6 ice cubes

1 measure vodka

2 measures pure pineapple juice

1 measure pure orange juice

¼ measure curaçao triple sec

1 teaspoon crème de banane

1 teaspoon grenadine

- Cut a triangle from the pineapple, leaving
the skin in place.
- Place the ice, vodka, pineapple juice,
orange juice, curaçao, crème de banane and
grenadine in the lower part of the shaker.
- Fit the upper part of the shaker and shake
vigorously for 8–10 seconds.
- Strain into a highball glass using a cocktail
strainer.
- Make a slit in the piece of pineapple
and fix it to the rim of the glass. Serve
immediately.

Screwdriver

Long drink to serve at any time

FOR 1 GLASS

5–6 ice cubes

1 measure vodka

3½ measures orange juice

1 segment unwaxed orange

• Place the ice, vodka and orange juice in the lower part of the shaker.
• Fit the upper part of the shaker and shake vigorously for 8–10 seconds.
• Strain into a highball glass using a cocktail strainer.
• Make a slit in the orange segment and fix to the rim of the glass. Serve immediately.

Some Screwdriver!

The Screwdriver (▷ left) is, to say the least, an original name for a cocktail. But it has always been the American custom to give names to drinks that have a bearing on their history. The name 'screwdriver' is reputed to have originated among Americans working on the oil platforms in Iran in the 1940s. Being short of spoons they stirred their drinks with whatever came to hand in their tool boxes…

Sea Breeze

Long drink to serve at any time

FOR 1 GLASS

5–6 ice cubes

1 measure vodka

2½ measures cranberry juice
(based on fruit concentrate)

1 measure pure grapefruit juice

⅛ unwaxed lime

• Place the ice, vodka and fruit juices in the lower part of the shaker.
• Fit the upper part of the shaker and shake vigorously for 8–10 seconds.
• Strain into a highball glass using a cocktail strainer.
• Lightly squeeze the lime segment over the glass and then add it to the drink. Serve immediately.

Variation: Bay Breeze

The Bay Breeze is made with pure pineapple juice instead of the grapefruit juice. Being sweeter it is ideal in the evening.

Sex on the Beach

Long drink to serve
at any time

FOR 1 GLASS

5–6 ice cubes

1 measure vodka

1½ measures cranberry juice
(based on fruit concentrate)

1½ measures pure orange juice

½ measure peach schnapps

- Place the ice and all the ingredients in the lower part of the shaker.
- Fit the upper part of the shaker and shake vigorously for 8–10 seconds.
- Strain into a highball glass using a cocktail strainer. Serve immediately.

Variation: Sex on the Beach # 2

In a Sex on the Beach # 2, ¼ measure of peach schapps is replaced by ¼ measure of crème de mûre and pure pineapple juice is used instead of orange juice, making a sweeter long drink that is ideal at any time.

Tetanka

Short drink to serve
in the evening

FOR 1 GLASS

3–4 ice cubes

1 measure bison grass-flavoured vodka

1½ measures pure apple juice

- Place the ice and all the ingredients in a rocks glass.
- Stir with a mixing spoon for 8–10 seconds. Serve immediately.

Woo Woo

Long drink to serve
at any time

FOR 1 GLASS

4–5 ice cubes

1 measure vodka

½ measure peach schnapps

3 measures cranberry juice
(based on fruit concentrate)

⅛ unwaxed lime

- Place the ice and all the ingredients except the lime segment in a highball glass.
- Stir with a mixing spoon for 8–10 seconds.
- Make a slit in the lime segment and fix it to the rim of the glass. Serve immediately.

Liqueur-based cocktails

Betty Blue

Short drink to serve
at any time

FOR 1 GLASS

5–6 ice cubes

1 measure vodka

⅛ measure peach schnapps

⅛ measure dry vermouth

2–3 drops blue curaçao

1 strip unwaxed orange peel (zest)

1 maraschino cherry

• Place the ice and all the ingredients except the orange peel and the cherry in a mixing glass.
• Stir with a mixing spoon for 8–10 seconds.
• Strain into a Martini glass using a cocktail strainer.
• Squeeze the orange peel over the glass to extract the oils but don't add it to the drink. Place the maraschino cherry in the glass. Serve immediately.

Black Russian

Short drink to serve
as a digestif

FOR 1 GLASS

3–4 ice cubes

1 measure vodka

½ measure coffee liqueur

• Place the ice and all the ingredients in a rocks glass.
• Stir with a mixing spoon for 8–10 seconds. Serve immediately.

Chocolate Martini

Short drink to serve as a digestif

FOR 1 GLASS

5–6 ice cubes

1 measure vodka

½ measure white crème de cacao

1 teaspoon brown crème de cacao

• Place the ice, vodka and the white crème de cacao in a mixing glass. Stir for 8–10 seconds.
• Strain into a Martini glass using a cocktail strainer.
• Slowly pour the brown crème de cacao into the centre of the drink; it should sink to the bottom of the glass. Serve immediately.

**Variation:
Chocolate Mint Martini**
This is made by replacing ¼ measure of the white crème de cacao with ¼ measure of white crème de menthe, and using green crème de menthe instead of the brown crème de cacao. It is ideal served after a chocolate dessert.

Gipsy Queen

Short drink to serve as a digestif

FOR 1 GLASS

3–4 ice cubes

1 measure vodka

½ measure Benedictine

2–3 drops orange bitters

- Place the ice and all the ingredients in a rocks glass.
- Stir with a mixing spoon for 8–10 seconds. Serve immediately.

 In this type of cocktail one uses double the quantity of spirit to liqueur to counterbalance the sweetness in the latter.

Godmother

Short drink to serve as a digestif

FOR 1 GLASS

3–4 ice cubes

1 measure vodka

½ measure amaretto

- Place the ice and all the ingredients in a rocks glass.
- Stir with a mixing spoon for 8–10 seconds. Serve immediately.

Red Russian

Short drink to serve as a digestif

FOR 1 GLASS

3–4 ice cubes

1 measure vodka

½ measure cherry brandy

1 maraschino cherry

- Place the ice, vodka and cherry brandy in a rocks glass.
- Stir with a mixing spoon for 8–10 seconds.
- Add the maraschino cherry. Serve immediately.

Variant: Green Russian

The Green Russian is made in the same way, using green crème de menthe instead of the cherry brandy – a fresher, short drink that is ideal as a digestif.

Vodka Stinger

Short drink to serve as a digestif

FOR 1 GLASS

3–4 ice cubes

1¼ measures vodka

½ measure white crème de menthe

• Place the ice and all the ingredients in a rocks glass.
• Stir with a mixing spoon for 8–10 seconds. Serve immediately.

The Vodka Stinger is also known as the White Spider. Its flavour is reminiscent of mint pastilles.

Smooth cocktails

On the trail of Hemingway

The Bloody Mary (▷ right), the precise origins of which are unknown, has been given any number of names: Mary Rose in 1939, Red Snapper in 1944 and Bloody Mary in 1946. Ernest Hemingway (pictured here) worked hard on making it widely known, even as far away as China. In a letter to Bernard Peyton in 1947 he wrote, 'When I introduced this cocktail in Hong Kong in 1941 I believe I contributed more than any other single factor – with the possible exception of the Japanese army – to the fall of this Crown Colony'.

Bloody Mary

Long drink to serve at any time

FOR 1 GLASS

5–6 ice cubes

1 measure vodka

3 measures tomato juice

1 teaspoon fresh lemon juice

1 teaspoon Worcestershire sauce

3 drops red Tabasco sauce

1 pinch celery salt

1 pinch black pepper

1 small stick (stalk) celery

• Place the ice and all the ingredients except the celery stick in a mixing glass. Stir with a mixing spoon for 8–10 seconds.
• Strain into a highball glass using a cocktail strainer.
• Wash the piece of celery and place it in the glass. Serve immediately.

Jungle Joe

Long drink to serve at any time

FOR 1 GLASS

5–6 ice cubes

1 measure vodka

3¼ measures full-fat milk

¼ measure crème de banane

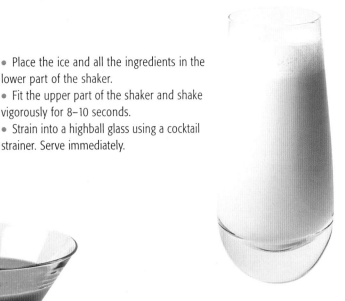

- Place the ice and all the ingredients in the lower part of the shaker.
- Fit the upper part of the shaker and shake vigorously for 8–10 seconds.
- Strain into a highball glass using a cocktail strainer. Serve immediately.

Velvet Hammer

Short drink to serve as a digestif

FOR 1 GLASS

5–6 ice cubes

¾ measure vodka

½ measure brown crème de cacao

½ measure single (light) cream

Few shavings plain dark (semi-sweet) chocolate

- Place the ice and all the ingredients except the chocolate shavings in the lower part of the shaker.
- Fit the upper part of the shaker and shake vigorously for 8–10 seconds.
- Strain into a Martini glass using a cocktail strainer. Sprinkle with the chocolate shavings. Serve immediately.

Variation:

Alexander The Great

The Alexander The Great is made by replacing ¼ measure of crème de cacao with ¼ measure of coffee liqueur. It has a slightly fuller flavour and is ideal after dessert.

White Russian

Short drink to serve as a digestif

FOR 1 GLASS

1¼ measures double (heavy) cream

4–5 ice cubes

¾ measure vodka

½ measure coffee liqueur

- Place the cream into the freezer for 5 minutes. Pour it into a bowl and beat with a fork until it thickens.
- Place the ice, vodka and coffee liqueur in a mixing glass.
- Stir with a mixing spoon for 8–10 seconds.
- Strain into a Martini glass using a cocktail strainer.
- Using the mixing spoon, pour on ½ measure of the whipped cream. Serve immediately.

Gin-based cocktails

Great Britain and the United States are the principal producers of gin.
▷ See also p. 295

Gin is, for the most part, a neutral spirit distilled from cereals and made principally in the Anglo-Saxon countries. This form of alcohol is either re-distilled – or simply flavoured – with juniper berries. A dozen or so other spices, such as cardamom seeds, angelica and coriander seeds add further touches to the bouquet. The subtle aromas of gin found in many cocktails are more or less pronounced according to the amount used. Gin mixes readily with all kinds of ingredients.

THE 10 INDISPUTABLE CLASSICS

It has long been associated with vermouth, as with dry vermouth in the Dry Martini (▷ p. 92) and the Journalist (▷ p. 93) or red vermouth in the Martinez (▷ p. 95). As a general rule the flavours of fruits blend admirably with gin. Since the invention of the first gin-based cocktails, lemon juice has been the favourite accompaniment, as in the famous Gin Fizz (▷ p. 100) or the Aviation (▷ p. 97). Red fruits also go well with the aroma of juniper, as the raspberries in a Raspberry Collins (▷ p. 104), and the cherries in the Desert Healer (▷ p. 99) demonstrate. And one must not forget the orange liqueurs such as the curaçao in the Breakfast Martini (▷ p. 98) and the Blue Bird (▷ p. 98), or the Grand Marnier Cordon Rouge in the Red Lion (▷ p. 111) and the French Kiss (▷ p. 114).

Dry cocktails

Astoria

Short drink to serve as an aperitif

FOR 1 GLASS

5–6 ice cubes

1 measure gin

¾ measure dry vermouth

2–3 drops orange bitters

1 strip unwaxed orange peel (zest)

- Place the ice, gin, vermouth and orange bitters in a mixing glass.
- Stir with a mixing spoon for 8–10 seconds.
- Strain into a Martini glass using a cocktail strainer.
- Cut the strip of orange peel with a paring knife. Over the glass, pinch it between the fingers to release the oils then drop it into the cocktail. Serve immediately.

Attaboy

Short drink to serve as an aperitif

FOR 1 GLASS

5–6 ice cubes

1 measure gin

½ measure dry vermouth

¼ measure grenadine

1 strip unwaxed lemon peel (zest)

- Place the ice, gin, vermouth and grenadine in the lower part of the shaker.
- Fit the upper part of the shaker and shake vigorously for 8–10 seconds.
- Strain into a Martini glass using a cocktail strainer.
- Cut the strip of lemon peel with a paring knife. Over the glass, pinch it between the fingers to release the oils then drop it into the cocktail. Serve immediately.

Bloodhound

Short drink to serve at any time

FOR 1 GLASS

4 fresh strawberries

5–6 ice cubes

¾ measure gin

¼ measure dry vermouth

¼ measure red vermouth

- Crush the strawberries with a pestle in the lower part of the shaker. Add the ice and all the other ingredients.
- Fit the upper part of the shaker and shake vigorously for 8–10 seconds.
- Strain into a Martini glass using a cocktail strainer and a pulp strainer. Serve immediately.

This cocktail was formerly made with raspberries rather than strawberries.

Bronx Terrace

Short drink to serve at any time

FOR 1 GLASS

5–6 ice cubes

1 measure gin

½ measure dry vermouth

¼ measure fresh lime juice

1 strip unwaxed lime peel (zest)

- Place the ice, gin, vermouth and lime juice in the lower part of the shaker.
- Fit the upper part of the shaker and shake vigorously for 8–10 seconds.
- Strain into a Martini glass using a cocktail strainer.
- Cut the strip of lime peel with a paring knife. Over the glass, pinch it between the fingers to release the oils then drop it into the cocktail. Serve immediately.

Claridge

Short drink to serve as an aperitif

FOR 1 GLASS

5–6 ice cubes

1 measure gin

½ measure dry vermouth

1 teaspoon curaçao triple sec

1 teaspoon apricot brandy

- Place the ice, gin, vermouth, curaçao and apricot brandy in a mixing glass.
- Stir with a mixing spoon for 8–10 seconds.
- Strain into a Martini glass using a cocktail strainer. Serve immediately.

Roosevelt, a great lover of dry cocktails

The Dry Martini (▷ p. 92) is for many the quintessential dry cocktail. Since 1904 it has been made in France from dry vermouth garnished with a green olive. The US President Franklin D Roosevelt (pictured here) was a fervent enthusiast. It is said that when Prohibition ended in 1933 his first act was to celebrate its passing with a Dry Martini.

Dry Martini

Short drink to serve
as an aperitif

FOR 1 GLASS

5–6 ice cubes

1⅘ measures gin

⅓ measure dry vermouth

1 green olive or 1 strip unwaxed
lemon peel (zest)

- Place the ice, gin and vermouth in a mixing glass.
- Stir with a mixing spoon for 8–10 seconds.

- Strain into a Martini glass using a cocktail strainer.
- Place the olive in the glass. Alternatively, cut the strip of lemon peel with a paring knife. Over the glass, pinch it between the fingers to release the oils then drop it into the cocktail. Serve immediately.

Variation: Extra-Dry Martini
The Extra-Dry Martini is made in the same way as the Vodka Martini Extra-Dry (▷ p. 67), using 1¾ measures of gin and ⅕ measure of dry vermouth. As a drier short drink, it makes an ideal aperitif.

A legendary quip for cinema buffs
The Dry Martini (▷ above) was already so popular at the end of the 1930s that it was the source of many slick retorts in Hollywood. In 1937, in Edward Sullivan's 'Every Day's a Holiday', May West played peach-skinned Fifi, a sparkling and extravagant confidence trickster who was driven out of New York for having sold Brooklyn Bridge. The wise cracking advice given by Larmadou Graves to Fifi was one of the most memorable: 'You should get out of those wet clothes and into a Dry Martini'.

Dubonnet Cocktail

Short drink to serve
as an aperitif

FOR 1 GLASS

3–4 ice cubes

1 measure gin

½ measure red Dubonnet

- Place the ice and all the ingredients in a rocks glass.
- Stir with a mixing spoon for 8–10 seconds. Serve immediately.

Variation: Diabola
By adding ¼ measure of orgeat syrup and making the drink in a shaker it becomes a Diabola, a short drink suitable for serving at any time. This recipe was created by Frank P Newman in Paris in the 1920s.

Floridita Bronx

Short drink to serve as an aperitif

FOR 1 GLASS

5–6 ice cubes

1 measure gin

¼ measure dry vermouth

¼ measure red vermouth

1 teaspoon orange curaçao

1 maraschino cherry

• Place the ice, both vermouths and the curaçao in a mixing glass.
• Stir with a mixing spoon for 8–10 seconds.
• Strain into a Martini glass using a cocktail strainer.
• Add the maraschino cherry to the drink. Serve immediately.

This variation of the Bronx (▷ p. 107) was invented in the 1920s in the Florida Bar, now known as the Floridita, in Havana, Cuba.

Gibson

Short drink to serve as an aperitif

FOR 1 GLASS

5–6 ice cubes

1½ measures gin

¼ measure dry vermouth

1 cocktail onion in vinegar

• Place the ice, gin and vermouth in a mixing glass.
• Stir with a mixing spoon for 8–10 seconds.
• Strain into a Martini glass using a cocktail strainer. Add the cocktail onion to the drink. Serve immediately.

Variation: Fino Martini
The Fino Martini is made by replacing the vermouth with dry sherry – a short drink that is perfect as an aperitif.

Journalist

Short drink to serve at any time

FOR 1 GLASS

5–6 ice cubes

¾ measure gin

¼ measure dry vermouth

¼ measure red vermouth

1 teaspoon fresh lemon juice

1 teaspoon orange curaçao

2–3 drops Angostura bitters

1 maraschino cherry

• Place the ice and all the ingredients except the cherry in the lower part of the shaker.
• Fit the upper part of the shaker and shake vigorously for 8–10 seconds
• Strain into a Martini glass using a cocktail strainer.
• Add the maraschino cherry to the drink. Serve immediately.

This classic from the 1920s owes its name to the habit formed by the journalists of the day of congregating in fashionable bars to gather and exchange news.

Leave it to Me

Short drink to serve at any time

FOR 1 GLASS

5–6 ice cubes

¾ measure gin

½ measure dry vermouth

1 teaspoon fresh lemon juice

1 teaspoon maraschino liqueur

1 teaspoon apricot brandy

1 strip unwaxed lemon peel (zest)

• Place the ice, gin, vermouth, lemon juice and both liqueurs in the lower part of the shaker.
• Fit the upper part of the shaker and shake vigorously for 8–10 seconds.
• Strain into a Martini glass using a cocktail strainer.
• Cut the strip of lemon peel with a paring knife. Over the glass, pinch it between the fingers to release the oils then drop it into the cocktail. Serve immediately.

Knickerbocker

Short drink to serve as an aperitif

FOR 1 GLASS

5–6 ice cubes

1 measure gin

⅓ measure dry vermouth

⅓ measure red vermouth

• Place the ice and all the ingredients in a mixing glass.
• Stir with a mixing spoon for 8–10 seconds.
• Strain into a Martini glass using a cocktail strainer. Serve immediately.

Variation: Rolls Royce

This is made by replacing the two kinds of vermouth with ¼ measure of Benedictine. A short drink with the aroma of herbs, ideal as a digestif.

London Fog

Short drink to serve as an aperitif

FOR 1 GLASS

3–4 ice cubes

1 measure still mineral water

½ measure Pernod

½ measure gin

• Place the ice in a rocks glass.
• First add the water, then the Pernod and finally the gin.
• Stir with a mixing spoon for 8–10 seconds. Serve immediately.

Lone Tree

Short drink to serve
at any time

FOR 1 GLASS

5–6 ice cubes

1 measure gin

½ measure dry vermouth

¼ measure maraschino liqueur

1 strip unwaxed lemon peel (zest)

- Place the ice, gin, vermouth and maraschino liqueur in a mixing glass.
- Stir with a mixing spoon for 8–10 seconds.
- Strain into a Martini glass using a cocktail strainer.
- Cut the strip of lemon peel with a paring knife. Over the glass, pinch it between the fingers to release the oils then drop it into the cocktail. Serve immediately.

Martinez

Short drink to serve
as an aperitif

FOR 1 GLASS

5–6 ice cubes

1 measure gin

½ measure red vermouth

1 teaspoon maraschino liqueur

3 drops Angostura bitters

1 strip unwaxed lemon
peel (zest)

- Place the ice, gin, vermouth, maraschino liqueur and Angostura bitters in a mixing glass.
- Stir with a mixing spoon for 8–10 seconds.
- Strain into a Martini glass using a cocktail strainer.
- Cut the strip of lemon peel with a paring knife. Over the glass, pinch it between the fingers to release the oils then drop it into the cocktail. Serve immediately

Parisian

Short drink to serve at any time

FOR 1 GLASS

5–6 ice cubes

1 measure gin

½ measure dry vermouth

¼ measure crème de cassis

1 strip unwaxed lemon peel (zest)

- Place the ice, gin, vermouth and crème de cassis in a mixing glass.
- Stir with a mixing spoon for 8–10 seconds.
- Strain into a Martini glass using a cocktail strainer.
- Cut the strip of lemon peel with a paring knife. Over the glass, pinch it between the fingers to release the oils then drop it into the cocktail. Serve immediately.

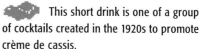 This short drink is one of a group of cocktails created in the 1920s to promote crème de cassis.

Pink Gin

Short drink to serve in the evening

FOR 1 GLASS

4–6 drops Angostura bitters

¾ measure Plymouth gin

• Place the Angostura bitters in a shot glass then pour in the gin.
• Serve immediately without stirring.

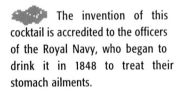 The invention of this cocktail is accredited to the officers of the Royal Navy, who began to drink it in 1848 to treat their stomach ailments.

Variation: Pink Gin & Tonic

This is obtained by preparing a Pink Gin in a highball glass and topping it up with tonic water – a long drink with a slightly bitter flavour, it is ideal in the late afternoon.

Turf

Short drink to serve
as an aperitif

FOR 1 GLASS

5–6 ice cubes

1 measure gin

½ measure dry vermouth

2–3 drops maraschino liqueur

2–3 drops absinthe-flavoured spirit

2–3 drops orange bitters

1 strip unwaxed lemon peel (zest)

• Place the ice and all ingredients except the lemon peel in a mixing glass.
• Stir with a mixing spoon for 8–10 seconds.
• Strain into a Martini glass using a cocktail strainer.
• Cut the strip of lemon peel with a paring knife. Over the glass, pinch it between the fingers to release the oils then drop it into the cocktail. Serve immediately.

Zaza

Short drink to serve
as an aperitif

FOR 1 GLASS

3–4 ice cubes

1 measure gin

½ measure red Dubonnet

3 drops Angostura bitters

• Place the ice and all the ingredients in a rocks glass.
• Stir with a mixing spoon for 8–10 seconds. Serve immediately.

 This cocktail was created by Frank P Newman between 1904 and 1907, at the Grand Hotel in Paris. Until World War I it was made with red vermouth instead of the Dubonnet.

Thirst-quenching cocktails

Alabama Fizz

Long drink to serve at any time

FOR 1 GLASS

8–10 ice cubes

1¼ measures gin

½ measure fresh lime juice

2 teaspoons sugar cane syrup

3–4 fresh mint leaves

2½ measures soda water
(club soda)

1 small fresh mint sprig

- Place 5–6 ice cubes in the lower part of the shaker then add the gin, lime juice, sugar cane syrup and mint leaves (without crushing them).
- Fit the upper part of the shaker and shake vigorously for 8–10 seconds.
- Place 3–4 ice cubes in a highball glass, then strain the contents of the shaker over them using a cocktail strainer.
- Add the soda water and then place the mint sprig in the glass. Serve immediately.

Aviation

Short drink to serve
at any time

FOR 1 GLASS

5–6 ice cubes

1 measure gin

⅛ measure fresh lemon juice

⅛ measure maraschino liqueur

1 maraschino cherry

- Place the ice, gin, lemon juice and maraschino liqueur in the lower part of the shaker.
- Fit the upper part of the shaker and shake vigorously for 8–10 seconds.
- Strain into a Martini glass using a cocktail strainer.
- Place the maraschino cherry in the glass. Serve immediately.

Blackout

Short drink to serve
at any time

FOR 1 GLASS

5–6 ice cubes

1 measure gin

½ measure fresh lime juice

¼ measure crème de mûre

- Place the ice, gin, lime juice and crème de mûre in the lower part of the shaker.
- Fit the upper part of the shaker and shake vigorously for 8–10 seconds.
- Strain into a Martini glass using a cocktail strainer. Serve immediately.

 This short drink appeared in the United States in the 1940s.

Blue Bird

Short drink to serve
at any time

FOR 1 GLASS

5–6 ice cubes

1 measure gin

⅛ measure fresh lemon juice

¼ measure curaçao triple sec

1 teaspoon blue curaçao

• Place the ice, gin, lemon juice and both kinds of curaçao in the lower part of the shaker.
• Fit the upper part of the shaker and shake vigorously for 8–10 seconds.
• Strain into a Martini glass using a cocktail strainer. Serve immediately.

This cocktail was created in 1927 to celebrate the land speed record established by Sir Malcolm Campbell in his car, the Bluebird.

Bramble

Short drink to serve
at any time

FOR 1 GLASS

3–4 crushed ice cubes
(▷ p. 59)

1 measure Plymouth gin

½ measure fresh lemon juice

¼ measure crème de mûre

1 teaspoon sugar cane syrup

½ slice unwaxed lemon

1 fresh blackberry

• Place the ice, gin, lemon juice, crème de mûre and sugar cane syrup in a rocks glass.
• Stir with a mixing spoon for 8–10 seconds.
• Add the lemon slice and the blackberry to the glass. Serve immediately.

Breakfast Martini

Short drink to serve in the morning

FOR 1 GLASS

5–6 ice cubes

1 measure gin

¼ measure fresh lemon juice

¼ measure curaçao triple sec

1 mixing spoon marmalade

1 strip unwaxed orange peel (zest)

• Place the ice, gin, lemon juice, curaçao and marmalade in the lower part of the shaker.
• Fit the upper part of the shaker and shake vigorously for 8–10 seconds.
• Strain into a Martini glass using a cocktail strainer and a pulp strainer.
• Cut the strip of orange peel with a paring knife. Over the glass, pinch it between the fingers to release the oils then drop it into the cocktail. Serve immediately.

Desert Healer

Long drink to serve at any time

FOR 1 GLASS

4–5 ice cubes

1 measure gin

1 measure fresh orange juice

½ measure cherry brandy

2 measures ginger beer or ginger ale

1 maraschino cherry

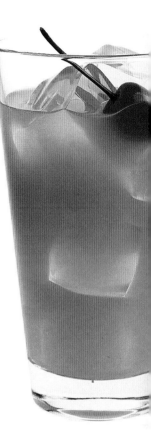

- Place the ice, gin, orange juice and cherry brandy in a highball glass.
- Stir with a mixing spoon for 8–10 seconds.
- Add the ginger beer and the maraschino cherry. Serve immediately.

Variation: Texas Fizz

Replace the cherry brandy with ¼ measure of fresh lemon juice and ¼ measure of grenadine, then top up (top off) with soda water (club soda) instead of ginger beer, making the Texas Fizz, a more acidic long drink; fine at any time.

Gimlet

Short drink to serve at any time

FOR 1 GLASS

3–4 ice cubes

1 measure Plymouth gin

½ measure lime cordial

- Place the ice and all the ingredients in a rocks glass.
- Stir with a mixing spoon for 8–10 seconds. Serve immediately.

A cocktail created for
Royal Navy personnel
The Gimlet (▷ left) was introduced aboard British warships by Surgeon General Sir Thomas D Gimlette, who served in the Royal Navy from 1879–1913. He had the idea that getting his men to drink lime cordial with gin could help combat scurvy, a disease caused by a lack of vitamin C.

Gin Fizz

Long drink to serve
at any time

FOR 1 GLASS

5–6 ice cubes

1¼ measures gin

½ measure fresh lemon juice

2 teaspoons sugar cane syrup

2½ measures soda water (club soda)

1 slice unwaxed lemon

1 maraschino cherry

- Place the ice, gin, lemon juice and sugar cane syrup in the lower part of the shaker.
- Fit the upper part of the shaker and shake vigorously for 8–10 seconds.
- Pour the contents of the shaker into a highball glass.
- Add the soda water and place the lemon slice and maraschino cherry in the glass. Serve immediately.

Variation: Silver Fizz

Replacing ½ measure of soda water (club soda) with ½ measure of beaten egg white results in a Silver Fizz, a smoother long drink, suitable for drinking at any time.

Green Hat

Long drink to serve
at any time

FOR 1 GLASS

4–5 ice cubes

1 measure gin

¼ measure green crème de menthe

3¼ measures soda water (club soda)

- Place the ice and all the ingredients in a highball glass.
- Stir with a mixing spoon for 8–10 seconds. Serve immediately.

Variation: Remsen Cooler

The Remsen Cooler, a sharper long drink that is excellent in late afternoon, is made by substituting fresh lemon juice for the crème de menthe and adding a strip of unwaxed lemon peel (zest) that has been pinched over the glass.

Jaizkibel

Short drink to serve
as an aperitif

FOR 1 GLASS

5–6 ice cubes

¾ measure gin

½ measure fresh
grapefruit juice

¼ measure Campari

1 teaspoon fresh lime juice

- Place the ice and all the ingredients in the lower part of the shaker.
- Fit the upper part of the shaker and shake vigorously for 8–10 seconds.
- Strain into a Martini glass using a cocktail strainer. Serve immediately.

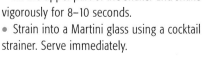

John Collins

Long drink to serve at any time

FOR 1 GLASS

4–5 ice cubes

1 measure gin

¾ measure fresh lemon juice

3 teaspoons sugar cane syrup

2¼ measures soda water (club soda)

½ slice unwaxed lemon

- Place the ice and all the ingredients except the lemon slice in a highball glass.
- Stir with a mixing spoon for 8–10 seconds.
- Add the lemon slice to the drink. Serve immediately.

 This cocktail is also called Tom Collins.

Variation: G.G.

The G.G., a sweeter long drink, ideal at any time, is made by replacing the sugar cane syrup with ¼ measure of blue curaçao and the soda water with 2½ measures of ginger ale. This cocktail was invented by Salvatore Calabrese around the year 2000 at the Lanesborough Hotel in London.

Macka

Long drink to serve as an aperitif

FOR 1 GLASS

4–5 ice cubes

1 measure gin

¼ measure dry vermouth

¼ measure red vermouth

¼ measure crème de cassis

2¾ measures soda water (club soda)

1 strip unwaxed lemon peel (zest)

- Place the ice and all the ingredients except the lemon peel in a highball glass.
- Stir with a mixing spoon for 8–10 seconds.
- Cut the strip of lemon peel with a paring knife. Over the glass, pinch it between the fingers to release the oils then drop it into the cocktail. Serve immediately.

Nicky's Fizz

Long drink to serve at any time

FOR 1 GLASS

4–5 ice cubes

1 measure gin

1 measure fresh grapefruit juice

2½ measures soda water (club soda)

- Place the ice, gin, grapefruit juice and soda water in a highball glass.
- Stir with a mixing spoon for 8–10 seconds. Serve immediately.

A few ideas for cocktail snacks to serve with
gin-based cocktails:

- Stilton, pear and celery canapés
- curried chicken pieces with mango chutney
- chicory barquettes filled with marinated
  smoked haddock
- mini brochettes of avocado and prawns (shrimp)
- madeleines flavoured with smoked China tea

▶ **recipes page 272**

Pink Lady

Short drink to serve at any time

FOR 1 GLASS

5–6 ice cubes

1 measure gin

½ measure fresh lemon juice

¼ measure grenadine

• Place the ice and all the ingredients in the lower part of the shaker.
• Fit the upper part of the shaker and shake vigorously for 8–10 seconds.
• Strain into a Martini glass using a cocktail strainer. Serve immediately.

Raspberry Collins

Long drink to serve at any time

FOR 1 GLASS

12–14 fresh raspberries

8–10 ice cubes

1 measure gin

¼ measure fresh lemon juice

2 teaspoons sugar cane syrup

2½ measures soda water (club soda)

½ slice unwaxed lemon

• Crush 12 raspberries in the lower part of the shaker.
• Add 5–6 ice cubes, the gin, lemon juice and sugar cane syrup.
• Fit the upper part of the shaker and shake vigorously for 8–10 seconds.
• Put 3–4 ice cubes in a highball glass then strain the contents of the shaker into it using a cocktail strainer and pulp strainer.
• Add the soda water.
• Place the lemon slice and the rest of the raspberries into the glass. Serve immediately.

Resolute

Short drink to serve at any time

FOR 1 GLASS

5–6 ice cubes

1 measure gin

½ measure fresh lemon juice

¼ measure apricot brandy

• Place the ice and all the ingredients in the lower part of the shaker.
• Fit the upper part of the shaker and shake vigorously for 8–10 seconds.
• Strain into a Martini glass using a cocktail strainer. Serve immediately.

 This short drink was very fashionable in the 1920s.

Shady Grove

Long drink to serve at any time

FOR 1 GLASS

4–5 ice cubes

1 measure gin

⅓ measure fresh lime juice

3 measures ginger ale

⅛ unwaxed lime

- Place the ice, gin, lime juice and ginger ale in a highball glass.
- Stir with a mixing spoon for 8–10 seconds.
- Place the lime segment in the glass. Serve immediately.

Variation: Bull-Dog

The Bull-Dog, a refreshing and fruity long drink that is ideal for late afternoon, is made by substituting fresh orange juice for the ginger ale.

Singapore Sling

Long drink to serve at any time

FOR 1 GLASS

5–6 ice cubes

1 measure gin

½ measure cherry brandy

⅓ measure fresh lemon juice

1 teaspoon Benedictine

2½ measures soda water (club soda)

½ slice unwaxed lemon

1 maraschino cherry

- Place the ice, gin, cherry brandy, lemon juice and Benedictine in the lower part of the shaker.
- Fit the upper part of the shaker and shake vigorously for 8–10 seconds.
- Pour into a highball glass. Add the soda water.
- Place the lemon slice and maraschino cherry in the glass. Serve immediately.

A popular long drink in Singapore

The Singapore Sling (▷ left) was created between 1910 and 1915 by Ngiam Tong Boon, at the Raffles Hotel (pictured below) in Singapore. The recipe, known in the 1920s as the Straits Sling, quickly gained popularity in the British Isles. Today, the Raffles Hotel serves a fruitier version called the Raffles Sling (▷ p. 111), made to a recipe suggested by a client in 1939.

Southside

Short drink to serve at any time

FOR 1 GLASS

5–6 ice cubes

1 measure gin

½ measure fresh lime juice

2 teaspoons sugar cane syrup

3–4 fresh mint leaves

1 strip unwaxed lime peel (zest)

- Place the ice, gin, lime juice, sugar cane syrup and mint leaves in the lower part of the shaker.
- Fit the upper part of the shaker and shake vigorously for 8–10 seconds.
- Strain into a Martini glass using a cocktail strainer.
- Cut the strip of lime peel with a paring knife. Over the glass, pinch it between the fingers to release the oils then drop it into the cocktail. Serve immediately.

Tamanaco Dry

Short drink to serve as an aperitif

FOR 1 GLASS

5–6 ice cubes

1½ measures gin

¼ measure light beer

- Place the ice and all the ingredients in a mixing glass.
- Stir with a mixing spoon for 8–10 seconds.
- Strain into a Martini glass using a cocktail strainer. Serve immediately.

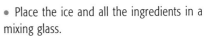 Originally called the Jack'artini, this cocktail was created in the 1950s by Jacques Hébrard at the Tamanaco Hotel in Caracas (Venezuela).

White Lady

Short drink to serve at any time

FOR 1 GLASS

5–6 ice cubes

1 measure gin

⅓ measure fresh lemon juice

⅓ measure curaçao triple sec

- Place the ice and all the ingredients in the lower part of the shaker.
- Fit the upper part of the shaker and shake vigorously for 8–10 seconds.
- Strain into a Martini glass using a cocktail strainer. Serve immediately.

A cocktail by this name, invented in 1919 by Harry McElhone, contained the following ingredients: Cognac, crème de menthe and curaçao triple sec.

Fruit-based cocktails

Bronx

Short drink to serve
at any time

FOR 1 GLASS

5–6 ice cubes

¾ measure gin

½ measure fresh
orange juice

¼ measure dry vermouth

¼ measure red vermouth

1 maraschino cherry

• Place the ice, gin, orange juice and
both kinds of vermouth in the lower part of
the shaker.
• Fit the upper part of the shaker and shake
vigorously for 8–10 seconds.
• Strain into a Martini glass using a cocktail
strainer.
• Add the maraschino cherry to the drink.
Serve immediately.

Abbey

Short drink to serve
at any time

FOR 1 GLASS

5–6 ice cubes

¾ measure gin

½ measure fresh orange juice

⅛ measure red vermouth

2–3 drops Angostura bitters

• Place the ice and all the ingredients in the
lower part of the shaker.
• Fit the upper part of the shaker and shake
vigorously for 8–10 seconds.
• Strain into a Martini glass using a cocktail
strainer. Serve immediately.

Colonial

Short drink to serve
at any time

FOR 1 GLASS

5–6 ice cubes

1 measure gin

½ measure fresh grapefruit juice

¼ measure maraschino liqueur

• Place the ice and all the ingredients
in the lower part of the shaker.
• Fit the upper part of the shaker and shake
vigorously for 8–10 seconds.
• Strain into a Martini glass using a cocktail
strainer. Serve immediately.

Variation: Dodge

The Dodge, a rather more bitter drink,
suitable for drinking at any time, is made
by replacing the maraschino liqueur with
curaçao triple sec.

Eurêka

Short drink to serve at any time

FOR 1 GLASS

5–6 ice cubes

1 measure gin

½ measure fresh orange juice

1 teaspoon fresh lemon juice

1 teaspoon grenadine

- Place the ice and all the ingredients in the lower part of the shaker.
- Fit the upper part of the shaker and shake vigorously for 8–10 seconds.
- Strain into a Martini glass using a cocktail strainer. Serve immediately.

Honolulu Punch

Long drink to serve at any time

FOR 1 GLASS

1 slice fresh pineapple

5–6 ice cubes

1 measure gin

2 measures pure pineapple juice

1 measure fresh orange juice

¼ measure fresh lemon juice

2 teaspoons sugar cane syrup

2–3 drops Angostura bitters

- Cut a triangular piece from the pineapple slice, leaving the skin in place.
- Place the ice and all the ingredients except the piece of pineapple in the lower part of the shaker. Fit the upper part of the shaker and shake vigorously for 8–10 seconds.
- Strain into a highball glass using a cocktail strainer.
- Cut a slit in the piece of pineapple and fix it to the rim of the glass. Serve immediately.

Lady Killer

Long drink to serve at any time

FOR 1 GLASS

5–6 ice cubes

¾ measure gin

1½ measures passion fruit juice (based on fruit concentrate)

1½ measures pure pineapple juice

⅓ measure curaçao triple sec

⅓ measure apricot brandy

1 segment unwaxed orange

- Place the ice, gin, fruit juices and both liqueurs in the lower part of the shaker.
- Fit the upper part of the shaker and shake vigorously for 8–10 seconds.
- Strain into a highball glass using a cocktail strainer.
- Make a slit in the orange segment and fix to the rim of the glass. Serve immediately.

Invented by Peter Roth, this long drink won first prize at the 1984 International Cocktail Competition organized by the International Bartenders' Association.

Miami Beach

Short drink to serve at any time

FOR 1 GLASS

5–6 ice cubes

1 measure gin

½ measure pure pineapple juice

1 teaspoon sugar cane syrup

1 fresh pineapple leaf

- Place the ice, gin, pineapple juice and sugar cane syrup in the lower part of the shaker.
- Fit the upper part of the shaker and shake vigorously for 8–10 seconds.
- Strain into a Martini glass using a cocktail strainer.
- Make a slit in the pineapple leaf and slot it onto the rim of the glass. Serve immediately.

Variation: Jinx

This colourful short drink, suitable for serving any time, is made with grenadine instead of the sugar cane syrup.

Monkey Gland

Short drink to serve at any time

FOR 1 GLASS

5–6 ice cubes

1 measure gin

½ measure fresh orange juice

1 teaspoon grenadine

3 drops absinthe-flavoured spirit

- Place the ice and all the ingredients in the lower part of the shaker.
- Fit the upper part of the shaker and shake vigorously for 8–10 seconds.
- Strain into a Martini glass using a cocktail strainer. Serve immediately.

Opal

Short drink to serve at any time

FOR 1 GLASS

5–6 ice cubes

1 measure gin

½ measure fresh orange juice

¼ measure curaçao triple sec

- Place the ice and all the ingredients in the lower part of the shaker.
- Fit the upper part of the shaker and shake vigorously for 8–10 seconds.
- Strain into a Martini glass using a cocktail strainer. Serve immediately.

Variation: Merry Widow

The Merry Widow, a short drink with a pronounced flavour of herbs, which makes an idea digestif, is made by replacing the curaçao triple sec with Benedictine and adding 2–3 drops of Angostura bitters.

Orange Blossom

Short drink to serve at any time

FOR 1 GLASS

5–6 ice cubes

¾ measure gin

¾ measure fresh orange juice

1 segment unwaxed orange

• Place the ice, gin and orange juice in the lower part of the shaker.
• Fit the upper part of the shaker and shake vigorously for 8–10 seconds.
• Strain into a rocks glass using a cocktail strainer.

• Make a cut in the orange segment and fix it to the rim of the glass. Serve immediately.

When served in a highball glass this cocktail is called Harvester.

Variation: Tropical Dawn
The Tropical Dawn, a bitter-flavoured short drink that is excellent in the late afternoon, is made by reducing the gin and orange juice by 1 teaspoon each and adding ¼ measure of Campari.

Paradise

Short drink to serve in the evening

FOR 1 GLASS

5–6 ice cubes

1 measure gin

½ measure fresh orange juice

¼ measure apricot brandy

• Place the ice and all the ingredients in the lower part of the shaker.
• Fit the upper part of the shaker and shake vigorously for 8–10 seconds.
• Strain into a Martini glass using a cocktail strainer. Serve immediately.

This short drink was created at the start of the 1920s. It is the best known of all the cocktails based on apricot brandy.

Queen Cocktail

Short drink to serve at any time

FOR 1 GLASS

5–6 ice cubes

¾ measure gin

¼ measure dry vermouth

¼ measure red vermouth

¼ measure fresh orange juice

¼ measure pure pineapple juice

• Place the ice and all the ingredients in the lower part of the shaker.
• Fit the upper part of the shaker and shake vigorously for 8–10 seconds.
• Strain into a Martini glass using a cocktail strainer. Serve immediately.

Raffles Sling

Long drink to serve at any time

FOR 1 GLASS

5–6 ice cubes

1 measure gin

2½ measures pure pineapple juice

½ measure cherry brandy

1 teaspoon curaçao triple sec

1 teaspoon Benedictine

1 teaspoon fresh lime juice

1 teaspoon grenadine

3 drops Angostura bitters

2 fresh pineapple leaves

• Place the ice and all the ingredients except the pineapple leaves in the lower part of the shaker.
• Fit the upper part of the shaker and shake vigorously for 8–10 seconds.
• Strain into a highball glass using a cocktail strainer.
• Make slits in the pineapple leaves and fix them to the rim of the glass. Serve immediately.

A short drink named after a distillery

The Red Lion (▷ below) might have been created in 1890 in a London pub (pictured here) of the same name. In actual fact, this cocktail was created in London in 1933 by Arthur A Tarling when he won the British Empire Cocktail Competition, organized by the Booth's Gin Company. The Red Lion is named after the oldest distillery run by Booth's at that time.

Red Lion

Short drink to serve at any time

FOR 1 GLASS

5–6 ice cubes

¾ measure gin

½ measure fresh orange juice

¼ measure Grand Marnier Cordon Rouge

1 teaspoon fresh lemon juice

• Place the ice, gin, orange juice, liqueur and lemon juice in the lower part of the shaker.
• Fit the upper part of the shaker and shake vigorously for 8–10 seconds.
• Strain into a Martini glass using a cocktail strainer. Serve immediately.

This short drink is the most popular of the cocktails made with Grand Marnier.

Liqueur-based cocktails

Acacias

Short drink to serve as a digestif

FOR 1 GLASS

5–6 ice cubes

1 measure gin

½ measure Benedictine

¼ measure kirsch

- Place the ice and all the ingredients in a mixing glass.
- Stir with a mixing spoon for 8–10 seconds.
- Strain into a Martini glass using a cocktail strainer. Serve immediately.

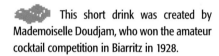 This short drink was created by Mademoiselle Doudjam, who won the amateur cocktail competition in Biarritz in 1928.

Alaska

Short drink to serve as a digestif

FOR 1 GLASS

3–4 ice cubes

1 measure gin

½ measure yellow Chartreuse

- Place the ice and all the ingredients in a rocks glass.
- Stir with a mixing spoon for 8–10 seconds. Serve immediately.

Bee's Knees

Short drink to serve as a digestif

FOR 1 GLASS

5–6 ice cubes

1 measure gin

½ measure fresh lemon juice

¼ measure liquid acacia honey

- Place the ice and all the ingredients in the lower part of the shaker.
- Fit the upper part of the shaker and shake vigorously for 8–10 seconds.
- Strain into a Martini glass using a cocktail strainer. Serve immediately.

Caruso

Short drink to serve
as a digestif

FOR 1 GLASS

5–6 ice cubes

1 measure gin

½ measure
dry vermouth

¼ measure green
crème de menthe

• Place the ice and all the ingredients in a mixing glass.
• Stir with a mixing spoon for 8–10 seconds.
• Strain into a Martini glass using a cocktail strainer. Serve immediately.

Variation: Knock-Out
Omitting ¼ measure of the gin and adding ¼ measure of absinthe-flavoured spirit results in the Knock-Out, a short drink with a strong aniseed flavour, ideal for ending the evening. It was invented in the 1920s by Jeff Dickson at the Salle Wagram in Paris.

Bijou

Short drink to serve
as a digestif

FOR 1 GLASS

5–6 ice cubes

1 measure gin

½ measure red vermouth

¼ measure green Chartreuse

2–3 drops orange bitters

• Place the ice and all the ingredients in a mixing glass.
• Stir with a mixing spoon for 8–10 seconds.
• Strain into a Martini glass using a cocktail strainer. Serve immediately.

Evolution

Short drink to serve
in the evening

FOR 1 GLASS

1½ measures gin

3–4 fresh mint leaves

¼ measure cherry brandy

- Place the gin in the freezer for 1 hour.
- Crush the mint leaves with the cherry brandy in a mixing glass.
- Strain into a Martini glass using a pulp strainer.
- Slowly pour the iced gin into the glass. Serve immediately.

Fallen Angel

Short drink to serve in the evening

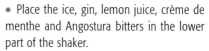

FOR 1 GLASS

5–6 ice cubes

1 measure gin

⅛ measure fresh lemon juice

⅛ measure white crème de menthe

2–3 drops Angostura bitters

- Place the ice, gin, lemon juice, crème de menthe and Angostura bitters in the lower part of the shaker.
- Fit the upper part of the shaker and shake vigorously for 8–10 seconds.
- Strain into a Martini glass using a cocktail strainer. Serve immediately.

French Kiss

Short drink to serve
as a digestif

FOR 1 GLASS

3–4 ice cubes

1 measure gin

½ measure Grand Marnier
Cordon Rouge

1 strip unwaxed orange peel
(zest)

- Place the ice, gin and liqueur in a rocks glass.
- Stir with a mixing spoon for 8–10 seconds.
- Cut the strip of orange peel with a paring knife. Over the glass, pinch it between the fingers to release the oils then drop it into the cocktail. Serve immediately.

Variation: Elegant

Elegant, a drier short drink that is ideal as an aperitif, is made by replacing ¼ measure of gin and ¼ measure of Grand Marnier Cordon Rouge with ½ measure of dry vermouth.

Just Try

Short drink to serve as a digestif

FOR 1 GLASS

5–6 ice cubes

1 measure gin

¼ measure dry vermouth

¼ measure yellow Chartreuse

¼ measure Grand Marnier Cordon Rouge

1 strip unwaxed orange peel (zest)

- Place the ice, gin, vermouth and both liqueurs in a mixing glass.
- Stir with a mixing spoon for 8–10 seconds.
- Strain into a Martini glass using a cocktail strainer.
- Cut the strip of orange peel with a paring knife. Over the glass, pinch it between the fingers to release the oils then drop it into the cocktail. Serve immediately.

Lemony Snicket

Short drink to serve as a digestif

FOR 1 GLASS

5–6 ice cubes

1 measure gin

¼ measure yellow Chartreuse

¼ measure limoncello

¼ measure fresh lemon juice

1 maraschino cherry

- Place the ice, gin, both liqueurs and the lemon juice in the lower part of the shaker.
- Fit the upper part of the shaker and shake vigorously for 8–10 seconds.
- Strain into a Martini glass using a cocktail strainer.
- Add the maraschino cherry to the glass. Serve immediately.

Princeton

Short drink to serve as a digestif

FOR 1 GLASS

5–6 ice cubes

1 measure gin

½ measure port

2–3 drops orange bitters

- Place the ice and all the ingredients in a mixing glass.
- Stir with a mixing spoon for 8–10 seconds.
- Strain into a Martini glass using a cocktail strainer. Serve immediately.

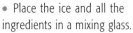

Spring Feeling

Short drink to serve as a digestif

FOR 1 GLASS

5–6 ice cubes

1 measure gin

½ measure fresh lemon juice

¼ measure green Chartreuse

- Place the ice, gin, lemon juice and liqueur in the lower part of the shaker.
- Fit the upper part of the shaker and shake vigorously for 8–10 seconds.
- Strain into a Martini glass using a cocktail strainer. Serve immediately.

Smooth cocktails

Alexander

Short drink to serve as a digestif

FOR 1 GLASS

5–6 ice cubes

¾ measure gin

½ measure white crème de cacao

½ measure single (light) cream

1 nutmeg

- Place the ice, gin, crème de cacao and cream in the lower part of the shaker.
- Fit the upper part of the shaker and shake vigorously for 8–10 seconds.
- Strain into a Martini glass using a cocktail strainer.
- Grate a pinch of nutmeg over the drink. Serve immediately.

Clover Club

Short drink to serve at any time

FOR 1 GLASS

1 egg white

5–6 ice cubes

1 measure gin

⅓ measure fresh lemon juice

1 teaspoon grenadine

- Place the egg white in a bowl and whisk for few seconds with a fork.
- Place the ice, gin, 1 teaspoon of the beaten egg, lemon juice and grenadine in the lower part of the shaker.
- Fit the upper part of the shaker and shake vigorously for 8–10 seconds.
- Strain into a Martini glass using a cocktail strainer. Serve immediately.

New Orleans was the birthplace of a certain style of jazz. The capital of Louisiana also saw the invention,

around 1888, of the Ramoz Gin Fizz (▷ right), a variation on the famous Gin Fizz (▷ p 100). Its creator, Henry C Ramos, was co-owner with his brother of an establishment that bore the name, among others, of the Gin Fizz Palace. It closed down at the start of Prohibition in 1919, at which time Henry Ramos revealed the recipe of the Ramos Gin Fizz, which up to then had remained secret.

Ramos Gin Fizz

Long drink to serve in the morning

FOR 1 GLASS

1 egg white

5–6 ice cubes

1 measure gin

⅓ measure fresh lemon juice

¼ measure fresh lime juice

2 teaspoons sugar cane syrup

2 teaspoons single (light) cream

3–4 drops orange flower water

2 measures soda water
(club soda)

- Place the egg white in a bowl and whisk with a fork.
- Place the ice, 3 teaspoons of the egg white and all the other ingredients except the soda water in the lower part of the shaker.
- Fit the upper part of the shaker and shake vigorously for 10 seconds.
- Strain into a highball glass using a cocktail strainer.
- Add the soda water. Serve immediately.

Red Snapper

Long drink to serve
at any time

FOR 1 GLASS

1 measure gin

3 measures tomato juice

1 teaspoon fresh lemon juice

1 teaspoon Worcestershire sauce

3 drops red Tabasco sauce

1 pinch celery salt

1 pinch black pepper

5–6 ice cubes

1 small stick (stalk) celery

- Place all the ingredients except the celery stick in a mixing glass. Stir with a mixing spoon for 8–10 seconds.
- Strain into a highball glass using a cocktail strainer.
- Wash the piece of celery and add it to the drink.

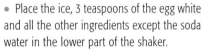 Fernand Petiot (ex-barman of Harry's Bar in Paris) renamed the Bloody Mary as the Red Snapper because the management of the Saint Regis Hotel in New York, where he started working in 1934, found the name Bloody Mary too colloquial for their customers. Originally made with vodka, the Red Snapper is now made with gin in order to offer an alternative to the Bloody Mary.

Whisky-based cocktails

Whisky is a form of alcohol distilled from cereals. In Scotland and Ireland it is made with barley; in the United States and Canada they use a mixture of cereals, predominantly maize (corn) or rye.

There are many kinds of whisky, differing vastly according to where they come from and the methods used to make them. Among the range of Scotch whiskies the most common are blended ones, which are a combination of grain whisky and malt whisky. Single malt whiskies, on the other hand, are made solely from malted barley.

A prime characteristic of Scotch whisky is its more or less pronounced peaty flavour that combines admirably with the herb aromas of the vermouth in a Rob Roy (▷ p. 123), or the herb-flavoured liqueurs in a Rusty Nail (▷ p. 135). Irish whiskeys, being less aromatic, are compatible with such varied ingredients as the coffee in Irish Coffee (▷ p. 139), or the lemon juice in an Irish Rose (▷ p. 127). The woody flavours of the American whiskeys (bourbon, rye) and those of Canada are enhanced by the aromatic bitters used in a Manhattan (▷ p. 122) and an Old-Fashioned (▷ p. 122). They also tend to attenuate the acidity of lemon juice in such drinks as Whiskey Sour (▷ p. 132) and California Lemonade (▷ p. 125).

▲
Scotland is the premier whisky producer in the world, followed by Japan, Canada, the United States and Ireland. Note that in the two latter countries it is spelled 'whiskey'.
▷ See also pp. 296–299

THE 10 INDISPUTABLE CLASSICS

Algonquin ▷ p. 132
Bobby Burns ▷ p. 134
Irish Coffee ▷ p. 139
Lynchburg Lemonade ▷ p. 130
Manhattan ▷ p. 122
Mint Julep ▷ p. 131
Old-Fashioned ▷ p. 122
Rusty Nail ▷ p. 135
Sazerac ▷ p. 123
Whiskey Sour ▷ p. 132

Dry cocktails

Blackthorn

Short drink to serve as an aperitif

FOR 1 GLASS

5–6 ice cubes

1 measure Irish whiskey

½ measure dry vermouth

2–3 drops absinthe-flavoured spirit

2–3 drops Angostura bitters

1 strip unwaxed lemon peel (zest)

- Place the ice and all the ingredients except the lemon peel in a mixing glass.
- Stir with a mixing spoon for 8–10 seconds.
- Strain into a Martini glass using a cocktail strainer.
- Cut the strip of lemon peel with a paring knife. Over the glass, pinch it between the fingers to release the oils then drop it into the cocktail. Serve immediately.

Churchill

Short drink to serve at any time

FOR 1 GLASS

5–6 ice cubes

1 measure Scotch whisky

½ measure red vermouth

1 teaspoon curaçao triple sec

1 teaspoon fresh lime juice

- Place the ice, whisky, vermouth, curaçao and lime juice in the lower part of the shaker.
- Fit the upper part of the shaker and shake vigorously for 8–10 seconds.
- Strain into a Martini glass using a cocktail strainer. Serve immediately.

European Beauty

Short drink to serve as an aperitif

FOR 1 GLASS

5–6 ice cubes

1¼ measures Scotch malt whisky

½ measure Dubonnet

1 strip unwaxed orange peel (zest)

- Place the ice, whisky and Dubonnet in a mixing glass.
- Stir with a mixing spoon for 8–10 seconds.
- Strain into a Martini glass using a cocktail strainer.
- Cut the strip of orange peel with a paring knife. Over the glass, pinch it between the fingers to release the oils then drop it into the cocktail. Serve immediately.

Hondarribia

Short drink to serve as an aperitif

FOR 1 GLASS

5–6 ice cubes

1 measure Scotch whisky

⅛ measure Campari

⅛ measure red vermouth

1 strip unwaxed lemon peel (zest)

- Place the ice, whisky, Campari and vermouth in a mixing glass.
- Stir with a mixing spoon for 8–10 seconds.
- Strain into a Martini glass using a cocktail strainer.
- Cut the strip of lemon peel with a paring knife. Over the glass, pinch it between the fingers to release the oils then drop it into the cocktail. Serve immediately.

Variation: Old Pal
Using Canadian whisky instead of Scotch, and dry vermouth instead of red, gives an Old Pal, a drier short drink, also suitable as an aperitif.

Gaslight

Short drink to serve at any time

FOR 1 GLASS

5–6 ice cubes

1 measure Scotch whisky

½ measure red vermouth

¼ measure orange curaçao

1 strip unwaxed orange peel (zest)

- Place the ice, whisky, vermouth and curaçao in a mixing glass.
- Stir with a mixing spoon for 8–10 seconds.
- Strain into a Martini glass using a cocktail strainer.
- Cut the strip of orange peel with a paring knife. Over the glass, pinch it between the fingers to release the oils then drop it into the cocktail. Serve immediately.

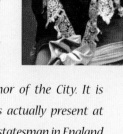

The most famous of the whiskey cocktails

The Manhattan (▷ p. 122) was invented in New York on the occasion of a dinner organized at the Manhattan Club on 18 November 1874 by Winston Churchill's mother, Jenny Churchill (1854–1921), photographed here, to celebrate the election of Samuel Jones Tilden as Governor of the City. It is doubtful, however, that Jenny Churchill was actually present at the banquet since she gave birth to the future statesman in England on 30 November of the same year.

Manhattan

Short drink to serve as an aperitif

FOR 1 GLASS

5–6 ice cubes

1¼ measures rye whiskey

½ measure red vermouth

2–3 drops Angostura bitters

1 maraschino cherry

- Place the ice, whiskey, vermouth and Angostura bitters in a mixing glass.
- Stir with a mixing spoon for 8–10 seconds.
- Strain into a Martini glass using a cocktail strainer.
- Add the maraschino cherry to the glass. Serve immediately.

Variation:

Perfect Manhattan

Replace ¼ measure of the red vermouth with ¼ measure of dry vermouth and you have a Perfect Manhattan – a drier short drink suitable for any time of the day.

The Old-Fashioned – a great classic

The song writer, Cole Porter (1892–1964) [pictured here] undoubtedly contributed to the popularity of the Old-Fashioned (▷ below) with his use of the name in the titles of several of his songs, including his first success, Old-Fashioned Garden, in 1919. This short drink was invented at the Pendennis Club in Louisville, Kentucky, sometime between 1900 and 1907. As to the recipe, it was the work of one of the members, Colonel James E Pepper, owner of a brand of Bourbon called 'Old 1776'.

Old-Fashioned

Short drink to serve at any time

FOR 1 GLASS

4–5 drops Angostura bitters

1 lump sugar

3–4 ice cubes

1¼ measures rye whiskey

½ measure still mineral water

1 strip unwaxed orange peel (zest)

1 maraschino cherry

- Drop the Angostura bitters onto the lump of sugar and then put it into a rocks glass and crush it with a pestle.
- Add the ice, whiskey and water. Stir with a mixing spoon for 10 seconds.
- Cut the strip of orange peel with a paring knife. Over the glass, pinch it between the fingers to release the oils then drop it into the cocktail. Add the maraschino cherry. Serve immediately.

Rob Roy

Short drink to serve
as an aperitif

FOR 1 GLASS

5–6 ice cubes

1¼ measures Scotch whisky

½ measure red vermouth

2–3 drops Angostura bitters

1 maraschino cherry

- Place the ice, whisky, vermouth and Angostura bitters in a mixing glass.
- Stir with a mixing spoon for 8–10 seconds.
- Strain into a Martini glass using a cocktail strainer.
- Add the maraschino cherry to the glass. Serve immediately.

Variation: Rory O'More

The Rory O'More, made with Irish whiskey instead of Scotch whisky, is less aromatic and is an ideal drink at any time of the day

Sazerac

Short drink to serve
at any time

FOR 1 GLASS

2–3 drops Peychaud's bitters

1 lump sugar

5–6 ice cubes

½ measure still mineral water

1¼ measures rye whiskey

3 drops absinthe-flavoured spirit

1 strip unwaxed lemon peel (zest)

- Drop the Peychaud's bitters onto the lump of sugar and place it in a mixing glass. Crush the bitters-soaked sugar with a pestle.
- Add the ice, water, whiskey and absinthe-flavoured spirit. Stir with a mixing spoon for 10 seconds.
- Cut the strip of lemon peel with a paring knife. Over the mixing glass, pinch it between the fingers to release the oils but don't place it in the drink.
- Strain into a rocks glass. Serve immediately.

Scoff-Law

Short drink to serve at any time

FOR 1 GLASS

5–6 ice cubes

1 measure Canadian whisky

½ measure dry vermouth

1 teaspoon fresh lemon juice

1 teaspoon grenadine

2–3 drops Angostura bitters

- Place the ice and all the ingredients in the lower part of the shaker.
- Fit the upper part of the shaker and shake vigorously for 8–10 seconds.
- Strain into a Martini glass using a cocktail strainer. Serve immediately.

Up-to-Date

Short drink to serve
at any time

FOR 1 GLASS

5–6 ice cubes

1 measure Canadian whisky

½ measure sherry

¼ measure Grand Marnier Cordon
Rouge

2–3 drops Angostura bitters

- Place the ice and all the ingredients in a
mixing glass.
- Stir with a mixing spoon for 8–10 seconds.
- Strain into a Martini glass using a cocktail
strainer. Serve immediately.

Whizz-Bang

Short drink to serve
at any time

FOR 1 GLASS

5–6 ice cubes

1 measure Scotch whisky

½ measure dry vermouth

1 teaspoon grenadine

1 teaspoon absinthe-flavoured spirit

2–3 drops orange bitters

- Place the ice and all the ingredients in a
mixing glass.
- Stir with a mixing spoon for 8–10 seconds.
- Strain into a Martini glass using a cocktail
strainer. Serve immediately.

Thirst-quenching cocktails

Cablegram

Long drink to serve
at any time

FOR 1 GLASS

4–5 ice cubes

1 measure rye whiskey

⅓ measure fresh lemon juice

1 teaspoon sugar cane syrup

3 measures ginger ale

1 slice unwaxed lemon

- Place the ice, whiskey, lemon juice, sugar
cane syrup and ginger ale in a highball glass.
- Stir with a mixing spoon for 8–10 seconds.
- Add the lemon slice to the glass.
Serve immediately.

 Popular in the 1920s, this long
drink is a good example of the happy union
of whiskey with ginger ale.

California Lemonade

Long drink to serve
at any time

FOR 1 GLASS

4–5 ice cubes

1 measure bourbon

¼ measure fresh lemon juice

¼ measure fresh lime juice

¼ measure grenadine

2¾ measures soda water (club soda)

• Place the ice and all the ingredients in a highball glass.
• Stir with a mixing spoon for 8–10 seconds. Serve immediately.

Commodore

Short drink to serve at any time

FOR 1 GLASS

5–6 ice cubes

1 measure Canadian whisky

½ measure fresh lime juice

2 teaspoons sugar cane syrup

2–3 drops orange bitters

• Place the ice and all the ingredients in the lower part of the shaker.
• Fit the upper part of the shaker and shake vigorously for 8–10 seconds.
• Strain into a Martini glass using a cocktail strainer. Serve immediately.

Creativity

Long drink to serve at any time

FOR 1 GLASS

4–5 ice cubes

¾ measure bourbon

¼ measure Grand Marnier Cordon Rouge

1 teaspoon lime cordial

3¼ measures ginger ale

2 fine slices unwaxed lime

2 maraschino cherries

• Place the ice, bourbon, Grand Marnier Cordon Rouge, lime cordial and ginger ale in a highball glass.
• Stir with a mixing spoon for 8–10 seconds.
• Add the lime slices and the maraschino cherries to the glass. Serve immediately.

Francis the Mule

Short drink to serve
at any time

FOR 1 GLASS

5–6 ice cubes

1 measure bourbon

¼ measure fresh lemon juice

¼ measure orgeat syrup

¼ measure cold espresso coffee

2–3 drops orange bitters

1 strip unwaxed lemon peel (zest)

- Place the ice and all the ingredients except the lemon peel in the lower part of the shaker.
- Fit the upper part of the shaker and shake vigorously for 8–10 seconds.
- Strain into a Martini glass using a cocktail strainer.
- Cut the strip of lemon peel with a paring knife. Over the glass, pinch it between the fingers to release the oils then drop it into the cocktail. Serve immediately.

Hemingway Sour

Short drink to serve
at any time

FOR 1 GLASS

5–6 ice cubes

1 measure bourbon

½ measure fresh lemon juice

¼ measure Drambuie

- Place the ice and all the ingredients in the lower part of the shaker.
- Fit the upper part of the shaker and shake vigorously for 8–10 seconds.
- Strain into a Martini glass using a cocktail strainer. Serve immediately.

Frisco

Short drink to serve
as a digestif

FOR 1 GLASS

5–6 ice cubes

1 measure bourbon

½ measure fresh lemon juice

¼ measure Benedictine

- Place the ice and all the ingredients in the lower part of the shaker.
- Fit the upper part of the shaker and shake vigorously for 8–10 seconds.
- Strain into a Martini glass using a cocktail strainer. Serve immediately.

Highland Cooler

Long drink to serve
at any time

FOR 1 GLASS

4–5 ice cubes

1 measure Scotch whisky

¼ measure fresh lemon juice

2 teaspoons sugar cane syrup

3 measures ginger ale

• Place the ice and all the ingredients in a highball glass.
• Stir with a mixing spoon for 8–10 seconds. Serve immediately.

Irish Rose

Short drink to serve
at any time

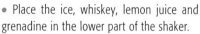

FOR 1 GLASS

5–6 ice cubes

1 measure Irish whiskey

⅓ measure fresh lemon juice

⅓ measure grenadine

1 strip unwaxed lemon
peel (zest)

• Place the ice, whiskey, lemon juice and grenadine in the lower part of the shaker.
• Fit the upper part of the shaker and shake vigorously for 8–10 seconds.
• Strain into a Martini glass using a cocktail strainer.
• Cut the strip of lemon peel with a paring knife. Over the glass, pinch it between the fingers to release the oils but don't add it to the glass. Serve immediately.

High Voltage

Short drink to serve at any time

FOR 1 GLASS

¼ unwaxed lime

3–4 ice cubes

1 measure Scotch whisky

¼ measure curaçao triple sec

1½ measures soda water (club soda)

• Squeeze the lime quarter over a rocks glass then drop it in.
• Add the ice and the other ingredients.
• Stir with a mixing spoon for 8–10 seconds. Serve immediately.

A few ideas for cocktail snacks to serve with whisky-based cocktails:

- cumin-flavoured Gouda canapés with cucumber and dried figs
- sweet potato crisps (chips), Gorgonzola dip and vegetable sticks
- mini brochettes of York ham with apricots
- mini club sandwich filled with coleslaw and bacon
- brownies with Morello cherries

▶ **recipes page 274**

Kentucky Tea

Long drink to serve
at any time

FOR 1 GLASS

4–5 ice cubes

1 measure bourbon

½ measure fresh lime juice

¼ measure orange curaçao

2¾ measures ginger ale

• Place the ice and all the
ingredients in a highball glass.
• Stir with a mixing spoon for 8–10 seconds.
Serve immediately.

Klondike Cooler

Long drink to serve
at any time

FOR 1 GLASS

4–5 ice cubes

1 measure rye whiskey

1 teaspoon sugar cane syrup

3¼ measures ginger ale

1 strip unwaxed lemon peel (zest)

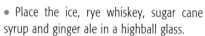

• Place the ice, rye whiskey, sugar cane
syrup and ginger ale in a highball glass.
• Stir with a mixing spoon for 8–10 seconds.
• Cut the strip of lemon peel with a paring
knife. Over the glass, pinch it between the
fingers to release the oils then drop it into
the cocktail. Serve immediately.

Lynchburg Lemonade

Long drink to serve
at any time

FOR 1 GLASS

4–5 ice cubes

1 measure Tennessee whiskey

½ measure fresh lemon juice

¼ measure curaçao triple sec

2¾ measures lemon-lime soda

½ slice unwaxed lemon

• Place the ice, whiskey, lemon juice, curaçao
and lemon-lime soda in a highball glass.
• Stir with a mixing spoon for 8–10 seconds.
• Add the lemon slice to the glass. Serve
immediately.

Mint Julep

Short drink to serve at any time

FOR 1 GLASS

6–8 fresh mint leaves

2 mixing spoons caster (superfine) sugar

3–4 ice cubes, crushed (▷ p. 59)

1¼ measures bourbon

- Wash the mint and dry it on kitchen paper (paper towels) then place in a rocks glass and crush lightly with a pestle.
- Add the sugar and the crushed ice.
- Add the bourbon and stir with a mixing spoon for 8–10 seconds. Serve immediately.

A harmonious mixture,
based on bourbon and mint

The Mint Julep (▷ left), a favourite of planters in the southern United States, is one of the oldest known cocktails. It was invented at the end of the eighteenth century in Virginia. The recipe was published in 1803 by John Davis, a British professor just back from a journey to study the American plantations. He recounts that the inhabitants of Virginia habitually drank this refreshing mint beverage at any time from morning onwards.

New Yorker

Short drink to serve
at any time

FOR 1 GLASS

5–6 ice cubes

1 measure bourbon

½ measure fresh lime juice

¼ measure grenadine

- Place the ice and all the ingredients in the lower part of the shaker.
- Fit the upper part of the shaker and shake vigorously for 8–10 seconds.
- Strain into a Martini glass using a cocktail strainer. Serve immediately.

Whiskey Sour
Short drink to serve in the evening

FOR 1 GLASS

3–4 ice cubes

1 measure bourbon

⅓ measure fresh lemon juice

⅓ measure sugar cane syrup

1 maraschino cherry

- Place the ice and all the ingredients except the maraschino cherry in the lower part of the shaker.
- Fit the upper part of the shaker and shake vigorously for 8–10 seconds.
- Pour the cocktail, without straining, into a rocks glass. Add the maraschino cherry. Serve immediately.

Fruit-based cocktails

Algonquin
Short drink to serve at any time

FOR 1 GLASS

5–6 ice cubes

¾ measure rye whiskey

¾ measure pure pineapple juice

¼ measure dry vermouth

- Place the ice and all the ingredients in the lower part of the shaker.
- Fit the upper part of the shaker and shake vigorously for 8–10 seconds.
- Strain into a rocks glass using a cocktail strainer. Serve immediately.

Beam Me Up Scotty
Long drink to serve at any time

FOR 1 GLASS

5–6 ice cubes

1¼ measures Scotch whisky

¾ measure fresh lemon juice

⅓ measure amaretto

⅓ measure cherry brandy

1¾ measures pure orange juice

- Place the ice and all the ingredients in the lower part of the shaker.
- Fit the upper part of the shaker and shake vigorously for 8–10 seconds.
- Strain into a highball glass using a cocktail strainer. Serve immediately.

Blood & Sand

Short drink to serve
at any time

FOR 1 GLASS

5–6 ice cubes

1 measure Scotch whisky

⅛ measure fresh orange juice

¼ measure cherry brandy

1 teaspoon red vermouth

• Place the ice and all the ingredients in the lower part of the shaker.
• Fit the upper part of the shaker and shake vigorously for 8–10 seconds.
• Strain into a Martini glass using a cocktail strainer. Serve immediately.

Ink Street

Short drink to serve
at any time

FOR 1 GLASS

5–6 ice cubes

¾ measure Canadian whisky

¾ measure fresh orange juice

¼ measure fresh lemon juice

• Place the ice and all the ingredients in the lower part of the shaker.
• Fit the upper part of the shaker and shake vigorously for 8–10 seconds.
• Strain into a Martini glass using a cocktail strainer. Serve immediately.

Polly Special

Short drink to serve
at any time

FOR 1 GLASS

5–6 ice cubes

¾ measure Scotch whisky

¾ measure fresh grapefruit juice

¼ measure curaçao triple sec

• Place the ice and all the ingredients in the lower part of the shaker.
• Fit the upper part of the shaker and shake vigorously for 8–10 seconds.
• Strain into a Martini glass using a cocktail strainer. Serve immediately.

Variation: Carlton

Using bourbon instead of Scotch whisky, and fresh orange juice instead of grapefruit juice, gives a Carlton, a less bitter short drink that is ideal at any time of the day.

Ward Eight

Short drink to serve
at any time

FOR 1 GLASS

5–6 ice cubes

1 measure rye whiskey

½ measure fresh orange juice

1 teaspoon fresh lemon juice

1 teaspoon grenadine

- Place the ice and all the ingredients in the lower part of the shaker.
- Fit the upper part of the shaker and shake vigorously for 8–10 seconds.
- Strain into a Martini glass using a cocktail strainer. Serve immediately.

This short drink from the 1920s was created in the Ward Eight district of Washington, which explains its name.

Liqueur-based cocktails

Bobby Burns

Short drink to serve
as a digestif

FOR 1 GLASS

5–6 ice cubes

1 measure Scotch whisky

⅓ measure Benedictine

⅓ measure red vermouth

- Place the ice and all the ingredients in a mixing glass.
- Stir with a mixing spoon for 8–10 seconds.
- Strain into a Martini glass using a cocktail strainer. Serve immediately.

Delmarva

Short drink to serve
in the evening

FOR 1 GLASS

5–6 ice cubes

1 measure rye whiskey

¼ measure white crème de menthe

¼ measure dry vermouth

¼ measure fresh lemon juice

- Place the ice and all the ingredients in the lower part of the shaker.
- Fit the upper part of the shaker and shake vigorously for 8–10 seconds.
- Strain into a Martini glass using a cocktail strainer. Serve immediately.

Godfather

Short drink to serve
as a digestif

FOR 1 GLASS
3–4 ice cubes
1 measure Scotch whisky
½ measure amaretto

- Place the ice and all the ingredients in a rocks glass.
- Stir with a mixing spoon for 8–10 seconds. Serve immediately.

 The Godfather is the most popular of the cocktails made with this bitter-almond flavoured Italian liqueur.

Kentucky Colonel

Short drink to serve as a digestif

FOR 1 GLASS
3–4 ice cubes
1 measure bourbon
½ measure Benedictine

- Place the ice and all the ingredients in a rocks glass.
- Stir with a mixing spoon for 8–10 seconds. Serve immediately.

Rusty Nail

Short drink to serve
as a digestif

FOR 1 GLASS
3–4 ice cubes
1 measure Scotch whisky
½ measure Drambuie

- Place the ice and all the ingredients in a rocks glass.
- Stir with a mixing spoon for 8–10 seconds. Serve immediately.

Variation: Golden Nail
Use Southern Comfort instead of Drambuie to make a Golden Nail; a short drink with aromas of peach that is ideal for drinking in the evening.

Tipperary

Short drink to serve
as a digestif

FOR 1 GLASS

5–6 ice cubes

1 measure rye whiskey

½ measure red vermouth

¼ measure green Chartreuse

- Place the ice and all the ingredients in a mixing glass.
- Stir with a mixing spoon for 8–10 seconds.
- Strain into a Martini glass using a cocktail strainer. Serve immediately.

Variation: Shamrock
Replace the red vermouth with dry vermouth, and use Irish whiskey instead of rye whiskey, and you have a Shamrock, a slightly drier short drink that is ideal as a digestif.

Twistin

Short drink to serve
at any time

FOR 1 GLASS

5–6 ice cubes

1 measure Canadian whisky

¼ measure peach schnapps

1 teaspoon manzana verde liqueur (▷ p. 38)

1 teaspoon lime cordial

1 strip unwaxed orange peel (zest)

1 maraschino cherry

- Place the ice and all the ingredients except the orange peel and maraschino cherry in a mixing glass.
- Stir with a mixing spoon for 8–10 seconds.
- Strain into a Martini glass using a cocktail strainer.
- Cut the strip of orange peel with a paring knife. Cut it into shreds and add to the glass. Add the maraschino cherry. Serve immediately.

Smooth cocktails

Boston Sour

Short drink to serve
at any time

FOR 1 GLASS

1 egg white

3–4 ice cubes

¾ measure bourbon

⅓ measure fresh lemon juice

2 teaspoons sugar cane syrup

½ slice unwaxed lemon

- Place the egg white in a bowl and whisk for a few seconds with a fork.
- Place the ice, bourbon, 2 teaspoons of beaten egg white, the lemon juice and sugar cane syrup in the lower part of the shaker.
- Fit the upper part of the shaker and shake vigorously for 8–10 seconds.
- Pour into a rocks glass without straining. Add the lemon slice. Serve immediately.

Elk's Own

Short drink to serve in the evening

FOR 1 GLASS

1 egg white

5–6 ice cubes

¾ measure rye whiskey

½ measure ruby port

1 teaspoon fresh lemon juice

1 teaspoon sugar cane syrup

- Place the egg white in a bowl and whisk for a few seconds with a fork.
- Place the ice, 2 teaspoons of beaten egg white and the other ingredients in the lower part of the shaker.
- Fit the upper part of the shaker and shake vigorously for 8–10 seconds.
- Strain into a Martini glass using a cocktail strainer. Serve immediately.

Millionaire

Short drink to serve in the evening

FOR 1 GLASS

1 egg white

5–6 ice cubes

1 measure rye whiskey

¼ measure fresh lemon juice

1 teaspoon curaçao triple sec

1 teaspoon grenadine

- Place the egg white in a bowl and whisk for a few seconds with a fork.
- Place the ice, 2 teaspoons of beaten egg white and the other ingredients in the lower part of the shaker.
- Fit the upper part of the shaker and shake vigorously for 8–10 seconds.
- Strain into a Martini glass using a cocktail strainer. Serve immediately.

Mocha Martini

Short drink to serve in the evening

FOR 1 GLASS

5–6 ice cubes

¾ measure bourbon

½ measure Irish cream

¼ measure brown crème de cacao

¼ measure cold espresso coffee

- Place the ice and all the ingredients in the lower part of the shaker.
- Fit the upper part of the shaker and shake vigorously for 8–10 seconds.
- Strain into a Martini glass using a cocktail strainer. Serve immediately.

Morning Glory Fizz

Long drink to serve in the morning

FOR 1 GLASS

1 egg white

5–6 ice cubes

1 measure Scotch whisky

⅓ measure fresh lemon juice

2 teaspoons sugar cane syrup

2½ measures soda water (club soda)

- Place the egg white in a bowl and whisk for a few seconds with a fork.
- Place the ice, 1 tablespoon of beaten egg white and all the other ingredients except the soda water in the lower part of the shaker.
- Fit the upper part of the shaker and shake vigorously for 8–10 seconds.
- Pour the contents of the shaker into a highball glass. Add the soda water. Serve immediately.

A warming Irish cocktail for American travellers

Irish coffee (▷ p. 139) was invented in 1943 at Foynes Airport in Ireland, from where aeroplanes took off to fly to New York via Montreal. During the winter they served the travellers hot tea laced with a little Irish whiskey, but the Americans preferred coffee. Barman Joe Sheridan therefore decided to invent a new, coffee-based drink for them and came up with Irish Coffee.

Mountain

Short drink to serve in the evening

FOR 1 GLASS

1 egg white

5–6 ice cubes

¾ measure rye whiskey

¼ measure dry vermouth

¼ measure red vermouth

1 teaspoon fresh lemon juice

- Place the egg white in a bowl and whisk for a few seconds with a fork.
- Place the ice, 2 teaspoons of beaten egg white, the rye whiskey, both vermouths and the lemon juice in the lower part of the shaker.
- Fit the upper part of the shaker and shake vigorously for 8–10 seconds.
- Strain into a Martini glass using a cocktail strainer. Serve immediately.

Hot cocktails

Blue Blazer
Long drink to serve in the winter

FOR 1 GLASS

1½ measures boiling water

1½ measures Scotch whisky

2 mixing spoons caster (superfine) sugar

1 strip unwaxed lemon peel (zest)

- Heat 2 metal beakers, with handles, by rinsing them out with boiling water.
- Pour the 1½ measures of boiling water into one of the beakers, then add the Scotch whisky.
- Ignite the mixture with a match and proceed to pour it from one beaker to the other several times as the alcohol burns, then pour it into a toddy glass.
- Add the sugar and stir with a mixing spoon until dissolved.
- Cut the strip of lemon peel with a paring knife. Over the glass, pinch it between the fingers to release the oils then drop it into the glass. Serve immediately.

Irish Coffee
Long drink to serve at any time

FOR 1 GLASS

1¼ measures double (heavy) cream

2 mixing spoons caster (superfine) sugar

3 measures hot espresso coffee

1 measure Irish whiskey

- Place the cream in the freezer for 5 minutes then beat it with a fork until it thickens.
- Place the sugar into a toddy glass and pour in the coffee, then add the Irish whiskey. Stir with a mixing spoon for 5–6 seconds. Using the same spoon, float about ½ measure of whipped cream on the top of the mixture.

Blue Blazer

This cocktail (▷ left) was invented by Jerry Thomas (1830–1885) at the beginning of the 1850s, when he was running the El Dorado bar at the Occidental Hotel in San Francisco. When a gold miner customer demanded a really special pick-me-up Jerry Thomas rose to the challenge, and his dexterity in manipulating the flaming liquid (see engraving) was instrumental in making the drink an instant hit with his customers.

Rum-based cocktails

Rum comes in a great many different varieties. The two main groups are industrial rum, made by sugar refineries, and *rhum agricole*, 'agricultural rum'. Industrial rum is distilled from molasses – a by-product of the process of refining sugar cane – while the *rhum agricole* is distilled from *vesou*, the juice of the sugar cane. When the almost clear rum has gone through an ageing process, it then becomes white rum, amber rum or old rum.

Rum is made in all the countries where sugar cane is produced: Brazil, the United States, Antilles, etc., but the most renowned rum comes from Cuba, Jamaica, Martinique and Puerto Rico.
▷ *See also pp. 300–301*

The quality of rum differs greatly according to the skills and customs of the rum-producing countries. Rum from Martinique and Guadeloupe is traditionally very aromatic, while the rum made at the sugar refineries in Puerto Rico, which is not aged, is much less so. Rum is a spirit that lends itself admirably to mixing with other ingredients. It is indispensable in the preparation of tropical cocktails and combines wonderfully well with fruit juices like the grapefruit juice in an Isle of Pines (▷ p. 149), or the lime juice in a Daiquiri (▷ p. 147) and a Mojito (▷ p. 151). It combines equally well with sweet ingredients like coconut milk, as in a Piña Colada (▷ p. 162) and a Pain Killer (▷ p. 162), or crème de cacao in a Mulata (▷ p. 167).

THE 10 INDISPUTABLE CLASSICS

Dry Cocktails

Cuban Manhattan

Short drink to serve as an aperitif

FOR 1 GLASS

5–6 ice cubes

1¼ measures amber Cuban rum

½ measure red vermouth

2–3 drops Angostura bitters

1 maraschino cherry

- Place the ice, rum, vermouth and Angostura bitters in a mixing glass.
- Stir with a mixing spoon for 8–10 seconds.
- Strain into a Martini glass using a cocktail strainer.
- Add the maraschino cherry to the glass. Serve immediately.

Variation: Martinican

The Martinican, a more aromatic short drink that is ideal for the evening, is made by using aged *rhum agricole*, 'agricultural rum', instead of the amber Cuban rum.

Presidente

Short drink to serve as an aperitif

FOR 1 GLASS

5–6 ice cubes

1 measure white Cuban rum

½ measure dry vermouth

1 teaspoon grenadine

1 strip unwaxed orange peel (zest)

1 maraschino cherry

- Place the ice, rum, vermouth and grenadine in a mixing glass.
- Stir with a mixing spoon for 8–10 seconds.
- Strain into a Martini glass using a cocktail strainer.
- Cut the strip of orange peel with a paring knife. Over the glass, pinch it between the fingers to release the oils but do not add it to the cocktail.
- Place the cherry in the glass. Serve immediately.

Redwood

Short drink to serve at any time

FOR 1 GLASS

3–4 ice cubes, crushed (▷ p. 59)

1¼ measures amber Jamaican rum

¼ measure crème de fraise

2–3 drops Angostura bitters

1 strip unwaxed lemon peel (zest)

- Place the crushed ice, rum, crème de fraise and Angostura bitters in a rocks glass.
- Stir with a mixing spoon for 8–10 seconds.
- Cut the strip of lemon peel with a paring knife. Over the glass, pinch it between the fingers to release the oils then drop it into the cocktail. Serve immediately.

Treacle

Short drink to serve
at any time

FOR 1 GLASS

2–3 drops Angostura bitters

1 lump sugar

3–4 ice cubes

1¼ measures dark Jamaican rum

½ measure pure apple juice

1 strip unwaxed lemon peel (zest)

• Drop the Angostura bitters onto the sugar then place it in a rocks glass and crush it with a pestle.
• Add the ice, rum and apple juice to the glass and stir with a mixing spoon for 10 seconds.
• Cut the strip of lemon peel with a paring knife. Over the glass, pinch it between the fingers to release the oils then drop it into the cocktail. Serve immediately.

Thirst-quenching cocktails

Añejo Highball

Long drink to serve
at any time

FOR 1 GLASS

4–5 ice cubes

1 measure amber Cuban rum

⅓ measure orange curaçao

⅓ measure fresh lime juice

3–4 drops Angostura bitters

2¾ measures ginger beer

½ slice unwaxed lemon

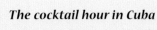

• Place the ice and all the ingredients except the lemon slice in a highball glass.
• Stir with a mixing spoon for 8–10 seconds.
• Place the lemon slice in the glass. Serve immediately.

The cocktail hour in Cuba

During Prohibition (1919–1933), many Americans didn't hesitate to travel to Cuba in order to enjoy drinking alcohol, notably cocktails. This trend was responsible for making bars in Havana, like the Floridita, Sloppy Joe's and the Bodeguita del Medio, very famous indeed. So much so that, in 1924, barmen on the island created the 'Club des Cantineros', the first organization dedicated to training bar personnel. At the end of the 1940s writer Ernest Hemingway and actor Spencer Tracy became regulars at the Floridita (on the left in the photograph, taken in 1954).

Bacardi Cocktail

Short drink to serve at any time

FOR 1 GLASS

5–6 ice cubes

1 measure white Puerto Rican rum (Bacardi)

½ measure fresh lime juice

¼ measure grenadine

1 strip unwaxed lime peel (zest)

- Place the ice, rum, lime juice and grenadine in the lower part of the shaker.
- Fit the upper part of the shaker and shake vigorously for 8–10 seconds.
- Strain into a Martini glass using a cocktail strainer.
- Cut the strip of lime peel with a paring knife. Over the glass, pinch it between the fingers to release the oils then drop it into the cocktail. Serve immediately.

Beja Flor

Short drink to serve in the evening

FOR 1 GLASS

5–6 ice cubes

1 measure cachaça rum

¼ measure crème de banane

¼ measure curaçao triple sec

½ measure fresh lime juice

- Place the ice and all the ingredients in the lower part of the shaker.
- Fit the upper part of the shaker and shake vigorously for 8–10 seconds.
- Strain into a Martini glass using a cocktail strainer. Serve immediately.

Black Rose

Short drink to serve at any time

FOR 1 GLASS

5–6 ice cubes

¾ measure white *rhum agricole*, 'agricultural rum'

2 teaspoons cold espresso coffee

2 teaspoons sugar cane syrup

- Place the ice and all the ingredients in the lower part of the shaker.
- Fit the upper part of the shaker and shake vigorously for 8–10 seconds.
- Strain into a Martini glass using a cocktail strainer. Serve immediately.

 This cocktail was created in the 1930s by Frank Meier at The Ritz Hotel's Cambon Bar in Paris, and was originally served as a long drink.

Boston Cooler

Long drink to serve
at any time

FOR 1 GLASS

4–5 ice cubes

1 measure amber Jamaican rum

⅛ measure fresh lime juice

1 teaspoon sugar cane syrup

3 measures ginger ale

1 slice unwaxed lemon

• Place the ice and all the ingredients except the lemon slice in a highball glass.
• Stir with a mixing spoon for 8–10 seconds. Place the lemon slice in the glass. Serve immediately.

Cable Car

Short drink to serve at any time

FOR 1 GLASS

5–6 ice cubes

¾ measure spiced rum

½ measure orange curaçao

⅛ measure fresh lemon juice

1 teaspoon sugar cane syrup

1 strip unwaxed orange peel (zest)

• Place the ice and all the ingredients except the orange peel in the lower part of the shaker.
• Fit the upper part of the shaker and shake vigorously for 8–10 seconds.
• Strain into a Martini glass using a cocktail strainer.
• Cut the strip of orange peel with a paring knife. Over the glass, pinch it between the fingers to release the oils then drop it into the cocktail. Serve immediately.

Caïpirinha

Short drink to serve
at any time

FOR 1 GLASS

½ unwaxed lime

3–4 ice cubes, crushed (▷ p. 59)

1¼ measures cachaça rum

2 mixing spoons caster (superfine) sugar

• Cut the lime half into 4 pieces, place the pieces in a rocks glass and crush them with a pestle.
• Add the crushed ice and all the other ingredients to the glass.
• Stir with a mixing spoon for 8–10 seconds. Serve immediately.

Variation: Caïpirissima
The Caïpirissima, a short drink with a lighter flavour, is made by replacing the cachaça rum with Puerto Rican rum. Ideal to drink at any time.

Citrus Cooler

Long drink to serve at any time

FOR 1 GLASS

5–6 ice cubes

¾ measure Puerto Rican rum

¾ measure fresh orange juice

¼ measure fresh lime juice

¼ measure curaçao triple sec

2½ measures lemon-lime soda

- Place the ice, rum, orange and lime juices, and the curaçao in the lower part of the shaker.
- Fit the upper part of the shaker and shake vigorously for 8–10 seconds.
- Pour into a highball glass without straining.
- Add the lemon-lime soda and stir. Serve immediately.

Cosmo-Ron

Short drink to serve
at any time

FOR 1 GLASS

5–6 ice cubes

¾ measure white Puerto Rican rum

¾ measure cranberry juice
(based on fruit concentrate)

1 teaspoon fresh lime juice

1 teaspoon orange curaçao

1 strip unwaxed lemon peel (zest)

- Place the ice, rum, cranberry juice, lime juice and the curaçao in the lower part of the shaker.
- Fit the upper part of the shaker and shake vigorously for 8–10 seconds.
- Strain the contents of the shaker into a Martini glass using a cocktail strainer.
- Cut the strip of lemon peel with a paring knife. Over the glass, pinch it between the fingers to release the oils then drop it into the cocktail. Serve immediately.

Cuba Libre

Long drink to serve at any time

FOR 1 GLASS

¼ unwaxed lime

4–5 ice cubes

1 measure white Cuban rum

3¼ measures cola

- Cut the lime quarter into 2 pieces, place in a highball glass and crush them with a pestle.
- Place the ice and the other ingredients in the glass.

- Stir with a mixing spoon for 8–10 seconds. Serve immediately.

 This cocktail first appeared in Cuba during the American Prohibition period. Some people now call it the Mentiroso (Spanish for liar) because Cuba is no longer *libre* (free).

Variation: Trinidad
Adding 3–4 drops of Angostura bitters gives a Trinidad – a slightly bitter long drink that is ideal to drink at any time.

Daiquiri

Short drink to serve
at any time

POUR 1 VERRE

5–6 ice cubes

1 measure white Cuban rum

½ measure fresh lime juice

2 teaspoons sugar cane syrup

• Place the ice and all the ingredients in the lower part of the shaker.
• Fit the upper part of the shaker and shake vigorously for 8–10 seconds.
• Strain into a Martini glass using a cocktail strainer. Serve immediately.

Variation: Daiquiri No 2

This is made by replacing 1 teaspoon of the white rum with 1 teaspoon of orange curaçao, and replacing 1 teaspoon of the lime juice with 1 teaspoon of orange juice. It is a sweeter short drink that is ideal in the afternoon.

Dark & Stormy

Long drink to serve at any time

FOR 1 GLASS

½ unwaxed lime

4–5 ice cubes

1 measure dark Jamaican rum

½ measure fresh lime juice

2 teaspoons sugar cane syrup

2¾ measures ginger beer

• Cut the lime half into 2 quarters, place them in a highball glass and crush them with a pestle.
• Add the ice and the other ingredients to the glass.
• Stir with a mixing spoon for 8–10 seconds. Serve immediately.

This cocktail is the national drink of Bermuda.

Doctor Funk

Long drink to serve
at any time

FOR 1 GLASS

4–5 ice cubes, crushed (▷ p. 59)

½ measure white Jamaican rum

½ measure white Cuban rum

⅛ measure fresh lime juice

¼ measure grenadine

1 teaspoon absinthe-flavoured
spirit

1¼ measures soda water
(club soda)

2 thin slices unwaxed lime

- Place the crushed ice and all the
ingredients except the lime slices in a
highball glass.
- Stir with a mixing spoon for 8–10 seconds.
- Place the lime slices in the glass. Serve
immediately.

Floridita Daiquiri

Short drink to serve
at any time

FOR 1 GLASS

5–6 ice cubes

1 measure white Cuban rum

⅛ measure fresh lime juice

1 teaspoon fresh grapefruit juice

1 teaspoon sugar cane syrup

1 teaspoon maraschino liqueur

- Place the ice and all the ingredients in the lower part of the
shaker.
- Fit the upper part of the shaker
and shake vigorously for 8–10 seconds.
- Strain into a Martini glass using a cocktail
strainer. Serve immediately.

 This cocktail is also known as a
Daiquiri No 3 and is attributed to barman
Benjamin Orbon, who is reputed to have
invented it in the 1930s in Cuba.

Frozen Daiquiri

Short drink to serve
at any time

FOR 1 GLASS

3–4 ice cubes, crushed (▷ p. 59)

1 measure white Cuban rum

½ measure fresh lime juice

1 teaspoon sugar cane syrup

1 teaspoon maraschino liqueur

- Place the crushed
ice and all the ingre-
dients in a blender.
- Blend at slow speed for
5–10 seconds then at high
speed for 15–30 seconds.
- Pour the contents of the blender
into a Martini glass. Serve immediately.

Hemingway Special

Short drink to serve
at any time

FOR 1 GLASS

3–4 ice cubes, crushed (▷ p. 59)

1¼ measures white Cuban rum

¼ measure fresh lime juice

1 teaspoon fresh grapefruit juice

1 teaspoon maraschino liqueur

- Place the crushed ice and all the ingredients in a blender.
- Blend at slow speed for 5–10 seconds then at high speed for 15–30 seconds.
- Pour the contents of the blender into a Martini glass. Serve immediately.

This cocktail was specially invented for writer Ernest Hemingway (1899–1961) by a Cuban barman called Antonio Melan.

Honeysuckle

Short drink to serve at any time

FOR 1 GLASS

5–6 ice cubes

¾ measure amber Jamaican rum

½ measure fresh lime juice

½ measure runny multi-floral honey

- Place the ice and all the ingredients in the lower part of the shaker.
- Fit the upper part of the shaker and shake vigorously for 8–10 seconds.
- Strain into a Martini glass using a cocktail strainer. Serve immediately.

Isle of Pines

Short drink to serve
at any time

FOR 1 GLASS

5–6 ice cubes

¾ measure white Cuban rum

¾ measure fresh grapefruit juice

2 teaspoons sugar cane syrup

- Place the ice and all the ingredients in the lower part of the shaker.
- Fit the upper part of the shaker and shake vigorously for 8–10 seconds.
- Strain into a Martini glass using a cocktail strainer. Serve immediately.

Variation: Pinerito

The Pinerito, a more colourful short drink that makes an ideal aperitif, is made with grenadine instead of the sugar cane syrup.

Jamaican Mule

Long drink to serve at any time

FOR 1 GLASS

⅛ unwaxed lime

4–5 ice cubes

1¼ measures spiced rum

¼ measure fresh lime juice

3–4 drops Angostura bitters

3 measures ginger beer

- Place the lime segment in a highball glass and crush it slightly with a pestle.
- Place the ice and the remaining ingredients in the glass.
- Stir with a mixing spoon for 8–10 seconds. Serve immediately.

Mai Tai

Short drink to serve at any time

FOR 1 GLASS

3–4 ice cubes, crushed (▷ p. 59)

¾ measure amber Jamaican rum

½ measure white *rhum agricole*, 'agricultural rum'

⅓ measure fresh lime juice

¼ measure orgeat syrup

1 teaspoon orange curaçao

⅛ unwaxed lime

1 small sprig fresh mint

- Place the crushed ice, both kinds of rum, the lime juice, orgeat syrup and curaçao in the lower part of the shaker.
- Fit the upper part of the shaker and shake vigorously for 8–10 seconds.
- Pour the shaker contents into a rocks glass. Make a slit in the lime segment and fix it to the rim of the glass. Add the mint sprig. Serve immediately.

Marama Rum Punch

Long drink to serve at any time

FOR 1 GLASS

8–10 ice cubes

¾ measure white Jamaican rum

½ measure curaçao triple sec

⅓ measure fresh lime juice

1 teaspoon orgeat syrup

3–4 drops Angostura bitters

2¾ measures lemon-lime soda

1 small sprig fresh mint

- Place 5–6 ice cubes, the rum, curaçao, lime juice, orgeat syrup and Angostura bitters in the lower part of the shaker.
- Fit the upper part of the shaker and shake vigorously for 8–10 seconds.
- Place 3–4 ice cubes in a highball glass then strain the contents of the shaker over them using a cocktail strainer.
- Add the lemon-lime soda and stir for 3–4 seconds with a mixing spoon.
- Wash the mint sprig and add to the glass. Serve immediately.

Mojito

Long drink to serve at any time

FOR 1 GLASS

8–10 fresh mint leaves

2 mixing spoons caster (superfine) sugar

4–5 ice cubes, crushed (▷ p. 59)

1 measure white Cuban rum

½ measure fresh lime juice

1½ measures soda water (club soda)

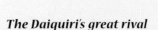

- Wash the mint leaves and place them in a highball glass.
- Crush them with a pestle, then add the sugar.
- Add the crushed ice and the other ingredients. Stir with a mixing spoon for 8–10 seconds. Serve immediately.

Variation: Mojito Criollo
Add 3–4 drops of Angostura bitters and you have the Mojito Criollo, a slightly bitter long drink that can be drunk at any time.

Montego Bay

Short drink to serve at any time

FOR 1 GLASS

5–6 ice cubes

1 measure amber *rhum agricole*, 'agricultural rum'

½ measure fresh lime juice

1 teaspoon sugar cane syrup

1 teaspoon curaçao triple sec

2–3 drops Angostura bitters

- Place the ice and all the ingredients in the lower part of the shaker.
- Fit the upper part of the shaker and shake vigorously for 8–10 seconds.
- Strain into a Martini glass using a cocktail strainer. Serve immediately.

The Daiquiri's great rival

The Mojito (▷ above) was created in Cuba during the American Prohibition period. It was modelled on the Mint Julep (▷ p. 131) that was, at that time, the favourite drink of the Americans staying on the island. The Mojito became popular thanks to the Bodeguita del Medio (pictured below), a bar whose motto was: 'Hemingway drinks Daiquiris at the Floridita and Mojitos at the Bodeguita!'

Periodista

Short drink to serve
at any time

  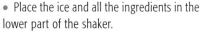

FOR 1 GLASS

5–6 ice cubes

1 measure white Cuban rum

½ measure fresh lime juice

1 teaspoon orange curaçao

1 teaspoon apricot brandy

• Place the ice and all the ingredients in the lower part of the shaker.
• Fit the upper part of the shaker and shake vigorously for 8–10 seconds.
• Strain into a Martini glass using a cocktail strainer. Serve immediately.

Pink Daiquiri

Short drink to serve at any time

  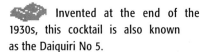

FOR 1 GLASS

5–6 ice cubes

1 measure white Cuban rum

½ measure fresh lime juice

1 teaspoon grenadine

1 teaspoon maraschino liqueur

3–4 drops Angostura bitters

• Place the ice and all the ingredients in the lower part of the shaker.
• Fit the upper part of the shaker and shake vigorously for 8–10 seconds.
• Strain into a Martini glass using a cocktail strainer. Serve immediately.

Invented at the end of the 1930s, this cocktail is also known as the Daiquiri No 5.

Planter's Punch

Long drink to serve
at any time

FOR 1 GLASS

4–5 ice cubes, crushed (▷ p. 59)

1½ measures dark Jamaican rum

½ measure fresh lime juice

¼ measure grenadine

2–3 drops Angostura bitters
(optional)

1¼ measures still mineral water

• Place the crushed ice and all the ingredients into a highball glass.
• Stir with a mixing spoon for 8–10 seconds. Serve immediately.

There are a number of versions of Planter's Punch. Here is one adapted from a recipe recommended in the seventeenth century: 1 measure of sweetener (grenadine), 2 measures of acidity (lime juice), 3 measures of strength (amber Jamaican rum) and 4 measures of mixer (still water and crushed ice).

Quarter Deck

Short drink to serve
at any time

FOR 1 GLASS

5–6 ice cubes

1 measure white Puerto Rican rum

⅓ measure fresh lime juice

⅓ measure sherry

• Place the ice and all the ingredients in the
lower part of the shaker.

• Fit the upper part of the shaker and shake
vigorously for 8–10 seconds.

• Strain into a Martini glass using a cocktail
strainer. Serve immediately.

Rumble

Long drink to serve at any time

FOR 1 GLASS

4–5 ice cubes

1 measure dark Jamaican rum

¼ measure coffee liqueur

3 measures soda water
(club soda)

½ unwaxed lime

• Place the ice, rum, coffee
liqueur and soda water in a
highball glass.

• Stir with a mixing spoon for
8–10 seconds.

• Cut the lime half into 4
pieces and add to the glass.
Serve immediately.

Suzie Taylor

Long drink to serve at any time

FOR 1 GLASS

4–5 ice cubes

1 measure amber Jamaican rum

¼ measure fresh lemon juice

3¼ measures ginger ale

½ slice unwaxed lemon

• Place the ice, rum, lemon juice and ginger
ale in a highball glass.

• Stir with a mixing spoon for 8–10 seconds.

• Place the lemon slice in the glass. Serve
immediately.

Variation: Mamy Taylor
This drier long drink, ideal at any time, is
made with gin instead of amber rum.

A few ideas for cocktail snacks to serve with rum-based cocktails:

- barquettes of red mullet (snapper) and fondue of (bell) peppers
- chicken and banana morsels
- prawn (shrimp) and pineapple à la Créole
- stir-fried vegetables with turmeric
- bite-sized vanilla slices

▶ recipes page 276

Ti Punch

Short drink to serve at any time

FOR 1 GLASS

⅛ unwaxed lime

1¼ measures white *rhum agricole*, 'agricultural rum'

½ measure sugar cane syrup

• Place the lime segment in a rocks glass and crush it with a pestle.
• Add the other ingredients to the glass.
• Stir with a mixing spoon for 8–10 seconds.
• Serve immediately accompanied by a glass of iced water, referred to as Ti Craze.

X.Y.Z.

Short drink to serve at any time

FOR 1 GLASS

5–6 ice cubes

1 measure white Puerto Rican rum

⅛ measure fresh lemon juice

⅛ measure curaçao triple sec

• Place the ice and all the ingredients in the lower part of the shaker.
• Fit the upper part of the shaker and shake vigorously for 8–10 seconds.
• Strain into a Martini glass using a cocktail strainer. Serve immediately.

Variation: Colombus
Replacing the curaçao triple sec with orange curaçao gives a Colombus, a sweeter short drink that is ideal for the evening.

Fruit-based cocktails

Aristo

Long drink to serve at any time

FOR 1 GLASS

5–6 ice cubes

1 measure aged Jamaican rum

1½ measures pure orange juice

1½ measures pure grapefruit juice

¼ measure fresh lemon juice

¼ measure grenadine

2–3 drops Angostura bitters

½ slice unwaxed lemon

• Place the ice and all the ingredients except the lemon slice in the lower part of the shaker.
• Fit the upper part of the shaker and shake vigorously for 8–10 seconds.
• Strain into a highball glass using a cocktail strainer.
• Make a slit in the lemon slice and fix it to the rim of the glass. Serve immediately.

Atomic Dog

Long drink to serve at any time

FOR 1 GLASS

5–6 ice cubes

½ measure white Puerto Rican rum

½ measure rum flavoured with coconut

¼ measure fresh lemon juice

¼ measure green melon liqueur

3 measures pure pineapple juice

- Place the ice and all the ingredients in the lower part of the shaker.
- Fit the upper part of the shaker and shake vigorously for 8–10 seconds.
- Strain into a highball glass using a cocktail strainer. Serve immediately.

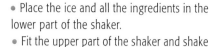

Baccarat

Long drink to serve at any time

FOR 1 GLASS

5–6 ice cubes

¾ measure white Cuban rum

1½ measures pure orange juice

1½ measures pure passion fruit juice

⅓ measure Benedictine

⅓ measure strawberry syrup

1 fresh strawberry

- Place the ice and all the ingredients except the strawberry in the lower part of the shaker.
- Fit the upper part of the shaker and shake vigorously for 8–10 seconds.
- Strain into a highball glass using a cocktail strainer.
- Wash the strawberry, cut a slit in it and fix it to the rim of the glass. Serve immediately.

Bahama Mama

Long drink to serve at any time

FOR 1 GLASS

5–6 ice cubes

½ measure dark Jamaican rum

½ measure rum flavoured with coconut

1¾ measures pure orange juice

1¾ measures pure pineapple juice

3–4 drops Angostura bitters

- Place the ice, both kinds of rum, the fruit juices and the Angostura bitters in the lower part of the shaker.
- Fit the upper part of the shaker and shake vigorously for 8–10 seconds.
- Strain into a highball glass using a cocktail strainer. Serve immediately.

Banana Daiquiri

Short drink to serve in the afternoon

FOR 1 GLASS

½ banana

3–4 ice cubes, crushed (▷ p. 59)

¾ measure white Cuban rum

1 teaspoon fresh lime juice

1 teaspoon sugar cane syrup

- Peel the banana half and cut into pieces.
- Place the crushed ice, the banana pieces and the other ingredients into a blender. Blend at slow speed for 5–10 seconds then at high speed for 15–30 seconds. Pour the contents of the blender into a Martini glass. Serve immediately.

Variation: Peach Daiquiri

Replace the banana half with half a peach and you have a Peach Daiquiri, a less sweet short drink that is ideal for afternoon drinking.

Batida Abaci

Long drink to serve at any time

FOR 1 GLASS

1 slice fresh pineapple about 1 cm (½ inch) thick

4–5 ice cubes, crushed (▷ p. 59)

1¼ measures cachaça rum

¼ measure fresh lime juice

2 teaspoons sugar cane syrup

- Peel the pineapple slice and cut it into pieces.
- Place the crushed ice, the pineapple pieces and all the other ingredients in a blender. Blend at slow speed for 5–10 seconds then at high speed for 15–30 seconds.
- Pour the contents of the blender into a highball glass. Serve immediately.

Bossa Nova

Long drink to serve at any time

FOR 1 GLASS

5–6 ice cubes

1 measure white Puerto Rican rum

2 measures pure pineapple juice

½ measure Galliano

¼ measure apricot brandy

¼ measure fresh lime juice

1 fresh pineapple leaf

- Place the ice and all the ingredients except the pineapple leaf in the lower part of the shaker.
- Fit the upper part of the shaker and shake vigorously for 8–10 seconds.
- Strain into a highball glass using a cocktail strainer.
- Make a slit in the pineapple leaf so that it fits over the rim of the glass. Serve immediately.

Caribbean Breeze

Long drink to serve
at any time

FOR 1 GLASS

5–6 ice cubes

1 measure amber Jamaican rum

1½ measures cranberry juice
(based on fruit concentrate)

1½ measures pure pineapple
juice

¼ measure crème de banane

¼ measure lime cordial

⅛ unwaxed lime

- Place the ice and all the ingredients except the lime segment in the lower part of the shaker.
- Fit the upper part of the shaker and shake vigorously for 8–10 seconds.
- Strain into a highball glass using a cocktail strainer.
- Cut a slit in the lime segment and fix it to the rim of the glass. Serve immediately.

Flamingo

Long drink to serve at any time

FOR 1 GLASS

5–6 ice cubes

1 measure white Cuban
rum

3 measures pure
pineapple juice

¼ measure fresh lime juice

¼ measure grenadine

- Place the ice and all the ingredients in the lower part of the shaker.
- Fit the upper part of the shaker and shake vigorously for 8–10 seconds.
- Strain into a highball glass using a cocktail strainer. Serve immediately.

Havana Beach

Short drink to serve at any time

FOR 1 GLASS

5–6 ice cubes

1 measure white Cuban rum

½ measure pure pineapple juice

1 teaspoon sugar cane syrup

- Place the ice and all the ingredients in the lower part of the shaker.
- Fit the upper part of the shaker and shake vigorously for 8–10 seconds.
- Strain into a Martini glass using a cocktail strainer. Serve immediately.

Hurricane

Long drink to serve in the evening

FOR 1 GLASS

4–5 ice cubes, crushed
(▷ p. 59)

½ measure white Puerto Rican rum

⅓ measure amber Cuban rum

⅓ measure dark Jamaican rum

1¼ measures pure orange juice

1¼ measures pure pineapple juice

⅓ measure fresh lime juice

1 teaspoon curaçao triple sec

1 teaspoon sugar cane syrup

1 teaspoon grenadine

• Place the crushed ice and all the ingredients in a blender. Blend at low speed for 5–10 seconds then at high speed for 15–30 seconds.

• Pour the contents of the blender into a highball glass. Serve immediately.

Island in the Sun

Long drink to serve at any time

FOR 1 GLASS

1 slice fresh pineapple, about 1 cm (½ inch) thick

5–6 ice cubes

1 measure amber Jamaican rum

2¾ measures pure pineapple juice

¼ measure Galliano

¼ measure apricot brandy

1 teaspoon fresh lemon juice

1 teaspoon sugar cane syrup

• Cut a triangular piece from the pineapple slice, leaving the skin on.
• Place the ice and the other ingredients in the lower part of the shaker.
• Fit the upper part of the shaker and shake vigorously for 8–10 seconds.
• Strain into a highball glass using a cocktail strainer.
• Make a slit in the piece of pineapple and fix it to the rim of the glass. Serve immediately.

Jam Daiquiri

Short drink to serve at any time

FOR 1 GLASS

3–4 ice cubes, crushed (▷ p. 59)

1 measure white Puerto Rican rum

⅓ measure fresh lime juice

1 teaspoon maraschino liqueur

2 mixing spoons blackcurrant jam (preserve)

• Place the cruhed ice and all the ingredients in a blender.
• Blend at low speed for 5–10 seconds then at high speed for 15–30 seconds.
• Pour the contents of the blender into a Martini glass. Serve immediately.

Joe Kanoo

Long drink to serve at any time

FOR 1 GLASS

5–6 ice cubes

1 measure white Jamaican rum

3¼ measures pure orange juice

¼ measure Galliano

1 segment unwaxed orange

- Place the ice and all the ingredients except the orange segment in the lower part of the shaker.
- Fit the upper part of the shaker and shake vigorously for 8–10 seconds.
- Strain into a highball glass using a cocktail strainer.
- Make a slit in the orange segment and fix it to the rim of the glass. Serve immediately.

Mary Pickford

Short drink to serve at any time

FOR 1 GLASS

5–6 ice cubes

1¼ measures white Cuban rum

½ measure pure pineapple juice

1 teaspoon grenadine

- Place the ice and all the ingredients in the lower part of the shaker.
- Fit the upper part of the shaker and shake vigorously for 8–10 seconds.
- Strain into a Martini glass using a cocktail strainer. Serve immediately.

Variation: National

Replacing the grenadine with apricot brandy gives a National, a sweeter short drink that is ideal for the evening.

Created for 'America's Sweetheart'

Born in Canada, Mary Pickford (1893–1979), pictured here, was one of the first stars of the silent screen. In 1919 she formed the movie company, Associated Artists, together with Douglas Fairbanks, whom she married, and Charlie Chaplin, who made a movie with her in Cuba. And it was there in Cuba that the short drink that bears her name (▷ above) was created for her by Fred Kaufman, a well-known barman during the Prohibition period.

Pain Killer

Long drink to serve
at any time

FOR 1 GLASS

4–5 ice cubes

1 measure white Puerto Rican rum

2¼ measures pure pineapple juice

¾ measure fresh orange juice

8 mixing spoons coconut milk (canned)

- Place the ice and all the ingredients in the lower part of the shaker.
- Fit the upper part of the shaker and shake vigorously for 8–10 seconds.
- Strain into a highball glass using a cocktail strainer. Serve immediately.

Variation: Blue Hawaiian

The Blue Hawaiian, a more colourful long cocktail to drink at any time, is made by replacing the orange juice with pure pineapple juice and adding ¼ measure of blue curaçao.

Piña Colada

Long drink to serve at any time

FOR 1 GLASS

1 slice fresh pineapple about
1 cm (½ inch) thick

5–6 ice cubes

1 measure white Puerto Rican rum

3 measures pure pineapple juice

8 mixing spoons coconut milk
(canned)

- Cut a triangular piece from the pineapple slice, leaving the skin on.
- Place the ice, rum, pineapple juice and coconut milk in the lower part of the shaker.
- Fit the upper part of the shaker and shake vigorously for 8–10 seconds.
- Strain into a highball glass using a cocktail strainer.
- Make a slit in the pineapple piece and fix it to the rim of the glass. Serve immediately.

Pearl Diver

Long drink to serve
at any time

FOR 1 GLASS

4–5 ice cubes, crushed (▷ p. 59)

½ measure white Puerto Rican rum

¼ measure amber Cuban rum

¼ measure dark Jamaican rum

1 measure fresh orange juice

½ measure fresh lime juice

½ measure fresh grapefruit juice

3–4 drops Angostura bitters

- Place the crushed ice and all the ingredients in a blender.
- Blend at low speed for 5–10 seconds then at high speed for 15–30 seconds.
- Pour the contents of the blender into a highball glass. Serve immediately.

Planteur

Long drink to serve at any time

FOR 1 GLASS

5–6 ice cubes

1 measure white *rhum agricole*, 'agricultural rum'

3¼ measures pure orange juice

¼ measure grenadine

1 segment unwaxed orange

- Place the ice, rum, orange juice and grenadine in the lower part of the shaker.
- Fit the upper part of the shaker and shake vigorously for 8–10 seconds.
- Strain into a highball glass using a cocktail strainer.
- Cut a slit in the orange segment and fix it to the rim of the glass. Serve immediately.

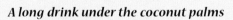 This cocktail is very popular in the French Antilles.

Rum Runner

Long drink to serve at any time

FOR 1 GLASS

5–6 ice cubes

1¼ measures amber Jamaican rum

2¾ measures pure pineapple juice

½ measure fresh lime juice

3–4 drops Angostura bitters

- Place the ice and all the ingredients in the lower part of the shaker.
- Fit the upper part of the shaker and shake vigorously for 8–10 seconds.
- Strain into a highball glass using a cocktail strainer. Serve immediately.

A long drink under the coconut palms

The combination of pineapple juice and coconut milk gives the Piña Colada (▷ left) a typically tropical character. Attributed to Ramon Marrero Perez, barman at the Caribe Hilton hotel in San Juan, Puerto Rica, it was invented in 1954, a short time after a commercial brand of coconut milk was first marketed in the Caribbean. Originally the name Piña Colada, meaning 'strained pineapple', just applied to fresh pineapple juice strained to remove the pulp.

Scorpion

Short drink to serve
at any time

FOR 1 GLASS

3–4 ice cubes, crushed
(▷ p. 59)

¾ measure white Puerto
Rican rum

½ measure Cognac

½ measure fresh orange
juice

⅛ measure fresh lemon juice

1 teaspoon orgeat syrup

• Place the crushed ice and all the ingredients in
a blender. Blend at low speed for 5–10 seconds
then at high speed for 15–30 seconds.
• Pour the contents of the blender into a rocks
glass. Serve immediately.

Sterling

Short drink to serve
at any time

FOR 1 GLASS

5–6 ice cubes

¾ measure amber
Jamaican rum

¾ measure fresh
orange juice

¼ measure Benedictine

• Place the ice and all the ingredients in the
lower part of the shaker.
• Fit the upper part of the shaker and shake
vigorously for 8–10 seconds.
• Strain into a Martini glass using a cocktail
strainer. Serve immediately.

Tropicana

Short drink to serve
at any time

FOR 1 GLASS

3–4 ice cubes

½ measure white Cuban rum

¼ measure cachaça rum

¼ measure pisco

¼ measure fresh lemon juice

⅛ measure lime cordial

1 teaspoon passion fruit syrup

• Place the ice and all the ingredients in the
lower part of the shaker.
• Fit the upper part of the shaker and shake
vigorously for 8–10 seconds.
• Pour the contents of the shaker into a
rocks glass. Serve immediately.

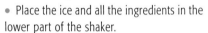 Rum from the Antilles and Brazil,
pisco from Chile and passion fruit syrup go
to make a truly exotic cocktail.

Voodoo

Long drink to serve
at any time

FOR 1 GLASS

5–6 ice cubes

1 measure amber Jamaican rum

2½ measures pure apple juice

½ measure red vermouth

¼ measure fresh lime juice

2 teaspoons sugar cane syrup

- Place the ice and all the ingredients
in the lower part of the shaker.
- Fit the upper part of the shaker and
shake vigorously for 8–10 seconds.
- Strain into a highball glass using a cocktail
strainer. Serve immediately.

Zombie

Long drink to serve
at any time

FOR 1 GLASS

5–6 ice cubes

¾ measure white Puerto
Rican rum

¾ measure dark Jamaican rum

¾ measure aged Cuban rum

¾ measure aged Jamaican rum

½ measure maraschino liqueur

½ measure fresh lime juice

¼ measure fresh grapefruit juice

1 teaspoon grenadine

1 teaspoon sugar cane syrup

3–4 drops Angostura bitters

3–4 drops absinthe-flavoured spirit

- Place the ice and all the ingredients in the
lower part of the shaker.
- Fit the upper part of the shaker and shake
vigorously for 8–10 seconds.
- Strain into a highball glass using a cocktail
strainer. Serve immediately.

At the heart of Polynesian beliefs

*The Zombie (▷ right) is one of the 'tiki' drinks drawn from
the Polynesian culture. Tikis are statues (pictured here)
representing the goddess of that name and, by extension,
objects bearing the same name that are thought to
protect against harm. Tiki cocktails, therefore, should
have the same prophylactic powers. The Zombie was
invented in 1934 by Donn Beach – better known as Don
The Beachcomber – for the opening of his first restaurant
in Hollywood.*

Liqueur-based cocktails

Centenario

Short drink to serve as a digestif

FOR 1 GLASS

5–6 ice cubes

1 measure white Cuban rum

¼ measure coffee liqueur

¼ measure fresh lime juice

1 teaspoon curaçao triple sec

1 teaspoon grenadine

- Place the ice and all the ingredients in the lower part of the shaker.
- Fit the upper part of the shaker and shake vigorously for 8–10 seconds.
- Strain into a Martini glass using a cocktail strainer. Serve immediately.

Black Widow

Short drink to serve as a digestif

FOR 1 GLASS

3–4 ice cubes

1 measure dark Jamaican rum

½ measure white crème de menthe

- Place the ice and all the ingredients in a rocks glass.
- Stir with a mixing spoon for 8–10 seconds. Serve immediately.

Mackinnon

Short drink to serve as a digestif

FOR 1 GLASS

5–6 ice cubes

1 measure amber Jamaican rum

½ measure Drambuie

¼ measure fresh lime juice

- Place the ice and all the ingredients in the lower part of the shaker.
- Fit the upper part of the shaker and shake vigorously for 8–10 seconds.
- Strain into a Martini glass using a cocktail strainer. Serve immediately.

Mulata

Short drink to serve as a digestif

FOR 1 GLASS

5–6 ice cubes

1 measure amber Cuban rum

½ measure brown crème de cacao

¼ measure fresh lime juice

1 strip unwaxed lime peel (zest)

- Place the ice, rum, crème de cacao and lime juice in the lower part of the shaker.
- Fit the upper part of the shaker and shake vigorously for 8–10 seconds.
- Strain into a Martini glass using a cocktail strainer.
- Cut the strip of lime peel with a paring knife. Over the glass, pinch it between the fingers to release the oils but do not add it to the cocktail. Serve immediately.

Yellow Bird

Short drink to serve as a digestif

FOR 1 GLASS

5–6 ice cubes

1 measure white Puerto Rican rum

¼ measure fresh lemon juice

¼ measure Galliano

¼ measure curaçao
triple sec

- Place the ice and all the ingredients in the lower part of the shaker.
- Fit the upper part of the shaker and shake vigorously for 8–10 seconds.
- Strain into a Martini glass using a cocktail strainer. Serve immediately.

Smooth cocktails

Baby Alexander

Short drink to serve as a digestif

FOR 1 GLASS

5–6 ice cubes

¾ measure amber Cuban rum

½ measure brown crème de cacao

½ measure single (light) cream

- Place the ice and all the ingredients in the lower part of the shaker.
- Fit the upper part of the shaker and shake vigorously for 8–10 seconds.
- Strain into a Martini glass using a cocktail strainer. Serve immediately.

Cubanita

Long drink to serve in the morning

FOR 1 GLASS

5–6 ice cubes

1¼ measures white Cuban rum

3 measures tomato juice

1 teaspoon fresh lemon juice

1 teaspoon Worcestershire sauce

2–3 drops red Tabasco sauce

1 pinch celery salt

1 pinch black pepper

- Place the ice and all the ingredients in a mixing glass.
- Stir with a mixing spoon for 8–10 seconds.
- Strain into a highball glass using a cocktail strainer. Serve immediately.

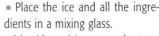 The Cubanita is a version of the Bloody Mary (▷ p. 86). At the end of the 1930s it was known as the Mary Rose.

Hot cocktails

Fish House Punch

Long drink to serve in the winter

FOR 1 GLASS

½ measure dark Jamaican rum

½ measure Cognac

⅛ measure fresh lemon juice

1 teaspoon crème de pêche (peach liqueur)

1 mixing spoon caster (superfine) sugar

1¾ measures boiling water

- Place all the ingredients into a heatproof toddy glass.
- Stir with a mixing spoon for 8–10 seconds. Serve immediately.

 This cocktail can also be drunk cold. It was invented in 1732 by members of the fishermen's club headquarters, the Fish House, in Philadelphia.

American Grog

Long drink to serve in the winter

FOR 1 GLASS

1 measure white Jamaican rum

⅛ measure fresh lemon juice

2 mixing spoons caster (superfine) sugar

⅛ unwaxed lemon

1 stick cinnamon

2–3 cloves

1¾ measures boiling water

- Place the rum, lemon juice and sugar in a heatproof toddy glass.
- Place the lemon segment, the cinnamon and the cloves in the glass.
- Add the boiling water. Stir with a mixing spoon for 8–10 seconds. Serve immediately.

This cocktail is attributed to Admiral Vernon, better known by his nickname of 'Old Grog', which referred to the coat he wore made of 'grogram' – a coarse fabric.

Hot Buttered Rum

Long drink to serve in the winter

FOR 1 GLASS

1 heaped teaspoon butter

2 mixing spoons caster (superfine) sugar

1 pinch grated nutmeg

1 pinch ground cinnamon

1 pinch ground cloves

1 measure white Puerto Rican rum

1 pinch salt

3 measures boiling water

- Using a spatula, cream together the butter, sugar and spices until smooth.
- Place this mixture in a heatproof toddy glass with the rum, salt and boiling water.
- Stir with a mixing spoon for 6–8 seconds. Serve immediately.

Variation:

Hot Buttered Rum Cow

Substituting boiling milk for the boiling water gives a Hot Buttered Rum Cow, a thicker, creamier drink that is ideal on winter evenings.

Tom & Jerry

Long drink to serve in the winter

FOR 1 GLASS

1 egg

2 mixing spoons caster (superfine) sugar

1 pinch ground cinnamon

1 pinch ground cloves

½ measure amber Jamaican rum

½ measure Cognac

1¾ measures boiling water

- Break the egg and separate the yolk from the white. Place the egg white in a bowl and whisk until stiff.
- Place the egg yolk, sugar and spices in a deep dish and, using a spatula, mix until creamy.
- Transfer this to a heatproof toddy glass, together with the rum and Cognac.
- Add the boiling water. Stir with a mixing spoon for 6–8 seconds.
- Top with a little of the whisked egg white. Serve immediately.

Predating the cartoon of that name

Contrary to what one might think, the cocktail Tom & Jerry (▷ left) was invented long before Bill Hanna and Joe Barbera's famous animated cartoon, made in 1940 (pictured here). This long drink was created in California in 1847 by Jerry Thomas (1830–1885), for a customer who wanted a drink based on egg and sugar. He was so proud of his creation that he gave it his own name but, finding this rather lacked resonance, he finally used the names of his two pet white mice.

Tequila-based cocktails

Mexico is the only country in the world to make tequila.
▷ See also p. 302

The Mexican spirit, tequila, is made from a variety of agave called Weber Blue. It is best to use 'Tequila 100% agave' – the name 'tequila' used by itself generally indicates a 'mixed tequila', that is one distilled from a minimum of 51% agave together with other added sugars. Both these main categories include various types: 'blanco' or 'silver' is tequila that has not undergone any ageing process; 'gold' or 'joven abocado' is a coloured, sweetened tequila; 'reposado' has spent two months in a tun or a cask, while tequila 'añejo' means it has been at least one year in cask.

Tequila is undoubtedly the type of alcohol in which the flavour of the original plant remains the most recognizable after distillation.

In the famous Margarita (▷ p. 176), the tequila is both sweetened by the curaçao triple sec and sharpened by the lime juice.

It harmonizes perfectly, too, with the grapefruit juice in an Ice-Breaker (▷ p. 184) or the orange juice in a Cactus Banger (▷ p. 183). The distinctive flavour of tequila is also a powerful counterbalance for sweet ingredients such as the crème de cassis in a Purple Pancho (▷ p. 177) or the coffee liqueur in a Brave Bull (▷ p. 189).

THE 10 INDISPUTABLE CLASSICS

Brave Bull ▷ p. 189
Cactus Banger ▷ p. 183
Chimayo ▷ p. 183
El Diablo ▷ p. 175
Ice-Breaker ▷ p. 184
Margarita ▷ p. 176
Strawberry Margarita ▷ p. 186
Tequila and Sangrita ▷ p. 173
Tequila Straight ▷ p. 173
Tequila Sunrise ▷ p. 186

Dry cocktails

California Dream

Short drink to serve as an aperitif

FOR 1 GLASS

5–6 ice cubes

1 measure tequila reposado 100% agave

⅓ measure dry vermouth

⅓ measure red vermouth

1 strip unwaxed lemon peel (zest)

- Place the ice, tequila and both vermouths in a mixing glass.
- Stir with a mixing spoon for 8–10 seconds.
- Strain into a Martini glass using a cocktail strainer.
- Cut the strip of lemon peel with a paring knife. Over the glass, pinch it between the fingers to release the oils then drop it into the cocktail. Serve immediately.

Variation: Rosita

In a Rosita 1 teaspoon of dry vermouth and 1 teaspoon of red vermouth are replaced with ¼ measure of Campari. This short bitter drink makes an excellent aperitif.

Mexico Manhattan

Short drink to serve as an aperitif

FOR 1 GLASS

5–6 ice cubes

1¼ measures tequila reposado 100% agave

½ measure red vermouth

2–3 drops Angostura bitters

1 maraschino cherry

- Place the ice and all the ingredients except the cherry in a mixing glass.
- Stir with a mixing spoon for 8–10 seconds.
- Strain into a Martini glass using a cocktail strainer.
- Add the maraschino cherry. Serve immediately.

Tequila and Sangrita

Short drink to serve at any time

FOR 3 GLASSES OF EACH

3 measures (3 x 1 measure) tequila añejo 100% agave

5–6 ice cubes

1¾ measures pure tomato juice

¾ measure fresh orange juice

¼ measure fresh lime juice

1 teaspoon Worcestershire sauce

1 teaspoon runny acacia honey

3–4 drops red Tabasco sauce

1 pinch salt

- Share the tequila between 3 shot glasses.
- Place the ice and the other ingredients in a mixing glass.
- Stir with a mixing spoon for 8–10 seconds.
- Strain this – the Sangrita – into 3 further shot glasses using a cocktail strainer.
- Serve immediately. This is drunk by sipping from each glass in turn – a little tequila followed by a little Sangrita, and so on.

 Mexicans tend to drink their tequila neat, either with a glass of Sangrita if consumed with a meal, or with a piece of lime, as in a Tequila Straight (▷ left).

Tequila Straight

Short drink to serve at any time

FOR 1 GLASS

1 measure tequila añejo 100% agave

1 pinch salt

⅛ unwaxed lime

- Place the tequila in a shot glass.
- Take the salt between the thumb and index finger and place a little on the tongue then knock back the spirit in one swallow and bite into the lime segment.

This way of drinking tequila is traditional in Mexico. The usual toast is: health, wealth, love and the time to enjoy them – each item being accompanied by another glass of tequila.

Tequini

Short drink to serve as an aperitif

FOR 1 GLASS

5–6 ice cubes

1⅔ measures tequila blanco 100% agave

⅓ measure dry vermouth

1 strip unwaxed lemon peel (zest)

- Place the ice, tequila and vermouth in a mixing glass.
- Stir with a mixing spoon for 8–10 seconds.
- Strain into a Martini glass using a cocktail strainer.
- Cut the strip of lemon peel with a paring knife. Over the glass, pinch it between the fingers to release the oils then drop it into the cocktail. Serve immediately.

Thirst-quenching cocktails

Agave Julep
Short drink to serve at any time

FOR 1 GLASS

8–10 fresh mint leaves

2 mixing spoons caster (superfine) sugar

3–4 ice cubes

1 measure tequila blanco 100% agave

⅓ measure fresh lime juice

• Wash the mint in cold water and place in a rocks glass.
• Crush the leaves with a pestle then add the sugar, ice, tequila and lime juice.
• Stir with a mixing spoon for 8–10 seconds. Serve immediately.

Alamo Splash
Long drink to serve at any time

FOR 1 GLASS

4–5 ice cubes

1 measure tequila blanco 100% agave

¾ measure fresh orange juice

2¾ measures lemon-lime soda

• Place the ice and all the ingredients in a highball glass.
• Stir with a mixing spoon for 8–10 seconds. Serve immediately.

Changuirongo
Short drink to serve at any time

FOR 1 GLASS

1 measure tequila blanco 100% agave

1¾ measures lemon-lime soda

¼ measure fresh lime juice

3–4 ice cubes

• Place the ice and all the ingredients in a rocks glass.
• Stir with a mixing spoon for 8–10 seconds. Serve immediately.

A long drink as red as the Devil

El Diablo (▷ right) only became well known about ten years ago. It was, however, invented in the 1940s, probably in the Mexican town of Mérida. It no doubt owes its name to the red colour brought to it by the crème de cassis. The recipe was published for the first time under the name of Mexican El Diablo, and it would seem that its origin was as a variation of a cocktail based on rum.

El Diablo

Long drink to serve at any time

FOR 1 GLASS

4–5 ice cubes

¼ unwaxed lime

1 measure tequila blanco 100% agave

¼ measure crème de cassis

3 measures ginger ale

- Cut the lime segment into 2 pieces and place them in a highball glass. Crush them with a pestle.
- Add the ice and the other ingredients.
- Stir with a mixing spoon for 8–10 seconds. Serve immediately.

Variation: Mexican Mule
Omit the crème de cassis to make a Mexican Mule, a more acidic long drink that is excellent at any time.

Frozen Margarita

Short drink to serve at any time

FOR 1 GLASS

3–4 ice cubes, crushed (▷ p. 59)

1 measure tequila blanco 100% agave

½ measure fresh lime juice

¼ measure curaçao triple sec

- Place the crushed ice and all the ingredients in a blender. Blend at low speed for 5–10 seconds then at high speed for 15–30 seconds.
- Pour the contents of the blender into a Martini glass. Serve immediately.

Variation: Blue Margarita
This is made by replacing the curaçao triple sec with blue curaçao. The Blue Margarita is a sweeter short drink that is ideal for the evening.

Margarita

Short drink to serve at any time

FOR 1 GLASS

Fine salt

5–6 ice cubes

1 measure tequila blanco 100% agave

½ measure fresh lime juice

¼ measure curaçao triple sec

- Frost the rim of the glass with fine salt (▷ p. 59).
- Place the ice and all the ingredients in the lower part of the shaker.
- Fit the upper part of the shaker and shake vigorously for 8–10 seconds.
- Strain into a Martini glass using a cocktail strainer. Serve immediately.

Variation: Stargarita

Replacing 1 teaspoon of the curaçao triple sec with 1 teaspoon of Campari gives a Stargarita, a short drink with a touch of bitterness that is ideal as an aperitif.

Japanese Slipper

Short drink to serve at any time

FOR 1 GLASS

5–6 ice cubes

1 measure tequila blanco 100% agave

½ measure fresh lime juice

¼ measure green melon liqueur

- Place the ice and all the ingredients in the lower part of the shaker.
- Fit the upper part of the shaker and shake vigorously for 8–10 seconds.
- Strain into a Martini glass using a cocktail strainer. Serve immediately.

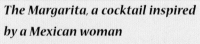

The Margarita, a cocktail inspired by a Mexican woman

Several legends about the origin of this drink (▷ above) feature a pretty Mexican woman. The best-known one maintains that it was invented in Acapulco in 1948 by Margarita Sames, who was organizing a reception and wished to offer her guests something new. Another version places its invention in the 1930s in Tijuana. Whatever the truth of the matter, the cocktail only became universally popular in the 1960s.

Mexicola

Long drink to serve
at any time

FOR 1 GLASS

¼ unwaxed lime

4–5 ice cubes

1 measure tequila blanco
100% agave

3¼ measures cola

- Cut the lime segment into 2 pieces and place them in a highball glass. Crush them with a pestle.
- Add the ice and the remaining ingredients.
- Stir with a mixing spoon for 8–10 seconds. Serve immediately.

Variation: Tijuana Tea

The Tijuana Tea is made by replacing ¼ measure of the cola with ¼ measure of curaçao triple sec. This results in a sweeter long drink that is ideal in the evening.

Purple Pancho

Short drink to serve
at any time

FOR 1 GLASS

3–4 ice cubes

1 measure tequila blanco
100% agave

½ measure fresh lime juice

¼ measure crème de cassis

- Place the ice and all the ingredients in a rocks glass.
- Stir with a mixing spoon for 8–10 seconds. Serve immediately.

Rude Cosmopolitan

Short drink to serve at any time

FOR 1 GLASS

5–6 ice cubes

¾ measure tequila blanco 100% agave

¾ measure cranberry juice
(based on fruit concentrate)

1 teaspoon fresh lime juice

1 teaspoon curaçao triple sec

1 strip unwaxed lime peel (zest)

- Place the ice, tequila, cranberry juice, lime juice and curaçao in the lower part of the shaker.
- Fit the upper part of the shaker and shake vigorously for 8–10 seconds.
- Strain into a Martini glass using a cocktail strainer.
- Cut the strip of lime peel with a paring knife. Over the glass, pinch it between the fingers to release the oils then drop it into the cocktail. Serve immediately.

Variation: Magic Bus

Replacing ⅓ measure of the cranberry juice with ⅓ measure of fresh orange juice gives a Magic Bus, a sweeter short drink that is suitable at any time.

A few ideas for cocktail snacks to serve with tequila-based cocktails:

- Tex-Mex chicken wings
- tortilla chips with fromage frais and red (bell) peppers
- cubes of raw pollack marinated in lime and orange juice
- guacamole and tomato sauce in multi-coloured layers
- chocolate-coated strawberries

▶ **recipes page 278**

Tequila Sunset

Short drink to serve
at any time

FOR 1 GLASS

3–4 ice cubes, crushed (▷ p. 59)

1 measure tequila blanco 100% agave

½ measure fresh lemon juice

1 teaspoon grenadine

- Place the crushed ice and all the ingredients in a blender. Blend at low speed for 5–10 seconds then at high speed for 15–30 seconds.
- Pour the contents of the blender into a rocks glass. Serve immediately.

T.N.T.

Long drink to serve
at any time

FOR 1 GLASS

⅛ unwaxed lime

4–5 ice cubes

1 measure tequila blanco 100% agave

3½ measures tonic water

- Place the lime segment in a highball glass.
- Add the ice and all the other ingredients.
- Stir with a mixing spoon for 8–10 seconds. Serve immediately.

Variation: Muppet

The Muppet – a long drink without any hint of bitterness that is ideal at any time – is made by using lemon-lime soda instead of tonic water.

Viva Villa

Short drink to serve
at any time

FOR 1 GLASS

5–6 ice cubes

1 measure tequila blanco 100% agave

½ measure fresh lime juice

2 teaspoons sugar cane syrup

- Place the ice and all the ingredients in the lower part of the shaker.
- Fit the upper part of the shaker and shake vigorously for 8–10 seconds.
- Strain into a Martini glass using a cocktail strainer. Serve immediately.

A tribute to Pancho Villa

The Viva Villa (▷ p. 180) was so-named in memory of Francisco 'Pancho' Villa (1878–1923), a poor peasant who, in 1910, joined the revolution against the dictator Porfirio Díaz in the north of Mexico. The revolutionary was head of the Northern division, an army of 50,000 men, and controlled a large part of the country in 1914. Beaten in 1915, Pancho carried on guerrilla activities until 1920. He was murdered.

Fruit-based cocktails

Acapulco

Long drink to serve at any time

FOR 1 GLASS

5–6 ice cubes

1 measure tequila reposado 100% agave

2 measures pure pineapple juice

1 measure fresh grapefruit juice

1 fresh pineapple leaf

- Place the ice, tequila and fruit juices in the lower part of the shaker.
- Fit the upper part of the shaker and shake vigorously for 8–10 seconds.
- Strain into a highball glass using a cocktail strainer.
- Cut a slit in the pineapple leaf and fix it to the rim of the glass. Serve immediately.

Agave Punch

Long drink to serve at any time

FOR 1 GLASS

5–6 ice cubes

1 measure tequila blanco 100% agave

2½ measures pure orange juice

½ measure fresh lemon juice

⅓ measure ruby port

1 teaspoon sugar cane syrup

- Place the ice and all the ingredients in the lower part of the shaker.
- Fit the upper part of the shaker and shake vigorously for 8–10 seconds.
- Strain into a highball glass using a cocktail strainer. Serve immediately.

Ambassador

Long drink to serve at any time

FOR 1 GLASS

5–6 ice cubes

1 measure tequila blanco 100% agave

3½ measures pure orange juice

- Place the ice and all the ingredients in the lower part of the shaker.
- Fit the upper part of the shaker and shake vigorously for 8–10 seconds.
- Strain into a highball glass using a cocktail strainer. Serve immediately.

Variation: Desert Glow

Replacing ½ measure of the orange juice with ½ measure of peach schnapps gives a Desert Glow – a fruitier long drink that is ideal at any time.

Arriba!

Short drink to serve at any time

FOR 1 GLASS

5–6 ice cubes

¾ measure tequila blanco 100% agave

¾ measure fresh orange juice

¼ measure orange curaçao

1 strip unwaxed orange peel (zest)

- Place the ice, tequila, orange juice and orange curaçao in the lower part of the shaker.
- Fit the upper part of the shaker and shake vigorously for 8–10 seconds.
- Strain into a Martini glass using a cocktail strainer.
- Cut the strip of orange peel with a paring knife. Over the glass, pinch it between the fingers to release the oils then drop it into the cocktail. Serve immediately.

Broadway Thirst

Short drink to serve at any time

FOR 1 GLASS

5–6 ice cubes

1 measure tequila blanco 100% agave

½ measure fresh orange juice

1 teaspoon fresh lemon juice

1 teaspoon sugar cane syrup

- Place the ice and all the ingredients in the lower part of the shaker.
- Fit the upper part of the shaker and shake vigorously for 8–10 seconds.
- Strain into a Martini glass using a cocktail strainer. Serve immediately.

Cactus Banger

Long drink to serve
at any time

FOR 1 GLASS

5–6 ice cubes

1 measure tequila blanco
100% agave

3¼ measures pure orange juice

¼ measure Galliano

1 segment unwaxed orange

- Place the ice and all the ingredients except the orange segment in the lower part of the shaker.
- Fit the upper part of the shaker and shake vigorously for 8–10 seconds.
- Strain into a highball glass using a cocktail strainer.
- Cut a slit in the orange segment and fix it to the rim of the glass. Serve immediately.

This cocktail is also known as the **Freddy Fudpucker.**

Chihuahua

Long drink to serve at any time

FOR 1 GLASS

Fine salt

5–6 ice cubes

1 measure tequila blanco 100% agave

3½ measures pure grapefruit juice

- Frost the rim of a highball glass with fine salt (▷ p. 59).
- Place the ice and all the ingredients in the lower part of the shaker.
- Fit the upper part of the shaker and shake vigorously for 8–10 seconds.
- Strain into the prepared highball glass using a cocktail strainer. Serve immediately.

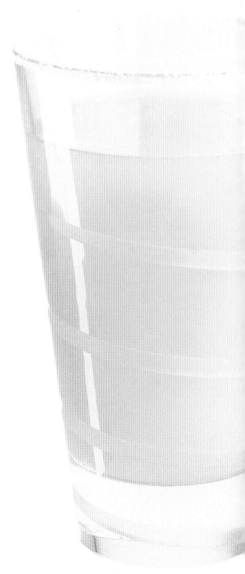

Chimayo

Short drink to serve at any time

FOR 1 GLASS

5–6 ice cubes

¾ measure tequila blanco 100% agave

¾ measure pure apple juice

¼ measure crème de cassis

- Place the ice and all the ingredients in the lower part of the shaker.
- Fit the upper part of the shaker and shake vigorously for 8–10 seconds.
- Strain into a Martini glass using a cocktail strainer. Serve immediately.

Coco Mexico

Long drink to serve
at any time

FOR 1 GLASS

5–6 ice cubes

1 measure tequila blanco
100% agave

3 measures pure pineapple juice

2 mixing spoons coconut milk
(canned)

1 fresh pineapple leaf

• Place the ice, tequila, pineapple juice
and coconut milk in the lower part of
the shaker.

• Fit the upper part of the shaker and
shake vigorously for 8–10 seconds.

• Strain into a highball glass using a
cocktail strainer.

• Cut a slit in the pineapple leaf and fix it to
the rim of the glass. Serve immediately.

Ice-Breaker

Short drink to serve at any time

FOR 1 GLASS

5–6 ice cubes

1 measure tequila blanco 100% agave

1 measure fresh grapefruit juice

1 teaspoon curaçao triple sec

1 teaspoon grenadine

• Place the ice and all the ingredients in the
lower part of the shaker.

• Fit the upper part of the shaker and shake
vigorously for 8–10 seconds.

• Strain into a rocks glass using a cocktail
strainer. Serve immediately.

Jungle Juice

Long drink to serve at any time

FOR 1 GLASS

5–6 ice cubes

1 measure tequila blanco 100% agave

1 measure fresh orange juice

1 measure pure pineapple juice

¾ measure cranberry juice
(based on fruit concentrate)

¾ measure lemon-lime soda

⅛ unwaxed lime

• Place the ice and all the ingredients except
the lime segment in the lower part of the
shaker.

• Fit the upper part of the shaker and shake
vigorously for 8–10 seconds.

• Strain into a highball glass using a cocktail
strainer.

• Lightly squeeze the lime segment into the
drink then cut a slit in it and fix it to the rim
of the glass. Serve immediately.

Mexican

Short drink to serve
at any time

FOR 1 GLASS

5–6 ice cubes

¾ measure tequila blanco
100% agave

¾ measure pure pineapple juice

1 teaspoon grenadine

- Place the ice and all the ingredients in the lower part of the shaker.
- Fit the upper part of the shaker and shake vigorously for 8–10 seconds.
- Strain into a Martini glass using a cocktail strainer. Serve immediately.

Variation: Mexicana

Preparing the cocktail in a highball glass and adding 2½ measures of pure pineapple juice, 1 teaspoon of grenadine and 1 teaspoon of fresh lime juice gives a Mexicana, a sweeter long drink that is ideal for evening drinking.

Piñata

Short drink to serve
at any time

FOR 1 GLASS

5–6 ice cubes

1 measure tequila blanco
100% agave

1½ measures pure pineapple juice

- Place the ice and all the ingredients in the lower part of the shaker.
- Fit the upper part of the shaker and shake vigorously for 8–10 seconds.
- Strain into a rocks glass using a cocktail strainer. Serve immediately.

Variation: Matador

Replacing ¼ measure of pineapple juice with 1 teaspoon of curaçao triple sec and 1 teaspoon of fresh lime juice gives a Matador – a drier short drink that is ideal at any time.

Playa del Mar

Short drink to serve at any time

FOR 1 GLASS

5–6 ice cubes

¾ measure tequila blanco
100% agave

⅓ measure cranberry juice
(based on fruit concentrate)

⅓ measure pure pineapple juice

1 teaspoon curaçao triple sec

1 teaspoon fresh lime juice

- Place the ice and all the ingredients in the lower part of the shaker.
- Fit the upper part of the shaker and shake vigorously for 8–10 seconds.
- Strain into a Martini glass using a cocktail strainer. Serve immediately.

Strawberry Margarita

Short drink to serve at any time

FOR 1 GLASS

4–5 fresh strawberries

3–4 ice cubes, crushed (▷ p. 59)

1 measure tequila blanco 100% agave

1 teaspoon curaçao triple sec

1 teaspoon fresh lime juice

- Wash the strawberries in cold water and set half of one fruit aside.
- Place the crushed ice, most of the strawberries and the other ingredients in a blender. Blend at low speed for 5–10 seconds then at high speed for 15–30 seconds.
- Strain the contents of the blender into a Martini glass. Add the remaining strawberry half. Serve immediately.

Variation: Pineapple Margarita

Replacing the strawberries with a 1 cm (½ inch) slice of fresh pineapple gives a Pineapple Margarita – a more refreshing short drink that is suitable at any time.

A very popular cocktail in the United States

The real origin of the Tequila Sunrise (▷ below) is unknown, but legend attributes its creation to a

barman whose boss woke him in the early hours of the morning after being out all night drinking with friends. The barman claimed to have waited until dawn before creating this drink, with its graduated colours that evoke the effect of the rising sun. The Tequila Sunrise was such a huge success in the United States that in 1988, a movie by Robert Twone starring Mel Gibson, Kurt Russell and Michelle Pfeiffer (pictured here) was given the same name.

Tequila Sunrise

Long drink to serve at any time

FOR 1 GLASS

5–6 ice cubes

1 measure tequila blanco 100% agave

3¼ measures pure orange juice

¼ measure grenadine

- Place the ice, tequila and orange juice in the lower part of the shaker.
- Fit the upper part of the shaker and shake vigorously for 8–10 seconds.
- Strain into a highball glass using a cocktail strainer.
- Pour in the grenadine. Serve immediately.

Tomahawk

Long drink to serve
at any time

FOR 1 GLASS

5–6 ice cubes

1 measure tequila blanco
100% agave

2 measures pure pineapple juice

1¼ measures cranberry juice
(based on fruit concentrate)

¼ measure curaçao triple sec

• Place the ice and all the ingredients in the lower part of the shaker.
• Fit the upper part of the shaker and shake vigorously for 8–10 seconds.
• Strain into a highball glass using a cocktail strainer. Serve immediately.

Vertigo

Long drink to serve at any time

FOR 1 GLASS

5–6 ice cubes

1 measure tequila reposado 100% agave

2½ measures cranberry juice
(based on fruit concentrate)

1 measure fresh orange juice

1 segment unwaxed orange

• Place the ice, tequila and the fruit juices in the lower part of the shaker.
• Fit the upper part of the shaker and shake vigorously for 8–10 seconds.
• Strain into a highball glass using a cocktail strainer.
• Cut a slit in the orange segment and fix it to the rim of the glass. Serve immediately.

Liqueur-based cocktails

Aguamiel

Short drink to serve in the evening

FOR 1 GLASS

5–6 ice cubes

¾ measure tequila reposado 100% agave

½ measure fresh lime juice

½ measure runny acacia honey

• Place the ice and all the ingredients in the lower part of the shaker.
• Fit the upper part of the shaker and shake vigorously for 8–10 seconds.
• Strain into a Martini glass using a cocktail strainer. Serve immediately.

Alice in Wonderland

Short drink to serve in the evening

FOR 1 GLASS

½ measure Grand Marnier Cordon Rouge

½ measure tequila blanco 100% agave

• Pour the liqueur into a shot glass.
• Add the tequila slowly, pouring it over a spoon so that it remains as a separate layer rather than mixing with the liqueur (▷ p. 58). Serve immediately.

Aztec Stinger

Short drink to serve as a digestif

FOR 1 GLASS

3–4 ice cubes

1 measure tequila blanco 100% agave

½ measure white crème de menthe

• Place the ice and all the ingredients in a rocks glass.
• Stir with a mixing spoon for 8–10 seconds. Serve immediately.

Variation: Cactus Cooler
Prepared in a highball glass with the addition of 3 measures of soda water (club soda) this becomes a Cactus Cooler, a more refreshing, long drink that is ideal in the late afternoon.

Banana Boat

Short drink to serve as a digestif

FOR 1 GLASS

5–6 ice cubes

1 measure tequila blanco 100% agave

½ measure fresh lime juice

¼ measure crème de banane

• Place the ice and all the ingredients in the lower part of the shaker.
• Fit the upper part of the shaker and shake vigorously for 8–10 seconds.
• Strain into a Martini glass using a cocktail strainer. Serve immediately.

Brave Bull

Short drink to serve as a digestif

FOR 1 GLASS

3–4 ice cubes

1 measure tequila blanco 100% agave

½ measure coffee liqueur

- Place the ice and all the ingredients in a rocks glass.
- Stir with a mixing spoon for 8–10 seconds. Serve immediately.

Variation:

South of the Border

The addition of ¼ measure of fresh lime juice gives a South of the Border. This slightly drier short drink, ideal for evening drinking, should be prepared in a shaker and served in a Martini glass.

Cactus Flower

Short drink to serve in the evening

FOR 1 GLASS

1 measure tequila blanco 100% agave

2–3 drops red Tabasco sauce

- Place the ingredients into a shot glass.
- Serve immediately, without stirring (the Tabasco sinks to the bottom of the glass).

 This cocktail is also known as the Prairie Fire.

Mockingbird

Short drink to serve as a digestif

FOR 1 GLASS

5–6 ice cubes

1 measure tequila reposado 100% agave

½ measure green crème de menthe

¼ measure fresh lime juice

- Place the ice and all the ingredients in the lower part of the shaker.
- Fit the upper part of the shaker and shake vigorously for 8–10 seconds.
- Strain into a Martini glass using a cocktail strainer. Serve immediately.

189

Speedy Gonzales

Short drink to serve at any time

FOR 1 GLASS

5–6 ice cubes

1 measure tequila blanco 100% agave

⅓ measure crème de mûre

⅓ measure green melon liqueur

- Place the ice and all the ingredients in a mixing glass.
- Fit the upper part of the shaker and shake vigorously for 8–10 seconds.
- Strain into a Martini glass using a cocktail strainer. Serve immediately.

Smooth cocktails

Bloody Maria

Long drink to serve in the morning

FOR 1 GLASS

5–6 ice cubes

1¼ measures tequila blanco 100% agave

1¾ measures pure tomato juice

¾ measure fresh orange juice

¼ measure fresh lime juice

1 teaspoon Worcestershire sauce

1 teaspoon runny acacia honey

3–4 drops red Tabasco sauce

1 pinch salt

- Place the ice and all the ingredients in a mixing glass.
- Stir with a mixing spoon for 8–10 seconds.
- Strain into a highball glass using a cocktail strainer. Serve immediately.

Frostbite

Short drink to serve in the evening

FOR 1 GLASS

5–6 ice cubes

¾ measure tequila blanco 100% agave

¾ measure single (light) cream

¼ measure white crème de cacao

1 nutmeg

- Place the ice, tequila, cream and crème de cacao in the lower part of the shaker.
- Fit the upper part of the shaker and shake vigorously for 8–10 seconds.
- Strain into a Martini glass using a cocktail strainer.
- Grate a sprinkling of nutmeg over the top. Serve immediately.

Hot cocktails

Gorilla Sweat
Long drink to serve in the winter

FOR 1 GLASS

1 heaped teaspoon butter

1 measure tequila blanco 100% agave

2 mixing spoons caster (superfine) sugar

1¾ measures boiling water

- Place the butter and the other ingredients into a heatproof toddy glass.
- Stir with a mixing spoon for 6–8 seconds. Serve immediately.

Mexican Coffee

Long drink to serve at any time

 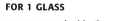

FOR 1 GLASS

1¼ measures double (heavy) cream

2 measures hot espresso coffee

1 measure tequila reposado 100% agave

2 teaspoons sugar cane syrup

- Place the cream in the freezer for 5 minutes.
- Place the cream in a bowl and whisk it with a fork until it thickens.
- Place the espresso coffee in a heatproof toddy glass. Add the tequila and sugar cane syrup.
- Stir with a mixing spoon for 3–4 seconds.
- Using the same spoon, float the cream on top. Serve immediately.

Mexican Tea
Long drink to serve in the winter

FOR 1 GLASS

1 measure tequila reposado 100% agave

2 mixing spoons caster (superfine) sugar

2 measures hot tea (Celon, for example)

1 strip unwaxed lime peel (zest)

- Place all the ingredients except the lime peel in a heatproof toddy glass.
- Stir with a mixing spoon for 8–10 seconds.
- Cut the strip of lime peel with a paring knife. Over the glass, pinch it between the fingers to release the oils then drop it into the cocktail. Serve immediately.

Brandy-based cocktails

The English word 'brandy' for the most part encompasses spirits distilled from wine, but it also covers those spirits that are distilled from fruit. It includes: Cognac, made from white wine grown in the Charentes region of France; pisco, a wine-based spirit made in Chile; Calvados from Normandy, distilled from cider and its American cousin Applejack, made in New Jersey and California. Kirsch, a spirit based on cherries, generally comes from Alsace, Switzerland and Germany.

A wide range of brandies are produced in many countries: France (Cognac, Armagnac, Calvados, kirsch), Spain (brandy distilled from sherry), Germany (kirsch, brandy), the United States (brandy, applejack), Chile (pisco).
▷ *See also pp. 303–305*

While most brandies are traditionally drunk as digestifs, they can also be combined with a wide range of flavours. Brandy mixes perfectly with fruit juices, such as the lemon juice in the famous Sidecar (▷ p. 201), orange juice in the Olympic (▷ p. 203), or pineapple juice in an East India (▷ p. 202). It makes a subtle alliance with such liqueurs as the crème de menthe in a Stinger (▷ p. 211), the coffee liqueur in a Brown Bear (▷ p. 205) or the Benedictine in a B & B (▷ p. 203).
And of course, brandy is completely at home with wine-based products like the vermouth in an Amber Twist (▷ p. 194) or the ruby port in a B & P (▷ p. 203) and American Beauty (▷ p. 194).

Dry cocktails

Amber Twist

Short drink to serve as an aperitif

FOR 1 GLASS

5–6 ice cubes

1 measure Cognac

½ measure dry vermouth

1 teaspoon apricot brandy

1 teaspoon curaçao triple sec

1 strip unwaxed orange peel (zest)

- Place the ice, Cognac, vermouth, apricot brandy and curaçao in a mixing glass.
- Stir with a mixing spoon for 8–10 seconds.
- Strain into a Martini glass using a cocktail strainer.
- Cut the strip of orange peel with a paring knife. Over the glass, pinch it between the fingers to release the oils then drop it into the cocktail. Serve immediately.

American Beauty

Short drink to serve as an aperitif

FOR 1 GLASS

2–3 fresh mint leaves

5–6 ice cubes

¾ measure Cognac

½ measure dry vermouth

¼ measure ruby port

¼ measure fresh orange juice

- Wash the mint leaves in cold water.
- Place the ice, Cognac, vermouth, port, orange juice and the mint leaves in the lower part of the shaker.
- Fit the upper part of the shaker and shake vigorously for 8–10 seconds.
- Strain into a Martini glass using a cocktail strainer and a pulp strainer. Serve immediately.

Gotham

Short drink to serve as an aperitif

FOR 1 GLASS

1¼ measures Cognac

½ measure Pernod

2–3 drops orange bitters

5–6 ice cubes

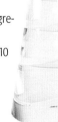

- Place the ice and all the ingredients in a mixing glass.
- Stir with a mixing spoon for 8–10 seconds.
- Strain into a Martini glass using a cocktail strainer. Serve immediately.

Variation: Bombay

The Bombay, a drier short drink suitable as an aperitif, is made by replacing the Pernod with ⅓ measure of vermouth and 1 teaspoon of orange curaçao.

Harvard

Short drink to serve as an aperitif

FOR 1 GLASS

5–6 ice cubes

1¼ measures Cognac

½ measure red vermouth

2–3 drops Angostura bitters

- Place the ice and all the ingredients in a mixing glass.
- Stir with a mixing spoon for 8–10 seconds.
- Strain into a Martini glass using a cocktail strainer. Serve immediately.

In the 1930s this cocktail was called a Metropolitan; in those days the recipe included 1 teaspoon of sugar cane syrup.

Variation: Star

Using Calvados instead of the Cognac gives a Star, a less woody-flavoured cocktail that is ideal as an aperitif.

Rose

Short drink to serve as an aperitif

FOR 1 GLASS

5–6 ice cubes

1 measure kirsch

½ measure dry vermouth

¼ measure cherry brandy

1 maraschino cherry

- Place the ice, kirsch, vermouth and cherry brandy in a mixing glass.
- Stir with a mixing spoon for 8–10 seconds.
- Strain into a Martini glass using a cocktail strainer.
- Add the maraschino cherry to the drink. Serve immediately.

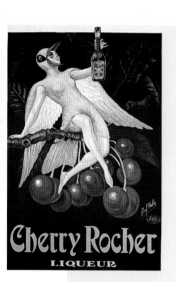

One of the oldest French cocktails

The Rose (▷ above), a short drink made with cherry brandy, was invented in Paris in 1906 by Johnny Milta, barman at the Chatam, Rue Daunou, a very popular area with Americans from that era on into the 1930s. The cocktail was invented for an American lady who loved roses. In 1922, artist Paul Mohr designed one of the best-known advertisements (pictured here) for the Cherry Rocher brand of cherry brandy.

T.N.T. No 2

Short drink to serve as an aperitif

FOR 1 GLASS

5–6 ice cubes

1¼ measures Cognac

⅓ measure orange curaçao

1 teaspoon absinthe-flavoured spirit

2–3 drops Angostura bitters

- Place the ice and all the ingredients in a mixing glass.
- Stir with a mixing spoon for 8–10 seconds.
- Strain into a Martini glass using a cocktail strainer. Serve immediately.

Thirst-quenching cocktails

Between the Sheets

Short drink to serve at any time

FOR 1 GLASS

5–6 ice cubes

½ measure Cognac

½ measure Puerto Rican rum

½ measure fresh lemon juice

¼ measure curaçao triple sec

- Place the ice and all the ingredients in the lower part of the shaker.
- Fit the upper part of the shaker and shake vigorously for 8–10 seconds.
- Strain into a Martini glass using a cocktail strainer. Serve immediately.

Variation: Nicky Finn
Replacing the rum with Pernod gives a Nicky Finn, an aniseed-flavoured short drink that is ideal in the late afternoon.

Brandy Highball

Long drink to serve at any time

FOR 1 GLASS

4–5 ice cubes

1 measure Cognac

3½ measures ginger ale

- Place the ice and all the ingredients into a highball glass.
- Stir with a mixing spoon for 8–10 seconds. Serve immediately.

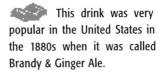 This drink was very popular in the United States in the 1880s when it was called Brandy & Ginger Ale.

Variation: B & S
Replacing the ginger ale with soda water (club soda) gives a B & S (Brandy & Soda), a long drink that is less sweet and is ideal at any time.

Cassisco

Long drink to serve
at any time

FOR 1 GLASS

4–5 ice cubes

1 measure Cognac

¼ measure crème de cassis

3¼ measures soda water
(club soda)

• Place the ice and all the
ingredients in a highball glass.
• Stir with a mixing spoon for 8–10
seconds. Serve immediately.

Variation: Kirsch & Cassis
Using kirsch instead of Cognac gives a
Kirsch & Cassis, a sweeter long drink that is
excellent at any time.

Dee-Light

Long drink to serve
at any time

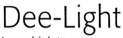

FOR 1 GLASS

¼ unwaxed lime

4–5 ice cubes

1 measure Cognac

2–3 drops crème de banane

3¼ measures lemon-lime soda

• Cut the lime quarter into 2
pieces and place them in a highball
glass. Crush them with a pestle.
• Add the ice and the other ingredients to
the glass.
• Stir with a mixing spoon for 8–10 seconds.
Serve immediately.

Depth Bomb

Short drink to serve
at any time

FOR 1 GLASS

5–6 ice cubes

½ measure Cognac

½ measure Calvados

½ measure fresh lemon juice

¼ measure grenadine

• Place the ice and all the ingredients in the
lower part of the shaker.
• Fit the upper part of the shaker and shake
vigorously for 8–10 seconds.
• Strain into a Martini glass using a cocktail strainer.
Serve immediately.

Georgia Mint Julep

Short drink to serve at any time

FOR 1 GLASS

8–10 fresh mint leaves

2 mixing spoons caster (superfine) sugar

3–4 ice cubes, crushed (▷ p. 59)

1 measure Cognac

• Wash the mint leaves in cold water then place them in a rocks glass and crush with a pestle.
• Add the sugar and fill the glass with the crushed ice.
• Add the Cognac and stir with a mixing spoon for 8–10 seconds. Serve immediately.

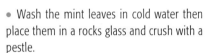 This is the oldest and best-loved of all America's cocktails.

Harvard Cooler

Long drink to serve at any time

FOR 1 GLASS

4–5 ice cubes

1 measure Calvados

¼ measure fresh lemon juice

2 teaspoons sugar cane syrup

3 measures soda water (club soda)

1 slice unwaxed lemon

• Place the ice and all the ingredients except the lemon slice into a highball glass.
• Stir with a mixing spoon for 8–10 seconds.
• Add the lemon slice. Serve immediately.

Horse's Neck

Long drink to serve at any time

FOR 1 GLASS

1 unwaxed lemon

4–5 ice cubes

1 measure Cognac

3–4 drops Angostura bitters

3½ measures ginger ale

• Using a paring knife cut the entire peel (zest) from the lemon in one long spiral and place this in a highball glass.
• Add the ice and the other ingredients.
• Stir gently with a mixing spoon for 8–10 seconds. Serve immediately.

A gangster's cocktail

The Jack Rose (▷ below), a great favourite with Humphrey Bogart (pictured here), was invented in New York between 1900 and 1910. It was supposedly created for gangster and gambler Jacob Rosenzweig, known to the Underworld as Bald Jack Rose. Another theory is that its original name was Jacque Rose, chosen because it is the exact colour of the Jacqueminot roses, created in 1853.

Jack Rose

Short drink to serve at any time

FOR 1 GLASS

5–6 ice cubes

1 measure Calvados

½ measure fresh lemon juice

¼ measure grenadine

- Place the ice and all the ingredients in the lower part of the shaker.
- Fit the upper part of the shaker and shake vigorously for 8–10 seconds.
- Strain into a Martini glass using a cocktail strainer. Serve immediately.

Normandy Cooler

Long drink to serve at any time

FOR 1 GLASS

4–5 ice cubes

¾ measure Calvados

1 measure soda water (club soda)

½ measure manzana verde liqueur (▷ p. 38)

2¼ measures pure apple juice

⅛ unwaxed lime

- Place the ice, Calvados, soda water, liqueur and apple juice in a highball glass.
- Stir with a mixing spoon for 8–10 seconds.
- Lightly squeeze the lime segment into the glass then add to the drink. Serve immediately.

Pisco Punch

Long drink to serve
at any time

FOR 1 GLASS

4–5 ice cubes

1 measure pisco

¾ measure pure pineapple juice

¼ measure fresh lemon juice

1 teaspoon sugar cane syrup

1 teaspoon orange curaçao

3–4 drops Angostura bitters

2¼ measures lemon-lime soda

1 fresh pineapple leaf

• Place the ice and all the ingredients except the pine-apple leaf in the lower part of the shaker.
• Fit the upper part of the shaker and shake vigorously for 8–10 seconds.
• Pour into a highball glass. Cut a slit in the pineapple leaf and fix it to the rim of the glass. Serve immediately.

 There are a number of different recipes for this cocktail; at the start of the 1900s it was made with pisco, orange curaçao, lemon juice and soda water (club soda).

Piscola

Long drink to serve
at any time

FOR 1 GLASS

4–5 ice cubes

1 measure pisco

1 teaspoon fresh lemon juice

3–4 drops Angostura bitters

3¼ measures cola

• Place the ice and all the ingredients in a highball glass.
• Stir with a mixing spoon for 8–10 seconds. Serve immediately.

Pisco Sour

Short drink to serve
at any time

FOR 1 GLASS

1 egg white

5–6 ice cubes

1 measure pisco

⅓ measure fresh lemon juice

2 teaspoons sugar cane syrup

2–3 drops Angostura bitters

• Beat the egg white for a few seconds with a fork.
• Place the ice, 1 teaspoon of egg white and the other ingredients in the lower part of the shaker.
• Fit the upper part of the shaker and shake vigorously for 8–10 seconds.
• Pour into a rocks glass. Serve immediately.

This cocktail is the national drink of Chile and Peru.

Sidecar

Short drink to serve at any time

FOR 1 GLASS

5–6 ice cubes

1 measure Cognac

⅛ measure fresh lemon juice

⅛ measure curaçao triple sec

1 strip unwaxed orange peel (zest)

• Place the ice, Cognac, lemon juice and curaçao in the lower part of the shaker.
• Fit the upper part of the shaker and shake vigorously for 8–10 seconds.
• Strain into a Martini glass using a cocktail strainer.
• Cut the strip of orange peel with a paring knife. Over the glass, pinch it between the fingers to release the oils then drop it into the cocktail. Serve immediately.

Variation: Apple Cart

Replacing the Cognac with Calvados gives an Apple Cart, a less woody-flavoured short drink that is ideal at any time.

In memory of an eccentric soldier

The Sidecar (▷ left) is one of the great classic short drinks. Legend has it that in 1931, when it first emerged at Harry's Bar in Paris, it was so called in homage to an army captain who habitually arrived at the bar in a sidecar! In fact, the recipe was invented in a French palace (either at Cannes or Paris) and was even introduced in London in 1922, by McGarry, head barman at Buck's Club.

Fruit-based cocktails

Apple Sunrise

Long drink to serve at any time

FOR 1 GLASS

4–5 ice cubes

1 measure Calvados

¼ measure crème de cassis

1 teaspoon fresh lemon juice

3 measures pure orange juice

• Place the ice and all the ingredients in a highball glass.
• Stir with a mixing spoon for 8–10 seconds. Serve immediately.

Castro Cooler

Long drink to serve at any time

FOR 1 GLASS

5–6 ice cubes

½ measure Calvados

2½ measures pure orange juice

½ measure amber Cuban rum

⅓ measure fresh lime juice

⅓ measure lime juice cordial

⅛ unwaxed lime

- Place the ice and all the ingredients except the lime segment in the lower part of the shaker.
- Fit the upper part of the shaker and shake vigorously for 8–10 seconds.
- Strain into a highball glass using a cocktail strainer.
- Cut a slit in the lime segment and fix it to the rim of the glass. Serve immediately.

East India

Short drink to serve at any time

FOR 1 GLASS

5–6 ice cubes

1 measure Cognac

½ measure pure pineapple juice

1 teaspoon orange curaçao

2–3 drops Angostura bitters

1 fresh pineapple leaf

- Place the ice and all the ingredients except the pineapple leaf in the lower part of the shaker.
- Fit the upper part of the shaker and shake vigorously for 8–10 seconds.
- Strain into a Martini glass using a cocktail strainer.
- Cut a slit in the pineapple leaf and fix it to the rim of the glass. Serve immediately.

El Ultimo

Long drink to serve at any time

FOR 1 GLASS

4–5 ice cubes

1 measure Cognac

¼ measure coconut liqueur

3¼ measures pure apple juice

- Place the ice and all the ingredients in a highball glass.
- Stir with a mixing spoon for 8–10 seconds. Serve immediately.

Olympic

Short drink to serve at any time

FOR 1 GLASS

5–6 ice cubes

1 measure Cognac

½ measure fresh orange juice

¼ measure orange curaçao

- Place the ice and all the ingredients in the lower part of the shaker.
- Fit the upper part of the shaker and shake vigorously for 8–10 seconds.
- Strain into a Martini glass using a cocktail strainer. Serve immediately.

Variation: Biarritz

The Biarritz – a short, more acidic, drink that is ideal for drinking any time, is made by replacing the orange juice with lemon juice.

Liqueur-based cocktails

B & B

Short drink to serve as a digestif

FOR 1 GLASS

3–4 ice cubes

1 measure Cognac

½ measure Benedictine

- Place the ice and all the ingredients in a rocks glass.
- Stir with a mixing spoon for 8–10 seconds. Serve immediately.

This cocktail was invented in 1937 at the Club 21 in New York. The initials B & B stand for Brandy and Benedictine.

Variation: April Shower

Replacing ¼ measure of Cognac and ¼ measure of Benedictine with ½ measure of fresh orange juice gives this more fruity short drink that is ideal at any time of the day. It is made in a shaker and served in a Martini glass.

B & P

Short drink to serve as a digestif

FOR 1 GLASS

1¼ measures Cognac

½ measure ruby port

- Place the ingredients in a rocks glass.
- Stir with a mixing spoon for 2–3 seconds. Serve immediately.

This is a very popular drink In Ireland. The initials B & P stand for Brandy and Port.

Variation: Port Flip

This smoother short drink is made by replacing 1 measure of Cognac with ½ measure of ruby port, 2 teaspoons of sugar cane syrup and 1 egg yolk. Good for hangovers.

Banana Bliss

Short drink to serve as a digestif

FOR 1 GLASS

3–4 ice cubes

1¼ measures Cognac

⅓ measure crème de banane

- Place the ice and all the ingredients in a rocks glass.
- Stir with a mixing spoon for 8–10 seconds. Serve immediately.

Variation:
Chocolate Bliss

Adding ½ measure of brown crème de cacao gives a Chocolate Bliss, a sweeter short drink that is ideal in the evening. It is prepared in a mixing glass and served in a Martini glass.

Black Jack

Short drink to serve as a digestif

FOR 1 GLASS

4–5 ice cubes

⅓ measure Cognac

¾ measure cold espresso coffee

⅓ measure kirsch

2 teaspoons sugar cane syrup

- Place the ice and all the ingredients in the lower part of the shaker.
- Fit the upper part of the shaker and shake vigorously for 8–10 seconds.
- Pour into a rocks glass. Serve immediately.

Bounty Boat

Short drink to serve as a digestif

FOR 1 GLASS

5–6 ice cubes

1 measure Cognac

½ measure brown crème de cacao

¼ measure coconut liqueur

- Place the ice and all the ingredients in a mixing glass.
- Stir with a mixing spoon for 8–10 seconds.
- Strain into a Martini glass using a cocktail strainer. Serve immediately.

Brown Bear

Short drink to serve as a digestif

FOR 1 GLASS

3–4 ice cubes

1 measure Cognac

½ measure coffee liqueur

• Place the ice and all the ingredients in a rocks glass.
• Stir with a mixing spoon for 8–10 seconds. Serve immediately.

 Another name for this cocktail is **Dirty Mother.**

Burgos

Short drink to serve as a digestif

FOR 1 GLASS

3–4 ice cubes

1¼ measures Cognac

5–6 drops Angostura bitters

• Place the ice and all the ingredients in a rocks glass.
• Stir with a mixing spoon for 8–10 seconds. Serve immediately.

Champs-Élysées

Short drink to serve as a digestif

FOR 1 GLASS

5–6 ice cubes

1 measure Cognac

½ measure yellow Chartreuse

¼ measure fresh lemon juice

2–3 drops Angostura bitters

• Place the ice and all the ingredients in the lower part of the shaker.
• Fit the upper part of the shaker and shake vigorously for 8–10 seconds.
• Strain into a Martini glass using a cocktail strainer. Serve immediately.

A few ideas for cocktail snacks to serve with brandy-based cocktails:

- panachés of rope-grown mussels with prosciutto ham
- Parmesan tuiles
- foie gras layered with artichokes and French (green) beans
- bite-sized, melting-soft pistachio cakes
- profiteroles with raspberries and whipped cream

▶ **recipes page 280**

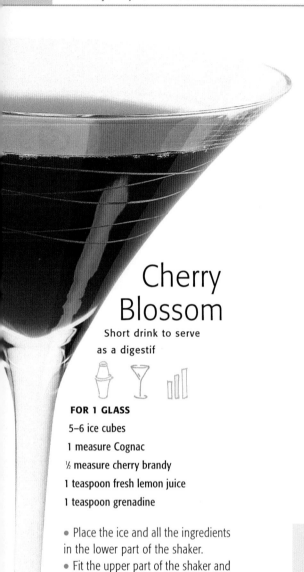

Corpse Reviver

Short drink to serve in the morning

FOR 1 GLASS

5–6 ice cubes

1 measure Cognac

⅛ measure Fernet-Branca liqueur

⅛ measure white crème de menthe

- Place the ice and all the ingredients in a mixing glass.
- Stir with a mixing spoon for 8–10 seconds.
- Strain into a Martini glass using a cocktail strainer. Serve immediately.

Variation: Apothecary

Replacing the Cognac with red vermouth gives an Apothecary, a less alcoholic short drink that is beneficial for hangover sufferers.

Cherry Blossom

Short drink to serve as a digestif

FOR 1 GLASS

5–6 ice cubes

1 measure Cognac

½ measure cherry brandy

1 teaspoon fresh lemon juice

1 teaspoon grenadine

- Place the ice and all the ingredients in the lower part of the shaker.
- Fit the upper part of the shaker and shake vigorously for 8–10 seconds.
- Strain into a Martini glass using a cocktail strainer. Serve immediately.

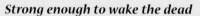

Strong enough to wake the dead

The Corpse Reviver (▷ above) is so strongly alcoholic that one could almost say that it revives the dead, as its name implies. In the 1890s, this type of cocktail was a form of 'pousse-café' – that is to say a mixture, served at room temperature, in which the alcohols were superimposed in layers. From the 1920s onward, the ingredients were served chilled and mixed as they are today.

Cuban

Short drink to serve
as a digestif

FOR 1 GLASS

5–6 ice cubes

1 measure Cognac

½ measure apricot brandy

¼ measure fresh lime juice

- Place the ice and all the ingredients in the lower part of the shaker.
- Fit the upper part of the shaker and shake vigorously for 8–10 seconds.
- Strain into a Martini glass using a cocktail strainer. Serve immediately.

French Connection

Short drink to serve as a digestif

FOR 1 GLASS

3–4 ice cubes

1 measure Cognac

½ measure Grand Marnier Cordon Rouge

1 strip unwaxed orange peel (zest)

- Place the ice, Cognac and Grand Marnier Cordon Rouge in a rocks glass.
- Stir with a mixing spoon for 8–10 seconds.
- Cut the strip of orange peel with a paring knife. Over the glass, pinch it between the fingers to release the oils then drop it into the cocktail. Serve immediately.

Highbinder

Short drink to serve
as a digestif

FOR 1 GLASS

3–4 ice cubes

1¼ measures Cognac

¼ measure crème de mûre

- Place the ice and all the ingredients in a rocks glass.
- Stir with a mixing spoon for 8–10 seconds. Serve immediately.

Japanese

Short drink to serve as a digestif

FOR 1 GLASS

5–6 ice cubes

1¼ measures Cognac

½ measure orgeat syrup

2–3 drops Angostura bitters

1 strip unwaxed lemon peel (zest)

● Place the ice, Cognac, orgeat syrup and Angostura bitters in the lower part of the shaker.
● Fit the upper part of the shaker and shake vigorously for 8–10 seconds.
● Strain into a Martini glass using a cocktail strainer.
● Cut the strip of lemon peel with a paring knife. Over the glass, pinch it between the fingers to release the oils but do not drop it into the cocktail. Serve immediately.

Honey Moon

Short drink to serve as a digestif

FOR 1 GLASS

5–6 ice cubes

1 measure Calvados

⅛ measure fresh lemon juice

¼ measure Benedictine

1 teaspoon orange curaçao

1 strip unwaxed lemon peel (zest)

● Place the ice and all the ingredients except the lemon peel in the lower part of the shaker.
● Fit the upper part of the shaker and shake vigorously for 8–10 seconds.
● Strain into a Martini glass using a cocktail strainer.
● Cut the strip of lemon peel with a paring knife. Over the glass, pinch it between the fingers to release the oils then drop it into the cocktail. Serve immediately.

Nikolaschka

Short drink to serve as a digestif

FOR 1 GLASS

1 measure Cognac

1 slice unwaxed lemon

2 mixing spoons caster (superfine) sugar

● Pour the Cognac into a tulip glass.
● Balance the slice of lemon on the top of the glass then carefully pile the sugar in a heap on top. Serve immediately.
● Savour it by first chewing the lemon and sugar then drinking the Cognac.

 This cocktail was all the rage in Germany at the start of the twentieth century.

Santina's Pousse-Café

Short drink to serve as a digestif

FOR 1 GLASS

1 teaspoon orange curaçao

¼ measure maraschino liqueur

⅓ measure Cognac

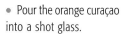

- Pour the orange curaçao into a shot glass.
- Pour the maraschino liqueur slowly over a mixing spoon, so that it floats on top of the curaçao (▷ p. 58).
- Pour the Cognac in exactly the same way. Serve immediately.

Stinger

Short drink to serve as a digestif

FOR 1 GLASS

3–4 ice cubes

1 measure Cognac

½ measure white crème de menthe

- Place the ice and all the ingredients in a rocks glass.
- Stir with a mixing spoon for 8–10 seconds. Serve immediately.

Variation: Chocolate Stinger

Omitting ¼ measure of crème de menthe and adding ½ measure of brown crème de cacao gives a Chocolate Stinger, a more aromatic short cocktail that is ideal as a digestif. The Chocolate Stinger was known as the Dimention in the 1930s.

The simplest of the digestifs

The Stinger (▷ above) gained the reputation in the 1900s in New York of being an excellent nightcap. In the 1956 movie High Society, which featured many of the stars of the time – Grace Kelly, Frank Sinatra (pictured here), Louis Armstrong and Bing Crosby – the latter sang the praises of the cocktail to Grace Kelly: 'It's a mixture of a few fresh flowers, called a Stinger. It takes away the burning sensation.'

Vanderbilt

Short drink to serve as a digestif

FOR 1 GLASS

5–6 ice cubes

1 measure Cognac

½ measure cherry brandy

2–3 drops Angostura bitters

1 maraschino cherry

- Place the ice and all the ingredients except the cherry in a mixing glass.
- Stir with a mixing spoon for 8–10 seconds.
- Strain into a Martini glass using a cocktail strainer.
- Add the maraschino cherry to the drink. Serve immediately.

Smooth cocktails

Brandy Alexander

Short drink to serve as a digestif

FOR 1 GLASS

5–6 ice cubes

¾ measure Cognac

½ measure brown crème de cacao

½ measure single (light) cream

1 nutmeg

- Place the ice, Cognac, crème de cacao and cream in the lower part of the shaker.
- Fit the upper part of the shaker and shake vigorously for 8–10 seconds.
- Strain into a Martini glass using a cocktail strainer.
- Grate a sprinkling of nutmeg on the top of the cocktail. Serve immediately.

Brandy Milk Punch

Short drink to serve as a digestif

FOR 1 GLASS

5–6 ice cubes

¾ measure Cognac

2 measures semi-skimmed milk

2 teaspoons sugar cane syrup

1 nutmeg

- Place the ice, Cognac, milk and sugar cane syrup in the lower part of the shaker.
- Fit the upper part of the shaker and shake vigorously for 8–10 seconds.
- Strain into a rocks glass using a cocktail strainer.
- Grate a sprinkling of nutmeg on top of the cocktail. Serve immediately.

Hot cocktails

Brandy Blazer

Long drink to serve in winter

FOR 1 GLASS

1½ measures boiling water

1½ measures Cognac

2 mixing spoons caster (superfine) sugar

1 strip unwaxed orange peel (zest)

- Heat 2 metal beakers with handles by scalding them.
- Pour the boiling water and then the Cognac into one beaker.
- Ignite the alcohol mixture with a match or lighter and, as it flames, pour the liquid from one beaker to the other 4–5 times before pouring it into a toddy glass.
- Add the sugar and stir with a mixing spoon until it dissolves.
- Cut the strip of orange peel with a paring knife. Over the glass, pinch it between the fingers to release the oils then drop it into the cocktail. Serve immediately.

Coffee Nudge

Long drink to serve in winter

FOR 1 GLASS

1 mixing spoon caster (superfine) sugar

¾ measure Cognac

1 teaspoon coffee liqueur

1 teaspoon brown crème de cacao

1½ measures hot espresso coffee

- Place the sugar in a toddy glass then add the Cognac, coffee liqueur, crème de cacao and coffee.
- Stir with a mixing spoon for 5–6 seconds. Serve immediately.

Variation: French Coffee

French Coffee, a less sweet short drink ideal for winter evenings, is made by replacing the coffee liqueur and the crème de cacao with ¼ measure of Cognac and I mixing spoon caster (superfine) sugar.

Maxim's Coffee

Long drink to serve in winter

FOR 1 GLASS

1 mixing spoon caster (superfine) sugar

1 measure Cognac

⅓ measure Benedictine

1 teaspoon Galliano

2 measures hot espresso coffee

- Place the sugar in a toddy glass then add the other ingredients.
- Stir with a mixing spoon for 5–6 seconds. Serve immediately.

Champagne-based cocktails

Champagne is produced
only in France.
▷ See also p. 306

Champagne is undoubtedly the most famous wine in the world. This sparkling white wine is produced in the strictly limited appellation area of Champagne. It is drunk 'frappé', that is to say at a temperature of 7–8°C/44–46°F, but never iced, which has a damaging effect on it.

The most celebrated of festive wines, Champagne – preferably Brut – brings sparkle, freshness and refinement to cocktails. It mixes harmoniously with neutral alcohols like the vodka in a Blue Champagne (▷ p. 219), but also with alcohol that has a woody flavour, like the Cognac in a Champagne Cocktail (▷ p. 217). Champagne also combines perfectly with red fruit flavours – the strawberry purée in the Rossini (▷ p. 225) and the Royal Highball (▷ p. 226), or the crème de cassis in a Kir Royal (▷ p. 218). Champagne also adapts itself admirably to the acidity of citrus fruits: the orange juice in the Mimosa (▷ p. 225) and the Jacuzzi (▷ p. 225), or the lemon juice in the Champagne Sour (▷ p. 220) and the French 75 (▷ p. 220). But it also harbours some pleasant surprises if it is mixed with aniseed (anise), like the Pernod in a Hemingway (▷ p. 218), or to an aperitif like Campari in the C.C. (▷ p. 216) and the Night & Day (▷ p. 229), or even with Irish stout in a Black Velvet (▷ p. 228).

THE 10 INDISPUTABLE CLASSICS

Dry cocktails

Alfonso

Short drink to serve as an aperitif

FOR 1 GLASS

3–4 drops Angostura bitters

1 lump sugar

2¼ measures Champagne Brut 'frappé'

¾ measure Dubonnet

- Drop the Angostura bitters onto the sugar lump then place it in a champagne flute.
- Pour in the Champagne and Dubonnet.
- Stir gently with a mixing spoon for 2–3 seconds without disturbing the sugar. Serve immediately.

Invented for King Alfonso III of Spain, this cocktail became popular in France and Great Britain at the start of the 1920s after the King visited Deauville.

Ambrosia

Short drink to serve at any time

FOR 1 GLASS

2¼ measures Champagne Brut 'frappé'

¼ measure Cognac

¼ measure Calvados

1 teaspoon fresh lemon juice

1 teaspoon curaçao triple sec

1 strip unwaxed orange peel (zest)

- Pour the Champagne, Cognac, Calvados, lemon juice and curaçao into a champagne flute.
- Stir gently with a mixing spoon for 2–3 seconds.
- Cut the strip of orange peel with a paring knife. Over the glass, pinch it between the fingers to release the oils then drop it into the cocktail. Serve immediately.

C.C.

Short drink to serve as an aperitif

FOR 1 GLASS

2½ measures Champagne Brut

½ measure Campari

- Pour the Champagne and Campari into a champagne flute.
- Stir gently with a mixing spoon for 2–3 seconds. Serve immediately.

Carol Channing

Short drink to serve at any time

FOR 1 GLASS

2¼ measures Champagne Brut

⅓ measure raspberry spirit

¼ measure crème de framboise

1 teaspoon sugar cane syrup

• Pour all the ingredients into a champagne flute.

• Stir gently with a mixing spoon for 2–3 seconds. Serve immediately.

This cocktail was invented in 1984 by Dick Bradsell in tribute to American actress Carol Channing who starred in *Gentlemen Prefer Blondes* (1949) and *Hello Dolly* (1964), among other movies.

Champagne Cocktail

Short drink to serve at any time

FOR 1 GLASS

3–4 drops Angostura bitters

1 lump sugar

2½ measures Champagne Brut 'frappé'

½ measure Cognac

• Drop the Angostura bitters onto the sugar lump then place it in a champagne flute.

• Add the Champagne and Cognac.

• Stir gently with a mixing spoon for 2–3 seconds without disturbing the sugar. Serve immediately.

Variation: Americana

In this cocktail the Cognac is replaced with bourbon, giving a more woody-flavoured short drink that is ideal at any time.

A legendary wine for a legendary movie

Casablanca, during World War II: the town welcomes many refugees who are trying to get to Portugal, like Ilsa Lund (Ingrid Bergman) and her husband, a Resistance hero. Rick Blaine (Humphrey Bogart), Ilsa's former lover, is the only one who can help them. Still in love with her, he hesitates for a long time but finally helps them escape, leaving himself with nothing but memories of the times when he and Ilsa drank Champagne together at the Belle Aurore in Paris (pictured here).

217

Ginger Champagne

Short drink to serve at any time

FOR 1 GLASS

1 piece fresh root ginger

2½ measures Champagne Brut 'frappé'

½ measure vodka

- Cut a very thin piece of ginger about 1 cm (½ inch) diameter and 1 mm (½₅ inch) thick. Place it in a champagne flute.
- Add the Champagne and vodka.
- Stir gently with a mixing spoon for 2–3 seconds. Serve immediately.

Ginger Champagne is a simplified version of the Benderitter, invented in Paris in 1995, by Colin Field at the Hemingway Bar of The Ritz Hotel. The Benderitter uses an infusion of vodka and ginger.

Hemingway

Short drink to serve as an aperitif

FOR 1 GLASS

2½ measures Champagne Brut 'frappé'

⅛ measure Pernod

- Pour the Champagne and Pernod into a champagne flute.
- Stir gently with a mixing spoon for 2–3 seconds. Serve immediately.

This cocktail is also known as Death in the Afternoon.

Variation:
Corpse Reviver No 2
Replacing 1 teaspoon of Pernod with 1 teaspoon of fresh lemon juice makes a Corpse Reviver No 2, a more refreshing short drink that is excellent at any time. This cocktail was invented in 1926 by Frank Meier at The Ritz Hotel's Cambon Bar in Paris.

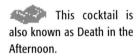

Kir Royal

Short drink to serve at any time

FOR 1 GLASS

2½ measures Champagne Brut 'frappé'

⅛ measure crème de cassis

- Pour the Champagne and crème de cassis into a champagne flute.
- Stir gently with a mixing spoon for 2–3 seconds. Serve immediately.

Variation: Kir Imperial
This is made with crème de framboise instead of the crème de cassis, making it a slightly drier short drink, ideal at any time.

Pimm's Royal

Short drink to serve
as an aperitif

FOR 1 GLASS

1 cucumber

2¼ measures Champagne
Brut 'frappé'

¾ measure Pimm's No 1

- Wash the cucumber in cold water. Using a paring knife, cut a piece of peel about 8 cm (3¼ inches) long by 1 cm (½ inch) wide.
- Pour the Champagne and Pimm's into a champagne flute.
- Stir gently with a mixing spoon for 2–3 seconds.
- Add the cucumber peel to the drink. Serve immediately.

Thirst-quenching cocktails

American Flyer

Short drink to serve
at any time

FOR 1 GLASS

2¼ measures Champagne Brut
'frappé'

½ measure aged Jamaican rum

1 teaspoon fresh lime juice

1 teaspoon sugar cane syrup

1 strip unwaxed lime peel (zest)

- Place the Champagne, rum, lime juice and sugar cane syrup in a champagne flute.
- Stir gently with a mixing spoon for 2–3 seconds.
- Cut the strip of lime peel with a paring knife. Over the glass, pinch it between the fingers to release the oils then drop it into the cocktail. Serve immediately.

Blue Champagne

Short drink to serve
at any time

FOR 1 GLASS

2¼ measures Champagne Brut
'frappé'

½ measure vodka

1 teaspoon blue curaçao

1 teaspoon fresh lemon juice

1 strip unwaxed lemon peel (zest)

- Pour the Champagne, vodka, curaçao and lemon juice into a champagne flute.
- Stir gently with a mixing spoon for 2–3 seconds.
- Cut the strip of lemon peel with a paring knife. Over the glass, pinch it between the fingers to release the oils then drop it into the cocktail. Serve immediately.

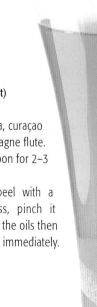

Champagne Julep

Short drink to serve
at any time

FOR 1 GLASS

4–6 fresh mint leaves, plus 1 fresh sprig mint

3 measures Champagne Brut 'frappé'

1 lump brown sugar

- Wash all the mint in cold water.
- Place the mint leaves in a mixing glass. Crush them lightly with a pestle then pour in the Champagne.
- Place the sugar lump in a champagne flute then add the contents of the mixing glass, straining them through a pulp strainer.
- Add the mint sprig to the glass. Serve immediately.

Champagne Sour

Short drink to serve
at any time

FOR 1 GLASS

2½ measures Champagne Brut 'frappé'

¼ measure fresh lemon juice

1 teaspoon sugar cane syrup

- Place all the ingredients in a champagne flute.
- Stir gently with a mixing spoon for 2–3 seconds. Serve immediately.

French 75

Long drink to serve
at any time

FOR 1 GLASS

4–5 ice cubes

3 measures Champagne Brut 'frappé'

¾ measure gin

⅓ measure fresh lemon juice

2 teaspoons sugar cane syrup

1 maraschino cherry

- Place the ice, Champagne, gin, lemon juice and sugar cane syrup in a highball glass.
- Stir gently with a mixing spoon for 2–3 seconds.
- Add the maraschino cherry to the glass. Serve immediately.

Variation: Diamond Fizz

Using gin instead of vodka gives a Diamond Fizz, a drier long drink that is suitable at any time.

Meringue

Short drink to serve
at any time

FOR 1 GLASS

¾ measure double (heavy) cream

2 measures Champagne Brut 'frappé'

½ measure limoncello

1 teaspoon lime cordial

- Whip the cream in a bowl with a fork until it thickens.
- Place the Champagne, limoncello and lime cordial into a champagne flute.
- Stir gently with a mixing spoon for 2–3 seconds.
- Float ⅛ measure of whipped cream on the top of the drink. Serve immediately.

Pick-Me-Up

Short drink to serve at any time

FOR 1 GLASS

2¼ measures Champagne Brut 'frappé'

⅓ measure Cognac

¼ measure fresh lemon juice

1 teaspoon grenadine

- Place all the ingredients in a champagne flute.
- Stir gently with a mixing spoon for 2–3 seconds. Serve immediately.

Variation: Barbotage

A Barbotage is made by replacing 1 teaspoon of Cognac and 1 teaspoon of lemon juice with ¼ measure of orange juice. This sweeter short drink is ideal at any time.

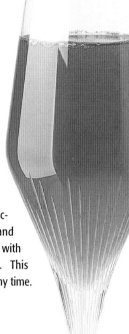

Christened with a military name

The French 75 (▷ opposite), which mixes Champagne with Anglo-Saxon gin, owes its name to a piece of artillery used in World War I: the French

75 mm cannon, known for its lightness. The original cocktail called the French 75 was not made with Champagne but with Calvados; in that form it survived until 1925, at which time Harry McElhone, owner of Harry's Bar, changed the recipe by making it with the famous sparkling wine.

A few ideas for cocktail snacks to serve with
Champagne-based cocktails:

- slices of queen (bay) scallops topped with caviar
- watercress mousse with roasted langoustines
- tartlets filled with toasted goat's milk cheese
  and pesto sauce
- squares of spiced bread with foie gras and
  cranberries
- orange crêpes soufflées in mini-gateau form

▶ **recipes page 282**

Fruit-based cocktails

Named after a Renaissance painter

The Bellini (▷ right) was invented in 1948 by Arrigo Cipriani, son of the proprietor of Harry's Bar in Venice. This cocktail pays tribute to the works of Giovanni Bellini (1430–1516), which were the subject of an exhibition in Venice in 1949. The orange-tinged rose colour of the peaches used in the recipe are reminiscent of the luminous colours in Bellini's paintings.

Bellini

Short drink to serve at any time

FOR 1 GLASS

2 yellow peaches

2 measures Champagne Brut 'frappé'

- Peel the peaches and cut in half to remove the stone (pit), then place them in a blender and blend to a purée.
- Place 1 measure of peach purée in a champagne flute and slowly pour on the Champagne.
- Stir gently with a mixing spoon for 2–3 seconds. Serve immediately.

Hawaii Sparkle

Short drink to serve at any time

FOR 1 GLASS

2 measures Champagne Brut 'frappé'

1 measure pure pineapple juice

- Place the Champagne and pineapple juice in a champagne flute.
- Stir gently with a mixing spoon for 2–3 seconds. Serve immediately.

Variation: Hawaii Breaker

Adding 3–4 drops of Angostura bitter gives a Hawaii Breaker, a slightly bitter short drink that is ideal at any time.

Jacuzzi

Short drink to serve at any time

FOR 1 GLASS

2 measures Champagne Brut 'frappé'

½ measure fresh orange juice

¼ measure gin

¼ measure peach schnapps

• Place all the ingredients in a champagne flute.
• Stir gently with a mixing spoon for 2–3 seconds. Serve immediately.

Mimosa

Short drink to serve at any time

FOR 1 GLASS

2 measures Champagne Brut 'frappé'

1 measure fresh orange juice

• Place the Champagne and orange juice in a champagne flute.
• Stir gently with a mixing spoon for 2–3 seconds. Serve immediately.

Variation: Buck's Fizz
Buck's Fizz is made by replacing 1 teaspoon of orange juice with 1 teaspoon of sugar cane syrup. This sweeter short drink, ideal for any time of the day, was invented in 1922 by McGarry, barman at Buck's Club in London.

Rossini

Short drink to serve at any time

FOR 1 GLASS

10–12 fresh strawberries

2 measures Champagne Brut 'frappé'

• Wash the strawberries in cold water and blend them to a purée in a blender, then place the purée in a champagne flute and slowly add the Champagne.
• Stir gently with a mixing spoon for 2–3 seconds. Serve immediately.

Royal Highball

Long drink to serve at any time

FOR 1 GLASS

10–12 fresh strawberries

4–5 ice cubes

3 measures Champagne Brut 'frappé'

½ measure Cognac

2 teaspoons sugar cane syrup

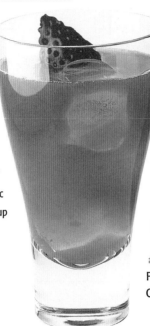

• Wash the strawberries in cold water and set half of one aside for decorating. Blend the remaining strawberries to a purée in a blender.

• Place the ice, Champagne, 1 measure of strawberry purée, Cognac and sugar cane syrup in a highball glass.

• Stir gently with a mixing spoon for 2–3 seconds.

• Add the strawberry half to the drink. Serve immediately.

This cocktail was invented in 1921 by Frank Meier for the opening of The Ritz Hotel's Cambon Bar in Paris.

Russian Spring Punch

Long drink to serve at any time

FOR 1 GLASS

4–5 ice cubes

3¼ measures Champagne Brut 'frappé'

¾ measure vodka

⅓ measure fresh lemon juice

¼ measure crème de cassis

1 teaspoon sugar cane syrup

1 slice unwaxed lemon

• Place the ice and all the ingredients except the lemon slice in a highball glass.

• Stir gently with a mixing spoon for 2–3 seconds.

• Add the lemon slice to the drink. Serve immediately.

Variation: French Spring Punch
Replace the vodka with Cognac and you have a French Spring Punch, a less dry long drink that is ideal at any time.

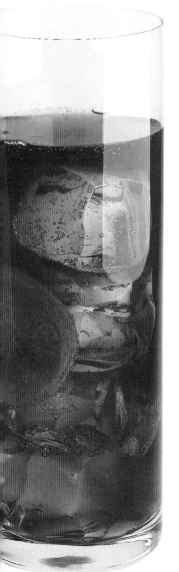

Saratoga

Short drink to serve at any time

FOR 1 GLASS

1¾ measures Champagne Brut 'frappé'

¾ measure pure pineapple juice

¼ measure Cognac

1 teaspoon maraschino liqueur

3–4 drops orange bitters

• Place all the ingredients in a champagne flute.

• Stir gently with a mixing spoon for 2–3 seconds. Serve immediately.

Serendipiti

Long drink to serve
at any time

FOR 1 GLASS

1 fresh sprig mint

¼ measure Calvados

4–5 ice cubes

3¾ measures Champagne
Brut 'frappé'

½ measure pure apple juice

- Wash the mint sprig and place it in a highball glass. Add the Calvados and lightly crush the mint with a pestle.
- Add the ice, Champagne and apple juice.
- Stir gently with a mixing spoon for 2–3 seconds. Serve immediately.

Tropical Hibiscus

Short drink to serve
at any time

FOR 1 GLASS

2 measures Champagne
Brut 'frappé'

1 measure cranberry juice
(based on fruit concentrate)

- Place the Champagne and cranberry juice in a champagne flute.
- Stir gently with a mixing spoon for 2–3 seconds. Serve immediately.

Valencia

Short drink to serve
at any time

FOR 1 GLASS

2 measures Champagne Brut 'frappé'

¾ measure fresh orange juice

¼ measure apricot brandy

- Place the Champagne, orange juice and apricot brandy in a champagne flute.
- Stir gently with a mixing spoon for 2–3 seconds. Serve immediately.

Variation: Golden Screw
Replacing ¼ measure of orange juice with ¼ measure of Cognac gives a Golden Screw, a drier drink for any occasion.

227

Liqueur-based cocktails

Black Pearl

Short drink to serve
in the evening

FOR 1 GLASS

2¼ measures Champagne
Brut 'frappé'

⅛ measure Cognac

⅛ measure coffee liqueur

• Place the Champagne, Cognac and
coffee liqueur in a champagne flute.
• Stir gently with a mixing spoon for
2–3 seconds. Serve immediately.

Black Velvet

Short drink to serve
at any time

FOR 1 GLASS

1½ measures Irish stout

1½ measures Champagne Brut 'frappé'

• Place the Irish stout in a champagne flute
then very slowly add the Champagne.
• Stir gently with a mixing spoon for 2–3
seconds. Serve immediately.

 When it was first invented in
1880, this cocktail was called Champagne
Velvet.

Midnight Moon

Short drink to wind up the evening

FOR 1 GLASS

2¼ measures Champagne Brut 'frappé'

¼ measure Cognac

¼ measure white crème de cacao

¼ measure amaretto

• Place all the ingredients in a champagne
flute.
• Stir gently with a mixing spoon for 2–3
seconds. Serve immediately.

Night & Day

Short drink to serve at any time

FOR 1 GLASS

2¼ measures Champagne Brut 'frappé'

⅓ measure Campari

⅓ measure Grand Marnier Cordon Rouge

- Place the Champagne, Campari and Grand Marnier Cordon Rouge in a champagne flute.
- Stir gently with a mixing spoon for 2–3 seconds. Serve immediately.

Ohio

Short drink to serve at any time

FOR 1 GLASS

2¼ measures Champagne Brut 'frappé'

⅓ measure rye whiskey

¼ measure red vermouth

1 teaspoon curaçao triple sec

3–4 drops Angostura bitters

- Place all the ingredients in a champagne flute.
- Stir gently with a mixing spoon for 2–3 seconds. Serve immediately.

Prince of Wales

Short drink to serve in the evening

FOR 1 GLASS

3–4 drops Angostura bitters

1 lump unrefined sugar

2¼ measures Champagne Brut 'frappé'

⅓ measure Cognac

⅓ measure curaçao triple sec

- Drop the Angostura bitters onto the sugar lump then place it into a champagne flute.
- Add the Champagne, Cognac and curaçao to the glass.
- Stir gently with a mixing spoon for 2–3 seconds without disturbing the sugar. Serve immediately.

Cocktails based on other forms of alcohol

Spain, France and Italy are all important producers of aperitifs. Liqueurs are made mostly in France, Italy and the Netherlands.
▷ See also pp. 307–311

Apart from the main types of alcohol that are served as the base for cocktails, other alcoholic drinks, more usually served as aperitifs or digestifs, can be used for the same purpose. These include: vermouth, made from white wine and a complex mixture of herbs and spices; bitters, based on alcohol and natural extracts of bitter and aromatic plants; the anises, produced by distilling or macerating star anise, green aniseed (anise), fennel, etc.; and not forgetting port,

sherry and liqueurs made from spirits, fruit, herbs and spices, and the crèmes – which are derived from liqueurs.

Vermouth is mixed with sherry in the Adonis (▷ p. 232), the Bamboo (▷ p. 233) or the Brazil (▷ p. 234). Bitters such as Campari, which unite happily with vermouth in the Americano (▷ p. 233) and the Negroni (▷ p. 235), are also excellent teamed with orange juice in the Garibaldi (▷ p. 241).

The anises, traditionally diluted with water as in the Absinthe Drip (▷ p. 232) or the Tomate à l'Absinthe (▷ p. 235), can be mixed with orange juice, as in the Tiger Tail (▷ p. 242).

And finally the crèmes and liqueurs go marvellously with the wine in a Kir (▷ p. 234) or with vermouth in a Vermouth-Cassis (▷ p. 236).

THE 10 INDISPUTABLE CLASSICS

Dry cocktails

Absinthe Drip

Short drink to serve as an aperitif

FOR 1 GLASS

½ measure absinthe-flavoured spirit

1 lump sugar

2½ measures still mineral water

• Place the absinthe-flavoured spirit in a wine glass.
• Place the sugar lump onto a perforated absinthe spoon and place this over the glass.
• Very slowly pour the water over the sugar, so that it dissolves completely as the glass is filled.
• Serve immediately, leaving it to your guest to stir their own drink.

Absinthe Veilleuse

Short drink to serve
as an aperitif

FOR 1 GLASS

3–4 ice cubes

5 measures chilled still mineral water

2 teaspoons sugar cane syrup

½ measure absinthe-flavoured spirit

• Place the ice and 2½ measures of chilled mineral water into a rocks glass.
• Place the remaining 2½ measures of mineral water and the sugar cane syrup into another rocks glass. Pour the absinthe-flavoured spirit over a mixing spoon so that it floats on top of the water (▷ p. 58).
• Ignite the spirit with a match or lighter. After 2–3 seconds, douse the flames by placing a saucer over the glass.
• Empty the ice and water from the first rocks glass and pour the contents of the second one into it. Serve immediately.

Adonis

Short drink to serve
as an aperitif

FOR 1 GLASS

5–6 ice cubes

1 measure fino sherry

¾ measure red vermouth

2–3 drops orange bitters

1 strip unwaxed orange peel (zest)

• Place the ice, sherry, vermouth and orange bitters in a mixing glass.
• Stir with a mixing spoon for 8–10 seconds.
• Strain into a Martini glass using a cocktail strainer.
• Cut the strip of orange peel with a paring knife. Over the glass, pinch it between the fingers to release the oils then drop it into the cocktail. Serve immediately.

Americano

Short drink to serve as an aperitif

FOR 1 GLASS

3–4 ice cubes

¾ measure Campari

¾ measure red vermouth

1 strip unwaxed lemon peel (zest)

- Place the ice, Campari and vermouth in a rocks glass.
- Stir with a mixing spoon for 8–10 seconds.
- Cut the strip of lemon peel with a paring knife. Over the glass, pinch it between the fingers to release the oils then drop it into the cocktail. Serve immediately.

Variation: Veneziano

The less bitter, long Veneziano is an Americano with 3 measures of white wine added and served in a highball glass as an aperitif.

A cocktail to please the tourists

The Americano (▷ left) saw the light of day at the start of Prohibition (1919–1933).

At that time many Americans took advantage of trips abroad to taste alcoholic drinks that they were forbidden at home. In Italy they discovered that Campari, which was prescribed as a tonic in the United States, could also be drunk as an aperitif but the flavour was rather too bitter for their taste. The Italian barmen got round this problem by serving them Campari mixed with red vermouth and calling it an 'Americano'. The drink became a classic and was marketed under a number of brands, including Poccardi (poster designed in 1923 by Leonetto Cappielo [1875–1942]).

Bamboo

Short drink to serve as an aperitif

FOR 1 GLASS

5–6 ice cubes

¾ measure dry vermouth

¾ measure fino sherry

2–3 drops orange bitters

1 strip unwaxed orange peel (zest)

- Place the ice, vermouth, sherry and orange bitters in a mixing glass.
- Stir with a mixing spoon for 8–10 seconds.
- Strain into a Martini glass using a cocktail strainer.
- Cut the strip of orange peel with a paring knife. Over the glass, pinch it between the fingers to release the oils then drop it into the cocktail. Serve immediately.

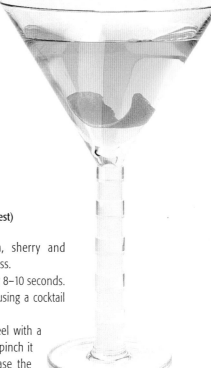

Dijon's own cocktail

*The Kir (▷ below) orig-
inated in Dijon in 1904,
created by café bar-
man Monsieur Faivre
from a combination of
the two local products
– white wine and crème de cassis (pictured here). Given
the name 'Blanc Cassis', the aperitif found favour and
was served by the local town council at its receptions
instead of Champagne. It was renamed the 'Kir' in 1951,
in honour of Canon Kir, a great lover of the drink and
mayor of the town from 1945–1968.*

Brazil

Short drink to serve as an aperitif

FOR 1 GLASS

5–6 ice cubes

¾ measure dry vermouth

¾ measure sherry

1 teaspoon absinthe-flavoured spirit

1 strip unwaxed lemon peel (zest)

• Place the ice and all the ingredients except the lemon peel in a mixing glass.
• Stir with a mixing spoon for 8–10 seconds. Strain into a Martini glass using a cocktail strainer.
• Cut the strip of lemon peel with a paring knife. Over the glass, pinch it between the fingers to release the oils then drop it into the cocktail. Serve immediately.

Kir

Short drink to serve
at any time

FOR 1 GLASS

⅛ measure crème de cassis

2½ measures chilled white Burgundy

• Place the crème de cassis in a wine glass and pour on the well-chilled white wine.
• Serve immediately.

Variation: Communard

This is made using red Côtes-du-Rhône instead of the white wine, giving a slightly less sweet short drink that is ideal at any time.

Negroni

Short drink to serve as an aperitif

FOR 1 GLASS

3–4 ice cubes

¾ measure Campari

¾ measure red vermouth

¼ measure gin

1 strip unwaxed lemon peel (zest)

- Place the ice, Campari, vermouth and gin in a rocks glass.
- Stir with a mixing spoon for 8–10 seconds.
- Cut the strip of lemon peel with a paring knife. Over the glass, pinch it between the fingers to release the oils then drop it into the cocktail. Serve immediately.

Variation: Cardinal

Replacing the red vermouth with dry vermouth gives a Cardinal, a drier short drink that makes an ideal aperitif.

Spritzer

Short drink to serve at any time

FOR 1 GLASS

1½ measures white wine (preferably Riesling)

1½ measures chilled soda water (club soda)

- Place the wine and very cold soda water in a wine glass.
- Serve immediately.

In the 1880s, this drink was also known as a Rhine Wine & Seltzer, especially in the United States.

Tomate à l'Absinthe

Short drink to serve as an aperitif

FOR 1 GLASS

½ measure absinthe-flavoured spirit

1¾ measures very cold still mineral water

1 teaspoon grenadine

- Place all the ingredients in a rocks glass.
- Stir with a mixing spoon for 8–10 seconds. Serve immediately.

Variation: Mauresque à l'Absinthe

Replacing the grenadine with orgeat syrup gives a Mauresque à l'Absinthe, an almond-flavoured short drink that is ideal as an aperitif.

Vermouth-Cassis

Short drink to serve as an aperitif

FOR 1 GLASS

3–4 ice cubes

1½ measures dry vermouth

⅓ measure crème de cassis

1 strip unwaxed lemon peel (zest)

- Place the ice, vermouth and crème de cassis in a rocks glass.
- Stir with a mixing spoon for 8–10 seconds.
- Cut the strip of lemon peel with a paring knife. Over the glass, pinch it between the fingers to release the oils then drop it into the cocktail. Serve immediately.

Thirst-quenching cocktails

American Lemonade

Long drink to serve
at any time

FOR 1 GLASS

¾ measure fresh lemon juice

3 measures chilled still mineral water

1¼ measures red Bordeaux wine

- Place the lemon juice and the very cold mineral water in a highball glass.
- Slowly add the red wine, pouring it over a mixing spoon so that it floats on the top (▷ p. 58). Serve immediately, leaving your guest to stir their own drink.

Apricot Cooler

Long drink to serve at any time

FOR 1 GLASS

4–5 ice cubes

¾ measure apricot brandy

⅓ measure fresh lemon juice

1 teaspoon grenadine

3¼ measures soda water (club soda)

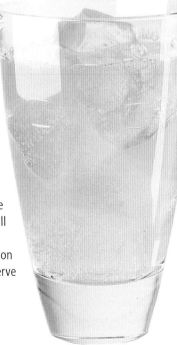

- Place the ice and all the ingredients in a highball glass.
- Stir with a mixing spoon for 8–10 seconds. Serve immediately.

Basic

Long drink to serve
at any time

FOR 1 GLASS

4–5 ice cubes

¾ measure crème de framboise

¾ measure fresh grapefruit juice

⅓ measure fresh lemon juice

⅓ measure orgeat syrup

2¼ measures tonic water

• Place the ice and all the ingredients in a highball glass.

• Stir with a mixing spoon for 8–10 seconds. Serve immediately.

Berry Sour

Short drink to serve
at any time

FOR 1 GLASS

4–5 ice cubes

½ measure crème de fraise

¼ measure crème de mûre

¾ measure fresh lemon juice

• Place the ice and all the ingredients in the lower part of the shaker.

• Fit the upper part of the shaker and shake vigorously for 8–10 seconds.

• Pour into a rocks glass. Serve immediately.

Cherry Cooler

Long drink to serve
at any time

FOR 1 GLASS

4–5 ice cubes

½ measure cherry brandy

½ measure maraschino liqueur

½ measure fresh lemon juice

3 measures soda water (club soda)

1 maraschino cherry

½ slice unwaxed lemon

• Place the ice and all the ingredients except the cherry and lemon slice into a highball glass.

• Stir with a mixing spoon for 8–10 seconds.

• Add the cherry and lemon slice to the drink. Serve immediately.

A few ideas for snacks to serve with cocktails based on other forms of alcohol:

- bite-sized pieces of polenta with Parma ham (prosciutto)
- bruschetta with mozzarella and artichokes
- prawns (shrimp) flavoured with almonds and paprika
- aubergine (eggplant) rolls with tomatoes and (bell) peppers
- cream of chestnut delight

▶ **recipes page 284**

Klondike Highball

Long drink to serve at any time

FOR 1 GLASS

4–5 ice cubes

½ measure red vermouth

½ measure dry vermouth

½ measure fresh lemon juice

2 teaspoons sugar cane syrup

2¾ measures ginger ale

1 segment unwaxed orange

• Place the ice and all the ingredients except the orange segment in a highball glass.

• Stir with a mixing spoon for 8–10 seconds.

• Add the orange segment to the drink. Serve immediately.

An immediate success

The Pimm's Cup (▷ below) was named after James Pimm, proprietor of an oyster bar in London. In the 1840s his restaurant used to serve its customers a cup based on gin, flavoured with herbs and spices. It was so well received that in 1859 he marketed it under the name of Pimm's. Twenty years later there were six different varieties of Pimm's on offer, based on gin, Scotch whisky, Cognac, rum, rye whiskey and vodka. Nowadays only the gin-based No 1 is still available.

Pimm's Cup

Long drink to serve at any time

FOR 1 GLASS

1 cucumber

4–5 ice cubes

1 measure Pimm's No 1

3½ measures soda water (club soda)

• Wash the cucumber in cold water. Using a paring knife, cut a very thin strip about 1 cm (½ inch) thick, 2 cm (¾ inch) wide and 10 cm (4 inches) long.

• Place the ice, Pimm's and soda water in a highball glass.

• Stir with a mixing spoon for 8–10 seconds.

• Add the strip of cucumber to the drink. Serve immediately.

Tampico

Long drink to serve
at any time

FOR 1 GLASS

4–5 ice cubes

½ measure Campari

½ measure curaçao triple sec

½ measure fresh lemon juice

3 measures tonic water

½ slice unwaxed orange

- Place the ice and all the ingredients except the orange slice in a highball glass.
- Stir with a mixing spoon for 8–10 seconds.
- Add the orange slice to the drink. Serve immediately.

Fruit-based cocktails

Fuzzy Navel

Long drink to serve at any time

FOR 1 GLASS

4–5 ice cubes

1 measure peach schnapps

3½ measures pure orange juice

1 segment unwaxed orange

- Place the ice, peach schnapps and orange juice in a highball glass.
- Stir with a mixing spoon for 8–10 seconds.
- Cut a slit in the orange segment and fix it to the rim of the glass. Serve immediately.

Garibaldi

Long drink to serve
at any time

FOR 1 GLASS

4–5 ice cubes

1 measure Campari

3½ measures pure orange juice

- Place the ice and Campari in a highball glass.
- Slowly pour in the orange juice. Serve immediately without stirring.

Variation: Bahamian

The Bahamian, a rather sweeter long drink, is made using pure pineapple juice instead of the orange juice. Ideal to drink at any time.

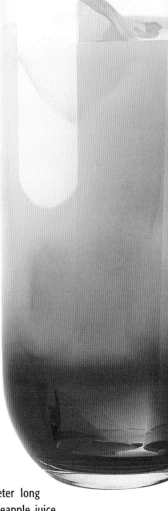

Sangria

Short drink to serve at any time

FOR 10 GLASSES

1 bottle (75 cl) Rioja wine

1½ measures Cognac

1½ measures curaçao triple sec

1½ measures fresh orange juice

6 lumps sugar

1 stick cinnamon

18 ice cubes

6¼ measures soda water (club soda)

10 slices unwaxed lime

10 slices unwaxed lemon

10 slices unwaxed orange

- Place all the ingredients except the ice, soda water and fruit slices in a salad bowl and stir well. Cover with clingfilm (plastic wrap) and leave in a refrigerator for at least 4 hours.
- Add the ice, soda water and fruit slices.
- Stir and serve, putting 1–2 ice cubes and a slice of each fruit in each wine glass.

Sangria, whose origins are unknown, is the Spanish national drink. There are many ways of preparing it.

Scarlett O'Hara

Short drink to serve at any time

FOR 1 GLASS

5–6 ice cubes

¾ measure Southern Comfort

¾ measure cranberry juice (based on fruit concentrate)

¼ measure fresh lime juice

- Place the ice and all the ingredients in the lower part of the shaker.
- Fit the upper part of the shaker and shake vigorously for 8–10 seconds.
- Strain into a Martini glass using a cocktail strainer. Serve immediately.

Variation: Spitfire

Replacing the cranberry juice with orange juice and adding 2–3 drops of absinthe-flavoured spirit gives a Spitfire, a more aniseed- (anise-) flavoured short drink for any time of the day.

Tiger Tail

Short drink to serve at any time

FOR 1 GLASS

3–4 ice cubes

½ measure Pernod

2 measures pure orange juice

- Place the ice and all the ingredients in a rocks glass.
- Stir with a mixing spoon for 8–10 seconds. Serve immediately.

Variation: Boccie Ball

The Boccie Ball is made by replacing the Pernod with amaretto. This almond-flavoured short drink is ideal at any time.

Liqueur-based cocktails

B-52

Short drink to serve in the evening

FOR 1 GLASS

¼ measure coffee liqueur

¼ measure Irish Cream

¼ measure Grand Marnier Cordon Rouge

• Place the coffee liqueur in a shot glass then float the Irish Cream on top using a mixing spoon (▷ p. 58).
• Add the Grand Marnier Cordon Rouge in the same way, making three layers in all. Serve immediately.

Variation: B-55

Replacing the Grand Marnier with absinthe-flavoured spirit gives a B-55, an aniseed- (anise-) flavoured short drink that is ideal for the evening.

Ferrari

Short drink to serve as a digestif

FOR 1 GLASS

3–4 ice cubes

¾ measure dry vermouth

¾ measure amaretto

• Place the ice and all the ingredients in a rocks glass.
• Stir with a mixing spoon for 8–10 seconds. Serve immediately.

Smooth cocktails

Banana Banshee

Short drink to serve as a digestif

FOR 1 GLASS

5–6 ice cubes

¾ measure crème de banane

½ measure white crème de cacao

½ measure single (light) cream

1 nutmeg

• Place the ice and all the ingredients except the nutmeg in the lower part of the shaker.
• Fit the upper part of the shaker and shake vigorously for 8–10 seconds.
• Strain into a Martini glass using a cocktail strainer.
• Grate a sprinkling of nutmeg over the top of the drink. Serve immediately.

Dusty Rose

Short drink to serve as a digestif

FOR 1 GLASS

5–6 ice cubes

¾ measure cherry brandy

½ measure white crème de cacao

½ measure single (light) cream

• Place the ice and all the ingredients in the lower part of the shaker.
• Fit the upper part of the shaker and shake vigorously for 8–10 seconds.
• Strain into a Martini glass using a cocktail strainer. Serve immediately.

Golden Cadillac

Short drink to serve as a digestif

FOR 1 GLASS

5–6 ice cubes

½ measure Galliano

½ measure white crème de cacao

½ measure single (light) cream

1 square plain dark (semi-sweet) chocolate (70%)

• Place the ice and all the ingredients except the chocolate in the lower part of the shaker.
• Fit the upper part of the shaker and shake vigorously for 8–10 seconds.
• Strain into a Martini glass using a cocktail strainer.
• Grate the chocolate over the drink with a nutmeg grater. Serve immediately.

Golden Dream

Short drink to serve as a digestif

FOR 1 GLASS

5–6 ice cubes

½ measure Galliano

½ measure fresh orange juice

¼ measure curaçao triple sec

½ measure single (light) cream

• Place the ice and all the ingredients in the lower part of the shaker.
• Fit the upper part of the shaker and shake vigorously for 8–10 seconds.
• Strain into a Martini glass using a cocktail strainer. Serve immediately.

Grasshopper

Short drink to serve as a digestif

FOR 1 GLASS

5–6 ice cubes

½ measure green crème de menthe

½ measure white crème de cacao

¾ measure single (light) cream

• Place the ice and all the ingredients in the lower part of the shaker.

• Fit the upper part of the shaker and shake vigorously for 8–10 seconds.

• Strain into a Martini glass using a cocktail strainer. Serve immediately.

Hot Shot

Short drink to serve as a digestif

FOR 1 GLASS

¼ measure Galliano

¾ measure double (heavy) cream

¼ measure hot espresso coffee

• Whip the cream in a bowl with a fork until it thickens.

• Place the Galliano and hot coffee in a shot glass.

• Float ¼ measure of the whipped cream on the top. Serve immediately.

Hot cocktail

Hot Wine

Long drink to serve as a digestif

FOR 7 GLASSES

½ unwaxed orange

½ unwaxed lemon

75 cl (1 bottle) red wine

8¾ measures still mineral water

2 measures sugar cane syrup

2 sticks cinnamon

2 mixing spoons cloves

• Cut the orange and lemon halves into slices.

• Place all the ingredients in a saucepan and leave to macerate for 30 minutes.

• Heat gently to simmering point – do not let it come fully to the boil.

• Ladle the drink into heat-proof toddy glasses. Serve immediately.

Alcohol-free cocktails

Fruit juices and syrups are produced on every continent, according to the raw materials found there.
▷ See also p. 312

Alcohol-free cocktails enjoyed considerable success in the United States during the Prohibition period. Their principal ingredients are fruit juices (freshly squeezed, commercial pure fruit juices, fruit nectar or juices reconstituted from concentrates) and certain vegetable juices. Some milkshakes too are, in fact, delicious non-alcoholic cocktails. Mastering the appropriate combinations is an essential factor in successful alcohol-free cocktail mixing.

Fruit juices and vegetable juices are often diluted with water or soda (club soda), and combined with syrups to produce a final flavour.

Syrups here play a similar role to that of liqueurs in alcoholic cocktails, adding sweetness and flavour to the drink and softening the natural acidity of citrus fruits. The grenadine in a Pussy Foot (▷ p. 267) or the sugar cane syrup in the Florida (▷ p. 250) and the Southside Cooler (▷ p. 253) are good examples. On the other hand, the juice of citrus fruits (lemon, lime, orange, grapefruit) tone down the sweetness of other juices, such as the passion fruit in the Yellow Bear (▷ p. 261), the pineapple juice in the Cinderella (▷ p. 255) or the carrot juice in a Rabbit Cooler (▷ p. 263).

THE TEN INDISPUTABLE CLASSICS

Thirst-quenching cocktails

Apple Pilar

Long drink to serve
at any time

FOR 1 GLASS

1 sprig fresh mint

4–5 ice cubes

1½ measures pure apple juice

2 teaspoons sugar cane syrup

2¾ measures ginger ale

- Wash the mint, place in a highball glass and crush slightly with a pestle.
- Add the ice and the remaining ingredients to the glass.
- Stir with a mixing spoon for 8-10 seconds. Serve immediately.

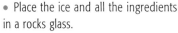 This recipe was created in 1994 by Colin Field at the Hemingway Bar of The Ritz Hotel in Paris. He named it after a fishing boat of which Ernest Hemingway was particularly fond, called the *Pilar*. This is on display at the writer's house in San Francisco de Paula in Cuba, now a museum.

Apple Sparkle

Short drink to serve
at any time

FOR 1 GLASS

3–4 ice cubes

1½ measures pure apple juice

¾ measure lemon-lime soda

1 teaspoon raspberry syrup

- Place the ice and all the ingredients in a rocks glass.
- Stir with a mixing spoon for 8–10 seconds. Serve immediately.

Asian Passion

Short drink to serve at any time

FOR 1 GLASS

3–4 ice cubes

¾ measure lychee (litchi) juice (based on fruit concentrate)

¾ measure passion fruit juice (based on fruit concentrate)

1 measure ginger ale

- Place the ice and all the ingredients in a rocks glass.
- Stir with a mixing spoon for 8–10 seconds. Serve immediately.

Bora Bora Brew

Long drink to serve at any time

FOR 1 GLASS

1 slice fresh pineapple, 1 cm (½ inch) thick

4–5 ice cubes

3 measures pure pineapple juice

1¼ measures ginger ale

¼ measure grenadine

- Cut a triangular piece from the unpeeled pineapple slice.
- Place the ice and the remaining ingredients into a highball glass.
- Stir with a mixing spoon for 8–10 seconds.
- Cut a slit in the piece of pineapple and fix it to the rim of the glass. Serve immediately.

Bull's Eye

Long drink to serve at any time

FOR 1 GLASS

4–5 ice cubes

1 measure fresh orange juice

2 teaspoons sugar cane syrup

3¼ measures ginger ale

1 slice unwaxed orange

- Place the ice, orange juice, sugar cane syrup and ginger ale in a highball glass.
- Stir with a mixing spoon for 8–10 seconds.
- Add the orange slice. Serve immediately.

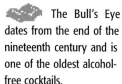 The Bull's Eye dates from the end of the nineteenth century and is one of the oldest alcohol-free cocktails.

Florida

Long drink to serve
at any time

FOR 1 GLASS

4–5 ice cubes

1½ measures pure orange juice

1 measure fresh grapefruit juice

1 measure soda water (club soda)

2 teaspoons sugar cane syrup

½ measure fresh lemon juice

• Place the ice and all the ingredients in a highball glass.
• Stir with a mixing spoon for 8–10 seconds. Serve immediately.

This alcohol-free cocktail was very popular at the start of the 1920s in London.

Grapefruit Cooler

Long drink to serve
at any time

FOR 1 GLASS

4–5 ice cubes

2 measures pure
grapefruit juice

2 measures soda water
(club soda)

½ measure grenadine

• Place the ice and all
the ingredients in a highball glass.
• Serve immediately with-
out stirring.

Iced Tea

Long drink to serve
at any time

FOR 1 GLASS

3¾ measures Ceylon tea

4–5 ice cubes

⅓ measure fresh
lemon juice

2 teaspoons sugar
cane syrup

1 slice unwaxed lemon

• Make the tea, then strain it and let it go cold.
• Place the ice, tea, lemon juice and sugar cane syrup in the lower part of the shaker.
• Fit the upper part of the shaker and shake vigorously for 8–10 seconds.
• Pour the mixture into a highball glass.
• Add the lemon slice to the drink. Serve immediately.

Lemonade

Long drink to serve at any time

FOR 1 GLASS

4–5 ice cubes

½ measure fresh lemon juice

2 teaspoons sugar cane syrup

3¾ measures still mineral water

½ slice unwaxed lemon

- Place the ice, lemon juice, sugar cane syrup and water in a highball glass.
- Stir with a mixing spoon for 8–10 seconds.
- Add the lemon slice to the drink. Serve immediately.

Mango Sparkle

Short drink to serve at any time

FOR 1 GLASS

3–4 ice cubes

1¼ measures mango juice
(based on fruit concentrate)

½ measure pure apple juice

¾ measure lemon-lime soda

1 slice unwaxed lime

- Place the ice, mango and apple juices and lemon-lime soda in a rocks glass.
- Stir with a mixing spoon for 8–10 seconds.
- Add the lime slice to the drink. Serve immediately.

Passion Cooler

Long drink to serve at any time

FOR 1 GLASS

4–5 ice cubes

2½ measures passion fruit juice
(based on fruit concentrate)

1½ measures lemon-lime soda

½ measure fresh lemon juice

- Place the ice and all the ingredients in a highball glass.
- Stir with a mixing spoon for 8–10 seconds. Serve immediately.

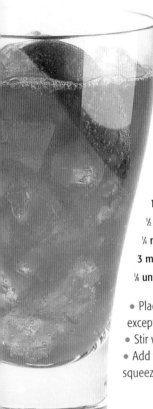

Planter's Punchless

Long drink to serve at any time

FOR 1 GLASS

4–5 ice cubes

1 measure pure apple juice

½ measure fresh lime juice

¼ measure grenadine

3 measures lemon-lime soda

⅛ unwaxed lime

• Place the ice and all the ingredients except the lime segment in a highball glass.
• Stir with a mixing spoon for 8–10 seconds.
• Add the lime segment to the drink without squeezing it. Serve immediately.

Purple Pash

Long drink to serve at any time

FOR 1 GLASS

4–5 ice cubes, crushed
(▷ p. 59)

2¾ measures lychee (litchi) juice (based on fruit concentrate)

1½ measures soda water (club soda)

⅛ measure raspberry syrup

1 slice unwaxed lime

• Place the crushed ice and all the ingredients except the lime slice in a highball glass.
• Stir with a mixing spoon for 8–10 seconds.
• Add the lime slice. Serve immediately.

Raspberry Squash

Short drink to serve at any time

FOR 1 GLASS

3–4 ice cubes

½ measure fresh lemon juice

1¾ measures soda water (club soda)

¼ measure raspberry syrup

1 slice unwaxed lemon

• Place the ice, lemon juice, soda water and raspberry syrup in a rocks glass.
• Stir with a mixing spoon for 8–10 seconds.
• Add the lemon slice to the drink. Serve immediately.

Variation: Lemon Squash
Replace the raspberry syrup with sugar cane syrup and you have Lemon Squash, a short drink with a more pronounced lemon flavour, ideal to drink at any time. This was one of the most popular short, non-alcoholic cocktails at the end of the nineteenth century.

Shirley Temple

Long drink to serve at any time

FOR 1 GLASS

4–5 ice cubes

2 measures ginger ale

2 measures lemon-lime soda

¼ measure grenadine

⅛ unwaxed lime

- Place the ice and all the ingredients except the lime segment in a highball glass.
- Stir with a mixing spoon for 8–10 seconds.
- Squeeze the lime segment over the glass then add it to the drink. Serve immediately.

A cocktail for a 'little princess'

The long drink called a Shirley Temple (▷ left) was so named in tribute to the child star (photographed here in 1934) of Hollywood movies in the 1930s, who President Franklin D Roosevelt congratulated on her 'contagious optimism'. Born in 1928 in California, she starred in 40 or so movies in the years between 1931 and 1949, including Walter Lang's 1939 movie, The Little Princess.

Southside Cooler

Long drink to serve at any time

FOR 1 GLASS

3–4 fresh mint leaves, plus 1 sprig fresh mint

8–10 ice cubes

½ measure fresh lime juice

2 teaspoons sugar cane syrup

3¾ measures soda water (club soda)

½ slice unwaxed lime

- Wash all the mint in cold water. Place 5–6 ice cubes, the mint leaves, lime juice and sugar cane syrup in the lower part of the shaker.
- Fit the upper part of the shaker and shake vigorously for 8–10 seconds.
- Place 3–4 ice cubes in a highball glass then strain the contents of the shaker into the glass, using both a cocktail strainer and a pulp strainer.
- Add the soda water, the lime slice and the mint sprig. Serve immediately.

Strawberry Cooler

Long drink to serve
at any time

FOR 1 GLASS

4 fresh strawberries

4–5 ice cubes

⅓ measure fresh lemon juice

2 teaspoons sugar cane syrup

2½ measures soda water (club soda)

- Wash the strawberries in cold water and save a quarter of one fruit for decoration.
- Crush the rest to a purée with a pestle.
- Place the ice, lemon juice, sugar cane syrup and strawberry purée in the lower part of the shaker.
- Fit the upper part of the shaker and shake vigorously for 8–10 seconds.
- Pour the mixture into a highball glass. Add the soda water and the strawberry quarter. Serve immediately.

Fruit-based cocktails

Baby Breeze

Long drink to serve
at any time

FOR 1 GLASS

1 slice fresh pineapple about 1 cm (½ inch) thick

4–5 ice cubes

2½ measures pure pineapple juice

1¾ measures cranberry juice (based on fruit concentrate)

¼ measure fresh lime juice

- Cut a triangular piece from the unpeeled pineapple slice.
- Place the ice and the remaining ingredients in the lower part of the shaker.
- Fit the upper part of the shaker and shake vigorously for 8–10 seconds.
- Pour the mixture into a highball glass.
- Cut a slit in the piece of pineapple and fix it to the rim of the glass. Serve immediately.

Banana Juicer

Long drink to serve
at any time

FOR 1 GLASS

4–5 ice cubes

2½ measures banana
nectar

2 measures pure
apple juice

¼ measure fresh lime
juice

- Place the ice and
all the ingredients in
the lower part of the
shaker.
- Fit the upper part of
the shaker and shake
vigorously for 8–10
seconds.
- Pour the mixture into a highball glass.
Serve immediately.

California Smoothie

Long drink to serve
at any time

FOR 1 GLASS

4 fresh strawberries

3–4 ice cubes, crushed
(▷ p. 59)

2¾ measures pure orange juice

2 teaspoons sugar cane syrup

- Wash the strawberries in cold water.
- Place the crushed ice and all the
ingredients in a blender.
- Blend at low speed for 20–30 seconds.
- Pour the contents of the blender into a
highball glass. Serve immediately.

Cinderella

Short drink to serve
at any time

FOR 1 GLASS

3–4 ice cubes

1¼ measures pure orange juice

1¼ measures pure pineapple juice

½ measure fresh lemon juice

- Place the ice and all the ingredients in
the lower part of the shaker.
- Fit the upper part of the shaker and shake
vigorously for 8–10 seconds.
- Pour the mixture into a rocks glass. Serve
immediately.

Cranberry Colada

Long drink to serve at any time

FOR 1 GLASS

4–5 ice cubes

3½ measures cranberry juice (based on fruit concentrate)

8 mixing spoons coconut milk (canned)

- Place the ice, cranberry juice and coconut milk in the lower part of the shaker.
- Fit the upper part of the shaker and shake vigorously for 8–10 seconds.
- Pour the mixture into a highball glass. Serve immediately.

Crazy Navel

Long drink to serve at any time

FOR 1 GLASS

4–5 ice cubes

2½ measures pure orange juice

1¾ measures peach nectar

¼ measure grenadine

1 segment unwaxed orange

- Place the ice and all the ingredients except the orange segment in the lower part of the shaker.
- Fit the upper part of the shaker and shake vigorously for 8–10 seconds.
- Pour the mixture into a highball glass.
- Add the orange segment to the drink. Serve immediately.

Gentle Breeze

Long drink to serve at any time

FOR 1 GLASS

4–5 ice cubes

2½ measures pure grapefruit juice

1¾ measures cranberry juice (based on fruit concentrate)

¼ measure fresh lime juice

1 slice unwaxed lime

- Place the ice and fruit juices in the lower part of the shaker.
- Fit the upper part of the shaker and shake vigorously for 8–10 seconds.
- Pour the mixture into a highball glass.
- Add the lime slice to the drink. Serve immediately.

Madras Special

Long drink to serve at any time

FOR 1 GLASS

4–5 ice cubes

2½ measures pure orange juice

1¾ measures cranberry juice (based on fruit concentrate)

¼ measure fresh lemon juice

1 slice unwaxed orange

- Place the ice and the fruit juices in the lower part of the shaker.
- Fit the upper part of the shaker and shake vigorously for 8–10 seconds.
- Pour the mixture into a highball glass.
- Add the orange slice to the drink. Serve immediately.

Mango Breeze

Long drink to serve at any time

FOR 1 GLASS

4–5 ice cubes

3¼ measures mango juice (based on fruit concentrate)

1 measure cranberry juice (based on fruit concentrate)

¼ measure fresh lime juice

- Place the ice and all the ingredients in the lower part of the shaker.
- Fit the upper part of the shaker and shake vigorously for 8–10 seconds.
- Pour the mixture into a highball glass. Serve immediately.

My Sky

Short drink to serve at any time

FOR 1 GLASS

1 red apple

3–4 ice cubes

1¾ measures pure apple juice

½ measure fresh lime juice

¼ measure orgeat syrup

- Wash the apple. Quarter it and cut 2 fine slices from one of the pieces.
- Place the ice, apple juice, lime juice and orgeat syrup in the lower part of the shaker.
- Fit the upper part of the shaker and shake vigorously for 8–10 seconds.
- Pour the mixture into a rocks glass.
- Add the fine slices of apple to the drink. Serve immediately.

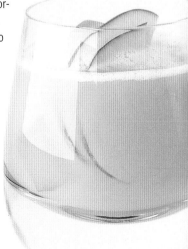

A few ideas for snacks to serve with alcohol-free cocktails:

- lettuce and tuna mousse purses
- sweet red (bell) pepper omelette (omelet)
- mini kebabs with courgette (zucchini), mint, feta cheese and black olives
- tzatziki with concassé of tomato
- a jumble of fruit dressed with orange flower water

▶ recipes page 286

The start of Prohibition

The ban on consuming alcohol began in 1845 in the state of Maine. The year 1869 saw the creation of the Prohibition Party and in 1893 the Anti-Saloons League launched an anti-alcohol propaganda campaign on a nationwide scale. On 16 January 1919, 36 states ratified an amendment banning the production, sale and consumption of alcoholic drinks of more than 0.5% Vol/1° proof. Finally, in October 1919 the National Prohibition Act was passed. Enforcement of this law gave rise to some spectacular measures, such as the police – seen here in the photo – emptying barrels of beer in the street.

Pain Cutter

Long drink to serve at any time

FOR 1 GLASS

4–5 ice cubes

1¾ measures pure orange juice

1¾ measures pure pineapple juice

8 mixing spoons coconut milk (cannned)

1 slice fresh pineapple, 5 mm (¼ inch) thick

• Place the ice, fruit juices and coconut milk in the lower part of the shaker.
• Fit the upper part of the shaker and shake vigorously for 8–10 seconds.
• Pour the mixture into a highball glass.
• Add the pineapple slice to the drink. Serve immediately.

Passion Breeze

Long drink to serve at any time

FOR 1 GLASS

4–5 ice cubes

1½ measures pure orange juice

1½ measures passion fruit juice (based on fruit concentrate)

1½ measures cranberry juice (based on fruit concentrate)

• Place the ice and all the ingredients in the lower part of the shaker.
• Fit the upper part of the shaker and shake vigorously for 8–10 seconds.
• Pour the mixture into a highball glass. Serve immediately.

Pink Banana

Short drink to serve
at any time

FOR 1 GLASS

3–4 ice cubes

2 measures banana nectar

¾ measure fresh
orange juice

¼ measure grenadine

• Place the ice and all the
ingredients in the lower
part of the shaker.
• Fit the upper part of the
shaker and shake vigorously
for 8–10 seconds.
• Pour the mixture into a rocks
glass. Serve immediately.

Virgin Colada

Long drink to serve
at any time

FOR 1 GLASS

4–5 ice cubes

3½ measures pure
pineapple juice

8 mixing spoons coconut
milk (cannned)

¼ slice fresh pineapple
about 5 mm (¼ inch) thick

• Place the ice and all
the ingredients except
the pineapple slice in
the lower part of the shaker.
• Fit the upper part of the shaker and shake
vigorously for 8–10 seconds.
• Pour the mixture into a highball glass.
• Add the pineapple slice to the drink.
Serve immediately.

Yellow Bear

Short drink to serve
at any time

FOR 1 GLASS

3–4 ice cubes

1¾ measures passion fruit juice
(based on fruit concentrate)

½ measure fresh lemon juice

¼ measure lime juice cordial

• Place the ice and all the ingredients in
the lower part of the shaker.
• Fit the upper part of the shaker and
shake vigorously for 8–10 seconds.
• Pour the mixture into a rocks glass.
Serve immediately.

Vegetable-based cocktails

Bunny Shame

Long drink to serve at any time

FOR 1 GLASS

5–6 ice cubes

4 measures pure carrot juice

¼ measure fresh lemon juice

1 teaspoon Worcestershire sauce

3–4 drops red Tabasco sauce

1 pinch celery salt

1 pinch black pepper

- Place the ice and all the ingredients in a mixing glass.
- Stir with a mixing spoon for 8–10 seconds.
- Strain into a highball glass using a cocktail strainer. Serve immediately.

This cocktail will please those who like highly flavoured drinks.

Cucumber Cooler

Long drink to serve at any time

FOR 2 GLASSES

½ cucumber

1 measure fresh lime juice

2 teaspoons sugar cane syrup

8–10 ice cubes

5 measures soda water (club soda)

- Wash the cucumber half in cold water and cut into pieces.
- Place the lime juice, sugar cane syrup and cucumber pieces into a blender.
- Blend at low speed for 5–10 seconds then at high speed for 15–30 seconds.
- Place the ice in 2 highball glasses.
- Pour half the contents of the blender into each glass. Add the soda water. Stir and serve immediately.

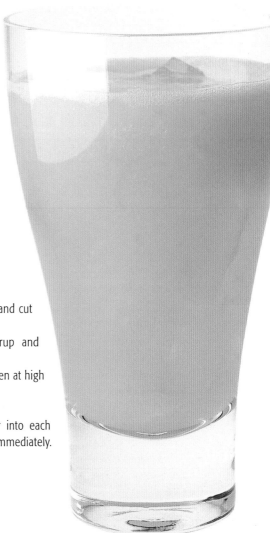

Holy Mary

Long drink to serve at any time

FOR 1 GLASS

5–6 ice cubes

4 measures pure tomato juice

1 teaspoon fresh lemon juice

1 teaspoon Worcestershire sauce

3–4 drops red Tabasco sauce

1 pinch celery salt

1 pinch black pepper

- Place the ice and all the ingredients in a mixing glass.
- Stir with a mixing spoon for 8–10 seconds.
- Strain into a highball glass using a cocktail strainer. Serve immediately.

This cocktail is also called a Virgin Mary or a Bloody Shame.

Rabbit Cooler

Long drink to serve at any time

FOR 1 GLASS

4–5 ice cubes

2¾ measures pure carrot juice

1½ measures soda water (club soda)

¼ measure fresh lime juice

1 strip unwaxed lime peel (zest)

- Place the ice, carrot juice, soda water and lime juice in a highball glass.
- Stir with a mixing spoon for 8–10 seconds.
- Cut the strip of lime peel with a paring knife. Over the glass, pinch it between the fingers to release the oils then drop it into the cocktail. Serve immediately.

1933, the end of American Prohibition

During Prohibition, the sale of alcoholic drinks was entirely in the hands of gangs – bootleggers – whose rivalry frequently became extremely violent. The St Valentine's Day Massacre, which took place in Chicago on 14 February 1929, was one example. These were the glory days of Al Capone and the Crime Syndicate, but also the great era of clandestine bars. Faced with the failure of Prohibition, President Franklin D Roosevelt proposed its abolition in his electoral programme of 1932. The amendment that finally ended it was voted in on 6 December 1933. The news provoked jubilant scenes among the opponents of Prohibition: in the photograph on the left, a New York crowd cheers as a truck-load of beer barrels leaves a brewery.

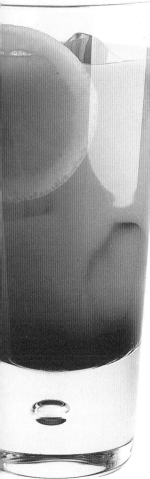

Rabbit Sunrise

Long drink to serve at any time

FOR 1 GLASS

4–5 ice cubes

3 measures pure carrot juice

1 measure fresh orange juice

1 teaspoon fresh lemon juice

¼ measure grenadine

1 slice lemon

• Place the ice, carrot juice, orange and lemon juices in a highball glass.
• Stir with a mixing spoon for 8–10 seconds.
• Slowly pour the grenadine into the centre of the glass.
• Add the lemon slice to the drink. Serve immediately.

Tomato & Cucumber Sparkle

Long drink to serve at any time

FOR 2 GLASSES

½ cucumber

1½ measures pure tomato juice

2 teaspoons sugar cane syrup

½ measure fresh lemon juice

8–10 ice cubes

4 measures soda water (club soda)

• Wash the cucumber half in cold water and cut into pieces.
• Place the tomato juice, sugar cane syrup, lemon juice and cucumber pieces in a blender.
• Blend at low speed for 5–10 seconds then at high speed for 15–30 seconds.
• Place the ice in 2 highball glasses. Pour half the contents of the blender into each glass. Add the soda water. Stir and serve immediately.

Smooth cocktails

Golden Scream

Short drink to serve as a digestif

FOR 1 GLASS

5–6 ice cubes

1 measure pure pineapple juice

½ measure single (light) cream

2 teaspoons sugar cane syrup

• Place the ice and all the ingredients in the lower part of the shaker.
• Fit the upper part of the shaker and shake vigorously for 8–10 seconds.
• Strain into a Martini glass using a cocktail strainer. Serve immediately.

Milky Mango

Long drink to serve
at any time

FOR 1 GLASS

1¾ measures mango nectar

2½ measures full-fat milk

¼ measure raspberry syrup

5–6 ice cubes

- Place the ice and all the ingredients in the lower part of the shaker.
- Fit the upper part of the shaker and shake vigorously for 8–10 seconds.
- Strain into a highball glass using a cocktail strainer. Serve immediately.

Parisette

Short drink to serve
at any time

FOR 1 GLASS

3–4 ice cubes

¼ measure grenadine

5 measures full-fat milk

- Place the ice, grenadine and milk in a highball glass.
- Stir with a mixing spoon for 4–5 seconds. Serve immediately.

Parson's Special

Long drink to serve at any time

FOR 1 GLASS

4–5 ice cubes

2 measures pure orange juice

⅓ measure fresh lemon juice

¼ measure grenadine

1 egg yolk

1¼ measures soda water (club soda)

1 slice unwaxed orange

1 slice unwaxed lemon

- Place the ice, orange juice, lemon juice, grenadine and egg yolk in the lower part of the shaker.
- Fit the upper part of the shaker and shake vigorously for 8–10 seconds.
- Pour the mixture into a highball glass. Add the soda water and stir
- Add the orange and lemon slices to the drink. Serve immediately.

Pink Pineapple

Long drink to serve
at any time

FOR 1 GLASS

4–5 ice cubes

2½ measures pure pineapple juice

1 measure soda water (club soda)

⅓ measure fresh lemon juice

⅓ measure egg white

¼ measure grenadine

- Place the ice and all the ingredients in the lower part of the shaker.
- Fit the upper part of the shaker and shake vigorously for 8–10 seconds.
- Pour the mixture into a highball glass. Serve immediately.

The use of a shaker, and particularly the addition of egg white, gives this long drink a frothy texture.

A medicinal cocktail?

The Prairie Oyster (▷ right) is much praised for its therapeutic value, especially as a remedy for headaches and all the other consequences of drinking to excess. This recipe appeared in London in the 1870s, but the cocktail would appear to have been invented in Germany, where it remained popular right up to the 1960s. To obtain maximum benefit from it, one is advised to take the whole drink into the mouth and then chew the egg yolk before swallowing.

Prairie Oyster

Short drink to serve
at any time

FOR 1 GLASS

1 egg yolk

1 teaspoon Worcestershire sauce

1 teaspoon vinegar

2 mixing spoons tomato ketchup

3–4 drops red Tabasco sauce

1 pinch black pepper

- Place all the ingredients in a rocks glass.
- Serve immediately, without stirring.

To stay as agile as a cat

The Pussy Foot (▷ right) was invented in 1920 by Robert Vermeire, barman at the Embassy Club in London. He created this alcohol-free cocktail (which originally included fresh mint) as a token of his admiration for 'Pussyfoot' Johnson, an ardent supporter of Prohibition in the United States. Johnson attempted to spread his propaganda in England in 1920, but his stay proved a short one as his ideas provoked considerable hostility among the English.

Pussy Foot

Long drink to serve at any time

FOR 1 GLASS

4–5 ice cubes

3¼ measures pure orange juice

¼ measure grenadine

¼ measure fresh lemon juice

¼ measure fresh lime juice

1 egg yolk

- Place the ice and all the ingredients in the lower part of the shaker.
- Fit the upper part of the shaker and shake vigorously for 8–10 seconds.
- Pour the mixture into a highball glass. Serve immediately.

Vanilla Milkshake

Long drink to serve at any time

FOR 1 GLASS

2 measures (2 scoops) vanilla ice cream

2½ measures milk

1 vanilla pod (bean)

- Place the ice cream and milk in a blender. Blend at slow speed for 15–20 seconds.
- Pour the mixture into a highball glass. Add the vanilla pod. Serve immediately.

Variation:
Strawberry Milkshake
Using strawberry ice cream instead of vanilla makes a strawberry milkshake, a more fruity long drink that is ideal at any time.

Cocktail snacks recipes

The art of cocktail mixing is inseparable from the pleasure of inviting a few friends for a festive gathering. Classic or unexpected, alcoholic or not, cocktails will always be more enjoyable if an assortment of cocktail snacks is served with them, especially if these are specifically chosen to bring out the qualities of the drinks – strength, sweetness, etc. And of course, the inadvisability of drinking alcohol on an empty stomach must also be borne in mind. A reasonable provision is six to eight items per person – perhaps a dozen or so if no meal is to be served. Only savoury cocktail snacks should be offered with pre-dinner aperitifs, particularly if the cocktails served are of a dry variety. Serving sweet items is only appropriate towards the end of an extended drinks gathering, or to accompany liqueur-based or smooth cocktails.

In the following pages recipes have been grouped by type of cocktail but of course, these combinations can be modified and others invented simply by alternating shapes and presentation (canapés, brochettes, 'verrines' [cocktail snacks served in small glasses], mini tartlets, garnished china spoons, etc.).

At all events, giving preference to produce in season, the judicious use of contrasting flavours, textures and colours is strongly recommended.

Each of the themes that follow offers a pretext for a gastronomic journey: salmon or herring with vodka to create a Nordic ambience, cheese and fruit combinations with gin-based drinks in the English style, coleslaw and bacon with whiskey to conjure up the North American tradition, Créole surprises with rum, guacamole and tequila to create a Mexican note, caviar and langoustines in sublimation of French Champagne, etc. There are so many possible combinations based on spices and herbs.

Most of the cocktail snacks can be made in advance, either completed the day before, or put together and then reheated just before serving. It is essential to leave plenty of time free to prepare the cocktails themselves, since these need to be served as soon as they are mixed.

Cocktail snacks to serve with vodka-based cocktails

1 Potato canapés with marinated salmon

FOR 4 PEOPLE (16 PIECES)
TO BE PREPARED 2 DAYS IN ADVANCE
PREPARATION TIME 30 MINS
COOKING TIME 15–20 MINS
MARINATING TIME 48 HRS

2 salmon fillets about 200 g (7 oz) each with skin on ▪ 3 medium Charlotte potatoes ▪ 2 sprigs fresh dill ▪ salt

FOR THE MARINADE

10 sprigs fresh dill ▪ 1½ tablespoons coarse sea salt ▪ 1 tablespoon granulated sugar ▪ ½ teaspoon crushed white peppercorns

FOR THE SAUCE

1½ tablespoons mild mustard ▪ ½ teaspoon granulated sugar ▪ 80 ml (3¼ fl oz, 5½ table-spoons) groundnut (peanut) oil ▪ 1 teaspoon wine vinegar

1 Prepare the marinade 2 days before. Wash and dry the dill and coarsely chop both the leaves and stalks. Mix with the salt, sugar and pepper.
2 Lay one salmon fillet, skin-side down, on 3 superimposed layers of cling-film (plastic wrap). Spread the marinade over the surface of the fish then lay the second fillet over it, skin-side up. Wrap the fillets in the clingfilm. Lay them in a deep dish, cover with a board and weigh down with a can of fruit or vegetables. Leave in the refrigerator for 48 hours, turning the fillets over every 12 hours.
3 On the day, cook the unpeeled potatoes in a pan of lightly salted boiling

water for 15–20 minutes. Leave them to cool, then store in the refrigerator.
4 When the potatoes are very cold, peel and cut into 16 rounds (circles) about 1 cm (½ inch) thick.
5 Unwrap the salmon fillets. Lay them skin-side down on a board and slice them finely, detaching the slices from the skin. Place 1 or 2 slices on each round of potato.
6 For the sauce, mix the mustard and sugar together. Pour on the oil slowly in a thin stream, stirring constantly, then add the vinegar.
7 Place a little of the sauce on each canapé. Garnish with dill. Serve the remaining sauce in a small dish.

2 Herring tartare and beetroot (beet) on canapés

FOR 4 PEOPLE (12 PIECES)
PREPARATION TIME 25 MINS

2 unsalted herring fillets in oil ▪ 1 small cooked beetroot (beet) ▪ 1 poppy seed, or multi-grain baguette ▪ 2 fresh chives

FOR THE SAUCE

150 g (5 oz, ⅔ cup) natural Greek (plain strained) yoghurt ▪ 5 fresh chives ▪ 2 shallots ▪ 1 teaspoon lemon juice ▪ salt and freshly ground black pepper

1 To prepare the sauce. Place the fromage frais, the chives, washed and chopped, the shallots, finely chopped, and the lemon juice in a bowl. Season with salt and pepper and mix.
2 Dry the herring fillets on kitchen paper (paper towels). Remove any bones with tweezers. Cut the herring fillets first into strips then into 5 mm (¼ inch) cubes.

3 Preheat the grill (broiler).
4 Peel the beetroot and cut into 5 mm (¼ inch) cubes.
5 Cut 12 slices of baguette and toast them on both sides.
6 Just before serving, spread each piece of toast with the cheese mixture. Divide the herring and beetroot cubes between them. Garnish with lengths of chives.

3 Cucumber 'tagliatelle' with taramasalata

FOR 4 PEOPLE (12 PIECES)
PREPARATION TIME 20 MINS

1 cucumber ▪ 125 g (4½ oz, scant ⅔ cup) taramasalata ▪ 1 tablespoon double (heavy) cream ▪ 25 g (1 oz) salmon roe caviar ▪ 2 sprigs fresh chervil ▪ fine salt

1 Wash and wipe the cucumber. Using a paring knife, peel it lengthways, leaving 1 cm (½ inch) bands unpeeled between each cut, then discard the peel. Cut off the ends. Cut 12 rounds (circles) of cucumber ½ cm (¼ inch) thick and lay them in a dish.

2 Using the paring knife, cut fine strips over the whole length of the remaining cucumber, leaving only the seedy centre part. Drop the strips into a bowl of salted iced water. Leave for 10 minutes.

3 Mix the taramasalata and cream together in a bowl.

4 Drain the cucumber strips in a sieve (strainer) and dry on kitchen paper (paper towels). Take 4 strips of cucumber and roll them around 2 fingers to form a little tub, tucking the ends under to form a base and ensuring the strip at the top of the tub has some green skin showing. Place each one on a round (circle) of cucumber. Fill with the taramasalata mixture using a small spoon.

5 Top with the salmon roe caviar. Sprinkle with tiny chervil sprigs. Refrigerate until needed.

4 Cherry tomatoes with two garnishes

FOR 4 PEOPLE (16 PIECES)
PREPARATION TIME 25 MINS
COOKING TIME 40 MINS

1 aubergine (eggplant) weighing 350 g (12 oz) ▪ 16 large cherry tomatoes ▪ 1 can diced mixed vegetables ▪ 2 tablespoons mayonnaise ▪ 6 sprigs fresh dill ▪ 1 medium onion ▪ 1 teaspoon lemon juice ▪ 3 tablespoons olive oil ▪ salt and freshly ground black pepper

1 Preheat the oven to 220°C (425°F, gas 7).

2 Wash the aubergine and dry with kitchen paper (paper towels). Line a roasting tin (pan) with foil and place the aubergine on it. Roast for 40 minutes, turning the aubergine 2 or 3 times.

3 Wash and wipe the tomatoes, leaving the stalks in place. Cut the top off each tomato to form a lid. Remove the flesh and seeds with a small spoon. Sprinkle the insides with a little salt then turn them upside down to drain on kitchen paper.

4 Drain the diced mixed vegetables in a sieve (strainer), rinse under cold running water then dry on kitchen paper.

5 Place 6 tablespoons of the diced mixed vegetables in a bowl, add the mayonnaise and mix. Wash the dill, roughly chop 3 sprigs and add to the bowl. Season with salt and pepper and mix again.

6 Peel the onion and grate it on a coarse grater into a bowl. Chop the remaining 3 sprigs of dill and add to the onion.

7 Remove the aubergine from the oven and cut it in half. Spoon the flesh into a sieve and press it with the back of a spoon. Then crush the flesh with a fork and add it to the bowl with the onion. Add the lemon juice and olive oil, season with salt and pepper and mix well.

8 Fill 8 tomatoes with the aubergine mixture and the remaining 8 tomatoes with the diced mixed vegetables. Replace the lids and serve.

5 Chopped pineapple and strawberries with rosemary

FOR 4 PEOPLE
PREPARATION TIME 20 MINS
MACERATION TIME 2 HRS

200 g (7 oz) strawberries ▪ 3 sprigs fresh rosemary about 10 cm (4 inches) long ▪ 50 g (2 oz, ¼ cup) brown sugar ▪ ½ pineapple

1 Wash and wipe the strawberries on kitchen paper (paper towels) before removing the stalks, then cut the fruit into pieces and place them in a large bowl.

2 Wash and dry the rosemary. Break off little leaves and mix with the strawberries in the bowl. Sprinkle with 2 tablespoons of sugar, cover with clingfilm (plastic wrap) and leave to marinate for 2 hours.

3 Peel the pineapple half and remove the 'eyes' with a sharp knife. Cut the flesh into small cubes on a deep plate to collect the juice. Sprinkle with the rest of the sugar.

4 Place a layer of pineapple in the base of 4 glasses, spread a layer of strawberries on top, then a second layer of pineapple and finally a layer of strawberries.

5 Strain the strawberry juice and mix with the pineapple juice. Pour it over the fruit. Decorate each glass with a rosemary sprig. Serve with small spoons.

Cocktail snacks to serve with gin-based cocktails

1 Stilton, pear and celery canapés

FOR 4 PEOPLE (8 PIECES)
PREPARATION TIME 15 MINS

1 stick (stalk) celery with leaves ▪ 1 pear ▪ 1 teaspoon lemon juice ▪ 150 g (5 oz) Stilton (or Roquefort) cheese ▪ 8 slices walnut bread

1 Wash and wipe the celery. Remove the leaves and peel the sticks to remove the threads from the surface. Cut the sticks into 7 cm (3 inch) lengths and then cut these into fine strips.
2 Peel the pear then halve it and remove the core. Cut each half into 8 segments and sprinkle with the lemon juice.
3 Using a fork, mash the cheese to a creamy consistency in a deep plate.
4 Spread the slices of bread with the cheese. Garnish each with 2 segments of pear and 2 strips of celery. Keep the canapés in a cool place until needed.

2 Curried chicken pieces with mango chutney

FOR 4 PEOPLE
PREPARE 2 DAYS IN ADVANCE
PREPARATION TIME 10 MINS + 10 MINS
COOKING TIME 1 HR + 20 MINS

300 g (11 oz) skinned chicken breast meat ▪ 1 onion ▪ 1 tablespoon olive oil ▪ 1 chicken stock cube (bouillon cube) ▪ 2 tablespoons ready-made curry paste or 1 tablespoon curry powder ▪ 100 ml (4 fl oz, 7 tablespoons) water ▪ 150 ml (¼ pint, ⅔ cup) coconut milk ▪ 4 sprigs fresh coriander (cilantro) ▪ salt and freshly ground black pepper

FOR THE MANGO CHUTNEY

1 very ripe mango ▪ 2 onions ▪ 1 tablespoon groundnut (peanut) oil ▪ 250 ml (9 fl oz, generous 1 cup) cider vinegar ▪ 150 ml (¼ pint, ⅔ cup) water ▪ ½ teaspoon ground ginger ▪ ¼ teaspoon grated nutmeg ▪ 2 cloves ▪ 150 g (5 oz, ⅔ cup) brown sugar ▪ salt and freshly ground black pepper

1 Prepare the mango chutney 2 days in advance. Peel the mango and cut into 1 cm (½ inch) cubes. Peel and chop the onions. Fry the onions in the oil over a high heat for 2 minutes. Add the vinegar, water, spices and sugar. Season with salt and pepper and bring to the boil. Leave to simmer for 30 minutes. Add the mango cubes and simmer for a further 30 minutes. Leave the chutney to cool then store in a sealed jar in the refrigerator.
2 On the day, cut the chicken breasts diagonally into strips about 1 cm (½ inch) thick, then cut into cubes. Season with salt and pepper.
3 Peel the onion and chop very finely.
4 Heat the oil in a sauté pan over a high heat. Add the chicken pieces and brown for 3 minutes then remove them from the pan. Add the chopped onion, the stock cube, crumbled, and the curry paste to the same pan and cook for 3 minutes, stirring constantly. Return the chicken to the pan and stir for 2 minutes. Add the water and coconut milk and stir again. Cook over a very low heat for 10 minutes. Leave to cool.
5 Divide the chicken mixture between 4 glasses and add a little of the mango chutney. Garnish with coriander leaves. Serve with small spoons.

3 Chicory barquettes filled with marinated smoked haddock

FOR 4 PEOPLE (12 PIECES)
PREPARATION TIME 20 MINS
MARINATING TIME 30 MINS
COOKING TIME 4 MINS

150 g (5 oz) smoked haddock with skin on ▪ 6 quails' eggs ▪ 1 head chicory ▪ salt and freshly ground black pepper

FOR THE MARINADE

2 tablespoons olive oil ▪ ½ teaspoon lemon juice ▪ ½ teaspoon green peppercorns ▪ salt

1 Wash the haddock in cold water. Dry it on kitchen paper (paper towels) then lay it on a board, skin-side down. Cut diagonally into fine slices, detaching them from the skin.

2 To make the marinade, place the oil and lemon juice in a bowl. Add the green peppercorns and crush with the back of a spoon. Salt lightly. Using a pastry brush, brush each fish slice with the marinade. Leave in a cool place for 30 minutes.

3 Cook the quails' eggs in boiling water for 4 minutes then place them in cold water to cool. When cold, peel and cut in half. Season with salt and pepper.

4 Cut the base of the chicory and separate the leaves, choosing the 12 best. Wash and dry them carefully, then top each with 4–5 strips of haddock and a half quails' egg.

4 Mini brochettes of avocado and prawns (shrimp)

FOR 4 PEOPLE (8 PIECES)
PREPARATION TIME 20 MINS

½ pink grapefruit ▪ 1 large avocado ▪ 1 tablespoon lemon juice ▪ 8 medium prawns (shrimp), shelled

FOR THE SAUCE

1 egg yolk ▪ 1 teaspoon mustard ▪ 150 ml (¼ pint, ⅔ cup) groundnut (peanut) oil ▪ 1 teaspoon lemon juice ▪ 1 tablespoon tomato ketchup ▪ few drops of Tabasco sauce ▪ salt and freshly ground black pepper

1 Peel the grapefruit with a sharp knife to remove all traces of pith. Take 4 segments and remove the membrane envelope, then cut in half lengthways. Season with salt and pepper.

2 Cut the avocado in half and remove the stone (pit). Using a Parisian ball cutter, cut 8 balls from the flesh, place them in a bowl and sprinkle with the lemon juice.

3 To prepare the sauce, mix the egg yolk and mustard together then pour on the oil in a thin stream, stirring constantly. Add the lemon juice then season with salt, pepper, tomato ketchup and Tabasco.

4 Thread 1 avocado ball, 1 piece of grapefruit and 1 prawn onto each cocktail stick (toothpick). Serve the sauce separately in a small dish.

5 Madeleines flavoured with smoked China tea

FOR 4 PEOPLE (12 PIECES)
PREPARATION TIME 10 MINS
COOKING TIME 15 MINS
RESTING TIME 3 HRS
CHILLING TIME 1 HR

115 g (4¼ oz, ½ cup plus 1 tablespoon) butter ▪ 2 tablespoons water ▪ ½ teaspoon smoked China tea leaves ▪ 2 eggs ▪ 100 g (4 oz, ½ cup) granulated sugar ▪ 115 g (4¼ oz, 1 cup plus 1 tablespoon) sifted plain (all-purpose) flour ▪ 2 pinches baking powder

1 Melt all but 1 tablespoon of the butter in a saucepan and leave to cool.

2 Boil the water in another small saucepan. Add the tea then remove from the heat. Cover and infuse for 2 minutes then pass through a tea-strainer into a bowl. Break the eggs into the bowl, add the sugar and, using a whisk, beat for 3 minutes.

3 In another bowl, mix all but 1 tablespoon of the flour with the baking powder, then sprinkle into the egg mixture, stirring with a wooden spoon until it forms a smooth mixture (batter). Gradually add the melted butter as you continue to stir. Leave to rest in the refrigerator for 3 hours.

4 Melt the remaining 1 tablespoon of butter and, using a pastry brush, paint the moulds (molds) in a madeleine tin (pan). Dust with the remaining flour then turn the tin upside down and tap to remove any excess flour.

5 Using a large spoon, almost fill each mould with the mixture, then place in the refrigerator for a further 1 hour.

6 Preheat the oven to 220°C (425°F, gas 7).

7 Bake for 15 minutes then remove from the oven, turn the tin upside down and tap the base to release the madeleines. Leave them to cool on a wire rack. Store at room temperature until needed.

Cocktail snacks to serve with whisky-based cocktails

1 Cumin-flavoured Gouda canapés with cucumber and dried figs

FOR 4 PEOPLE (12 CANAPÉS)
PREPARATION TIME 10 MINS

200 g (7 oz) cumin-flavoured Gouda cheese ■ 12 slices multi-grain baguette ■ ½ medium-sized cucumber ■ 2 pinches cumin seeds ■ 3 dried figs ■ freshly ground black pepper

1 Cut the cheese into 12 slices. Using a knife or pastry cutter, trim them to the same size as the slices of baguette.
2 Peel the cucumber and cut 12 thin slices lengthwise. Season them with pepper and a few cumin seeds.
3 Cut each fig into 4 pieces.

4 Place a round (circle) of cheese on each slice of baguette, then top with a slice of cucumber, folded in half, and a fig quarter.

2 Sweet potato crisps (chips), Gorgonzola dip and vegetable sticks

FOR 4 PEOPLE
PREPARATION TIME 30 MINS
COOKING TIME ABOUT 10 MINS

½ cucumber ■ 1 carrot ■ 2 sticks (stalks) celery ■ ½ cauliflower ■ 1 sweet potato, about 300 g (11 oz) ■ oil for deep-frying ■ 60 g (2¼ oz, ⅓ cup) pecan nuts

FOR THE GORGONZOLA DIP

100 ml (4 fl oz, 7 tablespoons) whipping cream ■ 200 g (7 oz) Gorgonzola cheese ■ 150 ml (¼ pint, ⅔ cup) double (heavy) cream ■ 1 teaspoon Worcestershire sauce ■ 5 sprigs fresh flat-leaf parsley ■ salt and freshly ground black pepper

1 Peel the cucumber half and the carrot and pull off the threads from the celery sticks. Wash them then cut into little sticks about 8 cm (3¼ inches) long and 1 cm (½ inch) wide. Break the cauliflower into little florets, then wash and dry them. Place all the vegetables in little bowls and store in the refrigerator.
2 For the dip: begin by placing a good sized bowl in the freezer for 5 minutes. Place the whipping cream in the chilled bowl and whisk it until very light and fluffy. Cut the Gorgonzola into pieces and mix together with the double cream and Worcestershire sauce. Wash the parsley, chop it and add to the

cheese mixture, season with salt and pepper. Blend to a purée then stir it into the whipped cream. Keep refrigerated.
3 Peel the sweet potato, wash and wipe it then cut into very fine slices. Preheat the deep-fat fryer. Deep-fry the slices a few at a time for 2–3 minutes. Drain on kitchen paper (paper towels).
4 Preheat the grill (broiler).
5 Chop the pecan nuts into small pieces. Spread the nuts on a baking sheet and place under the grill for 2–3 minutes.
6 Sprinkle the toasted nuts over the sweet potato crisps (chips) and serve together with the vegetable sticks and the Gorgonzola dip.

3 Mini brochettes of York ham with apricots

FOR 4 PEOPLE (24 PIECES)
PREPARATION TIME 10 MINS
COOKING TIME 10 MINS

150 ml (¼ pint, ⅔ cup) water ▦ 1 Earl Grey tea bag ▦ 4 dried apricots ▦ 1 slice York ham, about 1 cm (½ inch) thick

1 Bring the water to the boil in a small saucepan. As soon as it boils remove it from the heat and add the tea bag. Leave to infuse for 4 minutes then remove and discard the tea bag.
2 Return the pan to a low heat and add the dried apricots. Leave to simmer for 10 minutes until swollen. Drain them in a sieve (strainer) and leave to cool.

3 Remove the fat and rind from the ham and cut it into 24 cubes. Dry the apricots on kitchen paper (paper towels) and cut each into 6 pieces.
4 Thread 1 cube of ham and 1 piece of apricot onto each cocktail stick (toothpick). Place the mini brochettes in a bowl and cover with clingfilm (plastic wrap). Refrigerate until needed.

4 Mini club sandwich filled with coleslaw and bacon

FOR 4 PEOPLE (8 PIECES)
PREPARATION TIME 30 MINS
COOKING TIME ABOUT 3 MINS
CHILLING TIME 4 HRS

100 g (4 oz) bacon ▦ 1 teaspoon groundnut (peanut) oil ▦ 3 slices from a white loaf of bread

FOR THE COLESLAW

1 egg yolk ▦ 150 ml (¼ pint, ⅔ cup) groundnut (peanut) oil ▦ ½ teaspoon lemon juice ▦ 2 pinches cumin seeds (optional) ▦ 2 tablespoons double (heavy) cream ▦ 1 medium carrot ▦ ¼ white cabbage ▦ salt and freshly ground black pepper

1 To prepare the coleslaw, place the egg yolk in a bowl and stir vigorously with a wooden spoon while adding the oil in a thin stream. Sprinkle in the lemon juice. Season with salt, pepper and the cumin (if using). Stir in the cream. Peel and wash the carrot and grate it on a medium grater. Wash and dry the cabbage and slice it very finely. Add the vegetables to the sauce, mix and refrigerate for 4 hours.
2 Finely chop the bacon. Heat the oil in a small frying pan over a high heat. Add the chopped bacon and fry for 2–3 minutes, shaking the pan frequently, then drain on kitchen paper (paper towels).

3 Preheat the grill (broiler). Toast the slices of bread on both sides. Cut off the crusts and cut each slice into 8 small triangles.
4 Spread a layer of coleslaw on one triangle. Cover with a second triangle and spread this with coleslaw, then sprinkle on the bacon. Cover with a third triangle and pin together with a cocktail stick (toothpick). Repeat the process with the other triangles to make 8 pieces in all.

5 Brownies with Morello cherries

FOR 4 PEOPLE (16 PIECES)
PREPARATION TIME 15 MINS
COOKING TIME ABOUT 30 MINS

60 g (2¼ oz) plain dark (semi-sweet) chocolate ▦ 125 g (4½ oz, ½ cup plus 2 tablespoons) butter ▦ 2 eggs ▦ 200 g (7 oz, scant 1 cup) granulated sugar ▦ 50 g (2 oz, ½ cup) chopped pecan nuts ▦ 60 g (2¼ oz, ⅓ cup) sifted plain (all-purpose) flour ▦ 16 water-packed Morello cherries (or cherries in syrup).

1 Using a serrated knife, chop the chocolate on a board. Place all but 1 tablespoon butter, cut into pieces, with the chocolate in a small saucepan. Set this in a larger pan half-filled with hot water, to make a bain-marie. Place over a medium heat. Let the chocolate and butter melt gently then remove from the heat, stir well and leave to cool.
2 In a good-sized bowl, whisk the eggs and sugar together for 4 minutes. Pour on the chocolate mixture and add the chopped nuts, stirring with a wooden spoon. Incorporate the flour, sprinkling it in a fine rain while stirring vigorously.
3 Preheat the oven to 180°C (350°F, gas 4).
4 Butter a 20 cm (8 inch) square mould (mold) with the remaining 1 tablespoon of butter. Pour in the mixture (batter) in an even layer then tap the mould on the work surface (counter) to settle it down. Bake in the oven for 25 minutes.
5 Remove the cake from the oven and let it cool a little in the mould before turning out and leaving to cool completely. Cut it into 16 cubes.
6 Drain the cherries and place one on each brownie. Keep at room temperature.

Cocktail snacks to serve with rum-based cocktails

1 Barquettes of red mullet (snapper) and fondue of (bell) peppers

FOR 4 PEOPLE (8 BARQUETTES)
PREPARE THE DAY BEFORE
PREPARATION TIME 20 MINS
COOKING TIME ABOUT 12 + 30 MINS
MARINATING TIME 12 HRS

150 g (5 oz) red mullet (snapper) fillets ▪ 3 tablespoons olive oil ▪ 1 teaspoon red wine vinegar ▪ 1 tablespoons dry white wine ▪ 2 tablespoons water ▪ 1 sprig fresh thyme ▪ 1 sprig fresh rosemary ▪ 2 sprigs fresh parsley ▪ 1 bay leaf ▪ 4 pinches chilli powder ▪ ¼ green (bell) pepper ▪ ¼ red (bell) pepper ▪ 1½ teaspoons butter ▪ 75 g (3 oz) short-crust pastry (basic pie dough) ▪ salt and freshly ground black pepper ▪ fresh thyme flowers

1 Remove any bones remaining in the fish. Heat 1 tablespoon of oil in a frying pan over a high heat. Add the fish fillets and sauté for 1 minute on either side. Transfer them to a deep dish and season with salt and pepper. Add another tablespoon of oil to the pan. Add the vinegar, wine, water, herbs and 2 pinches of chilli powder. Bring to the boil and simmer for 10 minutes. Pour over the fish fillets, cover with clingfilm (plastic wrap) and refrigerate until the next day.
2 On the day, prepare the fondue of peppers: wash the peppers and cut into 3 mm (⅛ inch) cubes. Heat 1 tablespoon of oil in a frying pan. Add the peppers and cook for 10 minutes, adding 1–2 tablespoons of water as

necessary. Season with salt and pepper and 2 pinches of chilli powder.
3 Preheat the oven to 220°C (425°F, gas 7).
4 Butter 8 barquette moulds (molds) 8 cm (3¼ inches) long, and line them with pastry (dough). Prick the pastry with a fork then cover with a small piece of greaseproof (waxed) paper and some dried beans. Bake for 20 minutes. Remove the pastries from the moulds and leave to cool.
5 Drain the fish fillets and cut them into strips 5 mm (¼ inch) wide. Just before serving, spoon the fondue of peppers into the barquette moulds and top with the strips of fish. Garnish with thyme flowers.

2 Chicken and banana morsels

FOR 4 PEOPLE
PREPARATION TIME 10 MINS
COOKING TIME ABOUT 20 MINS

300 g (11 oz) chicken breast without skin ▪ 1 onion ▪ 2 cloves garlic ▪ 1 tablespoon olive oil ▪ 2 pinches ground cumin ▪ 200 g (7 oz) canned chopped tomatoes ▪ 150 ml (¼ pint, ⅔ cup) coconut milk ▪ 100 ml (4 fl oz, 7 tablespoons) water ▪ 1 small banana ▪ 1 tablespoon desiccated (shredded) coconut ▪ salt and freshly ground black pepper

1 Cut the chicken diagonally into 1 cm (½ inch) strips then cut into cubes. Season with salt and pepper.
2 Peel and chop the onion. Peel the garlic and crush it to a purée. Heat the oil in a sauté pan over a high heat. Add the chicken cubes and brown for 3 minutes. Remove them from the pan and add the onion, garlic and cumin to the pan. Stir for 2 minutes then add the tomatoes, coconut milk and water. Cook for 5 minutes, stirring

constantly. Bring to the boil and leave to simmer for 10 minutes.
3 Peel and slice the banana into rounds (circles). Place them in the sauté pan and stir well, then cover and remove from the heat.
4 Divide the chicken cubes between 4 large china spoons (or small dishes). Sprinkle with the desiccated coconut and serve hot, warm or cold, with cocktail sticks (toothpicks).

3 Prawn (shrimp) and pineapple à la Créole

FOR 4 PEOPLE (16 PIECES)
PREPARATION TIME 30 MINS
COOKING TIME ABOUT 20 MINS

1 large onion ▪ 3 tomatoes ▪ 2 cloves garlic ▪ 1 small fresh green chilli ▪ 1 tablespoon groundnut (peanut) oil ▪ 1 pinch saffron powder ▪ ½ pineapple ▪ salt and freshly ground black pepper ▪ 16 unshelled medium-sized prawns (shrimp)

1 Peel the onion. Cut it in half then slice finely. Wash the tomatoes and cut each into 8 segments. Peel the garlic cloves, cut them in half then crush to a purée. Wash and wipe the chilli. Cut it in half and remove the seeds, then chop finely.

2 Heat the oil in a sauté pan over a high heat. Add the onion slices and stir for 2 minutes, then add the tomato pieces, saffron, chopped chilli and garlic purée. Season with salt and pepper, stir well and leave to cook over a low heat for 10 minutes.

3 During this time, prepare the pineapple. Using a sharp knife, remove the flesh in even-sized pieces, starting 2 cm (¾ inch) from the skin. Collect the juice and add to the sauté pan.

4 Wash the prawns and drain them. Remove the heads and shells. Add the prawns to the sauté pan and leave to cook slowly for 5 minutes. Add the pineapple pieces, return to the boil, then remove from the heat. Leave to cool.

5 Thread cocktail sticks (toothpicks) with 1 piece of pineapple, 1 prawn and then another piece of pineapple. Serve these in the hollowed-out shell of the pineapple.

4 Stir-fried vegetables with turmeric

FOR 4 PEOPLE
PREPARATION TIME 20 MINS
COOKING TIME ABOUT 20 MINS

2 carrots ▪ ½ cucumber ▪ ½ cauliflower ▪ 100 g (4 oz) French (green) beans ▪ 1 large onion ▪ 2 cloves garlic ▪ 1 teaspoon ground ginger ▪ ½ teaspoon ground turmeric ▪ 1 pinch chilli powder ▪ 2 tablespoons groundnut (peanut) oil ▪ 1 tablespoon lemon juice ▪ salt

1 Peel the carrots and cucumber and cut into 4 cm (1½ inch) lengths. Remove the seeds from the cucumber. Cut the vegetables into little sticks.

2 Break the cauliflower into small florets. Top and tail (trim) the French beans and cut into 4 cm (1½ inch) lengths. Wash and drain them.

3 Peel and chop the onion.

4 Peel the garlic cloves and cut each into quarters. Place in a mortar with the ginger, turmeric, chilli powder and salt and crush to a purée with a pestle.

5 Heat 1 tablespoon of oil in a frying pan over a high heat. Mix together the carrot sticks, French beans and cauliflower florets, add them to the pan and cook for 10 minutes, stirring constantly. Transfer them to a bowl. Place the cucumber sticks in the pan and cook for 3 minutes then add them to the other vegetables.

6 Heat the remaining oil in the pan and add the onion. Brown for 2 minutes then add the garlic and spice mixture. Stir over the heat for 3 minutes.

7 Remove the pan from the heat and add the vegetables and lemon juice. Mix well and leave to cool. Store at room temperature until needed. Serve in 4 mini jars or small dishes, together with cocktail sticks (toothpicks).

5 Bite-sized vanilla slices

FOR 4 PEOPLE (8 PIECES)
PREPARATION TIME 20 MINS
COOKING TIME ABOUT 20 MINS

½ vanilla pod (bean) ▪ 250 ml (9 fl oz, generous 1 cup) milk ▪ 3 egg yolks ▪ 75 g (3 oz, 6 tablespoons) granulated sugar ▪ 1½ tablespoons flour ▪ 2 tablespoons butter ▪ 4 sheets filo (phyllo) pastry ▪ 2 tablespoons icing (confectioners') sugar

1 To prepare the cream, split the vanilla pod in half and scrape out the seeds. Place the seeds and pod into a saucepan with the milk and bring to the boil. In a bowl, mix the egg yolks with the sugar then mix in the flour. Pour on the boiling milk, whisking vigorously. Return the cream to the saucepan and stir over a low heat until the cream thickens. Remove from the heat, cover with clingfilm (plastic wrap) and leave to cool, then remove the vanilla pod.

2 Preheat the oven to 240°C (475°F, gas 9).

3 Melt the butter in a small saucepan over a low heat.

4 Lay one sheet of filo pastry on top of another and cut into 12 x 5 cm (2 inch) squares. Using a pastry brush, lightly brush the 24 squares with butter then sandwich them together in pairs. Do the same with the other 2 sheets of pastry. Line a baking sheet with greaseproof (waxed) paper and set the 24 double squares on it. Dredge them with 1 tablespoon of icing sugar and bake in the oven for 7–8 minutes. Leave them to cool.

5 Spread the cream onto 16 of the squares and pair them up, topping each pair with one of the remaining plain squares, spread with cream, to make 8 three-decked sandwiches. Dredge with the remaining icing sugar.

Cocktail snacks to serve with Tequila-based cocktails

1 Tex-Mex chicken wings

FOR 4 PEOPLE (16 PIECES)
PREPARATION TIME 20 MINS
COOKING TIME ABOUT 45 MINS
MARINATING TIME 2 HRS

16 chicken wings ▪ salt and freshly ground black pepper ▪ 2–3 sprigs fresh coriander (cilantro)

FOR THE MARINADE

2 onions ▪ 2 garlic cloves ▪ 2 tablespoons olive oil ▪ 2 small red chillies ▪ 200 g (7 oz) canned chopped tomatoes ▪ 150 ml (¼ pint, ⅔ cup) water ▪ 2 tablespoons wine vinegar ▪ 2 tablespoons sugar ▪ 1 teaspoon cayenne pepper ▪ salt

1 To prepare the marinade, peel the onions and garlic and chop them finely.

Heat the oil in a sauté pan over a medium heat. Add the chopped onion and garlic and cook, stirring constantly, for 5 minutes, or until softened.

2 Wash and wipe the chillies. Halve them and discard the seeds then chop them finely.

3 Add the chopped tomatoes, chopped chillies, water, vinegar, sugar and cayenne pepper to the sauté pan. Season with salt. Reduce the heat, cover and leave to simmer for 20 minutes. Leave to cool.

4 Place the chicken wings in a deep dish. Season with salt and pepper and pour the marinade over them. Leave to stand for 2 hours.

5 Preheat the oven to 200°C (400°F, gas 6).

6 Drain the chicken wings and place them onto a grill pan. Cook for 10 minutes then take them out and baste with more marinade. Return to the oven for a further 10 minutes.

7 Preheat the grill (broiler). Grill (broil) the wings for 3 minutes on each side.

8 Set the wings on a dish and garnish with the coriander. Serve warm or cold.

2 Tortilla chips with fromage frais and red (bell) peppers

FOR 4 PEOPLE
PREPARATION TIME 10 MINS
COOKING TIME 30 MINS

1 red (bell) pepper ▪ 300 g (11 oz, 1¼ cups) fromage frais or soured cream ▪ 3 pinches chilli powder ▪ 1 small red chilli ▪ 300 g (11 oz) tortilla chips ▪ salt and freshly ground black pepper

1 Preheat the oven to 220°C (425°F, gas 7).

2 Wash and wipe the pepper and place it on a baking sheet lined with foil. Cook for 30 minutes, turning it 2–3 times.

3 Seal the pepper in a plastic bag. When it has cooled take it out of the bag and cut it in half, then peel it and discard the stalk, seeds and any water generated during cooking. Cut the flesh into pieces then purée in a blender.

4 Mix the puréed pepper with the fromage frais in a large bowl, season with salt, pepper and chilli powder and mix. Garnish with the red chilli and keep refrigerated until the last minute.

5 Place the tortilla chips in a dish and serve with the fromage frais and pepper mixture as a dip.

3 Cubes of raw pollack marinated in lime and orange juice

FOR 4 PEOPLE
PREPARATION TIME 20 MINS
MACERATION TIME 4 HRS

200 g (7 oz) pollack fillets ▦ 4 limes (or lemons) ▦ 1 unwaxed orange ▦ 1 onion ▦ 2 cloves garlic ▦ 4 pinches chilli powder ▦ 6 fresh chives ▦ salt and freshly ground black pepper

1 Wash the fish under cold running water. Dry it on kitchen paper (paper towels). Remove any remaining bones with a pair of tweezers. Cut the fish into 5 mm (¼ inch) cubes and place them into a bowl.

2 Cut a lid from each lime and trim 5 mm (¼ inch) from the base so that they stand upright. Remove the pulp using a sharp knife then liquidize it in a blender to obtain 100 ml (4 fl oz, 7 tablespoons) of juice.

3 Finely cut the peel (zest) from the orange and cut into tiny sticks, then squeeze the orange to obtain 100 ml (4 fl oz, 7 tablespoons) of juice.

4 Pour the lime and orange juice over the cubes of fish.

5 Peel and chop the onion. Peel and crush the garlic. Add both these ingredients to the bowl containing the fish and stir well. Season with salt, pepper and chilli powder. Stir, cover with clingfilm (plastic wrap) and refrigerate for 4 hours.

6 Wash the chives and, using scissors, snip into short lengths over the fish. Mix well, then fill the hollowed-out limes with the mixture. Sprinkle the chopped orange peel over the top.

4 Guacamole and tomato sauce in multi-coloured layers

FOR 4 PEOPLE
PREPARATION TIME 20 MINS
COOKING TIME ABOUT 5 MINS

FOR THE TOMATO SAUCE

2 large tomatoes ▦ 1 small onion ▦ 1 clove garlic ▦ 1 small green chilli ▦ 1 tablespoon olive oil ▦ salt

FOR THE GUACAMOLE

8 sprigs fresh coriander (cilantro) [optional] ▦ 2 avocados ▦ 2 tablespoons olive oil ▦ 1 tablespoon lemon juice ▦ 2 pinches chilli powder ▦ salt and freshly ground black pepper ▦ 4 small green chillies

1 To prepare the tomato sauce, cut a cross in the base of each tomato with a sharp knife and plunge them for 30 seconds in boiling water. Drain then rinse under cold running water. Peel and cut into quarters. Remove the seeds.

2 Peel the onion and garlic. Cut them up into pieces. Wash and dry the chilli. Cut in half and remove the seeds. Place the tomato, onion, garlic and chilli in a blender and reduce to a purée. Season with salt.

3 Heat the oil in a frying pan over a high heat. Add the tomato sauce and cook for 5 minutes, stirring constantly with a wooden spoon. Leave to cool.

4 For the guacamole, wash and dry the coriander (if using). Strip the leaves from the stems and cut them up coarsely with scissors. Cut the avocados in half and remove the stones (pits) then peel and chop into pieces. Process the pieces in a blender with the oil, lemon juice, chilli powder and chopped coriander. Season with salt and pepper.

5 Fill 4 glasses with alternating layers of guacamole and tomato, ending with tomato. Garnish with the small green chillies. Serve together with small spoons.

5 Chocolate-coated strawberries

FOR 4 PEOPLE (12 PIECES)
PREPARATION TIME 10 MINS

12 strawberries ▦ 100 g (4 oz) plain dark (semi-sweet) chocolate

1 Wash the strawberries and dry carefully before removing the stalks.

2 With a serrated knife, chop the chocolate into small pieces and place it in a small saucepan. Set this in a larger pan half-filled with hot water, to form a bain-marie. Place the pan over a medium heat and allow the chocolate to melt without stirring it.

3 Remove the small pan from the water bath and stir the chocolate until smooth.

4 Working quickly, tilt the pan and prop it up with a cloth folded in 4. Dip the pointed end of each strawberry into the chocolate and twist to make sure it is well coated, then set onto a serving dish. Refrigerate the coated strawberries for 20 minutes to allow the chocolate to harden.

5 Remove the dish from the refrigerator and keep in a cool place until needed.

Cocktail snacks to serve with brandy-based cocktails

1 Panachés of rope-grown mussels with prosciutto ham

FOR 4 PEOPLE
PREPARATION TIME 20 MINS
COOKING TIME ABOUT 10 MINS

800 g (1¾ lb) rope-grown mussels ■ 1 shallot ■ 3 sprigs fresh flat-leaf parsley ■ 1½ teaspoons butter ■ 150 ml (¼ pint, ⅔ cup) dry white wine ■ 1 slice prosciutto ham, 1 cm (½ inch) thick ■ freshly ground black pepper

1 Scrape the mussels if necessary then wash in plenty of cold water and drain.

2 Peel the shallot and chop it very finely. Wash and dry the parsley and chop the leaves.

3 Melt the butter in a heavy-based casserole over a medium heat. Add the shallot and brown for 2 minutes, then add the white wine and bring to the boil. Leave to boil for 3–4 minutes to reduce the volume of liquid by one half.

4 Add the mussels to the casserole, cover and cook over a high heat for 3–4 minutes. Drain the mussels in a sieve (strainer) set over a bowl to catch the cooking liquid.

5 Take the mussels out of their shells and add them to the bowl containing the cooking liquid. Add the chopped parsley and mix well.

6 Remove the rind from the ham. Cut the meat into small cubes and add to the mussels in the bowl. Season with pepper and mix well.

7 Divide the mixture between 4 small dishes, moisten with the cooking liquid and serve, warm or cold, with small spoons or cocktail sticks (toothpicks).

2 Parmesan tuiles

FOR 4 PEOPLE (12 TUILES)
PREPARATION TIME 5 MINS
COOKING TIME ABOUT 6 MINS

60 g (2¼ oz, ⅓ cup) freshly grated Parmesan cheese ■ ½ teaspoon sifted plain (all-purpose) flour

1 Preheat the oven to 240°C (475°F, gas 9).
2 Place the Parmesan and flour in a bowl and, using a stainless steel spoon,

lift and stir until they are thoroughly mixed together.
3 Line a baking sheet with greaseproof (waxed) paper.
4 Take a heaped teaspoonful of the Parmesan mixture and place it on the sheet, using a spatula to form a disc about 7–8 cm (2¾–3¼ inches) in diameter. Repeat this process, making sure the 2 discs are well separated.
5 Bake in the oven for 3–4 minutes then remove and, using a spatula, lift the

2 tuiles and lay them over the rolling pin so that they take on a curved shape. Leave them to cool on a wire rack.
6 Repeat 5 more times.
7 Keep the tuiles in an airtight container until needed.

3 Foie gras layered with artichokes and French (green) beans

FOR 4 PEOPLE (8 PIECES)
PREPARATION TIME 30 MINS
COOKING TIME ABOUT 30 MINS

2 globe artichokes ▪ 1 lemon ▪ salt and freshly ground black pepper ▪ 60 g (2¼ oz) extra fine French (green) beans ▪ 200 g (7 oz) demi-conserve of foie gras (or paté de foie gras) ▪ 2 slices from a white loaf bread

1 Break off the stalks from the artichokes and pull out the filaments, then trim the bases. Squeeze the lemon and place both the juice and the skin into a pan with 2 litres (3½ pints, 9 cups) of water and bring to the boil. Add salt and the artichokes and boil for 30 minutes. Check that the artichokes are tender by piercing with the point of a knife, then take them out of the water and place them upside down in a sieve (strainer) to drain before washing them under cold running water.
2 Top and tail (trim) the French beans and wash them. Cook for 8 minutes in boiling salted water then drain and plunge the beans into plenty of iced water. When cold, drain and cut into 5 cm (2 inch) lengths.
3 Strip the leaves from the artichokes, remove the choke and, from the bases cut 8 x 5 cm (2 inch) squares about 5 mm (¼ inch) thick.

4 Cut the foie gras into 8 squares the same size as the artichoke squares. Cover with clingfilm (plastic wrap).
5 Preheat the grill (broiler).
6 Remove the crusts from the slices of bread and cut each into 4 squares. Toast them lightly on both sides.
7 Put a square of foie gras on each square of toast. Lightly season with salt and pepper. Cover with a square of artichoke and top with the French beans lined up neatly side by side. Serve cold.

4 Bite-sized melting-soft pistachio cakes

FOR 4 PEOPLE (12 PIECES)
PREPARATION TIME 20 MINS
COOKING TIME 40 MINS

175 g (6 oz, 1½ cups) blanched pistachio nuts ▪ 60 g (2¼ oz, ⅓ cup) corn flour ▪ 150 g (5 oz, ⅔ cup) granulated sugar ▪ 2 pinches salt ▪ 4 egg whites ▪ 1½ teaspoons butter ▪ 1 tablespoon icing (confectioners') sugar

1 Preheat the oven to 150°C (300°F, gas 2).
2 Place the pistachios in a blender and grind them to a powder, scraping them down from the sides of the goblet when necessary. Set 1 tablespoon of this powder aside for the decoration and place the rest in a bowl with the corn flour, 75 g (3 oz, 6 tablespoons) of sugar and a pinch of salt. Mix together.
3 Whisk the egg whites together with the second pinch of salt until they form stiff peaks then add the rest of the sugar.
4 Begin by delicately incorporating one-third of the whisked egg white into the sweetened ground pistachio mix, then gradually fold in the rest to achieve a smooth mixture.
5 Butter a deep 20 cm (8 inch) square cake tin (pan) and pour in the mixture (batter). Bake in the oven for 40 minutes.
6 When cooked, take the cake out of the oven and let it cool for 5 minutes before turning out onto a wire rack. Leave until completely cold.
7 Cut the pistachio cake into 12 small cubes. Dredge them with icing sugar using a fine sieve (strainer). Sprinkle them with the remaining ground pistachios and store at room temperature until needed.

5 Profiteroles with raspberries and whipped cream

FOR 4 PEOPLE (12 PIECES)
PREPARATION TIME 10 MINS

150 ml (¼ pint, ⅔ cup) whipping cream ▪ 1 tablespoon icing (confectioners') sugar ▪ 12 commercially made profiteroles ▪ 125 g (4½ oz) raspberries

1 Chill a bowl in the freezer for 5 minutes to make sure that the cream will whip easily.
2 Pass the icing sugar through a fine sieve (strainer) into a bowl.
3 Place the whipping cream in the chilled bowl and whip with an electric mixer. As soon as it begins to thicken add the sifted icing sugar. Continue beating until the whipped cream is thick and firm.
4 Cut a lid from each of the profiteroles and set the bases on a serving dish. Put 2–3 raspberries in each then add a spoonful of whipped cream. Replace the lids and store in a cool place until needed.

Cocktail snacks to serve with Champagne

1 Slices of queen (bay) scallops topped with caviar

FOR 4 PEOPLE
PREPARATION TIME 10 MINS
COOKING TIME ABOUT 10 MINS

12 fresh (or frozen) queen scallops ▪ 1 tablespoon butter ▪ salt and freshly ground black pepper ▪ 15 g (½ oz) caviar (or lump fish roe)

FOR THE SAUCE

3 tablespoons butter ▪ 1 tablespoon water ▪ 1 teaspoon lemon juice ▪ 1 tablespoon double (heavy) cream

1 Wash the scallops in cold water. Wipe them and remove the little hard side muscle. Cut each scallop into two discs, leaving the coral attached to one only.

2 Preheat the oven to 180°C (350°F, gas 4).

3 Melt the butter over a low heat and use a little of it to brush the base of a gratin dish. Lay the scallop slices in the dish, keeping them well separated. Brush them over lightly with the butter. Season with salt and pepper and bake in the oven for 2 minutes, then drain them on kitchen paper (paper towels).

4 For the sauce, divide the butter into hazelnut-sized pieces. Place the water in a small pan, bring to the boil and add the lemon juice. As soon as this has returned to the boil, add a few pieces of the butter and stir vigorously with a whisk. Add the rest of the butter in small stages. Add the cream and season with salt and pepper. Add the scallops and coat them delicately in the sauce. Leave to cool.

5 Divide the scallops between 4 china spoons, or small dishes, and sprinkle with the grains of caviar.

2 Watercress mousse with roasted langoustines

FOR 4 PEOPLE (4 PIECES)
PREPARATION TIME 20 MINS
COOKING TIME ABOUT 15 MINS

1 bunch watercress ▪ 1 tablespoon vinegar ▪ 1 tablespoon butter ▪ 200 ml (7 fl oz, scant 1 cup) double (heavy) cream ▪ salt and freshly ground black pepper ▪ 4 fresh (or frozen) langoustines ▪ 1 tablespoon olive oil ▪ 2 sprigs fresh chervil

1 Cut off the watercress stalks, wash the leaves thoroughly in water with added vinegar and squeeze them dry.

2 Melt the butter in a sauté pan over a medium heat. Add the watercress leaves and stir for 2 minutes. Add the cream, season with salt and pepper and leave to cook for 10 minutes, then process in a blender for 2–3 minutes.

3 Wash the langoustines in cold water. Drain thoroughly then shell them and remove the heads. Slide a knife down the back to remove the black thread.

4 Heat the oil in a small frying pan until smoking hot, then sear the langoustines for 2 minutes on each side. Season them with salt and pepper and drain on kitchen paper (paper towels). Cut in half along the length then cut each half into 2 pieces.

5 Divide the watercress mousse between 4 small glasses, or dishes. Place the langoustine pieces in the centre and garnish with chervil leaves. Serve warm, together with small spoons.

3 Tartlets filled with toasted goat's milk cheese and pesto sauce

FOR 4 PEOPLE (16 PIECES)
PREPARATION TIME 20 MINS
COOKING TIME ABOUT 20 MINS

200 g (7 oz) fresh, creamy goat's milk cheese ▓ 1 teaspoon fresh thyme leaves stripped from the stalk ▓ salt and freshly ground black pepper ▓ 1 tablespoon butter ▓ 175 g (6 oz) short-crust pastry (basic pie dough) ▓ 8 cherry tomatoes

FOR THE PESTO

15 leaves fresh basil ▓ 1 clove garlic ▓ 2 tablespoons pine nuts ▓ 3 tablespoons freshly grated Parmesan cheese ▓ 2 pinches coarse sea salt ▓ freshly ground black pepper ▓ 3 tablespoons olive oil

1 For the pesto, wash the basil leaves and pat them dry. Peel the garlic, cut it into pieces and put it in a blender. Add the basil, pine nuts, coarse salt and pepper. Blend for 2 minutes then add half of the oil. Blend again then add the rest of the oil and all the Parmesan. Continue processing until it forms a smooth purée. Keep the pesto in a bowl.
2 Preheat the oven to 180°C (350°F, gas 4).
3 Mash the goat's milk cheese with a fork and mix with the thyme in a deep plate. Season with salt and pepper.
4 Butter 16 tartlet tins (pans), 6 cm (2½ inches) in diameter, and line them

with pastry. Prick the pastry with a fork then line with greaseproof (waxed) paper and a layer of dried beans. Bake in the oven for 4 minutes.
5 Into each pre-cooked tartlet place ½ teaspoon pesto and 1 tablespoon goat's milk cheese mixture. Level the tops with a spatula then return to the oven and cook for a further 10 minutes. Heat the grill (broiler), and brown the tartlets under it for 2–3 minutes.
6 Cut each of the tomatoes into 6 pieces. Remove the tartlets from their tins and place 3 pieces of tomato in the centre of each. Serve hot or warm.

4 Squares of spiced bread with foie gras and cranberries

FOR 4 PEOPLE (16 CANAPÉS)
PREPARATION TIME 20 MINS

4 slices spiced bread ▓ 200 g (7 oz) demi-conserve of foie gras (or paté de foie gras) ▓ freshly ground black pepper ▓ 4 tablespoons cranberries (water-packed in a jar)

1 Cut the crusts from the spiced bread and cut each slice into 4 squares.

2 Cut the foie gras into 16 squares the same size as the spiced bread and lay one on each piece of spiced bread. Season with pepper and cover with clingfilm (plastic wrap).
3 Drain the cranberries and put them onto kitchen paper (paper towels).
4 Just before serving, remove the cling-film from the foie gras canapés and,

using a small spoon, carefully distribute the cranberries over half the surface of each of the 16 canapés.

5 Orange crêpes soufflées in mini-gateau form

FOR 4 PEOPLE (8 PIECES)
PREPARATION TIME 15 MINS
COOKING TIME ABOUT 35 MINS

FOR THE CREAM

3 tablespoons corn flour ▓ 2 tablespoons water ▓ 1½ teaspoons butter ▓ juice of 2 oranges ▓ juice of 1 lemon ▓ 165 g (5½ oz, scant ¾ cup) granulated sugar ▓ 2 eggs ▓ 50 g (2 oz, ½ cup) blanched whole almonds

FOR THE CRÊPE BATTER

3 eggs, separated ▓ 3 tablespoons sugar ▓ 5 tablespoons sifted plain (all-purpose) flour ▓ 150 ml (¼ pint, ⅔ cup) double (heavy) cream ▓ 2½ tablespoons butter

1 To prepare the cream, mix the corn flour with the water. Melt the butter in a small saucepan. In another pan place the orange and lemon juice with the sugar and

heat gently for 3 minutes. Add the eggs and whisk vigorously for 2 minutes then add the corn flour mixture and the butter and continue whisking until the cream comes away from the sides of the pan.
2 Brown the almonds in a dry frying pan, then chop them finely.
3 To prepare the crêpe batter, place the egg yolks and 1½ tablespoons of the sugar in a bowl. Beat for 2 minutes then add the flour. Mix well and add the cream. Place the egg whites in another bowl and whip them until quite stiff then add the remaining sugar. Delicately fold this into the egg yolk, cream and sugar mixture.
4 Heat 1½ teaspoons of butter in an 18 cm (7 inch) crêpe pan. Ladle in about

4 tablespoons of the batter and cook for 2–3 minutes. Turn it over and cook for a further 2–3 minutes. Meanwhile, add 1½ teaspoons of butter to a second 18 cm (7 inch) crêpe pan and begin another crêpe while the first is cooking. Continue in this way until you have 3 crêpes.
5 Spread a layer of cream on the first crêpe. Place a second crêpe on the top and spread that with cream, then top with the last crêpe. Using a spatula, spread the remaining cream around the edge of the cake and coat it with the chopped almonds. Keep it refrigerated until needed then cut into 8 pieces.

Cocktail snacks to serve with cocktails based on other forms of alcohol

1 Bite-sized pieces of polenta with Parma ham (prosciutto)

FOR 4 PEOPLE (16 PIECES)
PREPARATION TIME 15 MINS
COOKING TIME ABOUT 15 MINS

250 ml (9 fl oz, generous 1 cup) water ▥ salt and freshly ground black pepper ▥ 3 tablespoons olive oil ▥ 50 g (2 oz) pre-cooked polenta (cornmeal) ▥ 8 small fresh sage leaves ▥ 2 large slices Parma ham (prosciutto)

1 Bring the water to the boil in a small pan. Add salt and 1 tablespoon of oil. Sprinkle in the polenta in a fine rain, stirring vigorously all the time with a wooden spoon. Reduce the heat and cook the polenta for a further 3–4 minutes, stirring constantly.

2 Using a pastry brush, brush the inside of a gratin dish with 1 tablespoon of oil and pour in the polenta to a depth of 1 cm (½ inch). Level with a spatula and leave to cool at room temperature.

3 When the polenta is cold, cut it into rectangles about 3 cm (1¼ inches) long.

Place the remaining oil in a frying pan over a high heat and brown the polenta rectangles for about 3 minutes on each face. Drain on kitchen paper (paper towels).

4 Wash and dry the sage leaves. Remove the rind from the ham and cut it into as many strips as you have polenta pieces. Roll each polenta piece in a strip of ham. Season with pepper and lay a sage leaf on the top. Serve warm or cold, together with cocktail sticks (toothpicks).

2 Bruschetta with mozzarella and artichokes

FOR 4 PEOPLE (8 PIECES)
PREPARATION TIME 35 MINS
COOKING TIME ABOUT 40 MINS

50 g (2 oz) rocket (arugula) ▥ 8 slices from a small rustic loaf ▥ 1 clove garlic ▥ 1 tomato ▥ 16 slices mozzarella cheese ▥ salt and freshly ground black pepper ▥ 1 tablespoon dried oregano ▥ 1 tablespoon olive oil ▥ 8 pinches red chilli powder ▥ 16 pitted black olives

FOR THE ARTICHOKES ROMAN-STYLE

8 small purple artichokes ▥ 1 lemon ▥ 4 cloves garlic ▥ 8 sprigs fresh flat-leaf parsley ▥ 300 ml (11 fl oz, 1¼ cups) dry white wine ▥ 100 ml (4 fl oz, 7 tablespoons) water ▥ 3 tablespoons olive oil

1 To prepare the artichokes, half fill a salad bowl with water and add the juice of the lemon. Trim the stalks of the artichokes, leaving just 4 cm (1½ inches). Peel away the leaves down to the central cone and re-cut the base. Trim off the tops of the remaining leaves then cut the artichokes in half and take out the choke. Drop them into the acidulated water.

2 Peel the 4 garlic cloves, chop them finely with the parsley that has been washed. Place in a sauté pan with the wine, water and oil. Add the drained artichokes, season with salt and pepper

and bring to the boil. Leave to simmer for about 30 minutes then drain.

3 Preheat the grill (broiler).

4 Wash and dry the rocket.

5 Toast the bread slices on both sides. Peel the garlic and rub it on the toasted slices. Cut the tomato in half and rub that on the bread too then top each slice with 2 slices of mozzarella. Season with salt and pepper and sprinkle with oregano. Drizzle with oil and place under the grill to melt the cheese. Garnish each bruschetta with 2 pieces of artichoke, a sprinkle of chilli powder, some rocket and olives.

3 Prawns (shrimp) flavoured with almonds and paprika

FOR 4 PEOPLE (8 PIECES)
PREPARATION TIME 25 MINS
COOKING TIME 35 MINS

■ salt ■ 8 large fresh prawns (jumbo shrimp) ■ 1 slice stale rustic loaf ■ 1½ tablespoons olive oil ■ 2 sprigs fresh flat-leaf parsley ■ 2½ tablespoons ground almonds ■ 2 pinches paprika

FOR THE SAUCE

2 small tomatoes ■ 2 cloves garlic ■ 5 tablespoons ground almonds ■ 2½ table-spoons ground hazelnuts ■ 1 tea-spoon paprika ■ 2 tablespoons olive oil ■ 1 teaspoon sherry vinegar ■ salt and freshly ground black pepper

1 Preheat the oven to 200°C (400°F, gas 6).

2 To prepare the sauce, wash the tomatoes and place them in a gratin dish with the whole peeled garlic cloves. Bake in the oven for 35 minutes then process in a blender with the ground almonds, ground hazelnuts, paprika, oil, vinegar and seasoning until reduced to a purée. Pour the sauce into a small dish.

3 Place 1½ litres (2½ pints, 7 cups) of water in a pan, add a little salt and bring to the boil. Wash the prawns in cold water and drop them into the boiling water. Cook for 4 minutes then drain. Remove the heads and the shells and thread them onto small wooden skewers.

4 Cut the slice of bread into cubes. Heat 1 tablespoon of oil in a frying pan until smoking hot then drop in the cubes of bread and brown them for about 3 minutes. Drain on kitchen paper (paper towels).

5 Wash the parsley and chop finely. Place the cubes of fried bread in a blender with the ground almonds and parsley and process briefly. Place this mixture in a deep plate.

6 Using a pastry brush, brush the prawns with the remaining oil, roll them in the parsley, almond and crumbs mixture and sprinkle with paprika. Serve them arranged in a pyramid on a plate, with the dish of sauce for dipping placed conveniently beside it.

4 Aubergine (eggplant) rolls with tomatoes and (bell) peppers

FOR 4 PEOPLE (12 PIECES)
PREPARATION TIME 20 MINS
COOKING TIME 35 MINS

2 long, thin aubergines (eggplants) about 350 g (12 oz) ■ 3 tablespoons olive oil ■ salt and freshly ground black pepper ■ 4 tomatoes ■ 1 red (bell) pepper ■ 2 medium onions ■ 1 teaspoon balsamic vinegar

1 Preheat the oven to 220°C (425°F, gas 7).

2 Wash and wipe the aubergines. Cut off the ends but leave the skin on. Cut each into 6 long slices of equal thickness.

3 Line a large roasting tin (pan) with foil. Brush it with oil and lay the aubergine slices on it, side by side. Brush them with oil and season with salt.

4 Wash and wipe the tomatoes and the pepper. Cut the tomatoes into 6 wedges. Cut the pepper in half and remove the stalk and seeds. Cut each half into 6 strips. Peel the onions and cut each into 6 rounds (circles).

5 Distribute the pepper, tomatoes and onions evenly over the aubergine slices. Brush them with oil and season with salt.

6 Cook in the centre of the oven for 35 minutes. Sprinkle with the vinegar and season with pepper. Remove them from the roasting tin with a spatula and leave them to cool.

7 Remove the tomato pieces from the tin and crush them with a fork then discard the skins. Lay the slices of aubergine out flat and spread them with the tomato pulp. Place a piece of pepper and an onion round in the centre of each slice and roll it up around them. Arrange the rolls on a serving dish and keep at room temperature. Serve together with cocktail sticks (toothpicks).

5 Cream of chestnut delight

FOR 4 PEOPLE
PREPARATION TIME 10 MINS

200 ml (7 fl oz, scant 1 cup) whipping cream ■ 1 tablespoon icing (confectioners') sugar ■ 250 g (9 oz) can sweetened chestnut purée flavoured with vanilla ■ 40 g (1½ oz) store-bought meringue shells

1 Place a bowl into the freezer for 5 minutes to make sure that the cream will whip easily.

2 Sift the icing sugar through a fine sieve (strainer) into a bowl.

3 Pour the cream into the chilled bowl and whip with an electric mixer. When it begins to thicken, add the icing sugar and continue whipping until it is thick and firm.

4 Open the can of chestnut purée and, using a spoon, beat to a creamy, even texture.

5 Crush the meringue shells to crumbs and divide the crumbs between 4 glasses (or cups). Cover with a layer of chestnut cream then top with 2 tablespoons whipped cream. Store in the refrigerator until needed.

Cocktail snacks to serve with alcohol-free cocktails

1 Lettuce and tuna mousse purses

FOR 4 PEOPLE (8 PIECES)
PREPARATION TIME 20 MINS

1 unwaxed lemon ■ 200 g (7 oz) canned tuna in olive oil ■ 50 g (2 oz, ¼ cup) softened butter ■ 2 tablespoons olive oil ■ 1 teaspoon dried oregano ■ salt and freshly ground black pepper ■ 1 lettuce ■ 16 fresh lengths chives

1 Wash and dry the lemon and, using a sharp knife or vegetable peeler, remove the peel (zest) and chop it finely. Cut the lemon in half and squeeze it, reserving 2 tablespoons of the juice.
2 Place the tuna with its oil in a deep plate and crush with a fork then transfer it to a blender. Add the chopped lemon peel, the 2 tablespoons of lemon juice, butter, oil and oregano. Season with salt and pepper and blend for 4 or 5 minutes to obtain a thick purée. Place in a bowl and refrigerate.
3 Choose the 8 best lettuce leaves, wash and dry them on kitchen paper (paper towels). Wash and dry the chives.
4 Using a sharp knife, trim the spine on the back of each lettuce leaf to make it flat and supple.
5 Lay the leaves face-up on the work surface (counter). Place a spoonful of tuna purée in the centre of each and gather up the edges to form a little bag. Use 2 cocktail sticks (toothpicks) to hold each bag closed while you tie them up with 2 lengths of chives, then remove the cocktails sticks. Store in the refrigerator until needed.

2 Sweet red (bell) pepper omelette (omelet)

FOR 4 PEOPLE (16 PIECES)
PREPARATION TIME 10 MINS
COOKING TIME 1 HR

2 small red (bell) peppers ■ 6 eggs ■ salt and freshly ground black pepper ■ 1 teaspoon olive oil ■ 4 fresh lengths chives

1 Preheat the oven to 220°C (425°F, gas 7).
2 Wash and wipe the peppers and set them on a baking sheet lined with foil. Cook in the oven for 30 minutes, turning 2–3 times.
3 Remove the peppers from the oven, seal them in a plastic bag and leave to cool. When cold, take them out of the bag and cut them in half. Peel them and discard the stalks, seeds and any water generated during cooking. Cut the flesh into small cubes and sandwich between two layers of kitchen paper (paper towels) to remove all excess moisture.
4 Bring the oven back up to temperature.
5 Break the eggs and beat them in a bowl. Season with salt and pepper. Mix in the peppers.
6 Brush the inside of an 18 cm (7 inch) cake tin (pan) with oil. Pour in the egg mixture and cook in the oven for 30 minutes. Check that it is cooked by inserting the point of a knife, which should come out completely dry.
7 Turn the omelette out onto a plate. Leave it to cool before cutting it into 16 pieces. Store at room temperature until needed. Garnish with chives before serving.

3 Mini kebabs with courgette (zucchini), mint, feta cheese and black olives

FOR 4 PEOPLE (16 PIECES)
PREPARATION TIME 15 MINS
COOKING TIME ABOUT 6 MINS

1 courgette (zucchini) ▪ 1 tablespoon olive oil ▪ salt and freshly ground black pepper ▪ 8 leaves fresh mint ▪ 150 g (5 oz) feta cheese ▪ 16 pitted black olives ▪ 4 sprigs fresh mint

1 Wash and wipe the courgette. Using a paring knife, peel away strips of the skin along the length, leaving 1 cm (½ inch) unpeeled between each. Cut the courgette into 4 chunks about 5 cm (2 inches) long and then cut each chunk into 4 sticks.
2 Preheat the grill (broiler).
3 Line a baking sheet with foil and lay the courgette sticks on it. Brush them with oil and grill (broil) for 2–3 minutes. Turn them over and grill the other side for 2–3 minutes, then place in a bowl and season with salt and pepper.
4 Wash and dry the mint leaves and cut them up with scissors over the bowl. Mix well.
5 Cut the feta cheese into 16 cubes.
6 Thread 1 courgette stick, 1 cube of cheese and 1 olive onto each cocktail stick (toothpick). Place the mint sprigs in a serving dish and arrange the mini kebabs on them. Store at room temperature until needed.

4 Tzatziki with concassé of tomato

FOR 4 PEOPLE
PREPARATION TIME 15 MINS
RESTING TIME 30 MINS

¼ medium-sized cucumber ▪ salt and freshly ground black pepper ▪ 1 clove garlic ▪ 1 tablespoon olive oil ▪ ½ teaspoon lemon juice ▪ 200 g (7 oz, ¾ cup) natural Greek (plain strained) yogurt ▪ 1 tomato ▪ 2 fresh lengths chives

1 Peel the cucumber and remove the seeds with the point of a knife, then grate it into a bowl, using a coarse grater. Sprinkle with 3 pinches of salt and leave to sweat for 30 minutes. Rinse under cold running water for 2 minutes then squeeze it firmly in a cloth to press out the water. Transfer to a bowl.
2 Peel the garlic, cut into quarters and crush it to a purée. Add this to the cucumber in the bowl and stir in, together with the oil and lemon juice. Add the yogurt and mix well. Store in the refrigerator.
3 Using the point of a knife, cut a cross in the base of the tomato and plunge it into boiling water for 30 seconds. Drain off the water and rinse the tomatoes under cold running water. Skin and cut into quarters. Remove the seeds and cut the flesh into tiny cubes. Season with salt.
4 Wash and dry the chives. Divide the tzatziki between 4 Chinese spoons. Place a little heap of the chopped tomato on each spoon and, using scissors, snip the chives over each.

5 A jumble of fruit dressed with orange flower water

FOR 4 PEOPLE
PREPARATION TIME 30 MINS

1 green apple ▪ 1 teaspoon lemon juice ▪ 1 orange ▪ 1 pink grapefruit ▪ ½ pineapple ▪ 8 large strawberries ▪ 2 tablespoons brown sugar ▪ 1 unwaxed lime ▪ 4 tablespoons orange flower water

1 Wash the apple and cut marble-sized balls from it with a Parisian ball cutter. Place them in a bowl and coat them with the lemon juice.
2 Using a sharp knife, peel the orange and grapefruit, removing all the white pith and the inner membrane. Detach the segments one by one, sliding the knife inside the lateral membranes. Cut the grapefruit segments into 2 pieces. Add the orange segments and the grapefruit pieces to the bowl with the apple.
3 Peel the pineapple and remove the 'eyes' with the point of a knife. Cut the fruit into 1 cm (½ inch) slices then into triangles. Add these to the bowl.
4 Wash and wipe the strawberries then remove the stems. Cut each into 8 pieces and add to the bowl. Sprinkle the sugar carefully over the assorted fruits and mix gently.
5 Wash and dry the lime and remove the peel (zest) with a zester. Chop this very finely and mix in with the fruits. Pour over the orange flower water and stir the mixture again. Serve in 4 individual dishes.

Conversion table for the cocktail snacks recipes

LIQUID AND SOLID CAPACITY

Metric (g/ml)	Imperial (oz)	Cups/tablespoons
25 g/25 ml	1 oz	⅛ cup pre-cooked polenta (cornmeal)
50 g/50 ml	2 oz/2 fl oz	¼ cup brown sugar ½ cup pecan nuts, blanched whole almonds ¼ cup softened butter ¼ cup canned chopped tomatoes
60 g	2¼ oz	½ cup plain flour
75 g	3 oz	6 tablespoons granulated sugar
100 g/100 ml	4 oz/4 fl oz	7 tablespoons water ½ cup melted chocolate 1 cup sliced French (green) beans
115 g	4¼ oz	½ cup butter
125 g	4½ oz	½ cup taramasalata
150 g	5 oz/¼ pint	⅔ cup natural Greek (plain strained) yoghurt ⅔ cup brown or granulated sugar ⅔ cup groundnut (peanut) oil (or coconut milk)
200 g/200 ml	7 oz/7 fl oz	1 scant cup sugar 1 scant cup double (heavy) cream
300 g	11 oz	1¼ cups fromage frais or soured cream

This table indicates approximate conversions of common ingredients.

CONVERSION TABLES: METRIC, UK AND US

Liquid measures

Metric	UK fl oz	US cups
5 ml	teaspoon	teaspoon
15 ml	tablespoon	tablespoon
50 ml	2 fl oz	¼ cup
100 ml	4 fl oz	½ cup
150 ml	¼ pint	⅔ cup
225 ml	8 fl oz	1 cup
300 ml	½ pint	1¼ cups
600 ml	1 pint	2½ cups

Solid measures

Metric	UK/US
5 g	1 teaspoon
15 g	1 tablespoon
25 g	1 oz
100 g	4 oz
250 g	9 oz
300 g	11 oz

All measures are approximate because of rounding up or down. Only one set of measures should be followed in any recipe

COOKING TEMPERATURES

Gas Mark	Temp °C	Temp °F	Heat
½	120°C	250°F	very low
1	140°C	275°F	very low
2	150°C	300°F	low
3	160°C	325°F	low
4	180°C	350°F	moderate
5	190°C	375°F	moderate
6	200°C	400°F	medium
7	220°C	425°F	medium
8	230°C	450°F	hot
9	240°C	475°F	hot

These indications are valid for traditional ovens. For fan ovens consult the manufaturer's instructions.

For a deeper insight

The manufacture of alcoholic drinks and fruit juices

A look at the history of spirits and elixirs

Alcohol was a late-comer in the history of mankind. While ancient civilizations knew how to make wine and beer, and exploited them to the full, the rudimentary forms of distillation that existed were used only for the purpose of extracting aromas from plants and flowers.

In the Middle Ages, alchemists fired up their retorts in secretive attempts to discover the elixir of life; these efforts led to the discovery of new forms of alcohol. In 1309, Arnaud de Villeneuve, in *De Conservanda Juventute* – work he dedicated to King Robert of Naples – mentioned an 'eau-de-vie' or 'water of life' that he had distilled from wine. His pupil, Raymond Lulle, revealed how to separate the aqueous element out of the mixture to obtain a fiery spirit. In one of his writings he called a spirit a *quinta essentia* – a term that later on gave us the word 'quintessence'.

Spirits and elixirs, which were patiently created in monasteries or prepared by apothecaries, largely for medicinal purposes, gradually spread right across Europe.

The distillation techniques that were widely used, particularly by the Dutch, changed little over the centuries. In France, at the end of the eighteenth century, chemists Antoine Baumé, followed by Jean Antoine Chaptal and Antoine Augustin Parmentier, registered the first patents for a simple alembic through which the liquid was passed several times to obtain alcohol of a high degree. In 1801 a chemist in Montpellier, Édouard Adam, invented a new apparatus, which was the forerunner of the column still. This allowed the production of alcohol at a very high concentration (up to 90% Vol/180° proof) with a single distil-lation. Various improvements led on to the multi-column industrial installations.

During the nineteenth century, as the manufacturers' store of knowledge increased, the quality of spirits improved by leaps and bounds. Many people drank alcohol, often to forget their troubles. The alcohol produced at that time averaged about 50% Vol/100° proof, as against 40% Vol/80° proof today.

Very quickly, alcoholism became a problem in many countries. The year 1919 saw the start of Prohibition in the United States, which lasted for ten years before finally ending in failure. Alcohol consumption, though illegal, was widespread and very popular at that time and has continued to be so to this day. But while alcoholic drinks still have their same seductive powers, it is important to know how to enjoy them in moderation.

The basics of alcohol production

Ethyl alcohol (the kind we drink) is obtained by fermenting sugar-rich juices from fruit, cereals, plants or vegetables. Fermentation, caused by the action of yeasts, transforms sugar into alcohol (and carbon dioxide) and produces alcoholic liquids, such as wine or cider, that contain only a limited amount of alcohol. To obtain a higher concentration, these liquids must be distilled. Fermented liquids contain a combination of water and alcohol; liquids with a much higher alcohol content can be obtained by heating the fermented liquids and collecting the vapours, condensed by cooling. This is the basic principle on which the still works.

The term 'alcohol strength by volume' refers to the percentage of alcohol contained in 1 litre

(1¼ pints) of an alcoholic beverage. It is indicated by a number followed by the formula '% Vol'. To calculate the American proof rating multiply the % Vol value by two.

The raw materials

Alcohol can be obtained from many kinds of vegetable matter.

Fruit is the basis of many spirits. Cognac is made from white wine derived from grapes, Calvados from cider made from apples, kirsch from cherries, eau-de-vie de framboise and eau-de-vie de mirabelle from raspberries and wild plums respectively.

From cereals we make the various types of whisky, vodka and gin.

In hot countries spirits are made from tropical plants. Rum from the Antilles and cachaça from Brazil are both made from sugar cane, while in Mexico the local agave plant is used to make tequila.

Some vegetables can also be a source of alcohol; potatoes are still used in Poland to make certain types of vodka. Sugar beet gives a neutral alcohol, called potable spirit, which is used in the manufacture of many aperitifs and liqueurs.

Preparatory treatment

Whatever the raw material used, the manufacture of spirits is subject to the same series of procedures, beginning generally with some form of preparatory treatment.

Pressing is used to extract the juice from fruit prior to fermenting it.

Grain is cracked before being made into a mash.

Agave has to be pre-cooked, as have potatoes and non-malted cereals, in order to transform some of their complex sugars into simple sugars that ferment easily.

Crushing, whether of raw or cooked matter, reduces solids to a purée.

Mashing, which follows cracking or crushing, consists of adding water to allow the sugars in the solid raw materials, such as cereals, to be transformed into fermentable sugars.

Mixing consists of combining one or several products into a homogenous whole.

Dilution means either diluting a neutral alcohol so as to be able to distil it, or adding liquid to fibrous or thick matter to assist fermentation.

Fermentation

We have discussed how some spirits are obtained by distilling alcoholic liquids (wine or cider) that themselves result from fermentation. When using other materials, one must first encourage or provoke the fermentation of their juices.

Natural fermentation occurs when a liquid containing fermentable sugars is subjected to a certain temperature.

Artificial fermentation is needed when the raw material contains complex sugars, like starch, that do not ferment easily. After preparatory treatment (cooking or mashing) fermentation is started by adding yeasts, which are micro-organisms that feed on the sugars and turn them into ethyl-alcohol (and carbon dioxide).

Distillation

The alcohol content of a liquid obtained by fermentation is generally 8–10% Vol/16–20° proof. To produce a spirit, this alcohol content must be greatly increased by the process of distillation. A still is an apparatus that allows one to separate out the alcohol from an alcoholic liquid using vaporization. Until the start of the nineteenth century, using a simple pot still, two distillations were needed to produce alcohol at about 70% Vol/140° proof. A technical revolution took place in distilleries with the advent of the column alembic, also called a column still.

With a column still it is possible to produce alcohol at 70% Vol/140° proof with a single distillation.

The multiple-column still, made up of two or more columns, needs only a single distillation to produce alcohol at 96% Vol/192° proof.

Fine-tuning

Following distillation, the spirit may undergo different procedures aimed at improving it.

Filtration (or purification) is used to adjust the smell, taste and colour of a spirit. Tennessee whiskey is filtered through a specified depth of maple-wood charcoal.

Flavouring gives extra aromas to an alcohol with the addition of extracts of plants, fruits, herbs or spices.

Ageing is the irreplaceable traditional way of attaining the desired quality. Ageing in casks, for a more or less prolonged period, is used for many spirits. When it leaves the still the alcohol is colourless but, when in contact with wood that is permeable to the outside air, it takes on an amber colour and subtle aromas. When the spirit has reached its optimum state it is transferred to glass carboys and hermetically sealed.

Ageing in tuns (large beer casks) is a more gentle process than ageing in casks, because a tun has a capacity of 10,000 litres (2,200 gallons, 2,640 US gallons), whereas a cask holds no more than 700 litres (154 gallons, 185 US gallons).

Ageing in bottles does nothing to improve spirits.

Ageing in a carboy is used only for fruit alcohol such as kirsch or eau-de-vie de framboise. The carboys are left unsealed and so ageing takes place by oxidization, which leaves the spirit colourless.

Blending is the mixing of different categories of spirit. In the case of blended Scotch whisky, this is done to produce a lighter flavour.

Assemblage is a French word that, when used in respect of Champagne, means 'preparation of the cuvée'. *Assemblage* is the process of combining spirits having different flavours, smells and colour that belong to the same category but are from different years or vintages, and is carried out in order to maintain a constant style and quality.

Bottling

Some final procedures may take place prior to bottling.

Reduction serves to regulate the degree of alcohol in a spirit by adding the necessary quantity of de-mineralized water (spring or distilled). In the case of whisky, reduction may be done twice, first in order to comply with the legal degree of alcohol for spirit in cask (and avoid too much evaporation), then to adjust to the required degree depending on where it is to be sold.

Sweetening involves adding sugar to an alcoholic drink or a liqueur to sweeten the taste.

Colouring (with caramel, for example) helps to stress the maturity of a spirit or suggests the presence of fruit or herbs.

The final procedure is always that of clarification, to purify the product and eliminate any sediment.

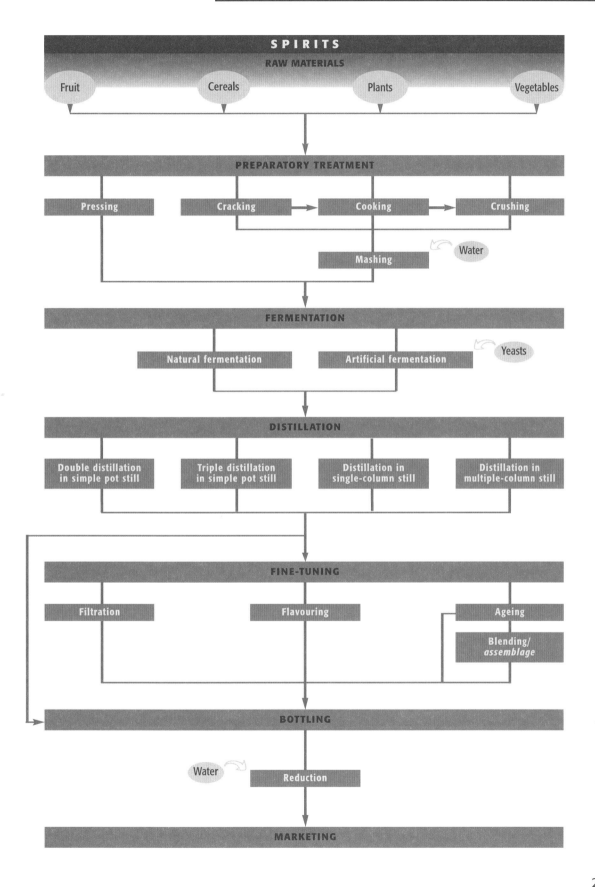

SPIRITS

RAW MATERIALS

Fruit — Cereals — Plants — Vegetables

PREPARATORY TREATMENT

Pressing — Cracking → Cooking → Crushing

Mashing — Water

FERMENTATION

Natural fermentation — Artificial fermentation — Yeasts

DISTILLATION

Double distillation in simple pot still — Triple distillation in simple pot still — Distillation in single-column still — Distillation in multiple-column still

FINE-TUNING

Filtration — Flavouring — Ageing

Blending/*assemblage*

BOTTLING

Water — Reduction

MARKETING

Vodka

Russia and Poland both claim to have invented vodka, a dispute that goes back several centuries. In Poland, the spirit was known as 'gorzalka' before it was accorded the name 'wodka', whereas in Russia the term vodka (literally 'little water') has always been used. Whatever the truth of the matter, this clear spirit is distilled from the fermented juice of potatoes, rye or a mixture of other cereals (wheat, maize [corn], malted barley, etc.). Vodka made in the sixteenth century was very different from that produced today. At that time vodka was distilled in inefficient pot stills and was flavoured with various plants to mask the roughness of the taste. Using column stills, it is now possible to produce vodka with a neutral flavour, purified further by filtration. In fact, vodka is considered one of the most neutral alcohols, in flavour, aroma and colour. Vodkas flavoured with fruit or plants do exist but are rarely used in cocktails. Unlike other forms of alcohol, there are no regulations governing the raw material, the geographic origin and the production process used. The only stipulation is that distillation should produce alcohol at 96% Vol/192° proof that is then generally reduced to 40% Vol/80° proof by the addition of de-mineralized water (spring or distilled). Nowadays vodka is produced in about 30 countries, the principal ones being Poland, Russia and the United States. Great Britain, Denmark, Finland, France, the Netherlands and Sweden also produce some.

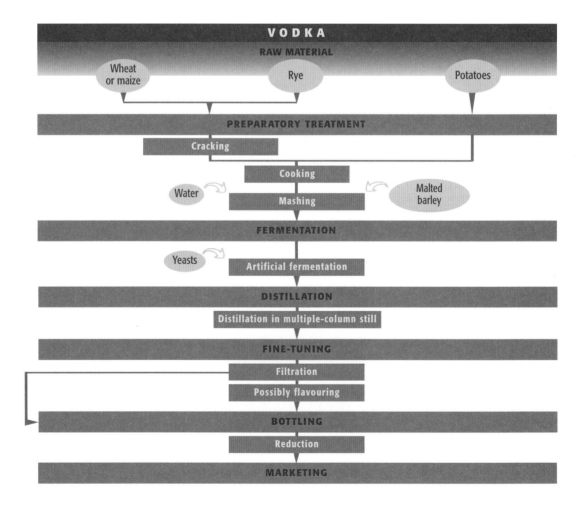

Gin

A treatise published in Amsterdam in 1622 was the first to mention a recipe for a juniper-flavoured spirit. The development of distillation in Holland contributed largely to the success of this drink, later named 'jenever'. When they returned from the Thirty Years War (1618–1648), the English soldiers, who had fought in Holland and acquired the taste for this spirit, created a demand for it under its new name of 'gin'. On his death in 1688, James II was succeeded by his son-in-law, Dutchman William III of Orange. The new Protestant king banned all imports from Catholic countries like France and thus encouraged local production of gin. What is more, he increased the tax on beer, which made gin the cheapest drink available. Excessive consumption of it became a national scourge in England – a situation that lasted for many decades.

Nowadays, gin is largely produced in the United States and Great Britain. There are several ways of making this cereal-based spirit (wheat or maize [corn] and barley, etc.). Ordinary gin is simply flavoured with juniper extract, whereas London gin is distilled together with juniper berries and other flavourings, like cardamom seed, angelica root, coriander seed, etc.

Plymouth gin is made in the same way as London gin but is covered by a controlled appellation of origin and can only be made in the British port after which it is named.

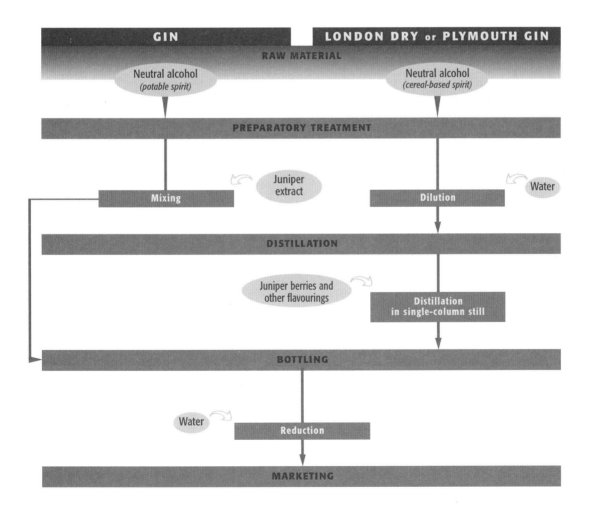

Scotch whisky

Scotland is the world's foremost producer of whisky. Whisky, whiskey, Scotch whisky, Irish whiskey, bourbon, rye – these various names are given to spirits that differ greatly in flavour, production methods, geographical origin and local traditions.

The first written reference to a spirit made from malt (germinated barley) produced in an abbey in Scotland, was in 1494. The Scottish production developed relatively slowly until the middle of the seventeenth century and then accelerated in the period up to 1824, the year when the first legal whisky distillery was established. Thirty or so years later, Andrew Usher, an employee of that distillery, had the idea of mixing the single malt whisky with a lighter one, made from other cereals – the 'single grain'. The latter was produced using the new column still, perfected in 1830 by Aeneas Coffey. The first blended Scotch thus saw the light of day.

Malt, or malted barley, is barley in which germination has been induced by soaking it in water to develop an enzyme that facilitates the transformation of the starches (complex, unfermentable sugars) into maltose (simple, fermentable sugar). Single malt Scotch whisky is made from malted barley, a proportion of which has been dried over a peat fire. It is distilled to 70–73% Vol/140–146° proof, whereas the single grain is distilled to 94.8% Vol/189.6° proof. After being reduced to 63% Vol/126° proof for the former and 67% Vol/134° proof for the latter, they are both matured for at least three years in used barrels.

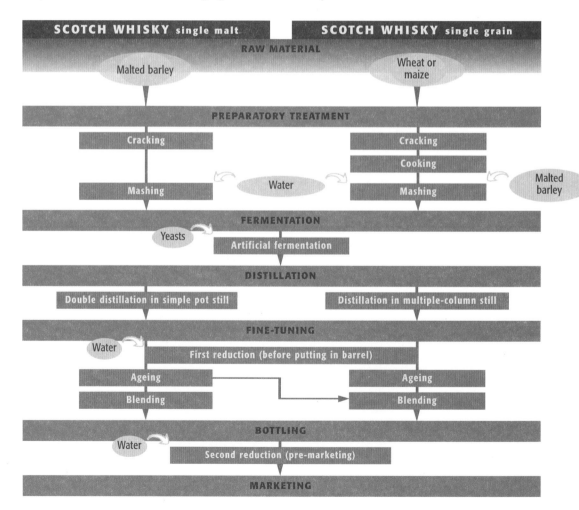

Irish whiskey

Legend attributes the appearance of whiskey in Ireland to the missionary Saint Patrick who, in the fifth century, brought back the art of distillation from a journey to Egypt. The spirit produced was called 'uisge beatha', or 'water of life' in the Celtic tongue; this could, therefore, have been the origin of the word whiskey.

At any rate, while one can find documentation on beer from the start of the sixth century, the first written mention of a cereal-based spirit in Ireland only appeared in 1556. The first distillery was established in 1608, but industrialized production only began after a law, passed in 1823, that gave preference to owners of stills with a capacity of at least 160 litres (35 gallons, 42 US gallons).

'Pure pot still' Irish whiskey differs from the Scotch single malt (▷ p. 296) in that, while it is made from a mixture of non-malted and malted barley, the malt is not dried over peat fires. When it leaves the still, the pure pot still whiskey is around 89–92% Vol/178–184° proof; the 'single grain' whiskey, made with other cereals, is 94.8% Vol/189.6° proof. Ageing, before which both are reduced to 70% Vol/140° proof, generally takes place in barrels that have previously contained Bourbon and lasts for a minimum of three years.

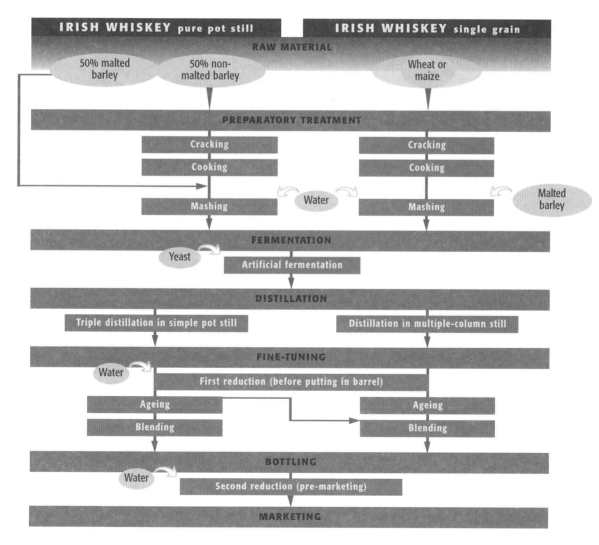

American whiskeys

At the end of the seventeenth century, when spirits like Cognac and rum were commonly imported into the United States, a cider distillery was opened in New Jersey. The distillation process had undoubtedly been brought to the United States by immigrants from Ireland or Scotland. However, it was not until the second half of the eighteenth century that the production of American whiskey got underway, with the first commercial distillery opening in 1783.

American whiskeys have to obey specific classifications: 'straight Bourbon' must be made from a mixture of cereals containing a minimum of 51% maize (corn), and must be produced in the United States; 'straight Tennessee' is specifically made with a minimum of 51% of the main cereal (usually maize), and can only be made in the State of Tennessee. It must be filtered through maple-wood charcoal before ageing; 'straight rye' is made by the same procedure as for 'straight bourbon', but the cereal used must be principally rye (51% minimum).

After distillation to a degree less than 80% Vol/160° proof, these 'straight' whiskeys must be reduced to 62.5% Vol/125° proof and undergo a minimum of two years in American oak barrels that have been charred internally.

Canadian whisky, Canadian rye whisky or simply rye whisky, are all names given to numerous brands of cereal-based spirits produced in Canada. The term 'straight rye' is only used for American rye whiskey. Canadian regulations do not impose minimum proportions for the type of cereals used, but in order to achieve the typical flavour of rye, this is always the major component.

PRINCIPAL CHARACTERISTICS OF THE DIFFERENT WHISKIES					
	Scotch whisky single malt	Irish whiskey pure pot still	American whiskey straight bourbon	American whiskey straight Tennessee	Canadian whisky
Raw Material	malted barley	malted barley and non-malted barley	minimum 51% maize, rye or wheat + malted barley	70% maize* and rye + malted barley	rye** and maize or wheat + malted barley
Fermentation	artificial	artificial	artificial	artificial	artificial
Distillation	double distillation	triple distillation	double or triple distillation	double distillation	simple distillation
Ageing	3 years minimum in used barrels	3 years minimum in used barrels	2 years minimum in new barrels	2 years minimum in new barrels	3 years minimum in new or used barrels

*Legally Tennessee whiskey must contain at least 51% of one cereal (maize or rye).
**Legally the typical rye characteristics must dominate in Canadian whisky though no actual minimum content is specified.

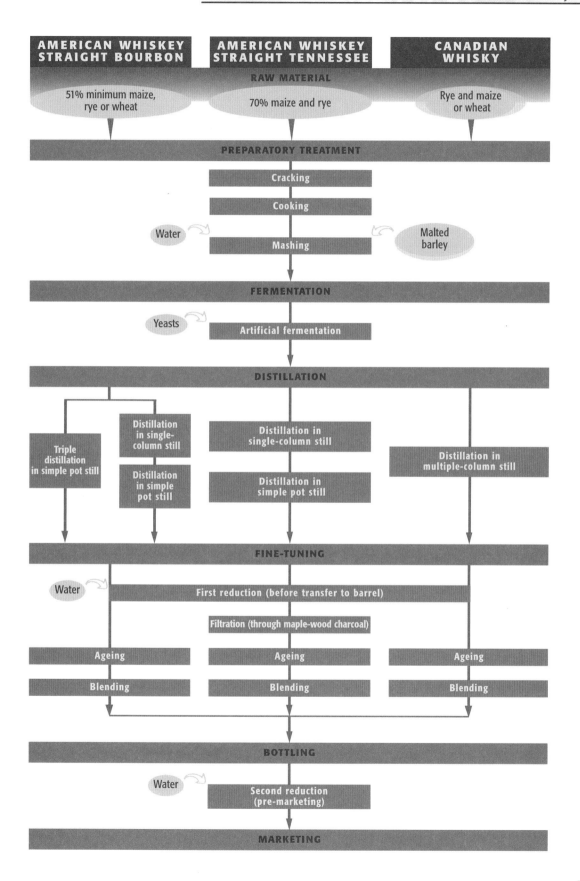

Sugar refinery rum

Industrial, or sugar refinery, rum – rum made from molasses – is made by distilling the by-products of sugar refining. In 1493, on his second voyage of discovery, Christopher Columbus introduced sugar cane plants from the Canary Islands to the island of Hispaniola (now Haiti and Dominican Republic). Sugar production took off rapidly as the Spanish and Portuguese conquerors set up sugar cane plantations in Mexico, Peru and Brazil. Later on the French and English took possession of the Antilles. Rum was mentioned for the first time at the beginning of the seventeenth century in Barbados, when rum rations were given to the sailors of the Royal Navy. The English influence contributed to the development of rum production and to its sale in Europe and the United States. By the end of the nineteenth century, American economic influence brought about an important increase in rum production in Cuba and Puerto Rico.

Straight from the still, industrial rum is between 65–96% Vol/130–192° proof. There are two kinds: Hispanic-type rums, made and filtered to obtain 'light rums' that are not very aromatic and contain 0.60–2.25 g (0.02–0.08 oz) of volatile elements per litre (1¾ pints); and the British-type rums which have more flavour and are sometimes termed 'high-aroma' rums. They contain in excess of 3.25 g (0.11 oz) of volatile elements per litre (1¾ pints).

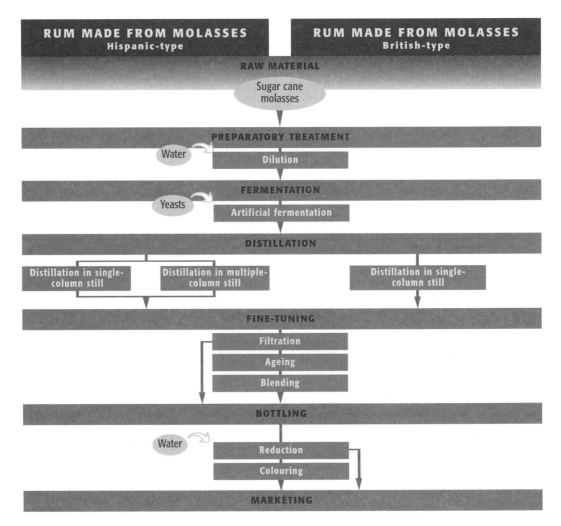

Rhum agricole, 'Agricultural rum'

While rum made by the sugar manufacturers from the by-product of refining sugar cane was already in production in the French Antilles in the middle of the seventeenth century, *Rhum agricole,* 'agricultural rum', known as distillery rum or *vesou* (sugar cane juice) rum, only appeared in the second half of the nineteenth century. At that time, the production of sugar from sugar beet, well established in mainland France, had caused a serious drop in the sale and production of sugar cane and consequently of rum (even though alcohol coming from the colonies to France had been exempted from tax since 1854).

Some sugar cane planters decided to by-pass the refineries and transform their own harvests into rum by distilling direct from the juice of the sugar cane.

In that way they came up with a new, more aromatic kind of rum – *rhum agricole.* From the 1880s onwards its production grew to significant proportions and in Martinique it now exceeds that of industrial rum.

After distillation the spirit is about 65–75% Vol/130–150° proof. In order to be called *rhum agricole* it must contain in excess of 2.25 g (0.08 oz) of volatile elements per litre (1¾ pints). *Rhum agricole* élevé sous bois (raised in wood) must be aged for at least one year in oak casks with a capacity of less than 650 litres (143 gallons, 172 US gallons). *Rhum agricole vieux* (aged 'agricultural rum') must have spent at least three years in oak casks.

For several years now, some of the Martinique rums are covered by a controlled appellation of origin (AOC).

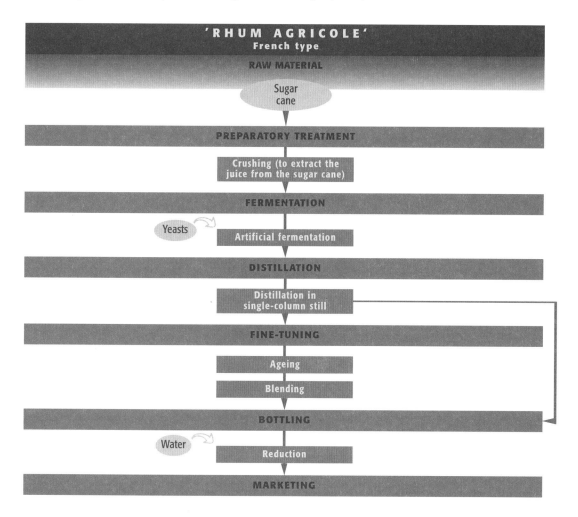

Tequila

Mention of a 'mescal wine' appeared in Mexico around 1620 but it was not until 1795 that the first distillery for mescal wine (or mezcal) was established. At the start of the twentieth century this name gave way to two distinct products: mescal and tequila. Mescal is made principally in the Oaxaca region, using eight different varieties of agave, of which agave A. *angustifolia* Haw. is the most common. Tequila is produced in the Jalisco region, using only agave A. *tequilana* Weber, a blue variety. Tequila is also the name of a town in the Jalisco region of western Mexico.

Shortly after the end of Prohibition, tequila made its first appearance on the American scene, via California, and gradually spread throughout the whole country. Thanks to – among other things – a song and numerous appearances in movies, tequila gradually became known the world over.

Tequila 100% agave is made exclusively with this tropical plant. Tequila without other qualification, or mixed tequila, may be made with no less than 51% agave together with sugars from other raw ingredients, such as sugar cane molasses. 'Blanco' (or silver) indicates a tequila that has undergone no ageing process whatsoever; 'gold' or 'joven abocado' is coloured and sweetened tequila. 'Reposado' is the name applied to tequila aged for at least two months in cask or tun; 'añejo' has spent a year or more in cask.

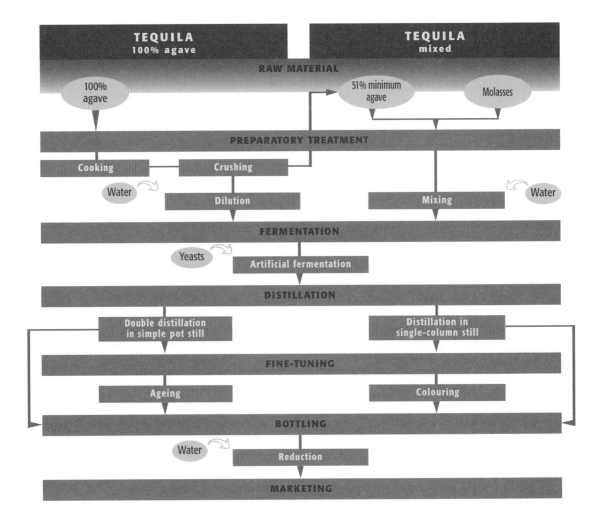

Cognac

The culture of vines in the Charente region of France dates back to the third century. The active sea and river port areas later encouraged the export of salt and wines produced in the area to England and the northern countries. As the wines did not travel well, in the seventeenth century the Dutch merchants were asked to distil them. The experiment was an irrefutable success and it was soon noted that the spirit produced in that way improved after a long period in oak barrels. Very quickly the name of Cognac – one of the most famous brandies – crossed frontiers and oceans. The phylloxera crisis, however, dealt a fatal blow to the vineyards – down from 280,000 hectares (692,000 acres) in 1875 to only 40,000 hectares (98,800 acres) twenty years later – and their replanting with new stock required a great effort lasting over several decades. Nowadays there are 80,000 hectares (198,000 acres) covering for the most part the Charente and Charente-Maritime region, now a controlled appellation of origin (AOC) zone. The predominant grape variety is Ugni Blanc.

In the temperate and ideally sunny climate, the geographical classifications of the six Crus – Grande Champagne, Petite Champagne, Borderies, Fins Bois, Bon Bois and Bois Ordinaires – are determined by the chalk and clay soil.

After distillation, the alcohol content of Cognac is 69–72% Vol/138–144° proof. It is aged in barrels, made of oak from central France, for at least two-and-a-half years for the VS (Very Special) or Three Star category, four-and-a-half years for VSOP (Very Superior Old Pale) or Réserve, and six-and-a-half years for XO (Extra Old) or Napoleon.

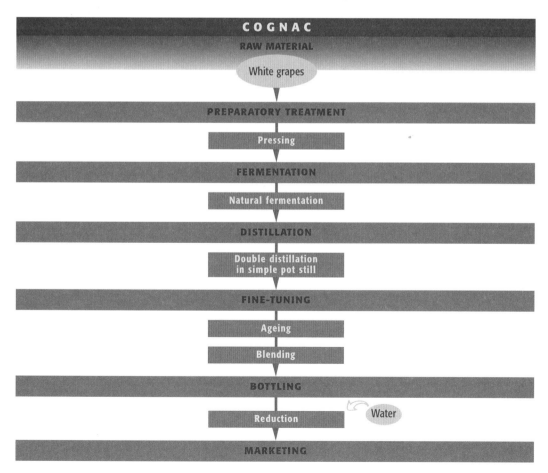

COGNAC

RAW MATERIAL

White grapes

PREPARATORY TREATMENT

Pressing

FERMENTATION

Natural fermentation

DISTILLATION

Double distillation in simple pot still

FINE-TUNING

Ageing

Blending

BOTTLING

Reduction — Water

MARKETING

Calvados

While cider was made in Normandy in Roman times, the first mention of a cider-based spirit occurred in Cherbourg in 1553. The name 'Calvados' did not come into use until much later, in the second half of the nineteenth century, and it wasn't until it was distributed as an alcohol ration to the soldiers during World War I, and then to the Allies who landed in Normandy in 1944, that Calvados became universally known.

Conditions for the production of Calvados are strictly regulated and limited to three distinct areas. The production zone for Calvados AOC – the least regulated – covers most of Basse-Normandie, with a few communes in the Mayenne and the Sarthe, and the Pays de Bray, in the Seine-Maritime region.

The Calvados Paye d'Auge AOC, essentially produced in the Calvados region, must undergo a double distillation in a simple pot still, of the type used in the Charentais, and must be aged for at least two years in oak barrels.

The Calvados Domfrontais AOC, produced in the Domfront region (Orne), is distinctive in that the basic raw material is only 70% apple juice, the other 30% being the juice of pears; it is aged for not less than three years.

Several dozens of apple varieties, classed as sour, sweet-sour and sweet-acid, are permitted in the production of Calvados AOC.

Calvados aged in wood is marketed under various different names: *Trois Pommes* (two years); Réserve (three years); Vielle Réserve (four years); Hors d'Age (six years).

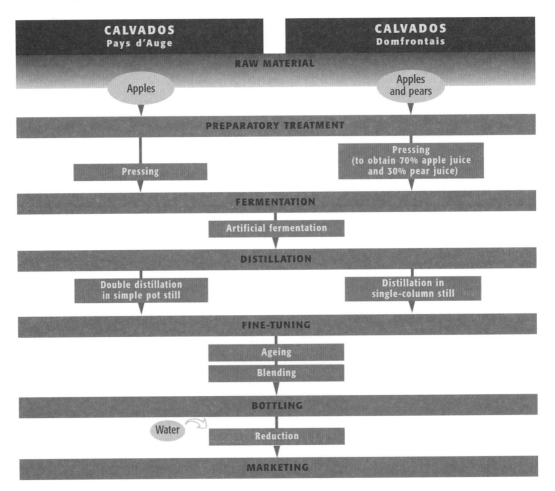

Fruit alcohols

Very little is to be found in ancient writings about the origins of fruit alcohols. We know that the Germanic roots of cherry alcohol, known by the name of kirsch or *Kirschwasser*, are to be found in the Rhine valley where its production was well established in the seventeenth century. At the start of the following century, distillation of kirsch began in Franche-Comté, Lorraine and Alsace, where they also began making eau-de-vie de quetsche (a variety of dark red plum). In fact, fruit spirit can be made from many types of fruit – apricots, wild berries, cherries, figs, raspberries, mirabelles (a small variety of plum), pears, plums, etc.

Production methods vary slightly. Here we look at those of eau-de-vie de cerise and eau-de-vie de framboise. The cherries are pressed, with or without

the stones (pits), to obtain a juice that is distilled following natural fermentation. Ageing formerly took place in ash casks that did not colour the spirit, but nowadays kirsch is aged for a few months in glass carboys.

Since raspberries do not produce a great deal of juice they are macerated in neutral alcohol (at least 100 kg [220 lb] to 20 litres [4.4 gallons, 5.3 US gallons] of alcohol). The resulting liquid is then distilled to a maximum 86% Vol/172° proof – the same as kirsch – and must also contain in excess of 2 g (0.07 oz) per litre (1¾ pints) of volatile elements. Eau-de-vie de framboise does not mature well in wood and it is always aged in glass carboys. As with kirsch, this ageing is due to oxidization, since the carboys are not hermetically sealed.

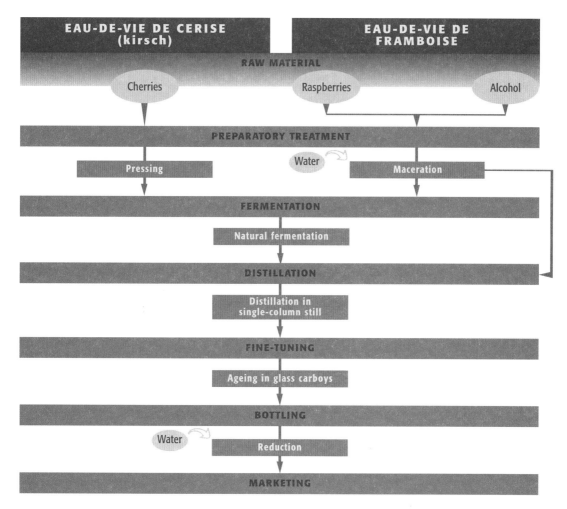

Champagne

Vineyards have been cultivated in the Champagne region since the early centuries A.D. but it was only at the end of the seventeenth century that Dom Pérignon, a Benedictine monk from the Abbaye d'Hautvillers, near Épernay, managed to produce a sparkling white wine which, two centuries later, earned him the title of the inventor of Champagne. The vineyards of the relatively small Champagne area are planted on slopes of chalky clay and benefit from a fresh climate. Three grape varieties are used in the making of Champagne – Pinot Noir and Pinot Meunier (black grapes with white juice) and Chardonnay (white grapes).

After an initial fermentation in vats, it is blended to combine the aromatic qualities of different wines in order to maintain consistency of quality and flavour. During the bottling process, a little *liqueur de tirage* – a mixture of sugar and wine yeasts – is added.

The second fermentation then begins, setting off the production of carbon dioxide. This is the *prise de mousse* (literally the taking on of effervescence), which lasts from two to six months. A light deposit forms which gradually accumulates in the neck of the bottles as they are regularly turned – either mechanically or by hand. This is then removed by the application of a liquid refrigerant to the neck of the bottle, which pushes out the cork and the impurities with it. The loss of content is made up with a *liqueur d'expédition* – a liquid containing more or less sweetening according to whether the Champagne is intended to be 'Brut', 'Sec' or 'Demi-sec'.

Traditionally, Champagne is the result of blending wines from different vintages (*assemblage*) but when a harvest yields a wine of a particular quality, the vintner may produce a cuvée millesimée by blending only wines from that year.

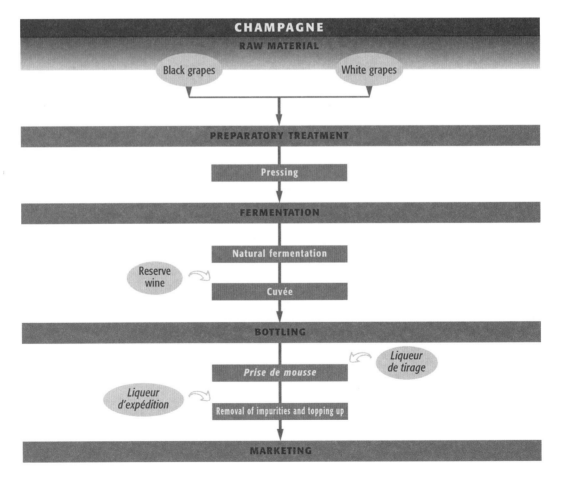

Vermouth and bitters

Vermouth – a member of the widespread aperitif family – is descended from a long line of aromatized wines known since antiquity for their medicinal properties. In the Middle Ages, spices imported into Venice gave rise to new preparations but it was in Piedmont in the seventeenth century that an 'absinthe wine' appeared and became popular in places as far apart as the Bavarian court and the dinner table of Louis XIV of France. In 1786, in Turin, Antonio Carpano offered his customers a red vermouth he had created, and soon after, an industry sprang up with the arrival of competitors Cinzano and Martini & Rossi. For his part, the Frenchman, Joseph Noilly, herbalist and maker of liqueurs, perfected his matured aromatic wine that later was to become the famous dry vermouth, Noilly Prat.

Around the same time a number of alcoholic drinks called 'bitters', such as the celebrated Campari, made their appearance in Italy. In France, the fashion for aperitifs was at its peak around 1900 but started to decline towards the middle of the twentieth century. Today, we are witnessing a return to favour of vermouths and bitters.

Distinction must be made between dry vermouth, which is virtually unsweetened and light in colour, and the sweeter red vermouth. Both are made from white wine with added alcohol and complex aromatic extracts.

Bitters are made from neutral alcohol and aromatic substances, and have a predominantly bitter flavour. The only permitted colouring agents are cochineal and caramel.

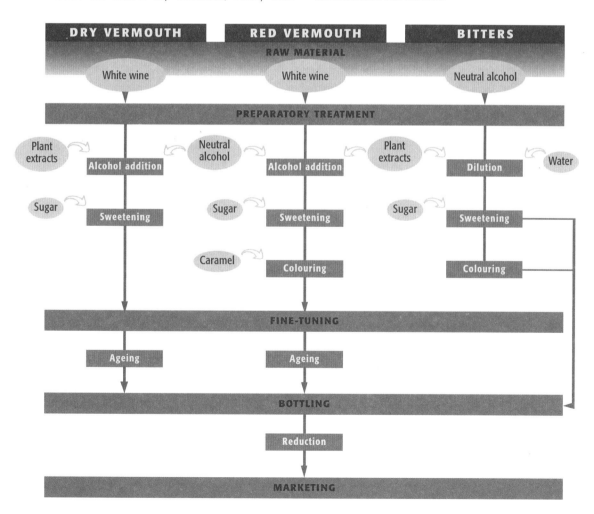

307

Port and sherry

In the eighteenth century English merchants, following the decision to impose a surcharge on imports of wines from Bordeaux, turned their sights on the Portuguese wines from the Douro valley. Situated in the north of Portugal, the production zone extends from the Spanish border to the town of Oporto. More than 100 types of vines are cultivated on the schistose soil. The production of port wine by the merchant-growers is achieved by a series of complicated operations. Alcohol is added to arrest the fermentation of the wine and to retain part of the sugar content. They then proceed to the blending process, mixing wines either from the same harvest or from different harvests. Wines blended together with those from the same harvest produce the following categories: vintage (matured for two years); late bottled vintage (LBV) (matured for four years); 'date of the harvest' (matured for

seven years). Blending wines from different vintages results in white port, red 'tawny' and 'ruby' ports, and 'old port' (ten years, 20 years, etc.).

Jerez, a fortified wine from the vine-growing region of Jerez de la Frontera, in Spain, also owes its success to the English, with whom it became popular at the start of the seventeenth century under the name of sherry. Sherry is produced using traditional methods. For a Fino, a thin film of mould (flor) must appear on the surface of the wine to start it fermenting. The addition of alcohol only takes place after classification of the various categories (Fino, Manzanilla, etc.). *Solera* is the Spanish word for a process of mixing a young wine and an old wine by transferring them back and forth from one cask to another. In addition to the light, dry Finos, there are also the stronger, darker-coloured Olorosos.

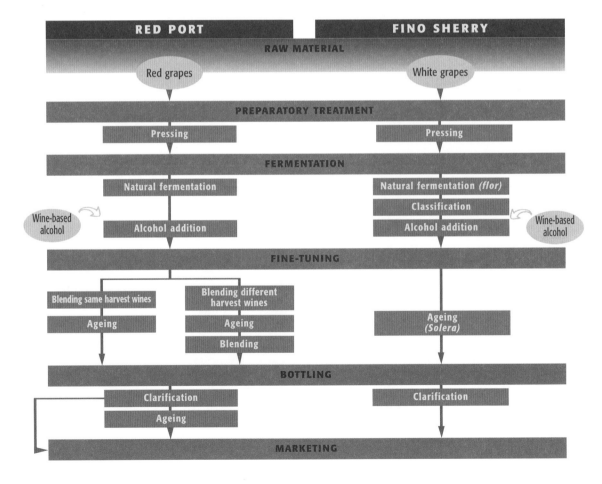

Aniseed (anises)

The aromatic plant absinthe was already known to the ancient Greeks, who considered it to have therapeutic properties and drank it either as an infusion or mixed with wine. Its name was given to a green alcoholic drink, created in Switzerland, and which Henri-Louis Pernod began manufacturing in his first distillery at Pontarlier, in the Doubs region, in 1805. It became very popular towards the end of the nineteenth century. It was poured through a lump of sugar, set on a slotted spoon held over the glass and then diluted with water. The fashion for this drink gave rise to a proliferation of absinthe products of dangerously poor quality. After a campaign denouncing its devastating effects on the nervous system, it was banned in France in 1915. A number of substitute products, such as Pernod and Pastis, have since been marketed. They all contain extracts of aniseed- (anise-) type plants, such as green anise and star anise. Some contain fennel and liquorice essence (Pastis), and others mint and coriander [cilantro] (Pernod).

In 1988 the production of absinthe was again legalized. The new formula, still based on absinthe and aniseed- (anise-) type plants, is similar to the old one and its alcohol content of 45–70% Vol/90–140° proof has been maintained; the noxious elements (such as thujone) are now present only in minute quantities.

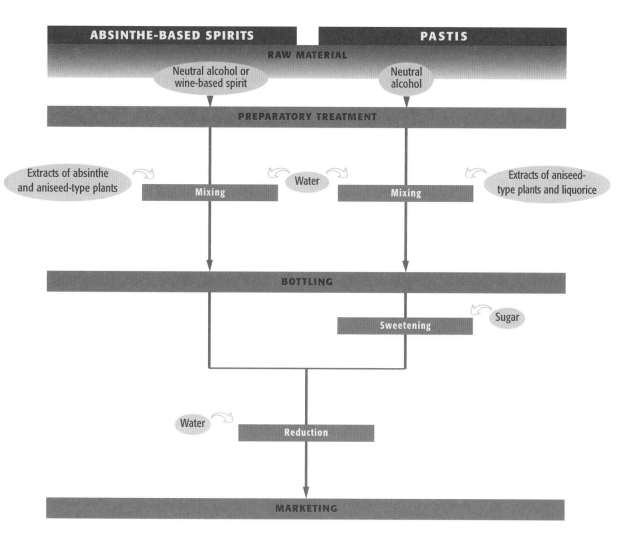

Liqueurs

Liqueurs are known to have existed well before the first appearance of spirits, obtained by distillation, in the thirteenth century. The oldest of these is Hippocras, which was very popular in the Middle Ages and was still drunk at the court of Louis XIV of France. It was a mixture of wine, cinnamon and honey, and its invention is attributed to Hippocrates, the ancient Greek physician.

In the course of the centuries other drinks appeared, based on hyssop, absinthe, sage, rosemary, aniseed (anise), etc. These were called 'herbal wines' and one of them, absinthe wine, is thought to be the ancestor of vermouth.

Later on, when the practice of distillation had reached the monasteries and apothecaries, most of the spirits produced would have been unsuitable as drinks and were above all seen as medicines. In the fifteenth century, the Italians were the first to attempt to remedy this inconvenience and, thanks to the subtle combining of a variety of substances, they managed to produce a drink that they named *liquori*. The arrival of Catherine de Médicis in France, after her marriage in 1532 to the future King Henri II, fostered the success of the Italian liqueurs, of which the best known was *rossoli* – made, it seems, from essence of flowers, predominantly roses.

In the seventeenth century, the production of liqueurs expanded and diversified, with curaçao, based on orange peel (zest), from Holland, cherry-based maraschino from Dalmatia, aniseed- (anise-) based anisette and green Chartreuse, made with herbs and spices, from France.

A century later the industry had powered ahead and new liqueurs, such as Grand Marnier Cordon Rouge (made from orange peel [zest] and Cognac), Benedictine (spices and herbs), cassis liqueur (blackcurrants) and cherry brandy came on the market.

Liqueurs are traditionally drunk as digestifs but some enthusiasts prefer them served with ice. They are also used in numerous cocktails.

The art of the liqueur-maker consists of choosing the ingredients with care, mixing them judiciously and deciding on how sweet the liqueur should be and how long it should be left to mature. The Italians are still the masters in this field: the famous limoncello, based on lemon peel (zest) from the Amalfi region of Campania; Galliano, made from herbs and flowers; and amaretto, flavoured with apricot kernels, are all good examples.

Colouring matter is often added to stimulate the customers' taste or suggest the presence of certain ingredients; cochineal produces red, saffron, caramel and honey add yellow tints and indigo gives a blue colour.

Liqueurs based on plants or fruit skins (like the orange peel [zest] in curaçao) are made by distilling neutral alcohol in which the plants, spices and/or fruit skins have macerated for several weeks. By law liqueurs must contain at least 100 g (4 oz) of sugar per litre (1¾ pints).

Crèmes are liqueurs with a high-sugar content. To be legally called crème de… (menthe, cacao, etc.), they must contain at least 250 g (9 oz) of sugar per litre (1¾ pints).

The fruit-based crèmes are made by macerating fruit in neutral alcohol. For a crème de cassis, for example, the minimum sugar requirement is raised to 400 g (14 oz) per litre (1¾ pints).

Novelties in the liqueur world are nowadays linked to progress in the aromatics industry. The creation of new flavours has made it possible to launch products – like manzana verde, flavoured with green apples – using flavours that are difficult to extract directly.

These liqueurs are made by flavouring and sweetening neutral alcohol, and must also contain a minimum of 100 g (4 oz) of sugar per litre (1¾ pints). The neutral alcohol used in their production is generally distilled from sugar beet.

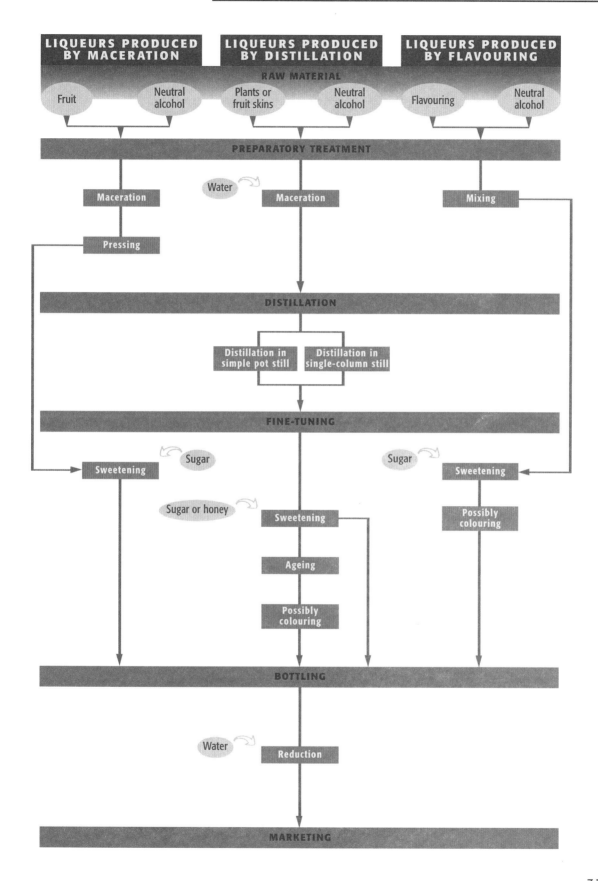

LIQUEURS PRODUCED BY MACERATION

LIQUEURS PRODUCED BY DISTILLATION

LIQUEURS PRODUCED BY FLAVOURING

RAW MATERIAL

Fruit

Neutral alcohol

Plants or fruit skins

Neutral alcohol

Flavouring

Neutral alcohol

PREPARATORY TREATMENT

Maceration

Water

Maceration

Mixing

Pressing

DISTILLATION

Distillation in simple pot still

Distillation in single-column still

FINE-TUNING

Sweetening

Sugar

Sugar

Sweetening

Sugar or honey

Sweetening

Possibly colouring

Ageing

Possibly colouring

BOTTLING

Water

Reduction

MARKETING

Fruit juices

There was a time when the consumption of fruit juice was limited to grape or apple juice, straight from the press at harvest time or during cider making. Keeping it longer than a few days was just not possible because it soon began to ferment.

Nowadays, thanks to refrigeration and, above all, pasteurization, a wide variety of fruit juices is available to the consumer in various forms.

'Fresh fruit juices', sold from refrigerated counters with a 'use-by' date of 15 days, are made simply by pressing the fruit and bottling it without additives or other treatment. Other types of fruit juice have been 'flash-pasteurized' – subjected briefly to a high temperature to sterilize them while retaining all their characteristics.

'Pure fruit juice' is 100% fruit juice and 'concentrate-based fruit juice' (or reconstituted juice) needs to have water added before being marketed and sold. It is made from fruit pressed in the country where it was grown and is subjected to a process of evaporation to save on transport and storage costs.

'Fruit nectars' are drinks made with a lower percentage of fruit (often those with very strong flavours or aromas) and are sweetened.

As to 'fruit drinks', there are no particular regulations for their manufacture.

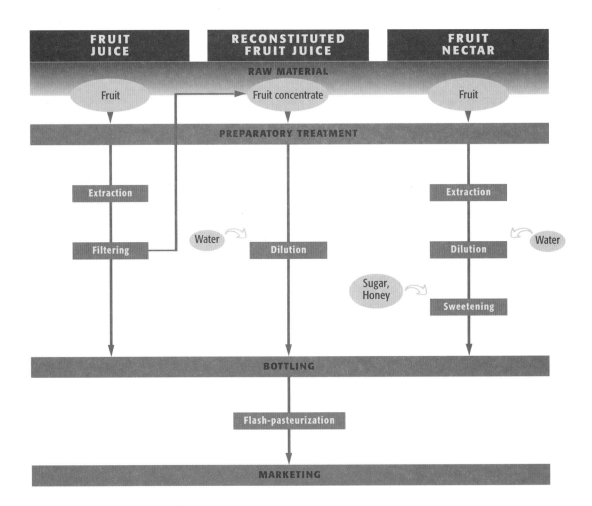

A glossary of bar terms

A

Absinthe-flavoured spirits: liqueur obtained by flavouring neutral alcohol with extract of absinthe. After a ban lasting for more than half a century, absinthe is now marketed under the name of 'spirit flavoured with extracts of absinthe' (45–70% Vol/90–140° proof). The noxious substances that occasioned the ban in 1915 are now present only in minute quantities.

After-dinner drink: a drink taken after a meal as a digestif.

Agave: name of a plant distilled to produce spirits in Mexico. Tequila 100% is made solely of the 'A. tequilana Weber blue' variety of agave.

Amaretto: Italian liqueur made by macerating apricot kernels in alcohol and adding water and sugar (25–28% Vol/50–56° proof). The best-known brand is Amaretto Disaronno, created in 1817.

Angostura bitters: concentrated, reddish-brown bitters, invented in 1824 by Dr Siegert in Ciudad Bolivar (formerly Angostura) in Venezuela, and produced nowadays in Trinidad in the British Antilles. It consists of rum flavoured with gentian and extracts of plants and spices (44.7% Vol/89.4° proof).

Aniseed- (Anise-) flavoured aperitif: predominantly aniseed- (anise-) flavoured spirit made from plant extracts (green anise, star anise, fennel, etc.) with alcohol, water and sugar added. Whether clear or coloured, all anises go cloudy when diluted with water or crushed ice. The two best-known brands are Pernod (45% Vol/90° proof), created in 1922 by Pernod Fils and Hémard, and Pastis Ricard (45% Vol/90° proof), invented by Paul Ricard in 1932.

Aperitif: name used to indicate alcoholic drinks with a dry, sometimes bitter, flavour that are taken to stimulate the appetite ('aperitif' comes from the Latin *aperire* – to open). It is also describes the convivial hour of day when people gather to drink them.

Applejack: spirit distilled from cider (similar to Calvados), which has been made in New Jersey on the east coast of the United States since the start of the eighteenth century. The most popular brand is 'Laird', founded in 1780 (40–50% Vol/ 80–100° proof).

Apricot brandy: liqueur made by macerating apricots in a wine-based spirit and adding at least 100 g (4 oz) of sugar per litre (1¼ pints) (24–30% Vol/ 48–60° proof).

Armagnac: wine-based spirit (white grapes) made in a part of Gascony, France, covered by a controlled appellation of origin (40% Vol/80° proof). The spirit is aged for a minimum of two years in oak casks before being marketed, either directly or blended with armagnacs from other vintages. Some vintages are more than 20 years old. Armagnac is seldom used in cocktails.

B

Bailey's
▶ *see* Irish cream

Banane (crème de): liqueur made from neutral alcohol flavoured with banana extract, coloured yellow and sweetened with at least 250 g (9 oz) sugar per litre (1¼ pints) (24–30% Vol/48–60° proof).

Base: spirit chosen for its smell, taste and colour around which a cocktail is constructed. It is one of the three components of a cocktail, the others being the modifier and the flavouring or colouring agents. It can be vodka, whisky, rum, brandy, etc.

Beer: alcoholic beverage obtained by fermenting the sugars in a must (▶ *see* **Must**) made from barley and flavoured with hops (4–7% Vol/ 8–14° proof).

Before dinner
▶ *see* Aperitif

Benedictine: amber-coloured liqueur based on plants, herbs and spices (angelica, coriander, hyssop, balm, myrrh, nutmeg, cloves, etc.), invented by Benedictine monks in the sixteenth century. It was first produced commercially at Fécamp, France, in 1863, by a certain Alexandre Le Grand (40% Vol/80° proof).

Bitter aperitif: alcoholic drink with a predominantly bitter taste, made of neutral alcohol flavoured with plant extracts. The best known is Campari (24% Vol/48° proof).

Bitter aromatic wines: alcoholic drinks made by flavouring a mixture of wine (minimum

75%) and neutral spirit with plant extracts and cinchona bark or gentian (14.5–22% Vol/29–44° proof). They include quinine tonic wines (Dubonnet, etc.) and vermouths.

Bitters: concentrated bitter liquids used a few drops at a time to flavour cocktails. Before 1900 there were a dozen or so different makes of bitters: the best-known today are Angostura, Peychaud's and orange bitters.

Blend: word used for the mixing of at least two spirits of different flavour, smell and colour. In Scotland, the word 'blend' is used to describe a mixture of malt and grain whiskies.

Blender: electric apparatus, used for puréeing ingredients, consisting of a motor topped by a container with a blade in its base. It is essential to the preparation of 'frozen' cocktails. The concept was patented in the United States in 1922 by Stephen Poplawski and put into production a few years later. A more reliable model was marketed in 1933 by Fred Osius and Fred Waring.

Boston shaker: term used for a cocktail shaker invented in the United States, made up of an upper and lower part that make a partial fit when put together. The lower part consists of a large glass, smaller in diameter than the metal beaker that fits over it. It has no built-in strainer.

Bourbon
▶ see Whiskey

Bowl
▶ see Cup

Brandy: generic English word for spirit distilled from wine, such as Cognac (white grapes) and pisco

(white grapes). Used together with the name of a fruit, the word means either a spirit distilled from that fruit or a liqueur containing that spirit. Apple brandy, for instance, refers to Calvados.

Bucks: family of cocktails that appeared in the 1920s. A buck is made with some form of spirit, lemon juice and ginger ale, garnished with a strip of lemon peel (zest).

C

Cacao (crème de): liqueur made by flavouring neutral alcohol with cocoa extract, with or without brown colouring, and adding at least 250 g (9 oz) sugar per litre (1¾ pints) (24–30% Vol/48–60° proof).

Cachaça
▶ see Rum

Calvados: spirit (minimum 40% Vol/80° proof) distilled from cider (mixed with 30% pear juice in the case of Calvados Domfrontais). The production area of the Calvados AOC is restricted largely to Basse-Normandie. Calvados Pays d'Auge AOC is mostly produced in the Calvados region and, after double distillation, it spends at least two years in cask. Calvados Domfrontais AOC must be aged for more than three years.

Campari: commercial brand of a bitter aperitif flavoured with extracts of roots, fruits, herbs and spices and coloured red (25% Vol/50° proof). This bitter was perfected by Gaspare Campari in the 1860s in Milan. It is the basis of the Americano cocktail, made with equal parts of Campari and red vermouth (▷ p. 233).

Canadian whisky
▶ see Whisky

Cassis (crème de): speciality of Dijon since 1845, made by macerating blackcurrants in neutral alcohol with added water and at least 400 g (14 oz) sugar per litre (1¾ pints) (15–20% Vol/30–40° proof).

Champagne: an AOC sparkling wine (about 12% Vol/24° proof) made to a very specific fermentation method in the wine-growing area around the city of Reims, France. The effervescence develops while it is ageing in bottles, following the start of a second fermentation. It is subsequently dosed with wine and amounts of sugar that are varied according to the desired category: Extra Brut, Brut, Sec or Demi-Sec.

Chartreuse: liqueur made by the Chartreuse monks to a recipe dating back to the early seventeenth century. It is flavoured with extracts from more than 100 herbs and spices (balm, hyssop, angelica leaves, cinnamon, saffron, etc.). There are two types: green Chartreuse (55% Vol/110° proof), created in 1764, and the rather sweeter yellow Chartreuse (40% Vol/80° proof), perfected in 1838. They are made at Voiron, near Grenoble, in the Grande-Chartreuse massif, France.

Cherry brandy: liqueur made by macerating cherries in wine-based spirit sweetened with at least 100 g (4 oz) sugar per litre (1¾ pints) (24–30% Vol/48–60° proof). The best-known brands are Cherry Heering, first produced in Denmark in 1818 (24.7% Vol/ 49.4° proof), and Cherry Rocher, created in the middle of the nineteenth century at La Côte-Saint-André, in Isère, France (24% Vol/48° proof).

Cobblers: family of cocktails that appeared in the United States at the start of the 1800s. A cobbler consists of a spirit sweetened with sugar and garnished with seasonal fruits.

Cocktail strainer: accessory for holding back the ice while pouring from a mixing glass or a Boston or continental shaker; used for cocktails that are served 'straight up'.

Coconut liqueur: liqueur made by flavouring rum (or a neutral alcohol) with an aromatic extract of coconut and at least 100 g (4 oz) sugar per litre (1¾ pints) (20–24% Vol/40°–48° proof).

Coconut milk: a thick, non-alcoholic liquid, made in the Caribbean since the 1950s from fresh coconut and sugar cane. The best-known brand is Coco Lopez, created in 1954 in Puerto Rico, in the Caribbean, and which inspired the famous Piña Colada (▷ p. 162).

Coffee liqueur: preparation obtained by flavouring neutral alcohol with coffee extract, brown colouring and at least 100 g (4 oz) sugar per litre (1¾ pints) (24–26.5% Vol/48–53° proof).

Cognac: spirit distilled from wine (white grapes) made in the Charentes region of France. Cognac is a controlled appellation of origin (AOC) and its entire production (harvesting, distillation and ageing) must take place exclusively within the designated area. It is blended according to a complex process that mixes spirits of different years and different crus (minimum 40% Vol/80° proof).

Cointreau: liqueur made by flavouring neutral alcohol with an aromatic extract of sweet and bitter orange peel (zest) (40% Vol/80° proof). It is made by the Cointreau company, founded in 1849, which created the famous curaçao triple sec in 1875 in Angers, France.

Cola: effervescent drink flavoured with plant extracts and coloured with caramel. The recipe was invented in the United States in the 1880s.

Coladas: family of cocktails that appeared in the 1950s. A colada consists of a spirit, coconut milk and fruit juice.

Collins: family of cocktails that appeared at the end of the 1860s in the United States, having been created in London in the 1800s. A collins is made up of some form of spirit, sugar, lemon juice and soda water (club soda). While it was originally just a large, double-sized fizz (➤ see **Fizzes**) made in a shaker, nowadays a collins, unlike a fizz, is made directly in the glass, using a higher proportion of lemon juice.

Coolers: family of cocktails – initially non-alcoholic – that appeared in the United States towards the end of the 1880s. A cooler consists of a spirit, sugar and ginger ale.

Cordial: name formerly applied in the United States to liqueurs. In the nineteenth century the word was used for both sweet drinks, such as curaçao and other liqueurs, and for syrups like lime cordial. Nowadays it is mainly used for syrups.

Corpse Reviver: name given to drinks used as cures for hangovers. It is also the name of a Cognac-based cocktail (▷ p. 208) with a very high alcohol content.

Cranberry: small, acidic red berry. Cranberry juice, unlike other fruit juices and nectars, is sharp and astringent.

Crème: term applied to liqueurs with a sugar content of more than 250 g (9 oz) per litre (1¾ pints). Crème de cassis must contain at least 400 g (14 oz) per litre (1¾ pints).

Crustas: family of cocktails invented by Joseph Santini at the City Exchange in New Orleans in the 1840s. A crusta is made up of a spirit, lemon juice, sugar and bitters, and is garnished with a strip of lemon peel (zest).

Cup: name used in English clubs and American taverns towards the end of the seventeenth century for a drink prepared in a punch bowl for serving to a large number of people.

Curaçao: name given to liqueurs made from neutral alcohol flavoured with essence of sweet orange peel (zest) together with that of bitter Seville oranges. The three types are curaçao triple sec (35–40% Vol/70–80° proof), blue curaçao (25% Vol/50° proof) and orange curaçao (30% Vol/60° proof). Cointreau is a brand of curaçao triple sec.

D

Daisies: family of cocktails that appeared in the United States in the 1870s. A daisy consists of a spirit, lemon juice, soda water (club soda), curaçao and sugar.

Dash: a small quantity, such as a few drops of bitters or a touch of syrup.

Digestif: term used to describe a drink that is taken after a meal to aid digestion.

Distillate: the liquid obtained when the vapours collected during distillation are condensed.

Drambuie: liqueur, whose origins go back to the eighteenth century, made by flavouring a blend of malt and grain Scotch whiskies with spices and heather honey (40% Vol/80° proof). It was made commercially from 1909 by Malcolm Mackinnon, to an undisclosed recipe.

Dry: term applied to cocktails with an astringent flavour either due to their high alcohol content or to the presence of tannin in such ingredients as American whiskey that is matured in oak barrels. Dry cocktails generally contain very little sweetening. When 'dry' forms part of the name of a cocktail, as in 'Dry Martini', it indicates a much greater quantity of spirit than vermouth.

Dubonnet: commercial brand of a bitter aromatic wine invented in Paris in 1846 by Joseph Dubonnet. The original had an alcohol content of 14.8% Vol/29.6° proof but another red Dubonnet and a white version, both 19% Vol/38° proof, were subsequently created for the American market.

E

Eau-de-vie: French word meaning alcoholic liquor or spirit.
► see Spirit

Eggnog: cocktails that became popular in the United States in the nineteenth century. An eggnog consists of a spirit, egg yolk, milk and sugar.

Extract: preparation made by thoroughly steeping a substance in water, spirit or ether, and concentrating the resulting solution. Aromatic substances obtained from plants, roots, spices or fruits are made in this way.

F

Fancy drink: describes excessively complicated, over-decorated drinks.

Fernet-Branca: a bitter aperitif invented in Milan in 1845 by Bernardino Branca. A drink with a very marked bitter flavour, Fernet-Branca is made by macerating more than 40 medicinal plants and aromatic herbs (aloes, camomile, gentian, quinine, saffron, sage, etc.) in neutral alcohol. Its alcohol content is 40% Vol/80° proof.

Fixes: family of cocktails that appeared in the United States before the 1860s. A fix is made from the same ingredients as the sours: a spirit with lemon juice and sugar, and garnished with seasonal berries.

Fizzes: family of cocktails that appeared in the United States in the 1870s. Like the collins, a fizz is made with spirit, lemon juice, soda water (club soda) and sugar. Unlike the collins, however, a fizz nowadays is made in a shaker.

Flair: name given to a spectacular technique of juggling the various objects (bottles, glasses, shakers, etc.) needed to make drinks during their preparation. There are 'flair' competitions, entered for the most part by professionals. There are two types of this phenomenon: 'working flair' or 'production flair', and 'exhibition flair', which, as its name implies, is a form of entertainment. The actions performed in the first kind allow the barman to prepare the drinks regardless of the amount contained in the bottles. In the second, the actions can only be performed with bottles containing no more than 60 ml (2 fl oz) of liquid.

Flamber: French culinary term used for setting light to an inflammable liquid or substance such as spirit or the oils in citrus peel (zest).

Flavouring and colouring agents: ingredients that give the final touches to the taste and colour of a cocktail. Together with the base and the modifier, these agents make up the three components of a cocktail. The flavouring agent is there to enhance the flavour of the basic alcohol or add something extra to it. It may be sweet (syrup or liqueur) or astringent (bitter aromatic wines or concentrated bitters).

Flips: family of cocktails that appeared in England before 1810. A flip is made with spirit, egg yolk and sugar, and is generally dusted with a little grated nutmeg.

Floater: term used when a layer of liquid is carefully superimposed on a previous, different layer, possibly with the help of a spoon.

Fortified wine: wine to which wine-based spirit has been added to increase its alcohol content and to create sweet wines that retain a certain sugar content. (Port and sherry are fortified wines.)

Fraise (crème de): liqueur made by macerating strawberries in neutral alcohol and adding at least 250 g (9 oz) sugar per litre (1¼ pints) (15–20% Vol/30–40° proof).

Framboise (crème de): liqueur made by macerating raspberries in neutral alcohol and adding at least 250 g (9 oz) sugar per litre (1¼ pints) (15–20% Vol/30–40° proof).

Frappé: term used for a cocktail poured into a Martini glass containing a generous amount of crushed ice. Before the invention of the blender, which permitted the preparation of 'frozen' drinks (▷ p. 57), this method made the coldest possible cocktail.

Frosting a glass: operation (▷ p. 59) that consists of moistening the rim of the glass, generally with lemon juice, and dipping it into a powder (sugar or fine salt).

Frozen: drinks having the consistency of a sorbet (sherbet), made by blending the ingredients with a good proportion of ice in an electric blender (▷ p. 57).

Fruit-based cocktails: drinks containing one or more types of fruit juice and tasting predominantly of fruit.

G

Galliano: liqueur invented in Tuscany, Italy, in 1896 by Arturo Vaccari. It is produced by flavouring alcohol with plant extracts (star anise, lavender, vanilla, etc.), and colouring it yellow (30% Vol/60° proof).

Gin: spirit obtained by flavouring neutral alcohol (usually cereal-based) with extract of juniper. London gin, which may be produced anywhere in the world, is distilled with juniper berries and other aromatic items (cardamom seeds, angelica root, coriander seeds, etc.). Plymouth gin is also made in the same way but, since it is covered by a form of controlled appellation of origin, may only be so named if it is produced at Plymouth, on the south coast of England.

Ginger ale: carbonated soft drink (soda) lightly flavoured with ginger. The best-known brand is Canada Dry, which was created in Toronto in 1904 by John J McLaughlin.

Ginger beer: non-alcoholic drink of British origin, produced in Jamaica for several centuries. It is made by bottling a liquid, based on fresh ginger, as soon as it begins to ferment. Ginger ale and ginger beer were once one and the same thing, but present-day ginger beer has a much more pronounced flavour of ginger. The main brands are D & G and Reed's.

Grand Marnier Cordon Rouge: created in 1880 by the Marnier-Lapostolle Company, this liqueur is made by combining the flavour of bitter oranges with rigorously selected Cognacs (40% Vol/80° proof).

Grenadine: formerly a syrup made from pomegranate seeds, it is now made with a sugar cane syrup flavoured with extracts of red berries and vanilla, and sometimes even lemon.

Grog: a hot drink made with rum, lemon juice, sugar and boiling water. The name is derived from the nickname given by sailors of the British Royal Navy to Admiral Edward Vernon, who forced them to dilute their rum rations with water.

H

Highballs: family of cocktails that appeared in the United States in the 1890s. A highball is made with a spirit, an effervescent drink and sometimes a strip of lemon peel (zest). Highball is also the name of a tall, straight-sided glass containing about 350 ml (12 fl oz). This 'long drink' glass is used for cocktails topped up with soda water (club soda) or fruit juices. It also goes under the names of collins glass or large tumbler.

Hot cocktails: mixtures that are served in a heatproof toddy glass, generally during cold weather.

I

Irish cream: liqueur of Irish origin made from Irish whiskey, fresh cream and cocoa (17% Vol/34° proof). The best-known brand is Bailey's, the first of this type of liqueur, invented in 1974.

Irish whiskey
 ► *see* Whisky, whiskey

J

Jigger: name for a type of spirit measure. The measures used for preparing cocktails vary from country to country. In France they are 20 ml (¾ fl oz) and 40 ml (1¼ fl oz), in Britain they are 25 ml (1 fl oz) and 50 ml (1¾ fl oz) and in the United States they are 20 ml (¾ fl oz) and 45 ml (1½ fl oz).

Juice: liquid obtained by pressing fruit or vegetables. It may be 100% pure juice or a concentrate diluted with water. Fruit nectars are thicker drinks with a lower fruit content, and added sugar and other ingredients. Banana nectar is one example.

Juleps: family of cocktails that appeared in the United States a little before 1800. A julep consists of some form of spirit, fresh mint leaves and sugar.

K

Kirsch: spirit distilled from cherries, chiefly made in France, Switzerland and Germany. Its flavour varies according to whether the cherries are crushed with or without their stones (pits). After distillation, kirsch is aged for several months in glass carboys.

Krupnik: traditional Polish liqueur made by flavouring vodka with spices and sweetening with honey, according to a recipe dating back several centuries (40% Vol/80° proof).

L

Lemon-lime soda: carbonated soft drink (soda) flavoured with extracts of lemon and lime. The best-known brand is 7 UP, which was invented in 1928 by Charles Grigg in the United States.

Lime cordial: syrup made with sugar and lime juice. It was invented by Lauchlan Rose of Edinburgh, Scotland, in 1865. The main brand is Rose's Lime Juice Cordial.

Limoncello: Italian liqueur produced in the Amalfi region, which became popular in the twentieth century. It is made by macerating lemon peel (zest) in neutral alcohol and adding sugar and water (30% Vol/60° proof). The best-known brand is Limoncello di Capri; it was created in 1988.

Liqueur: alcoholic drink consisting of a mixture of neutral alcohol or spirit, flavourings (fruits, plants, skins, seeds), sugar and possibly honey or glucose, with an alcohol content of at least 15% Vol/30° proof. A liqueur contains between 100–250 g (4–9 oz) of sugar per litre (1¾ pints); crèmes are much sweeter (up to 400 g [14 oz] sugar per litre [1¾ pints] for crème de cassis). Liqueurs may be based on different fruit or fruit skins; orange

(curaçao, Grand Marnier Cordon Rouge); cherry (cherry brandy, maraschino); apricot (apricot brandy); blackcurrant (crème de cassis), etc. Plants, too, may be used (Benedictine, Chartreuse, crème de menthe, Galliano).

Liqueur-based cocktail: a more or less sweet mixture, depending on the sugar content. This type of cocktail is served for preference as a digestif.

Long drink: any drink over 120 ml (4 fl oz) in volume.

Lychee (litchi) liqueur: neutral alcohol flavoured with extract of lychees and containing at least 100 g (4 oz) sugar per litre (1¾ pints) (20–24% Vol/40–48° proof). The best-known brand names are Soho in Europe and Dita in Asia.

M

Malibu: liqueur invented in 1980, made in Barbados from rum flavoured with extract of coconut and sweetened with at least 100 g (4 oz) sugar per litre (1¾ pints) (24% Vol/48° proof).

Malt: cereal in which germination has been artificially induced and then interrupted. It is subsequently dried, roasted and ground to a powder. In the industrial manufacture of alcoholic beverages, malted barley is the principal grain used, but some kinds of vodka are made with malted rye.

Manzana verde: Spanish liqueur made by flavouring neutral alcohol with extract of Granny Smith apples and adding a minimum of 100 g (4 oz) sugar per litre (1¾ pints) (18–20% Vol/36–40° proof). It is called apple schnapps in English, and the principal brands in France are Izarra and Vedrenne.

Maraschino cherries: cherries dyed red and used to garnish certain cocktails. When they first appeared at the end of the nineteenth century they were preserved in maraschino liqueur but today they are bottled in almond-flavoured syrup.

Maraschino liqueur: originally an Italian liqueur invented at Zara (now Zadar in Croatia) in 1821 by Girolamo Luxardo. It is made by distilling the fermented juice of bitter, wild cherries and adding at least 100 g (4 oz) sugar per litre (1¾ pints) (30–32% Vol/60–64° proof). The best brand is still Luxardo.

Martini
▶ see **Vermouth**

Martini glass: pedestal glass with a triangular profile recommended for serving short drinks 'straight up', 'frappé' and often 'frozen'. It gets its name from the famous Dry Martini (▷ p. 92), which is usually served in this type of glass. It is also called a cocktail glass.

Melocoton
▶ see **Peach schnapps**

Melon liqueur: green alcoholic drink made by flavouring neutral alcohol with an extract of winter melon (with yellow or greenish flesh) and at least 100 g (4 oz) sugar per litre (1¾ pints) (20–25% Vol/40–50° proof). It was created by the Japanese company Midori in 1978.

Menthe (crème de): liqueur of English origin consisting of neutral alcohol flavoured with mint extract, sweetened and often coloured green (21–24% Vol/42–48° proof). It became popular in the eighteenth century. Get 27 is a green crème de menthe, whereas Get 31 is colourless.

Mixing glass: large, slightly conical-shaped glass with a pouring lip, used to prepare cocktails that are intended to be served 'straight up', without ice in the glass, and are made from ingredients that mix easily. To prepare a single cocktail, it must hold at least 500 ml (17¼ fl oz); for two it requires a 650 ml (22½ fl oz) capacity.

Mixing spoon: a metal spoon for mixing cocktails either in a mixing glass or directly in the serving glass. It is also used in the preparation of shooters (▷ p. 58) or to measure quantities (it holds one teaspoonful). The stem, often ending in a small pestle for crushing mint leaves, etc., is twisted to give a better grip when coated with condensation caused by contact with the ice.

Mixologist: name given by fellow professionals to one who makes a contribution to the profession by researching new cocktail combinations, working techniques and bar history.

Mixology: word coined at the end of the 1890s in San Francisco, which means the sum total of knowledge about bars, techniques, history, etc.

Mocktail: word coined a few decades ago to describe a non-alcoholic cocktail.

Modifier: ingredient that gives a cocktail its consistency (fluid, creamy, thick, sparkling, etc.) and which governs whether the drink is short or long, depending on the quantities used. It is one of the three basic ingredients of a cocktail, the others being the flavouring or colouring agents, and the base. It can be vermouth, wine,

port, fruit juice, Champagne or even milk.

Mûre (crème de): liqueur made by macerating blackberries in neutral alcohol and adding at least 250 g (9 oz) sugar per litre (1¼ pints) (15–20% Vol/30–40° proof).

Must: name given to as yet unfermented grape juice from which wine is made; also to fruit and vegetable juices used in the production of alcoholic drinks.

N

Nectar
▶ *see* Juice

Neutral alcohol: this is alcohol distilled to a high degree (96% Vol/192° proof) to eliminate as much as possible of the taste, colour and smell of the raw material. Alcohol distilled from sugar beet it is known as potable spirit.

Nightcap: the last drink before going to bed.

Noilly Prat
▶ *see* Vermouth

O

On the rocks: drink poured over ice cubes in a 'rocks' glass.

Orange bitters: concentrated bitters with a predominant taste of orange. It is made by flavouring neutral alcohol with extracts of Seville or bitter oranges (30–40% Vol/60–80° proof).

Orgeat syrup: formerly made with a paste of ground sweet and bitter almonds, it is now produced by dissolving a sweetening agent in water flavoured with extracts of sweet and/or bitter almonds.

P

Pastis: alcoholic drink with a predominantly aniseed (anise) flavour made from plant extracts (green anise, star anise, fennel, etc.) and liquorice extract, together with alcohol, water and sugar (45% Vol/90° proof). The best-known brand is Ricard (45% Vol/90° proof), invented by Paul Ricard in 1932.

Peach schnapps (Melocoton): liqueur made from neutral alcohol flavoured with peach extract and containing at least 100 g (4 oz) sugar per litre (1¼ pints) (18–20% Vol/36–40° proof).

Peel: the oily outer layer of citrus fruit removed with a special paring knife. The peel (zest) of oranges, lemons or limes is used a great deal in the preparation of cocktails. To extract the aromatic oils they must be first squeezed firmly between the fingers over the cocktail glass.

Pernod
▶ *see* Aniseed- (Anise-) flavoured aperitif

Peychaud's bitters: concentrated bitters created by Antoine Peychaud in New Orleans in the 1830s based on a Créole recipe dating from 1793 (30% Vol/60° proof). The recipe is a closely guarded secret.

Pick-Me-Up: a drink believed to have fortifying properties.

Pimm's: a bitter aromatic drink invented by James Pimm in London in the 1840s and marketed from 1859 onwards. It is made by flavouring gin with herbs and spices (25% Vol/50° proof).

Pisco: Chilean spirit based on white grapes (known as Chilean brandy) and made by distilling fermented grape must. After distillation, pisco is marketed at different strengths (35, 40 or 45% Vol/70, 80 or 90° proof), either straight away or after a minimum of two months ageing. A spirit also called pisco is made in Peru, but by a different process resulting in a different flavour.

Plymouth gin
► see Gin

Port: wine fortified with grape-based alcohol, grown in the vineyards of the Douro Valley in Portugal (about 20% Vol/40° proof). Before ageing it is blended, either using wines from the same harvest to produce 'Vintage' and 'Late Bottled Vintage' (LBV), or wines from different harvests for 'Ruby' and 'Tawny' port. The vintage ports are made with wines from those years when the harvest was exceptionally good.

Potable spirit
► see Neutral alcohol

Pousse-cafés
► see Shooters

Prohibition: Period lasting from 1919–1933 during which the consumption of alcohol was prohibited in the United States. This ban applied to all drinks with an alcohol content of more than 0.5% Vol/1° proof. Some spirits and bitters with restorative qualities could, however, be sold legally when prescribed by a doctor.

Proof: scale used in the United States to indicate the degree of alcohol in a drink. Dividing this number by two gives the percentage of alcohol by volume (% Vol).

Puffs: family of cocktails that appeared in the United States in the 1890s. A puff consists of

a spirit, milk, sugar and sometimes soda water (club soda).

Pulp strainer: item used to strain liquids containing matter in suspension (notably fresh fruit pulp).

Punches: family of cocktails probably first recorded in Barbados in 1650. Punch is made in large quantities. Its composition is very varied and may contain the following ingredients: a spirit, a sweetener (sugar, syrup, liqueur, etc.), citrus fruit juice (lemon, lime, orange) and/or water (still, sparkling, soda water [club soda], tea, etc.).

R

Ricard
► see Pastis

Rickeys: family of cocktails that appeared in the United States around 1900. A rickey is made with some form of spirit, lime juice and soda water (club soda).

Rocks glass: glass used to serve spirits or short drinks with ice, the name being a shortened form of 'on the rocks'. It is also called an old-fashioned glass or a small tumbler.

Rum: spirit made by fermenting and then distilling either the molasses left after sugar cane is refined (industrial or sugar cane rum) or the juice of sugar cane (*rhum agricole*, 'agricultural' or distillery rum). Rum from Puerto Rico, Cuba and Jamaica is made from molasses and has a more or less woody flavour. *Rhum agricole* is the most aromatic among the different rums. They are all produced in several categories: white, amber, aged, etc. Cachaça is made in Brazil from either molasses or sugar cane juice.

Rye whiskey
► see Whisky, whiskey

S

Sangarees: family of cocktails that appeared in the British Antilles before the 1820s. A sangaree is made with a spirit, fortified wine and sugar and is dusted with grated nutmeg.

Scaffas: family of cocktails that originated in the United States before the 1860s. Prior to the 1930s, the ingredients were superimposed, shooter-style. A scaffa is made with a spirit, a liqueur and either a bitter aperitif or concentrated bitters.

Scotch whisky
► see Whisky, whiskey

Sec: French word for 'dry.'
► see Dry

Shaker: utensil indispensable to the preparation of some cocktails. It comes in two types: the two-part shaker (Boston or continental shakers) that has to be used with an ice strainer; and the three-part shaker that is equipped with an integral strainer.

Sherry: wine fortified with grape-based alcohol, produced in Andalucia in southern Spain, where it is called *Jerez*. It contains about 15% Vol/30° proof. Sherry is made strictly to traditional techniques. Fino sherry is light and dry; olorosos are darker in colour and stronger.

Shooters: cocktails served in a shot glass containing about 60 ml (2 fl oz), and designed to be 'knocked back' in one swallow. They are made up of three differently coloured liqueurs (or two liqueurs and a spirit) in separate, superimposed layers (▷ p. 58).

This type of drink was called a 'pousse-café' in the 1840s, at which time one drank the liqueurs one after the other.

Short drink: a cocktail of less than 120 ml (4 fl oz) in volume.

Shot glass: glass of which the small content (about 60 ml [2 fl oz]) and the concise shape is ideal for drinks that are intended for 'knocking back' in one go. Shooters are always served in this kind of glass. Shot glasses are also used for serving neat tequila or vodka.

Slings: family of cocktails that appeared in the United States before 1800s. A sling is made up of a spirit, sugar and still or sparkling water, topped with grated nutmeg.

Smashes: family of cocktails that appeared in the United States in the 1850s. A smash is made in much the same way as a julep – that is to say from spirit, sugar and fresh mint – but using less mint (two to three leaves only). It is garnished with orange slices or seasonal berries.

Smooth cocktail: mixture that is thick and/or nutritious, often containing cream, milk or egg.

Soda: American term for carbonated soft drinks made from purified water with added carbon dioxide, often flavoured with aromatic extracts. Sweetened to a greater or lesser degree, the main ones are ginger ale, lemon-lime soda, various colas, tonic water and ginger beer. Terms used in England are soda water (club soda) and 'mixers'.

Sours: family of cocktails that appeared in England in the eigthteenth century. A sour is made with a spirit, lemon juice and sugar.

Southern Comfort: liqueur invented in New Orleans in 1874 by M W Heron and has been on sale since 1889. It consists of American whiskey flavoured with ingredients that are kept secret and sweetened with at least 100 g (4 oz) sugar per litre (1¾ pints) (40% Vol/80° proof).

Speakeasy: clandestine drinking venue where alcohol was consumed illegally during the American Prohibition.

Spirit (Eau-de-Vie): drink made by distilling a fermented must (► see **Must**) made from a variety of raw materials. From fruit one obtains spirits like Cognac, Calvados, kirsch; cereals produce vodka, gin and whisky (or whiskey); plants produce tequila and rum; and vegetables (notably potatoes) are used to make vodka and potable spirit. Spirits may be aged or not, depending on the regulations applied.

Spirits: alcoholic drinks resulting from distillation and having particular characteristics (taste, aroma, colour) and a minimum alcohol content of 15% Vol/30° proof.

Straight up: expression used to indicate a drink that has been shaken or stirred, in a mixing glass, with ice that is then filtered out as it is poured into the glass.

Sugar cane syrup: sugar cane dissolved in water.

Syrup: substance made by dissolving sweeteners in water, with or without flavouring.

T

Tabasco: highly spiced sauce invented in 1868 in Louisiana by Edmund McIlhenny. Made from vinegar, chillies and salt, red Tabasco is the best known and the one most used in cocktails, but there is now also a green type, which is milder.

Tennessee whiskey
► see Whisky, whiskey

Tequila: Mexican spirit made from the tropical agave plant. The word 'tequila', used alone, indicates a spirit made from not less than 51% agave mixed with sugars from other raw materials. Tequila 100% agave is made solely with the 'A. *tequilana* Weber blue' variety of agave. The terms 'gold' or 'joven abocado' are used for coloured and sweetened tequila. Tequila blanco (or silver) has undergone no ageing process. Tequila reposado is matured for at least two months in tuns or large-capacity barrels. Tequila añejo is aged for at least one year in barrel.

Thirst-quenching: applied to drinks that slake the thirst; usually made with fruit juice and/or carbonated soft drinks (sodas).

Toddies: family of cocktails from the British Antilles around 1760. Formerly, they could be drunk either hot or cold, but nowadays we drink them hot, like grogs. A toddy consists of a spirit, sugar and boiling water. They are served in toddy glasses made from heatproof glass to withstand the addition of the boiling water. They contain about 250 ml (9 fl oz).

Tonic water: effervescent drink flavoured with quinine from the bark of the cinchona – a tree native to Peru. It was invented in the 1870s by the Schweppes company. Tonic waters fall into the category of sodas or mixers.

Triple Sec
▶ see Curaçao

Tumbler, large
▶ see Highballs (glass)

Tumbler, small
▶ see Rocks glass

U-V

Up
▶ see Straight up

Vermouth: a combination of at least 75% wine mixed with neutral alcohol and flavoured with extracts of plants (such as absinthe) and other, often bitter, aromatic substances. (Its alcohol content is 14.5–22% Vol/29–44° proof). There are many different types of vermouth, including the pale-coloured dry vermouth (50–60 g [2–2¼ oz] sugar per litre [1¼ pints]) and the sweeter red vermouth (100–150 g [4–5 oz] sugar per litre [1¼ pints]),

coloured with caramel. The best-known brands are Martini, created in 1863, and Noilly Prat, founded in 1813.

Vodka: spirit made by distilling a fermented must based on potatoes or rye, or a mixture of cereals (40% Vol/80° proof). The spirit is generally filtered through powdered-charcoal filters to remove as much of the flavours and aromas as possible. Some forms of vodka, rarely used in cocktails, are flavoured with fruit or plants. Among these are vodka flavoured with lemon, blackcurrant or bison grass.

W

Whisky, whiskey: spirit made – in the case of Scotch single malt whisky – by distilling malted barley. Irish 'pure pot still' whiskey uses malted and non-malted barley in roughly equal quantities (around 50%) and Canadian whisky uses a mixture

of cereals (predominantly rye). A mixture of at least 51% maize (corn) with other cereals goes into American 'straight bourbon', while Tennessee whiskey is made from mixed cereals – the predominant one being at least 51% – and is distinctive in that it is filtered through maple-wood charcoal.

Wine: drink made by fermenting grape juice or a grape must.

Worcestershire sauce: highly spiced preparation invented in 1837 in Worcestershire in England. The oldest and most popular is Lea & Perrins. The ingredients include vinegar, anchovies, tamarind, garlic and onion.

X-Z

Xérès: French name for sherry.
▶ see Sherry

Zest:
▶ see Peel

A cocktail bibliography

Old books
(before 1900)

BARNES (Albert), *The Complete Bartender*, Philadelphia, Crawford & Co., 1884, 64.

BEVIL (A. V.), *Barkeeper's Ready Reference*, 1871, 136.

BYRON (O. H.), *The Modern Bartender's Guide*, New York, Excelsior Publishing House, 1884, 114.

CAMPBELL (Chas. B.), *The American Barkeeper*, San Fancisco, Mullin Mahon & Co., 1867, 32.

DE SALIS (Mrs), *Drinks à la Mode*, London, Longmans, Green & Co., 1892, 100.

ENGEL (Leo), *American and Other Drinks*, London, Tinsley Brothers, 1878, 73.

FINNIGAN (M. J.), *The Reminder*, Worcester, Miles F. King Co., 1899, 93.

FOUQUET (Louis), *Bariana*, Paris, Émile Duvoye, 1896, 151.

GIBSON (Jos. W.), *Scientific Bar-Keeping*, New York, E. N. Cook & Co., 1884, 49.

GREEN (Herbert W.), *Mixed Drinks*, Indianapolis, Frank H. Smith, 1895, 168.

HANEY (Jesse), *Haney's Steward and Barkeeper's Manual*, New York, Jesse Haney & Co., 1869, 72.

JOHNSON (Harry), *New and Improved Bartender's Manual*, New York, Harry Johnson, 1882, 189.

JOHNSON (Harry), *New and Improved Illustrated Bartender's Manual*, New York, Harry Johnson, 1888, 197.

KAPPELLER (George J.), *Modern American Mixed Drinks*, New York, The Merriam Company, 1895, 120.

LAWLOR (C. F.), *The Mixicologist*, Cincinnati, A. E. Lawlor, 1897, 169.

McDONOUGH (Patsy), *McDonough's Bar-Keeper's Guide*, Rochester, Patsy McDonough, 1883, 49.

MEW (James) and ASHTON (John), *Drinks of the World*, London, The Leadenhall Press, 362.

MORSE EARLE (Alice), *Customs and Fashions in Old New England*, New York, Charles Scribner's Sons, 1893, 387.

NABER, ALFS and BRUNE, *Catalogue and Bartender's Guide*, San Francisco, 1884, 33.

ROBERTS (George Edwin), *Cups and their Customs*, London, John Van Voorst, 1863, 52.

ROBERTS (George Edwin), *Cups and their Customs*, 2nd edition, London, John Van Voorst, 1869, 62.

SCHMIDT (William), *The Flowing Bowl*, New York, Charles L. Webster & Co., 1892, 294.

SCHMIDT (William), *Fancy Drinks and Popular Beverages*, New York, Dick & Fitzgerald, 1891, 155. Reprinted 1896.

SPENCER (Edward), *The Flowing Bowl*, London, Grant Richards, 1899, 243.

STEVENS (B. A.), *Catalogue of Billiard and Bar Supplies*, Toledo, B. A. Stevens, 1896, 288.

TERRINGTON (William), *Cooling Cups and Dainty Drinks*, London, George Routledge & Sons, 1869, 223.

THOMAS (Jerry), *How to Mix Drinks*, New York, Dick & Fitzgerald, 1862, 244. Reprinted 1864 and 1876.

THOMAS (Jerry), *The Bar-Tender's Guide*, New York, Dick & Fitzgerald, 1876, 107.

THOMAS (Jerry), *The Bar-Tender's Guide*, New York, Dick & Fitzgerald, 1887, 130.

WEHMAN (Henry J.), *Wehman's Bartenders Guide*, New York, Henry J. Wehman, 1891, 95.

WINTER (G.), *How to Mix Drinks*, New York, G. Winter Brewing Co., 1884, 52.

Internationalization
(1900–1919)

The Cocktail Book, London, John MacQueen, 1903, 62.

First Annual Guide of Bartenders' Union, Detroit, 1916, 50.

BOOTHBY (Hon. Wm T.), *American Bartender*, 2nd edition, San Francisco, The San Francisco News Company, 1900, 98.

BOOTHBY (Hon. Wm T.), *The World's Drinks*, San Francisco, 1908, 140.

CHARLIE (Paul), *Recipes of American and Other Iced Drinks*, London, Farrow and Jackson Ltd, 1915, 80.

HISS (Emil), *The Standard Manual of Soda and Other Beverages*, Chicago, G. P. Engelhard & Company, 1900, 242.

GREEN (John), *Appelgreen's Bar Book*, 2nd edition, Chicago, The Hotel Monthly, 1904, 56.

LAMORE (Harry), *The Bartender*, New York, Richard K. Fox, 1901, 90.

LEWIS (V. B.), *The Buffet Guide*, Chicago, M. A. Donohue & Co., 1903, 180.

LEYBOLD (John) and SCHÖNFELD (Hans), *Lexicon der Getränke*, Cologne, 1913, 294.

LOWE (Paul E.), *Drinks as they are Mixed by Leading Bartenders*, Chicago, Frederick, Drake and Company, 1904, 135.

MUCKENSTURM (Louis), *Louis' Mixed Drinks*, Boston, H. M. Caldwell Co., 1906, 113.

NEWMAN (Frank P.), *American-Bar*, 2nd edition, Paris, Société Française d'Imprimerie, 1904, 111.

NEWMAN (Frank P.), *American-Bar*, 3rd edition, Paris, Société Française d'Imprimerie, 1907, 112.

RAWLING (Ernest P.), *Rawling's Book of Mixed Drinks*, San Francisco, Guild Press Publishers, 1914, 100.

SEUTER (Carl A.), *Der Mixologist*, Liepzig, P. M. Blüher's Velag, 1913, 103.

STUART (Thos), *Stuart Fancy Drinks*, New York, Excelsior Publishing House, 1904, 133.

Prohibition (1919–1933)

Bacardi and its Many Uses, Havana, Bacardi, 1931, 23.

Giggle Water, New York, Charles S. Warnock, 1928, 152.

ASBURY (Herbert), *The Bon Vivant's Companion*, New York, Alfred A. Knopf, 1928, 169.

BELTRAMO (Carlo), *Carlo's Cocktails*, Geneva, 1924, 98.

BOOTHBY (Hon. Wm T.), *World Drinks*, San Francisco, Boothby World Drinks Co., 1930, 160.

CHARLES of the Delmonicos, *Cheerio*, New York, Elf Publishing Company, 1928, 49.

CHICOTE (Pedro), *Mis Quinientos Cocktails*, Madrid, 1930, 298.

CRADDOCK (Harry), *The Savoy Cocktail Book*, London, Constable and Company Ltd, 1930, 287.

CRADDOCK (Harry), *The Savoy Cocktail Book*, 2nd edition, London, Constable and Company Ltd, 1933, 287.

CROCKETT (Albert Stevens), *The Old Waldorf Bar Days*, New York, Aventine Press, 1931, 243.

CUERVO (José), *Club de Cantineros de la Republica de Cuba*, Manual Oficial, Havana, Gerardo Corrales, 1930, 140.

DE BARALT (Blanche Z.), *Cuban Cookery Including Cuban Cocktails*, Havana, Hermes, 1931, 150.

JOHN of the Hotel Knickerbocker, *Happy Days*, New York, Felshin Publishing Co., 1931, 96.

JUDGE JUNIOR, *Here's How*, New York, The John Day Company, 1927, 63.

JUDGE JUNIOR, *Here's How Again!*, New York, The John Day Company, 1929, 63.

McELHONE (Harry), *Bar Flies and Cocktails*, Paris, Lecram Press, 1927, 101.

McELHONE (Harry), *ABC of Mixing Cocktails*, London, Dean & Son Ltd, 1930, 103.

PAUL of the Ramos, *Drinks as Mixed by Paul of the Well-Known Ramos*, Gin fizz Palace, New York, circa 1920, 25.

RIP, *Cocktails de Paris*, Paris, Demangel, 1929, 140.

STOCKBRIDGE (Bertha E. L.), *What to Drink*, New York, D. Appleton and Company, 1920, 177.

THOMAS (Henry William), *Life and Letters of Henry William Thomas, Mixologist*, Charles V. Wheeler, Washington, 1929, 64.

VERMEIRE (Robert), *Cocktails, How to Mix them*, London, Herbert Jenkins Ltd, 1922, 112.

VERMEIRE (Robert), *L'Art du Cocktail*, Brussels, Imprimerie de l'Office de Publicité, 1922, 128.

WATKEYS MOORE (Helen), *On Uncle Sam's Water Wagon*, New York, The Knickerbocker Press, 1919, 222.

WOON (Basil), *The Paris that's not in the Guide Books*, New York, Brentano's, 1926, 269.

WOON (Basil), *When it's Cocktail Time in Cuba*, New York, Horace Liveright, 1928, 284.

After Prohibition (1934–1945)

An Anthology of Cocktails, London, Booth Gin, 1934, 50.

Cocktails, La Havane, Bar 'La Florida', 1934, 70.

Cocktails, La Havane, Bar 'La Florida', 1937, 71.

Cocktails, La Havane, Bar 'La Florida', 1939, 75.

150 Recetas de Entemeses y Cock-tails, Mexico D. F., 1944, 83.

ASBURY (Herbert), *The French Quarter*, New York, Garden City, 1938, 462.

BROWNE (Charles), *The Gun Club Drink Book*, New York, Charles Scribner's & Sons, 1939, 190.

CLISBY (Arthur Stanley), *Famous New Orleans Drinks*, New Orleans, Harmanson, 1943, 96.

COTTON (Leo), *Old Mr Boston Official Bartender's Guide*, Boston, 1935, 143.

COTTON (Leo), *Old Mr Boston Official Bartender's Guide*, 2nd edition, Boston, 1940, 160.

CROCKETT (Albert Stevens), *The Old Waldorf-Astoria Bar Book*, New York, A. S. Crockett, 1935, 177.

DUFFY (Patrick Gavin), *The Official Mixer's Manual*, New York, Halcyon House, 1934, 299.

HAIMO (Oscar), *Cocktail Digest*, New York, 1944, 126.

LUPOÏU (Jean), *Cocktails*, Paris, Œuvres Françaises, 1938, 181.

MEIER (Frank), *The Artistry of Mixing Drinks*, Paris, Bishop & Sons, 1936, 182.

OSCAR OF THE WALDORF, *100 Famous Cocktails*, New York, Kenilworth Press, 1934, 46.

PORTA MINGOT (Raymond), *Gran Manual de Cocktails*, Buenos Aires, Corletta & Castro, 1936, 394.

POWNER (W. E.), *Tom and Jerry's Bartender's Guide*, Chicago, Charles T. Powner Co., 1934, 128.

Post World War II (1946–1975)

BAKER (Charles H.), *South American Gentleman's Companion*, New York, Crown Publishers, 1946, vol. II, 225.

BAKER (Charles H.), *The Gentleman's Companion*, New York, Crown Publishers, 1946, vol. II, 217.

BEEBE (Lucius), *The Stork Club Bar Book*, New York, Rinehart and Company, 1946, 136.

BERGERON (Victor), *Bartender's Guide*, New York, Doubleday & Company, 1947, 437.

BERGERON (Victor), *Traders Vic's Bartender's Guide Revised*, New York, Doubleday & Company, 1972, 442.

DE FOUQUIÈRES (André), **BUSSON** (Jean), **MORESTEL** (Yves) and **ANZINI** (Harry), *Cocktails*, Paris, Éditions du Lys, 1952, 135.

EMBURY (David A.), *The Fine Art of Mixing Drinks*, New York, Double Day & Company, 1948, 372.

LUPOÏU (Jean), *Cocktails*, Compiègne, Jean Lupoïu, 1955, 142.

PACE (Marcel), *Nos Meilleures Boissons*, Beaune, Marcel Pace, 1954, 138.

SCHRAEMLI (Harry), *Manuel du Bar*, Lucerne, Service d'Édition de l'Union Helvétia, 1965, 620.

TOWNSEND (Jack) and **MOORE McBRIDE** (Tom), *The Bartender's Book*, New York, Viking Press, 1951, 148.

United Kingdom Bartender's Guild, *Guide to Drinks*, London, UKBG, 1953, 4th edition, 1965, 296.

Recent books (1976–2004)

BITNER (Arnold) and **BEACH** (Phoebe), *Hawai'i Tropical Rum Drinks & Cuisine by Don the Beachcomber*, Hawai'i, Mutual Publishing, 2001, 111.

CALABRESE (Salvatore), *Classic Cocktails*, London, Prion Books, 1999, 192.

DeGROFF (Dale), *The Craft of the Cocktail*, New York, Clarkson Potter, 2002, 230.

DIAS BLUE (Anthony), *The Complete Book of Mixed Drinks*, New York, HarperCollins Publishers, 1993, 324.

DIFFORD (Simon), *Sauceguide to Cocktails*, London, Sauceguides, 2003, vol. IV, 256.

FIELD (Colin Peter), *Les Cocktails du Ritz*, Paris, Éditions du Chêne, 2001, 144.

HARRINGTON (Paul) and **MOORHEAD** (Laura), *Cocktail, The Drink Bible for 21st Century*, New York, Penguin Putnam Inc., 1998, 242.

JOHNSON (Byron A.) and **JOHNSON** (Sharon Peregrine), *Wild West Bartenders' Bible*, Texas Monthly Press, 1986, 274.

REA (Brian F.), *Brian's Booze Guide*, Burbank, The On Premise Institute, 1976, 96.

ROTH (Peter) and **BERNASCONI** (Carlo), *Das Jahrhundert-Mixbuch*, Falken, 1999, 351.

SCHUMANN (Charles), *American-bar*, New York, Abbeville Press, 1995, 408.

TISTLER (Duschan), *Categories of Mixed Drinks*, Passau, eCocktail, 2002, 182.

VAN HAGEN (Jan G.), *The Bols Book of Cocktails*, London, Toucan Books, 1992, 160.

Books on spirits

Des Apéritifs aux Spiritueux, Zurich, Éditions de la Fédération Suisse des Cafetiers, Restaurateurs and Hôteliers, 1988, 263.

Eaux-de-vie et Spiritueux, Paris, Éditions du Centre National de la Recherche Scientifique, 1985, 496.

Havana Club, Cuba: La Légende du Rhum, Toulouse, Éditions Bahia Presse, 100.

BARTY-KING (Hugh) and **MASSEL** (Anton), *Rum – Yesterday and Today*, London, Heinemann, 1983, 264.

BEGG (Desmond), *The Vodka Companion*, London, The Apple Press, 1998, 192.

BÉNITAH (Thierry), *Le Whisky*, Paris, Flammarion, 1999, vol. 1, 95. and vol. 2, 95.

BROOM (Dave), *Spirits & Cocktails*, 3rd edition, Carlton, 1998, 224.

CHAUSSÉE (Gérard), *Cassis*, Paris, Proxima, 2002, 96.

COATES (Geraldine), *Classic Gin*, London, Prion Books, 2000, 176.

DELAHAYE (Marie-Claude), *L'Absinthe*, coll. 'Arts et traditions populaires', Nancy, Berger-Levrault, 1983, 249.

DUMAY (Raymond), *Guide des Alcools*, Paris, Stock, 1973, 579.

DUPLAIS AÎNÉ (P.), *Traité des Liqueurs et de la Distillation des Alcools*, 2nd edition, Versailles, Beau Jeune, 1858, vol. I, 550.

DUPLAIS AÎNÉ (P.), *Traité des Liqueurs et de la Distillation des Alcools*, 2nd edition, Versailles, Beau Jeune, 1858, vol. II, 534.

EDWARDS (Walter N.), *The Beverages we Drink*, London, Ideal Publishing Union Ltd, 1898, 220.

FAHRASMANE (L.) and **GANOU-PARFAIT** (B.), *De la Canne au Rhum*, Paris, INRA Éditions, 1997, 104.

JALLAN (Daniel), *Son Excellence le Rhum en Martinique*, 4 M Impressions, 1994, 178.

JONES (Andrew), *The Aperitif Companion*, London, Apple Press, 1998, 192.

LICHINE (Alexis), *Encyclopédie des Vins & Alcools*, Aylesbury, Robert Laffont, coll. 'Bouquins', 1980. Reprinted 1995, 994.

MONZERT (L.), *The Independant Liquorist*, New York, Dick & Fitzgerald, 1866, 193.

MURRAY (Jim), *Classic Irish Whiskey*, London, Prion Books, 1997, 256.

PAGES (G.), *Les Eaux-de-vie et les Alcools*, Paris, Librairie Hachette, 1919, 166.

SALLÉ (Jacques and Bernard), *Larousse des Alcools*, Paris, Librairie Larousse, 1982, 240.

TCHUDI (Stephen N.), *Soda Poppery*, New York, Charles Scribner's Sons, 1985, 148.

WISNIEWSKI (Ian), *Classic Tequila*, London, Prion Books, 1998, 208.

Other sources

The Balance and Columbian Repository, Hudson (New York), 13 May 1806.

The New York Sun, New York (New York), 28 March 1882.

JOSEPHSON (Matthew), *Union House, Union Bar*, New York, Random House, 1956, 370.

ROULET (Claude), *Ritz – Une Histoire plus Belle que la Légende*, Paris, Quai Voltaire, 1998, 190.

Council Regulation No 1576/89/EEC of 29 May 1989, laying down general rules on the definition, description and presentation of spirit drinks. Amended by the following acts: No 3280/92/EEC and 3378/94/EC and Council ruling 95/1/EC.

Council Regulation No 1601/91/EEC of 10 June 1991, laying down general rules on the definition, description and presentation of aromatized wines, aromatized wine-based drinks and aromatized wine-product cocktails, and modified by Commission regulation No 122/94/EC.

Index of cocktail snacks

All the cocktail snacks recipes in this book are set out according to categories:
sweet or savoury.

Index of cocktails from A–Z

For ease of location, all the cocktail recipes and their variations given in this book are listed here in alphabetical order.

■ *The asterisks indicate the degree of alcohol in the drink: * = weak in alcohol;*

** = moderately alcoholic; *** = strongly alcoholic.

The alcohol-free cocktails are those not marked with asterisks.

■ *Cocktails that are served hot are marked with a ★.*

Havana Beach 159**
Hawaii Breaker 224*
Hawaii Sparkle 224*
Hemingway 218**
Hemingway Sour 126**
Hemingway Special 149**
Henrietta Wallbanger 79**
High Voltage 127**
Highbinder 209**
Highland Cooler 127*
Holy Mary 263
Hondarribia 121**
Honey Moon 210**
Honeysuckle 149*
Honolulu Punch 108*
Horse's Neck 198**
Hot Buttered Rum 169** ★
Hot Buttered Rum Cow 169** ★
Hot Shot 245*
Hot Wine 245* ★
Hurricane 160**

I, J

Ice-Breaker 184**
Iced Tea 250
Ink Street 133*
Irish Coffee 139** ★
Irish Rose 127*
Island in the Sun 160**
Isle of Pines 149*
Jack Rose 199**
Jacuzzi 225**
Jaizkibel 100*
Jam Daiquiri 160**
Jamaican Mule 150**
Japanese 210**
Japanese Slipper 176**
Jinx 109**
Joe Kanoo 161**
John Collins 101**
Journalist 93**
Jungle Joe 87**
Jungle Juice 184*
Just Try 115***

K

Kamikaze 71*
Kentucky Colonel 135**
Kentucky Tea 130**
Killer Punch 72**
Kir 234*
Kir Imperial 218*
Kir Royal 218*

Kirsch & Cassis 197**
Klondike Cooler 130**
Klondike Highball 240*
Knickerbocker 94**
Knock-Out 113***
Koolaid 72*
Kremlin Cooler 72*

L

Lady Killer 108**
Leave it to Me 94**
Lemon Drop 72**
Lemon Squash 252
Lemonade 251
Lemony Snicket 115**
London Fog 94**
Lone Tree 95**
Long Island Iced Tea 73***
Long Island Lemonade 73***
Lychee Martini 80*
Lynchburg Lemonade 130**

M

Macka 101**
Mackinnon 166**
Madras 80*
Madras Special 257
Magic Bus 177*
Mai Tai 150**
Mamy Taylor 153*
Mango Breeze 257
Mango Sparkle 251
Manhattan 122***
Marama Rum Punch 150**
Margarita 176**
Martinez 95**
Martinican 142***
Mary Pickford 161**
Matador 185**
Mauresque à l'Absinthe 235*
Maxim's Coffee 213** ★
Melon Martini 65**
Meringue 221**
Merry Widow 109**
Metropolitan 65*
Mexican 185*
Mexican Coffee 191** ★
Mexican Mule 175*
Mexican Tea 191** ★
Mexicana 185*
Mexico Manhattan 172***
Mexicola 177*
Miami Beach 109**

Midnight Moon 228**
Milky Mango 265
Millionnaire 137**
Mimosa 225*
Mint Julep 131**
Mocha Martini 137**
Mockingbird 189***
Mojito 151**
Mojito Crillo 151**
Monkey Gland 109**
Montego Bay 151**
Morning Glory Fizz 138**
Moscow Mule 73**
Mountain 138**
Mulata 167**
Muppet 180*
My Sky 257

N

Napoli 74**
National 161**
Negroni 235*
New Yorker 131*
Nicky Finn 196**
Nicky's Fizz 101*
Night & Day 229**
Nikolaschka 210**
Normandy Cooler 199**

O

Ohio 229**
Old Pal 121**
Old-Fashioned 122**
Olympic 203**
Opal 109**
Orange Blossom 110**

P

Pain Cutter 260
Pain Killer 162**
Paradise 110**
Parisette 265
Parisian 95**
Parson's Special 265
Passion Breeze 260
Passion Cooler 251
Peach Daiquiri 158*
Pearl Diver 162**
Perfect Manhattan 122***
Periodista 152**
Pick-Me-Up 221*
Pimm's Cup 240*

Index of cocktails by their main ingredients

All the cocktail recipes and variations of them given in this book are listed according to their main ingredients, making a clear distinction between alcoholic cocktails and non-alcoholic ones.

■ *The asterisks indicate the degree of alcohol in the drink: * = weak in alcohol;*
** = moderately alcoholic; *** = strongly alcoholic.
The alcohol-free cocktails have no asterisks.
■ *Cocktails that are served hot are marked with a ★.*

ALCOHOLIC COCKTAILS

In each of these recipes, any other alcoholic drinks used in their preparation are bracketed.

Absinthe-flavoured spirits

Absinthe Drip 232*
Absinthe Veilleuse 232*
B-55 (coffee liqueur, Irish cream) 243*
Blackthorn (Irish whiskey, dry vermouth, Angostura bitters) 120***
Brazil (dry vermouth, sherry) 234*
Doctor Funk (white Jamaican rum, white Cuban rum) 148**
Knock-Out (gin, dry vermouth, green crème de menthe) 113***
Mauresque à l'Absinthe 235*
Monkey Gland (gin) 109**
Sazerac (rye whiskey, Peychaud's bitters) 123**
Spitfire (Southern Comfort) 242*
T.N.T. No 2 (Cognac, orange curaçao, Angostura bitters) 196***
Tomate à l'Absinthe 235*
Turf (gin, dry vermouth, maraschino liqueur, orange bitters) 96**
Whizz-Bang (Scotch whisky, dry vermouth, orange bitters) 124**

Zombie (white Puerto Rican rum, dark Jamaican rum, aged Cuban rum, aged Jamaican rum, maraschino liqueur, Angostura bitters) 165***

Amaretto

Beam Me Up Scotty (Scotch whisky, cherry brandy) 132***
Boccie Ball 242*
Ferrari (dry vermouth) 243*
Godfather (Scotch whisky) 135**
Godmother (vodka) 85**
Killer Punch (vodka, green melon liqueur) 72**
Koolaid (vodka, green melon liqueur) 72*
Midnight Moon (Champagne, Cognac, white crème de cacao) 228**

Angostura bitters

Abbey (gin, red vermouth) 107*
Alfonso (Champagne, Dubonnet) 216*
Americana (Champagne, bourbon) 217**
Añejo Highball (amber Cuban rum, orange curaçao) 143**
Aristo (aged Jamaican rum) 156**

Bahama Mama (dark Jamaican rum, coconut-flavoured rum) 157**
Blackthorn (Irish whiskey, dry vermouth, absinthe-flavoured spirit) 120***
Burgos (Cognac) 205**
Champagne Cocktail (Champagne, Cognac) 217**
Champs-Elysées (Cognac, yellow Chartreuse) 205***
Cuban Manhattan (amber Cuban rum, red vermouth) 142***
Double Vision (blackcurrant-flavoured vodka, lemon-flavoured vodka) 70*
East India (Cognac, orange curaçao) 202**
Fallen Angel (gin, white crème de menthe) 114**
Harvard (Cognac, red vermouth) 195***
Hawaii Breaker (Champagne) 224*
Honolulu Punch (gin) 108*
Horse's Neck (Cognac) 198**
Jamaican Mule (spiced rum) 150**
Japanese (Cognac) 210**
Journalist (gin, dry vermouth, red vermouth, orange curaçao) 93**
Manhattan (rye whiskey, red vermouth) 123***

Marama Rum Punch (white Jamaican rum, curaçao triple sec) 150**
Martinez (gin, red vermouth, maraschino liqueur) 95**
Martinican (aged *rhum agricole* ['agricultural rum'], red vermouth) 142***
Merry Widow (gin, Benedictine) 109**
Mexico Manhattan (tequila reposado, red vermouth) 172***
Mojito Criollo (white Cuban rum) 151**
Montego Bay (amber *rhum agricole* ['agricultural rum'], curaçao triple sec) 151**
Moscow Mule (vodka) 73*
Ohio (Champagne, rye whiskey, red vermouth) 229**
Old-Fashioned (rye whiskey) 122**
Pearl Diver (white Puerto Rican rum, amber Cuban rum, dark Jamaican rum) 162**
Perfect Manhattan (rye whiskey, red vermouth, dry vermouth) 122***
Pink Daiquiri (white Cuban rum, maraschino liqueur) 152**
Pink Gin (Plymouth gin) 96*
Pink Gin & Tonic (Plymouth gin) 96*
Pisco Punch (pisco, orange curaçao) 200**
Pisco Sour (pisco) 200**
Piscola (pisco) 200*
Planter's Punch (dark Jamaican rum) 152***
Prince of Wales (Champagne, Cognac, curaçao triple sec) 229**
Raffles Sling (gin, cherry brandy, curaçao triple sec, Benedictine) 111**
Redwood (amber Jamaican rum, crème de fraise) 142**
Rob Roy (Scotch whisky, red vermouth) 123***
Rory O'More (Irish whiskey, red vermouth) 123***
Rum Runner (amber Jamaican rum) 163**
Star (Calvados, red vermouth) 195***
T.N.T. No 2 (Cognac, orange curaçao, absinthe-flavoured spirit) 196***

Treacle (dark Jamaican rum) 143**
Trinidad (white Cuban rum) 146*
Up-to-Date (Canadian whisky, sherry, Grand Marnier Cordon Rouge) 124***
Vanderbilt (Cognac, cherry brandy) 212***
Zaza (gin, red Dubonnet) 96**
Zombie (white Puerto Rican rum, dark Jamaican rum, aged Cuban rum, aged Jamaican rum, maraschino liqueur, absinthe-flavoured spirit) 165***

Apricot brandy

Amber Twist (Cognac, dry vermouth, curaçao triple sec) 194**
Apricot Cooler 236*
Bossa Nova (white Puerto Rican rum, Galliano) 158**
Claridge (gin, dry vermouth, curaçao triple sec) 91**
Cuban (Cognac) 209**
Golden Screw (Champagne, Cognac) 227**
Island in the Sun (amber Jamaican rum, Galliano) 160**
Lady Killer (gin, curaçao triple sec) 108**
Leave it to Me (gin, dry vermouth, maraschino liqueur) 94**
National (white Cuban rum) 161**
Paradise (gin) 110**
Periodista (white Cuban rum, orange curaçao) 152**
Resolute (gin) 104**
Valencia (Champagne) 227*

Banane (crème de)

Banana Banshee (white crème de cacao) 243*
Banana Bliss (Cognac) 204**
Banana Boat (tequila blanco) 188**
Beja Flor (cachaça rum, curaçao triple sec) 144**
Caribbean Breeze (amber Jamaican rum) 159**

Chocolate Bliss (Cognac, brown crème de cacao) 204**
Dee-Light (Cognac) 197*
Jungle Joe (vodka) 87**
San Francisco (vodka, curaçao triple sec) 81**

Beer

Tamanaco Dry (gin) 106***
Black Velvet (Champagne) 228*

Benedictine

Acacias (gin, kirsch) 112***
April Shower (Cognac) 203*
B & B (Cognac) 203**
Baccarat (white Cuban rum) 157**
Bobby Burns (Scotch whisky, red vermouth) 134***
Frisco (bourbon) 126**
Gipsy Queen (vodka, orange bitters) 85**
Honey Moon (Calvados, orange curaçao) 210**
Kentucky Colonel (bourbon) 135**
Maxim's Coffee (Cognac, Galliano) 213** ★
Merry Widow (gin, Angostura bitters) 109**
Raffles Sling (gin, cherry brandy, curaçao triple sec, Angostura bitters) 111**
Rolls Royce (gin, dry vermouth, red vermouth) 94**
Singapore Sling (gin, cherry brandy) 105**
Sterling (amber Jamaican rum) 164**

Brandy

► *See* calvados, Cognac, kirsch, pisco

Cacao, crème de (brown)

Alexander The Great (vodka, coffee liqueur) 87*
Baby Alexander (amber Cuban rum) 167**

Bounty Boat (Cognac, coconut liqueur) 204**

Brandy Alexander (Cognac) 212**

Chocolate Bliss (Cognac, crème de banane) 204**

Chocolate Martini (vodka, white crème de cacao) 84**

Chocolate Stinger (Cognac, white crème de menthe) 211**

Coffee Nudge (Cognac, coffee liqueur) 213** ★

Mocha Martini (bourbon, Irish cream) 137**

Mulata (amber Cuban rum) 167**

Velvet Hammer (vodka) 87*

Cacao, crème de (white)

Alexander (gin) 116*

Banana Banshee (crème de banane) 243*

Chocolate Martini (vodka, brown crème de cacao) 84**

Dusty Rose (cherry brandy) 244*

Frostbite (tequila blanco) 190**

Golden Cadillac (Galliano) 244*

Grasshopper (green crème de menthe) 245*

Midnight Moon (Champagne, Cognac, amaretto) 228**

Calvados

Ambrosia (Champagne, Cognac, curaçao triple sec) 216**

Apple Cart (curaçao triple sec) 201**

Apple Sunrise (crème de cassis) 201**

Castro Cooler (amber Cuban rum) 202**

Depth Bomb (Cognac) 197**

Harvard Cooler 198**

Honey Moon (Benedictine, orange curaçao) 210**

Normandy Cooler (manzana verde liqueur) 199**

Serendipiti (Champagne) 227**

Star (red vermouth, Angostura bitters) 195***

Campari

Americano (red vermouth) 233*

Bahamian 241*

C.C. (Champagne) 216*

Cardinal (dry vermouth, gin) 235*

Fiesta (vodka, curaçao triple sec) 65*

Garibaldi 241*

Hondarribia (Scotch whisky, red vermouth) 121**

Jaizkibel (gin) 100*

Negroni (red vermouth, gin) 235*

Night & Day (Champagne, Grand Marnier Cordon Rouge) 229**

Old Pal (Canadian whisky, dry vermouth) 121**

Rosita (tequila reposado, dry vermouth, red vermouth) 172**

Stargarita (tequila blanco, curaçao triple sec) 176**

Tampico (curaçao triple sec) 241*

Testa Rossa (vodka) 75*

Tropical Down (gin) 110**

Veneziano (red vermouth, white wine) 233**

Cassis (crème de)

Apple Sunrise (Calvados) 201**

Ballet Russe (vodka) 67**

Burgundy Juicer (vodka) 69**

Cassisco (Cognac) 197**

Cassisina (vodka) 70**

Chimayo (tequila blanco) 183**

Communard (red Côtes-du-Rhône wine) 234*

El Diablo (tequila blanco) 175**

French Spring Punch (Champagne, Cognac) 226***

Kir (white Burgundy wine) 234*

Kir Royal (Champagne) 218*

Kirsch & Cassis (kirsch) 197**

Macka (gin, dry vermouth, red vermouth) 101**

Parisian (gin, dry vermouth) 95**

Purple Pancho (tequila blanco) 177**

Russian Spring Punch (Champagne, vodka) 226***

Vermouth-Cassis (dry vermouth) 236*

Champagne

Alfonso (Angostura bitters, Dubonnet) 216*

Ambrosia (Cognac, Calvados, curaçao triple sec) 216**

American Flyer (aged Jamaican rum) 219**

Americana (Angostura bitters, bourbon) 217**

Barbotage (Cognac) 221*

Bellini 224*

Black Pearl (Cognac, coffee liqueur) 228**

Black Velvet (Irish stout) 228*

Blue Champagne (vodka, blue curaçao) 219**

Buck's Fizz 225*

C.C. (Campari) 216*

Carol Channing (eau-de-vie de framboise, crème de framboise) 217**

Champagne Cocktail (Angostura bitters, Cognac) 217**

Champagne Julep 220*

Champagne Sour 220*

Corpse Reviver No 2 (Pernod) 218**

Diamond Fizz (vodka) 220***

French 75 (gin) 220***

French Spring Punch (Cognac) 226***

Ginger Champagne (vodka) 218**

Golden Screw (Cognac, apricot brandy) 227**

Hawaii Breaker (Angostura bitters) 224*

Hawaii Sparkle 224*

Hemingway (Pernod) 218**

Jacuzzi (gin, peach schnapps) 225**

Kir Imperial (crème de framboise) 218*

Kir Royal (crème de cassis) 218*

Meringue (limoncello) 221**

Midnight Moon (Cognac, white crème de cacao, amaretto) 228**

Mimosa 225*

Night & Day (Campari, Grand Marnier Cordon Rouge) 229**

Ohio (rye whiskey, red vermouth, curaçao triple sec, Angostura bitters) 229**

Pick-Me-Up (Cognac) 221*

Pimm's Royal (Pimm's No 1) 219**

Prince of Wales (Angostura bitters, Cognac, curaçao triple sec) 229**

Rossini 225*

Royal Highball (Cognac) 226***

Russian Spring Punch (vodka, crème de cassis) 226***

Saratoga (Cognac, maraschino liqueur, orange bitters) 226*

Serendipiti (Calvados) 227**

Tropical Hibiscus 227*

Valencia (apricot brandy) 227*

Chartreuse, green

Bijou (gin, sweet vermouth, orange bitters) 113***

Shamrock (Irish whiskey, dry vermouth) 136***

Spring Feeling (gin) 116**

Tipperary (rye whiskey, red vermouth) 136***

Chartreuse, yellow

Alaska (gin) 112***

Champs-Elysées (Cognac, Angostura bitters) 205***

Just Try (gin, dry vermouth, Grand Marnier Cordon Rouge) 115***

Lemony Snicket (gin, limoncello) 115**

Cherry brandy

Beam Me Up Scotty (Scotch whisky, amaretto) 132***

Blood & Sand (Scotch whisky, red vermouth) 133**

Cherry Blossom (Cognac) 208**

Cherry Cooler (maraschino liqueur) 237*

Desert Healer (gin) 99**

Dusty Rose (white crème de cacao) 244*

Evolution (gin) 114***

Raffles Sling (gin, curaçao triple sec, Benedictine, Angostura bitters) 111**

Red Russian (vodka) 85**

Rose (kirsch, dry vermouth) 195**

Singapore Sling (gin, Benedictine) 105**

Vanderbilt (Cognac, Angostura bitters) 212***

Coconut liqueur

Bounty Boat (Cognac, brown crème de cacao) 204**

El Ultimo (Cognac) 202**

Coconut milk

Blue Hawaiian (white Puerto Rican rum, blue curaçao) 162**

Chi Chi (vodka) 79*

Coco Mexico (tequila blanco) 184**

Pain Killer (white Puerto Rican rum) 162**

Piña Colada (white Puerto Rican rum) 162**

Coffee liqueur

Alexander The Great (vodka, brown crème de cacao) 87*

B-52 (Irish cream, Grand Marnier Cordon Rouge) 243*

B-55 (Irish cream, absinthe-flavoured spirit) 243*

Black Pearl (Champagne, Cognac) 228**

Black Russian (vodka) 84**

Brave Bull (tequila blanco) 189**

Brown Bear (Cognac) 205**

Centenario (white Cuban rum, curaçao triple sec) 166**

Coffee Nudge (Cognac, brown crème de cacao) 213** ★

Espresso Martini (vodka) 71*

Rumble (dark Jamaican rum) 153**

South of the Border (tequila blanco) 189**

White Russian (vodka) 87*

Cognac

Amber Twist (dry vermouth, apricot brandy, curaçao triple sec) 194**

Ambrosia (Champagne, Calvados, curaçao triple sec) 216**

American Beauty (dry vermouth, ruby port) 194**

April Shower (Benedictine) 203*

B & B (Benedictine) 203**

B & P (ruby port) 203**

B & S 196*

Banana Bliss (crème de banane) 204**

Barbotage (Champagne) 221*

Between the Sheets (Puerto Rican rum, curaçao triple sec) 196**

Biarritz (orange curaçao) 203**

Black Jack (kirsch) 204**

Black Pearl (Champagne, coffee liqueur) 228**

Bombay (dry vermouth, orange curaçao, orange bitters) 194***

Bounty Boat (brown crème de cacao, coconut liqueur) 204**

Brandy Alexander (brown crème de cacao) 212**

Brandy Blazer 213*** ★

Brandy Highball 196*

Brandy Milk Punch 212*

Brown Bear (coffee liqueur) 205**

Burgos (Angostura bitters) 205**

Cassisco (crème de cassis) 197**

Champagne Cocktail (Champagne, Angostura bitters) 217**

Champs-Elysées (yellow Chartreuse, Angostura bitters) 205***

Cherry Blossom (cherry brandy) 208**

Chocolate Bliss (crème de banane, brown crème de cacao) 204**

Chocolate Stinger (white crème de menthe, brown crème de cacao) 211**

Coffee Nudge (coffee liqueur, brown crème de cacao) 213** ★

Corpse Reviver (Fernet-Branca, white crème de menthe) 208***

Cuban (apricot brandy) 209**

Dee-Light (crème de banane) 197*

Long Island Lemonade (vodka, gin, Puerto Rican rum) 73***

Lynchburg Lemonade (Tennessee whiskey) 130**

Magic Bus (tequila blanco) 177*

Marama Rum Punch (white Jamaican rum, Angostura bitters) 150**

Margarita (tequila blanco) 176**

Matador (tequila blanco) 185**

Metropolitan (blackcurrant-flavoured vodka) 65*

Millionnaire (rye whiskey) 137**

Montego Bay (amber *rhum agricole* ['agricultural rum'], Angostura bitters) 151**

Nicky Finn (Cognac, Pernod) 196**

Ohio (Champagne, rye whiskey, red vermouth, Angostura bitters) 229**

Opal (gin) 109**

Pineapple Margarita (tequila blanco) 186**

Playa del Mar (tequila blanco) 185*

Polly Special (Scotch whisky) 133*

Prince of Wales (Champagne, Angostura bitters, Cognac) 229**

Raffles Sling (gin, cherry brandy, Benedictine, Angostura bitters) 111**

Rude Cosmopolitan (tequila blanco) 177*

San Francisco (vodka, crème de banane) 81**

Sangria (Roija wine, Cognac) 242*

Sidecar (Cognac) 201**

Stargarita (tequila blanco, Campari) 176**

Strawberry Margarita (tequila blanco) 186*

Tampico (Campari) 241*

Tijuana Tea (tequila blanco) 177**

Tomahawk (tequila blanco) 187**

White Lady (gin) 106**

X.Y.Z. (white Puerto Rican rum) 156**

Yellow Bird (white Puerto Rican rum, Galliano) 167**

Drambuie

Hemingway Sour (bourbon) 126**

Mackinnon (amber Jamaican rum) 166**

Rusty Nail (Scotch whisky) 135**

Dubonnet

Alfonso (Champagne, Angostura bitters) 216*

European Beauty (Scotch malt whisky) 120**

Diabola (gin) 92**

Dubonnet Cocktail (gin) 92**

Zaza (gin, Angostura bitters) 96**

Fernet-Branca

Apothecary (red vermouth, white crème de menthe) 208**

Corpse Reviver (Cognac, white crème de menthe) 208***

Fraise (crème de)

Berry Sour (crème de mûre) 237*

Redwood (amber Jamaican rum, Angostura bitters) 142**

Framboise (crème de)

Basic 237*

Carol Channing (Champagne, eau-de-vie de framboise) 217**

Kir Imperial (Champagne) 218*

Framboise (eau-de-vie de)

Carol Channing (Champagne, crème de framboise) 217**

Galliano

Bossa Nova (white Puerto Rican rum, apricot brandy) 158**

Cactus Banger (tequila blanco) 183**

Golden Cadillac (white crème de cacao) 244*

Golden Dream (orange, curaçao triple sec) 244*

Harvey Wallbanger (vodka) 79**

Henriette Wallbanger (vodka) 79**

Hot Shot 245*

Island in the Sun (amber Jamaican rum, apricot brandy) 160**

Island in the Sun (amber Jamaican rum, apricot brandy) 160**

Joe Kanoo (white Jamaican rum) 161**

Maxim's Coffee (Cognac, Benedictine) 213** ★

Napoli (vodka) 74**

Yellow Bird (white Puerto Rican rum, curaçao triple sec) 167**

Gin

Abbey (red vermouth, Angostura bitters) 107*

Acacias (Benedictine, kirsch) 112***

Alabama Fizz 97**

Alaska (yellow Chartreuse) 112***

Alexander (white crème de cacao) 116*

Astoria (dry vermouth, orange bitters) 90**

Attaboy (dry vermouth) 90**

Aviation (maraschino liqueur) 97**

Bee's Knees 112*

Bijou (sweet vermouth, green Chartreuse, orange bitters) 113***

Blackout (crème de mûre) 97**

Bloodhound (dry vermouth, red vermouth) 90*

Blue Bird (blue curaçao, curaçao triple sec) 98**

Breakfast Martini (curaçao triple sec) 98**

Bronx (dry vermouth, red vermouth) 107**

Bronx Terrace (dry vermouth) 91**

Bull-Dog 105**

Cardinal (Campari, dry vermouth) 235*

Caruso (dry vermouth, green crème de menthe) 113**

Claridge (dry vermouth, curaçao triple sec, apricot brandy) 91**

Clover Club 116*

Colonial (maraschino liqueur) 107**

Desert Healer (cherry brandy) 99**

Diabola (red Dubonnet) 92**

Krupnik

Polish Martini (vodka, bison grass-flavoured vodka) 81*

Limoncello

Lemony Snicket (gin, yellow Chartreuse) 115**

Meringue (Champagne) 221**

Lychee (litchi) liqueur

Lychee Martini (vodka) 80*

Manzana verde liqueur

Apple Martini (vodka) 78*

Frisky Bison (bison grass-flavoured vodka) 71*

Normandy Cooler (Calvados) 199**

Twistin (Canadian whisky, peach schnapps) 136**

Maraschino liqueur

Aviation (gin) 97**

Cherry Cooler (cherry brandy) 237*

Colonial (gin) 107**

Floridita Daiquiri (white Cuban rum) 148**

Frozen Daiquiri (white Cuban rum) 148**

Hemingway Special (white Cuban rum) 149**

Jam Daiquiri (white Puerto Rican rum) 160**

Leave it to Me (gin, dry vermouth, apricot brandy) 94**

Lone Tree (gin, dry vermouth) 95**

Martinez (gin, red vermouth, Angostura bitters) 95**

Pink Daiquiri (white Cuban rum, Angostura bitters) 152**

Santina's Pousse-Café (Cognac, orange curaçao) 211**

Saratoga (Champagne, Cognac, orange bitters) 226*

Turf (gin, dry vermouth, absinthe-flavoured spirit, orange bitters) 96**

Zombie (white Puerto Rican rum, dark Jamaican rum, aged Cuban rum, aged Jamaican rum, Angostura bitters, absinthe-flavoured spirit) 165***

Melon liqueur, green

Atomic Dog (white Puerto Rican rum, coconut-flavoured rum) 157**

Japanese Slipper (tequila blanco) 176**

Killer Punch (vodka, amaretto) 72**

Koolaid (vodka, amaretto) 72*

Speedy Gonzales (tequila blanco, crème de mûre) 190**

Menthe, crème de (green)

Caruso (gin, dry vermouth) 113**

Chocolate Mint Martini (vodka, white crème de menthe) 84***

Grasshopper (white crème de cacao) 245*

Green Hat (gin) 100**

Green Russian (vodka) 85**

Knock-Out (gin, dry vermouth, absinthe-flavoured spirit) 113***

Mockingbird (tequila reposado) 189***

Menthe, crème de (white)

Apothecary (red vermouth, Fernet-Branca) 208**

Aztec Stinger (tequila blanco) 188**

Black Widow (dark Jamaican rum) 166**

Cactus Cooler (tequila blanco) 188**

Chocolate Mint Martini (vodka, green crème de menthe) 84***

Chocolate Stinger (Cognac, brown crème de cacao) 211**

Corpse Reviver (Cognac, Fernet-Branca) 208***

Delmarva (rye whiskey, dry vermouth) 134**

Fallen Angel (gin, Angostura bitters) 114**

Stinger (Cognac) 211**

Vodka Stinger (vodka) 86**

Mûre (crème de)

Berry Sour (crème de fraise) 237*

Blackout (gin) 97**

Bramble (Plymouth gin) 98**

French Martini (vodka) 79*

Highbinder (Cognac) 209**

Purple Haze (vodka) 74*

Purple Hooter (vodka) 74*

Sex on the Beach # 2 (vodka, peach schnapps) 83**

Speedy Gonzales (tequila blanco, green melon liqueur) 190**

Uncle Vanya (vodka) 75**

Orange bitters

Adonis (fino sherry, red vermouth) 232*

Astoria (gin, dry vermouth) 90**

Bamboo (dry vermouth, fino sherry) 233*

Bijou (gin, sweet vermouth, green Chartreuse) 113***

Bombay (Cognac, dry vermouth, orange curaçao) 194***

Commodore (Canadian whisky) 125**

Francis the Mule (bourbon) 126*

Gipsy Queen (vodka, Benedictine) 85**

Gotham (Cognac, Pernod) 194***

Princeton (gin, ruby port) 115**

Saratoga (Champagne, Cognac, maraschino liqueur) 226*

Scoff-Law (Canadian whisky, dry vermouth) 123**

Turf (gin, dry vermouth, maraschino liqueur, absinthe-flavoured spirit) 96**

Whizz-Bang (Scotch whisky, dry vermouth, absinthe-flavoured spirit) 124**

Peach schnapps

Aquamarine (vodka, blue curaçao) 78**

Betty Blue (vodka, dry vermouth, blue curaçao) 84**
Desert Glow (tequila blanco) 182**
Fuzzy Navel 241*
Jacuzzi (Champagne, gin) 225**
Sex on the Beach (vodka) 83**
Sex on the Beach # 2 (vodka, crème de mûre) 83**
Twistin (Canadian whisky, manzana verde liqueur) 136**
Woo Woo (vodka) 83**

Pêche (crème de)

Fish House Punch (dark Jamaican rum, Cognac) 168** ★

Pernod

Corpse Reviver No 2 (Champagne) 218**
Gotham (Cognac, orange bitters) 194***
Hemingway (Champagne) 218**
London Fog (gin) 94**
Nicky Finn (Cognac, curaçao triple sec) 196**
Tiger Tail 242*

Peychaud's bitters

Sazerac (rye whiskey, absinthe-flavoured spirit) 123**

Pimm's No 1

Pimm's Cup 240*
Pimm's Royal (Champagne) 219**

Pisco

Pisco Punch (orange curaçao, Angostura bitters) 200**
Pisco Sour (Angostura bitters) 200**
Piscola (Angostura bitters) 200*
Tropicana (white Cuban rum, cachaça rum) 164**

Port, ruby

Agave Punch (tequila blanco) 181**
American Beauty (Cognac, dry vermouth) 194**
B & P (Cognac) 203**
Elk's Own (rye whiskey) 137**
Port Flip (Cognac) 203*
Princeton (gin, orange bitters) 115**

Rum

■ Aged *rhum agricole*, 'agricultural rum'
Martinican (red vermouth, Angostura bitters) 142***

■ Aged Cuban rum
Zombie (white Puerto Rican rum, dark Jamaican rum, aged Jamaican rum, maraschino liqueur, Angostura bitters, absinthe-flavoured spirit) 165***

■ Aged Jamaican rum
American Flyer (Champagne) 219**
Aristo (Angostura bitters) 156**
Zombie (white Puerto Rican rum, dark Jamaican rum, aged Cuban rum, maraschino liqueur, Angostura bitters, absinthe-flavoured spirit) 165***

■ Amber *rhum agricole*, 'agricultural rum'
Montego Bay (curaçao triple sec, Angostura bitters) 151**

■ Amber Cuban rum
Añejo Highball (orange curaçao, Angostura bitters) 143**
Baby Alexander (brown crème de cacao) 167**
Castro Cooler (Calvados) 202**
Cuban Manhattan (red vermouth, Angostura bitters) 142***
Hurricane (white Puerto Rican rum, dark Jamaican rum, curaçao triple sec) 160**

Mulata (brown crème de cacao) 167**
Pearl Diver (white Puerto Rican rum, dark Jamaican rum, Angostura bitters) 162**

■ Amber Jamaican rum
Boston Cooler 145*
Caribbean Breeze (crème de banane) 159**
Honeysuckle 149*
Island In the Sun (Galliano, apricot brandy) 160**
Mackinnon (Drambuie) 166**
Mai Tai (white *rhum agricole* ['agricultural rum'], orange curaçao) 150**
Redwood (crème de fraise, Angostura bitters) 142**
Rum Runner (Angostura bitters) 163**
Sterling (Benedictine) 164**
Suzie Taylor 153**
Tom & Jerry (Cognac) 169** ★
Voodoo (red vermouth) 165**

■ Cachaça rum
Batida Abaci 158**
Beja Flor (crème de banane, curaçao triple sec) 144**
Caïpirinha 145**
Tropicana (white Cuban rum, pisco) 164**

■ Coconut-flavoured rum
Atomic Dog (white Puerto Rican rum, green melon liqueur) 157**
Bahama Mama (dark Jamaican rum, Angostura bitters) 157**

■ Dark Jamaican rum
Bahama Mama (coconut-flavoured rum, Angostura bitters) 157**
Black Widow (white crème de menthe) 166**
Dark & Stormy 147**
Fish House Punch (Cognac, crème de pêche) 168** ★
Hurricane (white Puerto Rican rum, amber Cuban rum, curaçao triple sec) 160**

Pearl Diver (white Puerto Rican rum, amber Cuban rum, Angostura bitters) 162**

Planter's Punch (Angostura bitters) 152***

Rumble (coffee liqueur) 153**

Treacle (Angostura bitters) 143**

Zombie (white Puerto Rican rum, aged Cuban rum, aged Jamaican rum, maraschino liqueur, Angostura bitters, absinthe-flavoured spirit) 165***

■ **Puerto Rican rum**

Between the Sheets (Cognac, curaçao triple sec) 196**

Caïpirissima 145**

Citrus Cooler (curaçao triple sec) 146*

Long Island Iced Tea (vodka, gin, curaçao triple sec) 73***

Long Island Lemonade (vodka, gin, curaçao triple sec) 73***

■ **Spiced rum**

Cable Car (orange curaçao) 145*

Jamaican Mule (Angostura bitters) 150**

■ **White *rhum agricole*, 'agricultural rum'**

Black Rose 144*

Mai Tai (amber Jamaican rum, orange curaçao) 150**

Planteur 163**

Ti Punch 156***

■ **White Cuban rum**

Baccarat (Benedictine) 157**

Banana Daiquiri 158*

Centenario (coffee liqueur, curaçao triple sec) 166**

Cuba Libre 146*

Cubanita 168**

Daiquiri 147**

Daiquiri No 2 (orange curaçao) 147**

Doctor Funk (white Jamaican rum, absinthe-flavoured spirit) 148**

Flamingo 159**

Floridita Daiquiri (maraschino liqueur) 148**

Frozen Daiquiri (maraschino liqueur) 148**

Havana Beach 159**

Hemingway Special (maraschino liqueur) 149**

Isle of Pines 149*

Mary Pickford 161**

Mojito 151**

Mojito Criollo (Angostura bitters) 151**

National (apricot brandy) 161**

Peach Daiquiri 158*

Periodista (orange curaçao, apricot brandy) 152**

Pinerito 149*

Pink Daiquiri (maraschino liqueur, Angostura bitters) 152**

Presidente (dry vermouth) 142**

Trinidad (Angostura bitters) 146*

Tropicana (cachaça rum, pisco) 164**

■ **White Jamaican rum**

American Grog 168** ★

Doctor Funk (white Cuban rum, absinthe-flavoured spirit) 148**

Joe Kanoo (Galliano) 161**

Marama Rum Punch (curaçao triple sec, Angostura bitters) 150**

■ **White Puerto Rican rum**

Atomic Dog (coconut-flavoured rum, green melon liqueur) 157**

Bacardi Cocktail 144**

Blue Hawaiian (coconut milk, blue curaçao) 162**

Bossa Nova (Galliano, apricot brandy) 158**

Colombus (orange curaçao) 156**

Cosmo-Ron (orange curaçao) 146*

Hot Buttered Rum 169** ★

Hot Buttered Rum Cow 169** ★

Hurricane (amber Cuban rum, dark Jamaican rum, curaçao triple sec) 160**

Jam Daiquiri (maraschino liqueur) 160**

Pain Killer (coconut milk) 162**

Pearl Diver (amber Cuban rum, dark Jamaican rum, Angostura bitters) 162**

Piña Colada (coconut milk) 162**

Quarter Deck (sherry) 153**

Scorpion (Cognac) 164**

X.Y.Z. (curaçao triple sec) 156**

Yellow Bird (Galliano, curaçao triple sec) 167**

Zombie (dark Jamaican rum, aged Cuban rum, aged Jamaican rum, maraschino liqueur, Angostura bitters, absinthe-flavoured spirit) 165***

Sherry

Brazil (dry vermouth, absinthe-flavoured spirit) 234*

Quarter Deck (white Puerto Rican rum) 153**

Up-to-Date (Canadian whisky, Grand Marnier Cordon Rouge, Angostura bitters) 124***

■ **Fino sherry**

Adonis (red vermouth, orange bitters) 232*

Bamboo (dry vermouth, orange bitters) 233*

Fino Martini (gin) 93***

Southern Comfort

Golden Nail (Scotch whisky) 135**

Scarlett O'Hara 242*

Spitfire (absinthe-flavoured spirit) 242*

Tequila

■ **Tequila añejo**

Tequila and Sangrita 173*

Tequila Straight 173*

■ **Tequila blanco**

Agave Julep 174**

Agave Punch (ruby port) 181**

Alamo Splash 174*

Alice in Wonderland (Grand Marnier Cordon Rouge) 188*

Ambassador 182*

Arriba! (orange curaçao) 182**
Aztec Stinger (white crème de menthe) 188**
Banana Boat (crème de banane) 188**
Bloody Maria 190**
Blue Margarita (blue curaçao) 175**
Brave Bull (coffee liqueur) 189**
Broadway Thirst 182**
Cactus Banger (Galliano) 183**
Cactus Cooler (white crème de menthe) 188**
Cactus Flower 189*
Changuirongo 174*
Chihuahua 183*
Chimayo (crème de cassis) 183**
Coco Mexico (coconut milk) 184**
Desert Glow (peach schnapps) 182**
El Diablo (crème de cassis) 175**
Frostbite (white crème de cacao) 190**
Frozen Margarita (curaçao triple sec) 175**
Gorilla Sweat 191** ★
Ice-Breaker (curaçao triple sec, grenadine) 184**
Japanese Slipper (green melon liqueur) 176**
Jungle Juice 184*
Magic Bus (curaçao triple sec) 177*
Margarita (curaçao triple sec) 176**
Matador (curaçao triple sec) 185**
Mexican 185*
Mexican Mule 175*
Mexicana 185*
Mexicola 177*
Muppet 180*
Piñata 185*
Pineapple Margarita (curaçao triple sec) 186**
Playa del Mar (curaçao triple sec) 185*
Purple Pancho (crème de cassis) 177**
Rude Cosmopolitan (curaçao triple sec) 177*
South of the Border (coffee liqueur) 189**

Speedy Gonzales (crème de mûre, green melon liqueur) 190**
Stargarita (curaçao triple sec, Campari) 176**
Strawberry Margarita (curaçao triple sec) 186*
T.N.T. 180*
Tequila Sunrise 186*
Tequila Sunset 180**
Tequini (dry vermouth) 173***
Tijuana Tea (curaçao triple sec) 177**
Tomahawk (curaçao triple sec) 187**
Viva Villa 180**

▥ Tequila reposado
Acapulco 181*
Aguamiel 187**
California Dream (dry vermouth, red vermouth) 172**
Mexican Coffee 191** ★
Mexican Tea 191** ★
Mexico Manhattan (red vermouth, Angostura bitters) 172***
Mockingbird (green crème de menthe) 189***
Rosita (dry vermouth, red vermouth, Campari) 172**
Vertigo 187**

Vermouth

▥ Dry vermouth
Algonquin (rye whiskey) 132**
Amber Twist (Cognac, apricot brandy, curaçao triple sec) 194**
American Beauty (Cognac, ruby port) 194**
Astoria (gin, orange bitters) 90**
Attaboy (gin) 90**
Bamboo (fino sherry, orange bitters) 233*
Betty Blue (vodka, peach schnapps, blue curaçao) 84**
Blackthorn (Irish whiskey, absinthe-flavoured spirit, Angostura bitters) 120***
Bloodhound (gin, red vermouth) 90*
Bombay (Cognac, orange curaçao, orange bitters) 194***

Brazil (sherry, absinthe-flavoured spirit) 234*
Bronx (gin, red vermouth) 107**
Bronx Terrace (gin) 91**
California Dream (tequila reposado, red vermouth) 172**
Cardinal (Campari, gin) 235*
Caruso (gin, green crème de menthe) 113**
Claridge (gin, curaçao triple sec, apricot brandy) 91**
Delmarva (rye whiskey, white crème de menthe) 134**
Dry Martini (gin) 92***
Elegant (gin, Grand Marnier Cordon Rouge) 114**
Extra-Dry Martini (gin) 92***
Ferrari (amaretto) 243*
Floridita Bronx (gin, red vermouth, orange curaçao) 93**
Gibson (gin) 93***
Journalist (gin, red vermouth, orange curaçao, Angostura bitters) 93**
Just Try (gin, yellow Chartreuse, Grand Marnier Cordon Rouge) 115***
Klondike Highball (red vermouth) 240*
Knickerbocker (gin, red vermouth) 94**
Knock-Out (gin, green crème de menthe, absinthe-flavoured spirit) 113***
Leave it to Me (gin, maraschino liqueur, apricot brandy) 94**
Lone Tree (gin, maraschino liqueur) 95**
Macka (gin, red vermouth, crème de cassis) 101**
Mountain (rye whiskey, red vermouth) 138**
Old Pal (Canadian whisky, Campari) 121**
Parisian (gin, crème de cassis) 95**
Perfect Manhattan rye whiskey, red vermouth, Angostura bitters) 122***
Presidente (white Cuban rum) 142**
Queen Cocktail (gin, red vermouth) 110*

Rolls Royce (gin, red vermouth, Benedictine) 94**

Rose (kirsch, cherry brandy) 195**

Rosita (tequila reposado, red vermouth, Campari) 172**

Scoff-Law (Canadian whisky, orange bitters) 123**

Shamrock (Irish whiskey, green Chartreuse) 136***

Tequini (tequila blanco) 173***

Turf (gin, maraschino liqueur, absinthe-flavoured spirit, orange bitters) 96**

Vermouth-Cassis (crème de cassis) 236*

Vodka Martini dry (vodka) 67**

Vodka Martini Extra-Dry (vodka) 67***

Whizz-Bang (Scotch whisky, absinthe-flavoured spirit, orange bitters) 124**

■ **Red vermouth**

Abbey (gin, Angostura bitters) 107*

Adonis (fino sherry, orange bitters) 232*

Americano (Campari) 233*

Apothecary (Fernet-Branca, white crème de menthe) 208**

Blood & Sand (Scotch whisky, cherry brandy) 133**

Bloodhound (gin, dry vermouth) 90*

Bobby Burns (Scotch whisky, Benedictine) 134***

Bronx (gin, dry vermouth) 107**

California Dream (tequila reposado, dry vermouth) 172**

Churchill (Scotch whisky, curaçao triple sec) 120**

Cuban Manhattan (amber Cuban rum, Angostura bitters) 142***

Floridita Bronx (gin, dry vermouth, orange curaçao) 93**

Gaslight (Scotch whisky, orange curaçao) 121***

Harvard (Cognac, Angostura bitters) 195***

Hondarribia (Scotch whisky, Campari) 121**

Journalist (gin, dry vermouth, orange curaçao, Angostura bitters) 93**

Klondike Highball (dry vermouth) 240*

Knickerbocker (gin, dry vermouth) 94**

Macka (gin, dry vermouth, crème de cassis) 101**

Manhattan (rye whiskey, Angostura bitters) 123***

Martinez (gin, maraschino liqueur, Angostura bitters) 95**

Martinican (aged *rhum agricole* ['agricultural rum'], Angostura bitters) 142***

Mexico Manhattan (tequila reposado, Angostura bitters) 172***

Mountain (rye whiskey, dry vermouth) 138**

Negroni (Campari, gin) 235*

Ohio (Champagne, rye whiskey, curaçao triple sec, Angostura bitters) 229**

Perfect Manhattan (rye whiskey, dry vermouth, Angostura bitters) 122***

Queen Cocktail (gin, dry vermouth) 110*

Rob Roy (Scotch whisky, Angostura bitters) 123***

Rolls Royce (gin, dry vermouth, Benedictine) 94**

Rory O'More (Irish whiskey, Angostura bitters) 123***

Rosita (tequila reposado, dry vermouth, Campari) 172**

Star (Calvados, Angostura bitters) 195***

Tipperary (rye whiskey, green Chartreuse) 136***

Veneziano (Campari, white wine) 233**

Voodoo (amber Jamaican rum) 165**

■ **Sweet Vermouth**

Bijou (gin, green Chartreuse, orange bitters) 113***

Vodka

Alexander The Great (brown crème de cacao, coffee liqueur) 87*

Apple Martini (manzana verde liqueur) 78*

Aquamarine (peach schnapps, blue curaçao) 78**

Balalaïka (curaçao triple sec) 67**

Ballet Russe (crème de cassis) 67**

Bay Breeze 82*

Berry Blush 68*

Betty Blue (peach schnapps, dry vermouth, blue curaçao) 84**

Black Russian (coffee liqueur) 84**

Bloody Mary 86**

Blue Champagne (Champagne, blue curaçao) 219**

Blue Lagoon (blue curaçao) 68**

Blue Lagoon Highball (blue curaçao) 68**

Bull-Frog 68*

Burgundy Juicer (crème de cassis) 69**

Caipirovska 69**

Cape Cod Cooler 69*

Cape Codder 69*

Cassisina (crème de cassis) 70**

Chi Chi (coconut milk) 79*

Chocolate Martini (white crème de cacao, brown crème de cacao) 84**

Chocolate Mint Martini (white crème de menthe, green crème de menthe) 84***

Clockwork Orange 70**

Cosmopolitan (curaçao triple sec) 64**

Cucumber Martini 64**

Diamond Fizz (Champagne) 220***

Espresso Martini (coffee liqueur) 71*

Fiesta (curaçao triple sec, Campari) 65*

French Martini (crème de mûre) 79*

Ginger Champagne (Champagne) 218**

Gipsy Queen (Benedictine, orange bitters) 85**

Godmother (amaretto) 85**

Green Russian (green crème de menthe) 85**

Harvey Wallbanger (Galliano) 79**

Henrietta Wallbanger (Galliano) 79**

Bobby Burns (Benedictine, red vermouth) 134***
Churchill (red vermouth, curaçao triple sec) 120**
Gaslight (red vermouth, orange curaçao) 121***
Godfather (amaretto) 135**
Golden Nail (Southern Comfort) 135**
High Voltage (curaçao triple sec) 127**
Highland Cooler 127*
Hondarribia (Campari, red vermouth) 121**
Morning Glory Fizz 138**
Polly Special (curaçao triple sec) 133*
Rob Roy (red vermouth, Angostura bitters) 123***
Rusty Nail (Drambuie) 135**
Whizz-Bang (dry vermouth, absinthe-flavoured spirit, orange bitters) 124**

■ **Tennessee whiskey**
Lynchburg Lemonade (curaçao triple sec) 130**

Wine, red

American Lemonade 236*
Communard (crème de cassis) 234*
Hot Wine 245* ★
Sangria (Cognac, curaçao triple sec) 242*

Wine, white

Kir (crème de cassis) 234*
Spritzer 235*
Veneziano (Campari, red vermouth) 253**

ALCOHOL-FREE COCKTAILS

The main ingredients required to prepare each of these cocktails are indicated in brackets.

Apple juice

Apple Pilar (fresh mint, ginger ale) 248
Apple Sparkle (lemon-lime soda, raspberry syrup) 248
Banana Juicer (banana nectar, lime juice) 255
Mango Sparkle (mango juice, lemon-lime soda) 251
My Sky (lime juice, orgeat syrup) 257
Planter's Punchless (lime juice, grenadine, lemon-lime soda) 252

Banana nectar

Banana Juicer (apple juice, lime juice) 255
Pink Banana (orange juice, grenadine) 261

Carrot juice

Bunny Shame (lemon juice, Worcestershire sauce, Tabasco sauce, celery salt) 262
Rabbit Cooler (soda water [club soda], lime juice) 263
Rabbit Sunrise (orange juice, lemon juice, grenadine) 264

Coconut milk

Cranberry Colada (cranberry juice) 256
Pain Cutter (orange juice, pineapple juice) 260
Virgin Colada (pineapple juice) 261

Cranberry juice

Baby Breeze (pineapple juice, lime juice) 254
Cranberry Colada (coconut milk) 256
Gentle Breeze (grapefruit juice, lime juice) 256
Madras Special (orange juice, lemon juice) 257
Mango Breeze (mango juice, lime juice) 257
Passion Breeze (orange juice, Passion fruit juice) 260

Cucumber

Cucumber Cooler (lime juice, soda water [club soda]) 262
Tomato & Cucumber Sparkle (tomato juice, lemon juice, soda water [club soda]) 264

Egg

■ **Egg white**
Pink Pineapple (pineapple juice, soda water [club soda], lemon juice, grenadine) 266

■ **Egg yolk**
Parson's Special (orange juice, lemon juice, grenadine, soda water [club soda]) 265
Prairie Oyster (Worcestershire sauce, vinegar, Tabasco sauce, tomato ketchup) **266**
Pussy Foot (orange juice, grenadine, lemon juice, lime juice) 267

Fresh mint

Apple Pilar (apple juice, ginger ale) 248
Southside Cooler (lime juice, soda water [club soda]) 253

Ginger ale

Apple Pilar (apple juice, fresh mint) 248
Asian Passion (lychee [litchi] juice, passion fruit juice) 249
Bora Bora Brew (pineapple juice, grenadine) 249
Bull's Eye (orange juice) 249
Shirley Temple (lemon-lime soda, grenadine, lime) 253

Grapefruit juice

Florida (orange juice, soda water [club soda], lemon juice) 250
Gentle Breeze (cranberry juice, lime juice) 256
Grapefruit Cooler (soda water [club soda], grenadine) 250

Passion fruit juice

Asian Passion (lychee [litchi] juice, ginger ale) 249
Passion Breeze (orange juice, cranberry juice) 260
Passion Cooler (lemon-lime soda, lemon juice) 251
Yellow Bear (lemon juice, lime juice cordial) 261

Peach nectar

Crazy Navel (orange juice, grenadine) 256

Pineapple juice

Baby Breeze (cranberry juice, lime juice) 254
Bora Bora Brew (ginger ale, grenadine) 249
Cinderella (orange juice, lemon juice) 255

Golden Scream (single [light] cream) 264
Pain Cutter (orange juice, coconut milk) 260
Pink Pineapple (soda water [club soda], lemon juice, egg white, grenadine) 266
Virgin Colada (coconut milk) 261

Raspberry syrup

Apple Sparkle (apple juice, lemon-lime soda) 248
Milky Mango (mango nectar, milk) 265
Purple Pash (lychee [litchi] juice, soda water [club soda]) 252
Raspberry Squash (lemon juice, soda water [club soda]) 252

Strawberry

California Smoothie (orange juice) 255

Strawberry Cooler (lemon juice, soda water [club soda]) 254

■ **Strawberry ice cream**
Strawberry Milkshake (milk) 267

Tea, Ceylon

Iced Tea (lemon juice) 250

Tomato juice

Holy Mary (lemon juice, Worcester sauce, Tabasco sauce, celery salt) 263
Tomato & Cucumber Sparkle (cucumber, lemon juice, soda water [club soda]) 264

Vanilla ice cream

Vanilla Milkshake (milk) 267

Index of cocktails by their appropriate time of drinking

Depending on the ingredients contained in it, a cocktail may be more enjoyable at certain times of the day, or in certain seasons. This index lists the recipes for cocktails and their variations contained in this book according to the most appropriate time to drink them.

■ *The asterisks indicate the degree of alcohol in the drink: * = weak in alcohol;*

** = moderately alcoholic; *** = strongly alcoholic.

The alcohol-free cocktails are those not marked with asterisks.

■ *Cocktails that are served hot are marked with a ★.*

To serve as an aperitif

Absinthe Drip 232*
Absinthe Veilleuse 232*
Adonis 232*
Alfonso 216*
Amber Twist 194**
American Beauty 194**
Americano 233*
Astoria 90**
Attaboy 90**
Bamboo 233*
Blackthorn 120***
Bombay 194***
Brazil 234*
C.C. 216*
California Dream 172**
Cardinal 235*
Claridge 91**
Cuban Manhattan 142***
Dry Martini 92***
Dubonnet Cocktail 92**
Elegant 114**
European Beauty 120**
Extra-Dry Martini 92***
Fino Martini 93***
Floridita Bronx 93**
Gibson 93***
Gotham 194***
Harvard 195***
Hemingway 218**
Hondarribia 121**
Jaizkibel 100*
Knickerbocker 94**
London Fog 94**
Macka 101**

Manhattan 122***
Martinez 95**
Mauresque à l'Absinthe 235*
Mexico Manhattan 172***
Negroni 235*
Old Pal 121**
Pimm's Royal 219**
Pinerito 149*
Presidente 142**
Rob Roy 123***
Rose 195**
Rosita 172**
Star 195***
Stargarita 176**
T.N.T. No 2 196***
Tamanaco Dry 106***
Tequini 173***
Testa Rossa 75*
Tomate à l'Absinthe 235*
Turf 96**
Veneziano 233**
Vermouth-Cassis 236*
Vodka Martini Dry 67**
Vodka Martini Extra-Dry 67***
Zaza 96**

To serve as a digestif

Acacias 112***
Alaska 112***
Alexander 116*
Alexander The Great 87*
Aztec Stinger 188**
B & B 203**
B & P 203**
Baby Alexander 167**

Banana Banshee 243*
Banana Bliss 204**
Banana Boat 188**
Bee's Knees 112*
Bijou 113***
Black Jack 204**
Black Russian 84**
Black Widow 166**
Bobby Burns 134***
Bounty Boat 204**
Brandy Alexander 212**
Brandy Milk Punch 212*
Brave Bull 189**
Brown Bear 205**
Burgos 205**
Caruso 113**
Centenario 166**
Champs-Élysées 205***
Cherry Blossom 208**
Chocolate Martini 84**
Chocolate Mint Martini 84***
Chocolate Stinger 211**
Cuban 209**
Dusty Rose 244*
Ferrari 243*
French Connection 209**
French Kiss 114***
Frisco 126**
Gipsy Queen 85**
Godfather 135**
Godmother 85**
Golden Cadillac 244*
Golden Dream 244*
Golden Scream 264
Grasshopper 245*

Green Russian 85**
Highbinder 209**
Honey Moon 210**
Hot Shot 245*
Hot Wine 245** ★
Japanese 210**
Just Try 115***
Kentucky Colonel 135**
Lemony Snicket 115**
Mackinnon 166**
Merry Widow 109**
Mockingbird 189***
Mulata 167**
Nikolaschka 210**
Princeton 115**
Red Russian 85**
Rolls Royce 94**
Rusty Nail 135**
Santina's Pousse-Café 211**
Shamrock 136***
Spring Feeling 116**
Stinger 211**
Tipperary 136***
Vanderbilt 212***
Velvet Hammer 87*
Vodka Stinger 86**
White Russian 87*
Yellow Bird 167**

To serve in the morning

Bloody Maria 190**
Breakfast Martini 98**
Corpse Reviver 208***
Cubanita 168**
Morning Glory Fizz 138**
Ramos Gin Fizz 117*

To serve in the afternoon

Banana Daiquiri 158*
Bull-Dog 105**
Cactus Cooler 188**
Cape Cod Cooler 69*
Daiquiri No 2 147**
Nicky Finn 196**
Peach Daiquiri 158*
Pink Gin & Tonic 96*
Remsen Cooler 100*
Tropical Down 110**

To serve in the evening

Aguamiel 187**
Alice in Wonderland 188*
B-52 243*
B-55 243*

Bay Breeze 82*
Beja Flor 144**
Black Pearl 228**
Blue Margarita 175**
Cactus Flower 189*
Chocolate Bliss 204**
Columbus 156**
Delmarva 134**
Elk's Own 137**
Espresso Martini 71*
Evolution 114***
Fallen Angel 114**
Fiesta 65*
Frisky Bison 71*
Frostbite 190**
Golden Nail 135**
Hurricane 160**
Kamikaze 71*
Knock-Out 113***
Long Island Iced Tea 73***
Long Island Lemonade 73***
Martinican 142***
Mexicana 185*
Midnight Moon 228**
Millionnaire 137**
Mocha Martini 137**
Mountain 138**
National 161**
Paradise 110**
Pink Gin 96*
Prince of Wales 229**
Purple Haze 74*
South of the Border 189**
Tetanka 83*
Tijuana Tea 177**
Uncle Vanya 75**
Whiskey Sour 132*

To serve to hangover sufferers

Apothecary 208**
Port Flip 203*

To serve in winter

American Grog 168** ★
Blue Blazer 139*** ★
Brandy Blazer 213*** ★
Coffee Nudge 213** ★
Fish House Punch 168** ★
French Coffee 213* ★
Gorilla Sweat 191** ★
Hot Buttered Rum 169** ★
Hot Buttered Rum Cow 169** ★
Maxim's Coffee 213** ★

Mexican Tea 191** ★
Tom & Jerry 169** ★

To serve at any time

Abbey 107*
Acapulco 181*
Agave Julep 174**
Agave Punch 181**
Alabama Fizz 97**
Alamo Splash 174*
Algonquin 132**
Ambassador 182*
Ambrosia 216**
American Flyer 219**
American Lemonade 236*
Americana 217**
Añejo Highball 143**
Apple Cart 201**
Apple Martini 78*
Apple Pilar 248
Apple Sunrise 201**
Apple Sparkle 248
Apricot Cooler 236*
April Shower 203*
Aquamarine 78**
Aristo 156**
Arriba! 182**
Asian Passion 249
Atomic Dog 157**
Aviation 97**
B & S 196*
Baby Breeze 254
Bacardi Cocktail 144**
Baccarat 157**
Bahama Mama 157**
Bahamian 241**
Balalaïka 67**
Ballet Russe 67**
Banana Juicer 255
Barbotage 221*
Basic 237*
Batida Abaci 158**
Beam Me Up Scotty 132***
Bellini 224*
Berry Blush 68*
Berry Sour 237*
Betty Blue 84**
Between-the-Sheets 196**
Biarritz 203**
Black Rose 144*
Black Velvet 228*
Blackout 97**
Blood & Sand 133**
Bloodhound 90*
Bloody Mary 86**

Photograph acknowledgements

Photography of cocktails, cocktail snacks and bar interiors in Paris
Photography by Nicolas Bertherat © Coll. Larousse
Design by Coco Jobard

Photography of material and filmed sequences
Pages 15, 43–44, 46, 53–59 Olivier Ploton © Coll. Larousse

Photographs of products
Page 269 G+S Photography © Coll. Larousse

Additional photography
Page 12 Jean Noël De Soye – p. 16 CORBIS – p. 18 P. Harholt/CORBIS – p. 19, 208 Underwood and
Underwood/CORBIS – p. 20 D.R. – p. 21 ROGER-VIOLLET – p. 22, 143 AKG – p. 23, 66, 92, 169, 186, 211,
217 Coll. CHRISTOPHE L – p. 26 RyKoff Coll./CORBIS – p. 34 Selva/LEEMAGE – p. 35, 39, 267
KHARBINE/TAPABOR – p. 36 LEEMAGE – p. 37 ab© Costa/LEEMAGE – p. 42, 48, 91, 121, 161, 199, 253,
260, 263 Bettmann/CORBIS – p. 60 M. Voyeux/EDITING – p. 62 Grant Peter/Camera Press/ GAMMA/HFP –
p. 64 SIPA PRESS – p. 73 D.R. – p. 80, 82, 176 Lake County Museum/CORBIS – p. 86 T. Johnson/MAGNUM –
p. 88 D. Majorel/SIC – p. 99, 122, 201 Hulton Deutsch/CORBIS – p.105, 131, 140 B. Krist/CORBIS –
p. 111 R.Horrox/CORBIS – p. 113 Cavalli/SIPA PRESS – p. 117 B. Smith/CORBIS – p. 118 Iliona /TOP –
p. 151 P. Gutman/CORBIS – p. 138, 181, 195 and 221 Coll. Larousse – p. 163 D. Muench/CORBIS – p. 165
D.G. Houser/CORBIS – p. 170 Michel SETBOUN – p. 175, 234 LEEMAGE – p. 192 H. Amiard/TOP – p. 214
Jean Noël De Soye/Madame Figaro – p. 224 M.G. Mayer/CORBIS – p. 230 M.J. Jarry/J.F. Tripelon/TOP –
p. 233 KHARBINE/TAPABOR. Paris, ADAGP 2004 – p. 246 R. Alcock/Maison Madame Figaro.

The bars shown at the beginning of sections and chapters are, in page order :
Harry's Bar in Venice (pages 12–13) – the Man Ray in Paris (pages 60–61) – the bar of the Ice Hotel in
Sweden (page 62) – the Apparemment Café in Paris (page 88) – the bar of the Saint James Club in Paris
(page 118) – la Bodeguita del Medio in Havana (page 140) – the bar of the Peninsular Hotel in Hong Kong
(page 170) - the Hemingway Bar of The Ritz Hotel in Paris (page 192) – the bar of the Plaza Athénée in Paris
(page 214) – La Bocca in Paris (page 230) – the Chai 33 in Paris (page 246).

Acknowledgements
*The designer would like to offer most sincere thanks to the following people for their kind collaboration
with the production of the illustrations:*
Laurence Becquart for the various trade names belonging to the ARC INTERNATIONAL GROUP (Salviati, Mikasa,
Studio Nova, Cristal d'Arques, Luminarc, Arcoroc), Martine Collombier-Mautin for LEONARDO and ASA
SÉLECTION, Jean-Paul Genovese for TRANSEXIM – AINSI DE SUITE, Jean Marc Knoll for LSA INTERNATIONAL,
Anne Krief for CHRISTOFLE, Christine Labrune and Josiane Bonnardel for JARS CERAMISTES, Anne and Guy Du
Martray for PORCELAINE DE SOLOGNE, Bruno Miremont for L'ENTREPÔT, Anne Schuhmacher for BACCARAT.

For the interior shots of the Paris bars
The bar of the Georges restaurant, 19 rue Beaubourg, 75001 Paris (pages 76–77)
The bar of the Hotel Montalembert, 3 rue de Montalembert, 75007 Paris (pages 102–103)
The bar of the Closerie des Lilas, 171 boulevard du Montparnasse, 75006 Paris (pages 128–129)
The bar of the Hotel Bel-ami, 7/11 rue Saint Benoît, 75006 Paris (pages 154–155)
The Barrio Latino, 48 rue du faubourg Saint-Antoine, 75011 Paris (pages 178–179)
The Hemingway Bar and the Cambon Bar of The Ritz Hotel, 15 place Vendôme, 75001 Paris
(pages 206–207 and 222–223)
The Étienne-Marcel bar, 34 rue Étienne-Marcel, 75002 Paris (pages 238–239)
The Kong, 1 rue du Pont-Neuf, 75001 Paris (pages 258–259).